Literary Realism
and the
Ekphrastic Tradition

Literary Realism and the Ekphrastic Tradition

Mack Smith

The Pennsylvania State University Press
University Park, Pennsylvania

Library of Congress Cataloging-in-Publication Data

Smith, Mack, 1948–
    Literary realism and the ekphrastic tradition / Mack Smith.
        p.   cm.
    Includes bibliographical references and index.
    ISBN 0-271-02819-X
    1. Literature—History and criticism.   2. Ekphrasis.   3. Realism
in literature.   I.   Title.
PN56.E45S55   1995
809.3'912—dc20   93-41181
                                                                CIP

Published by The Pennsylvania State University Press,
University Park, PA 16802-1003

It is the policy of The Pennsylvania State University Press to use acid-free paper
for the first printing of all clothbound books. Publications on uncoated stock
satisfy the minimum requirements of American National Standard for Information Sciences—Permanence of Paper for Printed Library Materials, ANSI
Z39.48–1984.

CONTENTS

In memory of Sylvan Karchmer

PREFACE

I shall, for the moment, put aside the self-doubts expressed by the prologuist of *Don Quixote* and his desire to present his text "naked and unadorned, without the ornament of a prologue or the countless train of customary sonnets, epigrams and eulogies it is the fashion to place at the beginning of books" (26). The prefatory adornment that serves my text most is a brief discussion of its genesis and evolution, for like Cervantes' prologuist, I cannot claim that it is directly descended from me alone, as a "child of my brain"; the most I can claim is that I am its "stepfather," for many of my theories are more directly descended from others and many that are original to me have been nurtured by colleagues, teachers, and friends.

Although the present form of my text bears little resemblance either to my original organizing theory or to my original readings of the primary works treated here, I am thankful for the ways in which they allowed me to develop a more comprehensive theory while still using several of their more salient points. I am indebted to Terrence Doody for his careful attention to my readings of Cervantes, Austen, Tolstoy, Joyce, and Pynchon as well as his guiding insights into the theory of the novel. Walter Isle helped me to formulate a theory of self-reflexivity while accommodating my more specific focus on the novel's representation of an ekphrastic art form as a reflexive device of mimetic self-definition. I remember still the excitement of my discovery of the profusion of novelistic texts containing the paradigmatic scene of characters debating over the mimetic accuracy of a represented art form. The dissertation resulting from my central insights and from the guidance of Professors Isle and Doody provided a nucleus from which I was able to develop my wider formulation of the history of realism in the novel. While I am proud of that early, ambitious text, its central blindness typifies many critical texts of an era that interpreted novelistic self-consciousness as a sign of fiction's liberation from the broader conditions of cultural production.

My work took a major theoretical shift during my stay at the School of Criticism and Theory at Northwestern University, where, under the tutelage of Michael Riffaterre, I came to see the trope of *ekphrasis* as an important signifying element of a grammar of mimesis. My theory of ekphrastic systems, the network of represented art forms that helps to define a novel's representational norms, parallels Riffaterre's notion of mimesis as an intertextual function of the text that works to convey the illusion of extratextual reference. What especially interests me, however, about Riffaterre's theory is his notion of hypogram, the semiotic matrix expressing a dominant cultural stereotype. Implicit in the theory of hypogram is that the metalanguage evoked by such mimetic grammatical units as ekphrastic system's does not signify solely an intertextual meaning derived just from a sequence of literary texts; rather, the metalanguage produced within novelistic texts mirrors the production of other cultural signifying systems.

It was fortunate that, during my stay at the School of Criticism and Theory, I was able to learn also from Richard Rorty, whose patient and caring interest in the work of the participants is one of my fondest memories of the summer. Rorty influenced my thinking on how cultural signifying systems are organized around central precepts. Although Rorty's theory of conceptual schemes cannot be conflated entirely with the paradigms of Thomas Kuhn or the epistemes of Michel Foucault, their similarities were helpful in allowing me to see the regulative nature of a metalanguage that informs all discursive practices. I was able to see more fully how the metalanguage derived from ekphrastic debates within novels not only defines what referential function the novelistic text uses but also prescribes, by means of parody, the mimetic formulations of other texts. The character debates over the verisimilitude of an ekphrastic art form I then came to see as clashes between a valorized mimetic norm and one that the text seeks to reject. What these scenes symbolize are conflicts between competing paradigms of representation that reflect changes in broader historical epistemes. Furthermore, what is at stake in these debates is not just the dramatization of the victory of one character's views over another's but, rather, what discourse can convey the most accurate illusion of what we define to be "the real."

My view of how such devices as parody and character debate over ekphrastic representations signal a shift in representational conventions borrows heavily from the Russian formalist theories of naturalization and estrangement. However, I prefer to emphasize those elements of formalism that detail how artistic changes parallel social and cultural transformations. I presented a summary of my theory of literary historical change at the MLA forum, "Sociological Approaches to Literature," at the 1986 convention. After reading my paper, "Realism: The Paradigm of Competing Paradigms," I was pleased to become acquainted with the respondent to my panel, Remi Clignet, whose then recent *Structures of Artistic Revolutions* paralleled so closely my own interests. His enthusiastic response to my work was most gratifying, and I appreciate his later reading of my longer manuscript and his support for my project throughout the years. His kind effort on my behalf restores my faith in the academic discipline as a community of scholars working toward a common, humanistic goal. His views also helped me formulate more clearly a theory of artistic paradigm shifts.

My project crystallized most fully, however, during a National Endowment for the Humanities summer seminar conducted by John Carlos Rowe titled "American Literature and Literary Theory." I am indebted to the endowment and to the University of California, Irvine, which sponsored me as a visiting scholar for three successive summers after my NEH stay in order that I might use its facilities to complete my manuscript. Professor Rowe's reading of my project enabled me to focus more clearly on the ways in which the paradigmatic character debates over linguistic reference are embedded within the terms of the dominant language philosophy of the historical period in which the novels were written. I began to see that although the terms changed, in each period the conflict over the accuracy of representations emerged as an opposition between correspondence and coherence theories of truth and meaning. Thus, a continuing motif appeared within language and representational philosophies as different as the scholastic, humanist, empiricist, Kantian transcendentalist, logical positivist, and finally the poststructuralist. I also appreciate Professor Rowe's demonstration in my discussions with him and in his *Theoretical Dimensions of Henry James* that the procedures of several theoretical models now in vogue are not necessarily antithetical; each model has its use, but when reaching an aporia in its critical praxis, it must be supplemented by another. I am sincerely grateful to Professor Rowe for his encouragement, support, and faith in my project in the several years it has taken me to complete it.

I have been helped and influenced by others too numerous to mention. But I give special thanks to Wallace Martin and Bainard Cowan, whose careful readings and suggestions influenced my final revision. I am also grateful to Gerald Graff for his very helpful insights into my work. I thank Murray Krieger, whose works influenced my own from the very beginning. Even though we disagree over the nature of the ekphrastic artifact, I enjoyed and benefited greatly from our discussion in Irvine. I would also like to thank James Kinneavy for taking interest in my work and for sending materials and references regarding the classical, medieval, and Renaissance uses of ekphrasis. I want to express gratitude to Kathryn Hume for her continuing friendship and for her reading and providing helpful commentary on sections of my theoretical chapter and portions of my *Ulysses* and *Gravity's Rainbow* chapters. I have also benefited from our discussions on Pynchon. I appreciate the very lengthy commentary Khachig Tölölyan gave to an early version of my essay on film in *Gravity's Rainbow*.

I am grateful for the assistance Berry College has provided in the form of release time from my teaching duties and my responsibilities as head of the Department of English. I also appreciate the college's financial support of my residencies at the University of California. A very special note of gratitude goes to my student workers who have given me valuable assistance in preparing my manuscript. Rachel Clark's proofreading skills, knowledge of computers, organizational abilities, and patience saved me literally months of work. I would also like to thank Julie Boatwright, Lisa Southerland, Tonya Couch, Kathy Gann, and Alisa Ezell for their help. I am especially grateful to my wife, Sue Silverman Smith, who applied her keen eye to a careful proofreading of the final draft of my manuscript. Special thanks go to Philip Winsor, senior editor at Penn State Press, for his help throughout the publication process.

I thank *Twentieth-Century Literature*, *Renascence*, *Massachusetts Studies in English*, and *Pynchon Notes* for allowing me to reprint portions of my previously published works. A note on the editions that I use: I include parenthetical references to both the 1961 Random House and the 1986 Vintage "corrected" texts of *Ulysses*. Because I prefer their translations, I use the J. M. Cohen version of *Don Quixote* and the Rosemary Edmonds version of *Anna Karenina*. I use the standard Chapman edition of *Emma* and the Viking/Compass edition of *Gravity's Rainbow*.

CHAPTER ONE

Ekphrasis and the Realist Novel:
The Paradigm of Competing Paradigms

From Correspondence to Discourse

Throughout literary history, the concept of realism has been revised constantly. In *Keywords* Raymond Williams traces the concept's complex semantic history and refuses ultimately to limit it according to any of the isolated historical definitions. Similarly, Roman Jakobson complains that the word has become so polysemous that "theoreticians and historians of art—in particular, of literature—are acting as if the term were a bottomless sack into which everything and anything could be conveniently hidden away" (45). The semantic debates in literary theory over the term "realism" place it in a position similar to those of the terms "truth" and "reality" in philosophy; each is defined in as many ways as there are conflicting systems of knowledge based upon them. However, in spite of these semantic and hence theoretical shifts, literary history reveals a pattern in change itself, a structure in the succession of unifying principles temporarily forming consensuses among the contemporary communities of scholars and artists concerning what is meant by realism as "fidelity to reality." With some notable differences, these theories of consensuses concerning realism in literature bear a relation to those in philosophy and science. Critiquing theories of knowledge as a quasi-visual faculty, Richard Rorty describes consensuses epistemologically as "privileged representations," which are temporary "foundations of knowledge" (*Philosophy* 163). Thomas Kuhn, describing consensus in science, adopts the term "paradigm," defined as "universally recognized scientific achievements that for a time provide model problems and solutions to a community of practitioners" (viii). Both Rorty and Kuhn argue that shifts in consensus are revolutionary and not evolutionary. An outdated consensus disappears not because of incremental changes; the shift to a new model, according to Kuhn, "requires the reconstruction of prior theory and the re-evaluation of prior fact" (7). Similarly, Fredric Jameson's account of Russian formalist theories of literary history shows paradigms of realism as undergoing an "artistic permanent revolution" demanding "a kind of consent to change and to the inevitable wearing out of once-new procedures" (*Prisonhouse* 90).

With a consensus theory of knowledge in mind, I offer several postulates about the current status of realism in literary theory. First, a shift in realist paradigms has taken place in this century from an empirical, correspondence theory of signification to a foundational model emphasizing discourse and a coherence theory of meaning. This shift therefore implies a different interpretive methodology for evaluating novelistic realism. Instead of correspondent conceptions of literary language transmitting nonverbal phenomena and a novel "reflecting" the world, a realism of discourse interprets the ways in which specific literary conventions provide assumptions and rationalizations about the world constituted in the act of reading.[1] Second, this discourse theory of realism has transformed the role of narrative description, once the definitional core of representational and referential theories and now viewed for its performative function. And last, I contend that this most recent shift is not exceptional—that, in fact, many realist novels reflect some historically and culturally specific manifestation of the opposition matching a correspondence theory against a coherence, or constructivist, theory of truth and linguistic meaning.

Using the postulates above, one can therefore define a realist novel as a novelistic text that incorporates devices of rhetorical appeal that serve to make claims of verisimilitude and that thematizes the representational

---

1. I use the term "discourse" in the sense that it is used by Gerard Genette: the description of the act of enunciation, the rhetorical means by which the text is communicated. Structuralist theory divides narrative into two parts—the events and existents (*histoire*) and the act of enunciating (*discours*).

accuracy of its paradigm of linguistic meaning. A study of influential realist novels shows that the precise philosophy of representation upon which the text's realist assumptions have been constructed is often foregrounded thematically in descriptive scenes, which establish verisimilar truth-claims. Therefore a realist text refers as much to its own philosophic origin and processes of validation as it does to an extratextual reality. In fact, one of the guiding premises of this study is that a text's realist assumptions must be interpreted within the conceptual framework of the historical paradigm of representation that governs its language use. Significantly, a discourse theory of realism reveals that these descriptive conventions of verisimilitude serve a juridical function in validating the truth-claims of mimetic paradigms that are governed by the perpetual dialectic of oppositional theories of coherence and correspondence.

While writing primarily from a constructivist perspective, I nonetheless contend that the debate is undecidable because the two theories form a binary opposition in which each term depends upon and cannot entirely discredit the other. On the one hand, correspondence and denotation are presuppositions for every speech-act situation upon which conceptual schemes can be constructed. Quite simply, a coherence theory cannot disprove or abandon entirely the possibility of a referent's existence, the possibility that talk can be talk about something. The fact that reference cannot be proven and may in fact be illusory does not invalidate its use as a speech-act presupposition. Even Jacques Derrida halts his attack upon referentiality short of denying its existence. He has commented that his intention is to problematize "a certain naïve relationship to the signified or the referent, to sense or meaning" (*Positions* 74), and in doing so, he does not deny *any* connection of language to reality. He says, "To distance oneself from the habitual structure of reference, to challenge or complicate our common assumptions about it, does not amount to saying that there is *nothing* beyond language" ("Interview" 124). On the other hand, there is no way of empirically validating that signs correspond to or mirror a particular reality that is unmodified by or perhaps even created by the semiotic system. Arguing from this perspective, Nelson Goodman contends that "there is . . . no such thing as the real world, no unique ready-made absolute reality apart from and independent of all versions and visions" (269). This debate is rendered further undecidable by the means through which I show that a realist paradigm establishes its truth-claims. Denying that a paradigm has unmediated access to external, empirical validation, the only viable means by which it can establish truth-conditions is by textually representing the oppositional other and proving it false. André Gide calls attention to this conflictive element in realism by calling it "a rivalry between the real world and a [false] representation of it" (Levin 53). However, this falsifiability method of establishing truth-claims makes the opposing paradigm present in the text that would attempt to deny its representational status. In the chain of signification, the absent term must be made present to confirm the present term's validity. A final reason why no realist text can entirely discredit or abandon the binary opposite of its governing paradigm is inherent within the concept of fictional realism itself. An assumption behind realism is that a text strives to make claims about a world apart from it and language; however, to do so, it must involve itself in the process of constructing worlds through language, which ultimately problematizes the concept of a reality entirely apart from texts. In fact, because of its conflicting sympathies between word and world, a realist text will often support the guiding assumptions of its governing paradigm on a textual level but subvert its more extreme implications subtextually. The aporia in these theories explains why change occurs and why the succession of consensuses in realism is not a progressive one toward absolute knowing.

The most recent shift, beginning early in the century, is currently reflected in structuralist and poststructuralist questioning of what Derrida calls naïve theories of reference and denotation. An empirical, correspondence theory of literary description implies a representational model in which a verbal sign and an external referent are joined logically by denotation. Similar to an early Wittgensteinian picture theory of language, in which a correspondent relation is posited by the similarity of the structure of language and the world, the representing and the represented, this theory of literature assumes a stability in denotative reference, an unproblematic relation between sign and referent. However, the referential status of denotation has been problematized by a generation of structuralist and poststructuralist theorists. Roland Barthes, speaking in this tradition, criticizes denotative reference as privileging one system of meaning over others that can be revealed through connotation. He argues that by valorizing denotation as "hearth, center, guardian, refuge, light of truth" (S/Z 9), one limits a text's play of signification, creating illusions of unitary and singular references. In spite of restraints upon play, the connotative references behind the denotative sign constantly remind one of the instability of communicative and reading acts that are always subject to supplementation or substitution—psychologically by the individuated consciousnesses of authors and readers and linguistically by the galaxy of signifiers clustering about every sign. Derrida goes much further than Barthes in exploring the implications of the arbitrary relations of the Saussurean sign. Equatable with Barthes's denotation, Derrida's theory of logocentrism shows how contextual determinants limit a sign's meaning by making the arbitrary relation of signifier and signified seem essential, seem in fact not to be between a signifier and signified at all but between the sign and a singular, external referent. Presiding over Derrida's critique of logocentrism is his critique of presence, a perceptual model depending upon denotation's making present a unitary and particular referent with every sign instead of the connotative play of relational signifiers. In the context of Barthes's and Derrida's critiques of denotation, logocentrism, and presence, I contend that it is through description, the mode most associated with denotation and presence, that connotation most succinctly reveals a text's discursive praxis.[2] In identifying description as a fundamental principle of discourse, I treat it not as unmotivated or value-free but rather as the rhetorical trope ekphrasis, a digressive description used as an appeal to narrative credibility. Thus, in aligning novelistic realism with a broader *rhetorical* tradition, I establish its basis in the practices of discourse.

Realistic Paradigm Shifts

My theory of literary historical change is derived not only from Kuhn's paradigm theory but also from Michel Foucault's theories of episteme and discursive formation. In spite of numerous differences, both the Kuhnian paradigm and the Foucaultian episteme provide models of knowledge that are consensual rather than empiricist, and both detail how a consensus model is formed and maintained. Kuhn's model is particularly instructive in elaborating a scientific paradigm's birth, development, and extinction, which he describes in two stages, revolutionary science and normal science. A normal science period allows ractitioners to work because of the acceptance of an established model and "the assumption that the scientific community knows what the world is like" (5). However, the slightest indeterminacy in these supposedly unquestioned beliefs commits normal science practitioners to defend constantly a discourse that "suppresses fundamental novelties because they are necessarily subversive of basic commitments" (5). Kuhn's second stage, revolutionary science, begins when an anomaly reveals a flaw in the problem-solution model of tradition-bound normal science.

2. Barthes's use of the category of connotation was more than likely borrowed from the Danish linguist Louis Hjemslev, who first posited the notion of connotation as a second-order signifying system.

The novel, or radical, model adopted to contend with the anomaly represents a shift not just in world view but in basic determinations of "what should count as an admissible problem or as a legitimate problem solution" (6). Giving a fuller view than Kuhn of social determinants, Foucault's epistemic theory describes the regulative nature of paradigms, or discursive formations, which, in establishing authoritarian dominance, "constitute a system of control in the production of discourse, fixing its limits through the action of an identity taking the form of a permanent reactivization of the rules" ("Discourse on Language" 224). In spite of these and other differences, both Kuhn and Foucault show how a regulative model is established and supplanted through struggle—the struggle of tradition to maintain dominance and of innovation to be culturally legitimated.[3]

The history of aesthetics also reveals a consistent pattern of struggle between competing representational paradigms, roughly defined as tradition and innovation. Adapting Kuhn's theories to a sociology of artistic change, Remi Clignet argues that both artists and scientists are "equally susceptible to tensions between tradition and innovation," since the work of both "is shaped by standardized sets of prescriptions concerning the definition and treatment of reality" (40).[4] In science, the conflict ultimately is over definitional rights to some manifestation of physical reality, whereas in literary and other artistic modes, innovator and traditionalist struggle over rights to the term "realism." In fact, the struggle of competing groups to appropriate this term lies at the heart of the conflicts between representational paradigms. As Jakobson writes, "Classicists, sentimentalists, the romanticists to a certain extent, even the 'realists' of the nineteenth century, the modernists to a large degree and, finally, the futurists, expressionists, and their like have more than once steadfastly proclaimed faithfulness to reality, maximum verisimilitude—in other words, realism—as the guiding motto of their artistic program" (39). It is ironic, though, that realism has been appropriated by both traditionalist and innovator. Goodman comments upon this

3. The theories of Kuhn and Foucault cannot be conflated completely. A chief difference is that between their accounts of how rules provide the coherence for a paradigm, or discursive formation. Foucault defines discursive practice as rule governed; Kuhn defines the formation of a paradigm as the result of shared goals, practices, and results, and not as the result of a transcendental set of rules. For a fuller discussion of differences between Kuhn and Foucault on the subject of paradigm and discursive formations, see Herbert Dreyfus and Paul Rabinow, *Michel Foucault: Beyond Structuralism and Hermeneutics.*

4. Clignet's *The Structure of Artistic Revolutions* is a significant contribution to the study of the sociology of artistic forms. Clignet argues that art and science can be studied with similar methodologies, that Kuhn's description of the properties of scientific paradigms—symbolic generalizations, models, and exemplars—apply to artistic paradigms as well.

discrepancy when he notes that realism has meant "familiarity," "the standard mode of representation," and "a new mode of representation . . . so fresh and forceful as to achieve what amounts to a revelation" (269). However, this discrepancy becomes easier to understand by examining the life cycle of a realistic paradigm to see how it occupies both traditionalist and innovational roles.

The life cycle of a mimetic model follows a pattern similar to that of a Kuhnian paradigm. A revolutionary, innovative model becomes traditional once its representations are fully incorporated within a cultural lexicon of realistic conventions. Ironically, these realistic conventions become extinct not long after their universal acceptance, presaging the paradigm's collapse. Richard Harvey Brown summarizes the process in this way: "Art or science 'describes reality' only to the extent that its metaphoric construction of experience has become frozen. 'Realistic representation' appears as such only when a given genre or paradigm has become commonplace or prosaic, a frozen or dead metaphor that is taken for literal description" (227). Brown implies that the illusion of correspondent reference in realistic description depends upon a broad acceptance of a paradigm's conventions. However, in later stages this conventionality becomes too apparent, and the artificiality inhibits the reader from viewing a text's signs as references to the literally real.

The dialectical turns of this cycle, tradition and innovation, can be described in the Russian formalist terms of naturalization and defamiliarization. When the image of the world postulated by a realist text is naturalized, it is, in Jonathan Culler's terms, brought "into relation with a type of discourse or model which is, already, in some sense, natural and legible" (*Structuralist* 138). The shared conventions of a paradigm, or model, are, according to Michael Riffaterre, "rationalizations," which "reduce everything that is strange in the text to something known and familiar" (*Text* 2). Rationalizations, supplied and motivated by the familiar ideology of a social model, facilitate naturalization by operating through conventions that serve to denote "the real." By fulfilling generic expectations through conventional events and existents, a realist text guarantees recognition. A paradigmatic model, however, ultimately pays a price for an audience's spontaneous recognition. First, the reader identifies these conventions as solely literary signs, which are therefore distanced from the objects they presumably signify. Second, repeatedly portraying objects with static, conventional images causes immediacy to be lost, thus evoking habitual responses, called automatization by the Russian formalists. Victor Shklovsky writes, "As perception becomes habitual . . . the object, perceived thus in the manner of prose perception, fades and does not leave a first impression; ultimately even the essence of what it was is forgotten" (Lemon and Reis 11). In order to retrieve this loss of presence, a text must ironically "make objects 'unfamiliar,' " so that automatized sensibilities can perceive the fictional as essentially real.

The most ambitious Russian formalist attempt to apply the concepts of defamiliarization and naturalization to literary history is Juri Tynjanov's systemic formalism, which not only posits a history of artistic change but also supplements Shklovsky's immanent definition of literariness by acknowledging the formative influence of culture.[5] Tynjanov conceives of naturalization and defamiliarization as opposing impulses of a literary historical dialectic in which a dynamic, innovative expression, rising in response to an automatized mode, also becomes automatic in readers' responses and is soon replaced by a newer expression that is dynamic in relation to the now traditional one (Steiner 121). Tynjanov writes that this paradigm of literary historical change evolves in four stages: "(1) the contrastive principle of construction dialectically rises in respect to the automatized principle of construction; (2) it is applied—the constructive principle seeks the easiest application; (3) it spreads over the maximal number of phenomenon; (4) it is automatized and gives rise to a contrastive principle of construction" (Steiner 121). Peter Steiner, arguing that these stages of literary change parallel cultural changes, writes, "Among all the pretenders to dominance in the literary system, the one that converges with the developmental tendencies of the overall cultural system becomes the victor" (112). The cultural influence on the selection of signs and their organization is the only extralinguistic, correspondent relation that a coherentist or constructivist perspective will allow. From this view, language reflects its cultural and political origins more than it disinterestedly corresponds to an objective, extralinguistic reality. And the historical struggle of cultures to shape language in the forms of tradition and innovation can be read archaeologically in the hidden, rhetorical subtext of what the text purports to be real.

Tynjanov's overview of an artistic paradigm shift foreshadows Kuhn's concept of revolutionary and normal science, but with one significant difference: as Clignet notes, "the banishment of ideas, models, and

---

5. The conflict between an immanent, or intrinsic, definition of literary development and an extrinsic, or cultural, definition was manifest in the writings of Shklovsky and Tynjanov and in the correspondences between them. Shklovsky developed his theory by describing the distinction between art and *byt* (everyday life) as absolute, so that artistic change took place because of a struggle between older and newer forms of art and not because of a form's inability to keep pace with cultural change. Tynjanov, on the other hand, questioning the absolute distinction between art and *byt*, argued for the pervasiveness of extraliterary influences. In my discussion of Shklovsky and Tynjanov I am indebted to Peter Steiner, *Russian Formalism: A Metapoetics*.

exemplars deemed to be invalid tends to be total and irreversible in the sciences but not in the arts" (41). Art and literature, much more tolerant of the coexistence of rival paradigms, often elevate older formulations to the status of a sustaining tradition rather than relegate them to a lexicon of outworn beliefs. My examination of realist novels shows that while it is possible to speak of realist conventions that are more or less adequate according to a given paradigm, one should take care in stepping out of that paradigm of knowledge to speak of an objective, progressivist series of realist paradigms giving increasingly accurate fictional approxima-tions of the real. But the basic parallel with Kuhn and Foucault remains— the relation of individual works to a system of literature or realism is culturally determined. In this context "realism" can be described as a term that rival representational paradigms define separately and then contend with one another to culturally legitimate.

The Realist Novel and the Ekphrastic Art Form

An interesting element of the cultural struggle of paradigmatic realisms is that it is often incorporated within texts and can be interpreted intrinsically. On an extrinsic, intraliterary level there occurs during a late historical period of a mimetic paradigm what Menachem Brinker calls "moments of crisis" that "are accompanied by radical changes in the modes made use of by art in its representation of reality" (256). Brinker suggests that the struggle appears on an intrinsic, textual level with the introduction of devices that "create an impression of fidelity to the real world by stressing prior representations' thorough dependence upon conventions of style and genre"; among these are "critical polemics as well as parodistic elements incorporated into the fiction itself . . . to expose the artificiality of antecedent conventions" (254). Brinker is correct in assuming that the conflict between paradigmatic realisms is internalized within novels proposing an innovative change in representa-tional models, the equivalent of Kuhn's revolutionary science. However, I contend that the conflict is also internalized within novels justifying a traditional representational norm.[6] The novels I examine incorporate a central device to render thematically paradigm conflict and validate

6. Brinker's essay gives a helpful and succinct summary of the historical shifts in realist conventions by synthesizing Russian formalist theories with those of Nelson Goodman and Roland Barthes. I disagree, however, with his identifying revolutionary texts as the only ones that parodically and self-consciously represent mimetic conventions to further their realist agendas.

truth-claims. In many revisionist novels, characters supporting a false, restrictive view of conventional representation are set against those who see reality with greater clarity; often the narration traces the dramatic progress of a character from a false, "dominant" view to the true, "emerging" one consistent with the text's own mimesis. Conversely, a text from a "normal" historical period shows mimetic views diverging from a currently prescribed norm as products of an eccentric or deluded sensibility. I stress as important this dramatic element of the textual struggle of representational paradigms. The novels I examine dramatize the consequences of confining life according to the false truth-claims of a discredited discourse.

The most interesting device through which this conflict is internalized is the representation within the text of a work of art to be critically interpreted by several characters. Through character debate over verisimilitude and proper interpretation, a text questions artistic representation in a manner implying that its own mimesis is truthful. This convention, the description of a work of art, serves the intertextual function of realistic self-definition throughout literary history. As a revolutionary trope it is both a focal point for a struggle in which a new "emerging" revision of realism grows out of its rejected heritage, and a device used to stabilize a prevailing norm. The origin of this convention is in classical rhetoric—the ekphrasis of epic and poetry.

In its original use as defined in the *Progymnasma* of Hermogenes, ekphrasis entails any elaborate digressive description embedded within rhetorical discourse: "an account in detail . . . of persons, actions, times, places, seasons, and many other things" (Baldwin 35). Thus it can be a narrative within a narrative, as Callimachus in the *Hecale* includes the story of Ericthonius within the central story of Theseus, or it can serve as an extended description of nature, as Dion of Prusa uses it to idealize pastoral life in the *Euboean Discourse*.[7] One of the most typical and

---

7. The studies of ekphrasis have largely been of its use in poetry. There are several interesting ones that provide helpful descriptions and definitions of the various ways the trope has been used by poets. See, for example, Jean Hagstrum, *The Sister Arts: The Tradition of Literary Pictorialism from Dryden to Gray*; Emilie L. Bergmann, *Art Inscribed: Essays on Ekphrasis in Spanish Golden Age Poetry*; Diane Chaffee, "Visual Art in Literature: The Role of Time and Space in Ekphrastic Creation"; John Hollander, "The Poetics of *Ekphrasis*"; Murray Krieger, "The Ekphrastic Principle and the Still Movement of Poetry, or *Laokoön* Revisited"; Michael Davidson, "*Ekphrasis* and the Postmodern Painter Poem"; and George Kurman, "*Ekphrasis* in Epic Poetry." Interesting studies of ekphrasis and fictional or nonfictional narratives include David Carrier, "Ekphrasis and Interpretation: Two Modes of Art History Writing"; Fritz Gysin, "Paintings in the House of Fiction: The Example of Hawthorne"; and Svetlana Leontieff Alpers, "*Ekphrasis* and Aesthetic Attitudes in Vasari's *Lives*."

instructive uses of ekphrasis is as the description of a work of art graphically representing figures from mythology, history, or everyday life to provide an implicit, didactic commentary upon the narrative within which they are incorporated. The artifact classical writers most often use to embed these figures is a carpet or tapestry. For example, Catullus, in his *epyllion* (miniature epic) *Carmen* LXIV, comments upon the marriage of Peleus and Thetis by illustrating a tapestry describing Theseus's desertion of Ariadne; and Ovid shows conflicting views of divinity by describing the respective tapestries of Minerva and Arachne in *Metamorphoses*. Jason's cloak in the *Argonautica* of Apollonius Rhodius portrays several myths that compose an interpretive background to the central narrative. Similar to the description of tapestries are Longus's painting that opens his *Daphnis and Chloe*; Virgil's mural of the Trojan War, which causes Aeneas to weep in the *Aeneid*; Moschus's flower basket in *Europa*; and Homer's shield of Achilles in the *Iliad*.

For the representational tradition of the novel, perhaps the most relevant example of ekphrasis in classical literature is Ovid's tale of Arachne in *Metamorphoses*. In the weaving contest between Minerva and Arachne, Ovid compares two different modes of rendering. Minerva's tapestry is a representation of divine order, for her subject, the Parnassian hierarchy, is arranged in a design of severest order and symmetry. On the other hand, Arachne weaves a tapestry exhibiting no such symmetry, and she chooses as her subject the various metamorphoses of gods into animals in their pursuit of earthly maidens. The tapestry is described by G. Karl Galinsky as a "swirling depiction of the love of gods for mortal women, and as such it is a thematic restatement of the stories which Ovid had told in the earlier books of *Metamorphoses*" (82). Its structural design is a loosely related series "not fitted into a rigid, formal pattern, but the unity consists of the general theme, and the succession of the various stories is associative" (83). As such, Arachne's tapestry provides a hidden code for interpreting the poem that contains it, for the *Metamorphoses* can be considered a series of *epyllia* loosely linked together, telling the same stories woven by the ill-fated seamstress.

Similar to the story of Arachne in *Metamorphoses*, many ekphrastic scenes in novels contrast forms of art illustrating different modes of rendering. Either two textual artifacts representing the aesthetic views of two characters are paired in a debate on artistic representation, or a single artifact informs this debate. The debate, an interpretive code for the text's mimesis, is often replicated in corresponding scenes throughout the narrative and creates an ekphrastic system in which literary language refers, through these interpolated artifacts, to the rhetorical dimension of its mimesis. The numerous examples of such ekphrastic scenes in the genre reflect a cultural struggle over verisimilitude in the linguistic representation of reality, either by proposing newer, more accurate mimetic modes or by defending traditional ones. Moreover, the extensive use of ekphrasis in novelistic history calls into question the limited definition given it by the tradition of *ut pictura poesis* as a description of a work of *spatial* art. According to Emilie Bergmann, this limited definition came into currency about the fourth century (1). I believe that the prevalence of this usage in the eighteenth through the twentieth centuries is due to its serving particular aesthetic agendas. For reasons I outline later in this chapter, I return to the original definition of ekphrasis so that it encompasses a descriptive scene within the novelistic text in which there is a representation of any work of art. This more extended definition is warranted by the differences between novelistic and poetic discourses as well as recent theoretical questioning of poetic presence, a crucial element of *ut pictura poesis*.[8]

As descriptions of works of art, ekphrases within key realist texts are used to foreground linguistic debates over the truth-claims of referential and linguistic paradigms, making language their primary theme. I examine five novels to show how their realist assumptions are based upon a governing paradigm of representation and also how through ekphrastic scenes they thematically render the struggle between correspondence and coherence. Harry Levin writes that "realism . . . has often originated in parody" (*Gates* 47), and by parodying the romance, Miguel de Cervantes' *Don Quixote* is the prototype of the realistic novel. A paradigmatic ekphrastic scene is thus the debate between the Canon and the barber in *Don Quixote* over the respective virtues of histories and romances. Having characterized narrative features intrinsic to both forms, Cervantes thematizes them within myriad ekphrases, most notably Master Peter's puppet show, a scene in which several narrative modes and voices compete for dominance. This struggle between narrators can be read in terms of the shift in the Renaissance debate over referentiality matching a traditional scholastic paradigm against an emerging empirical and humanist one. The tradition of scholasticism assumed a natural, divine

---

8. I do not argue against the usefulness of studies emphasizing ekphrasis as the description of spatial art forms. I feel, however, that this limited definition circumscribes its further and wider theoretical use. Definitions of ekphrasis as the description of spatial art forms include Hagstrum's: "literary descriptions of works of graphic art" (18n). Wendy Steiner, in *The Colors of Rhetoric: Problems in the Relation Between Modern Literature and Painting*, writes that ekphrasis creates a "pregnant moment . . . in which poetry is to imitate the visual arts by stopping time" (14). Of these definitions of ekphrasis, Emilie Bergmann concedes, "Although most studies, including this one, refer to the description of visual works of art . . . the present usage has only been applied since the fourth century, A. D." (1).

correspondence between signs and their referents in the essences of things, and the text's empirical corrective of Don Quixote's textualizing signs within an ideal, chivalric code can be interpreted superficially as Cervantes' critique of this belief. However, in spite of the numerous real-world correctives of Don Quixote's excesses, I argue that the text implicitly problematizes the status of *all* discourses suggesting empirically correspondent relations. Ekphrases such as Master Peter's puppet show and the thematizing of competing narrative voices illustrate Cervantes' approval of the liberating play of language and worldmaking that came from the humanist celebration of creativity. Also, by representing a myriad of discourses conceivably to stabilize discursive relations, *Don Quixote* proves undecidable the historical debate between the terms of a binary opposition.

Another important example for the genre is Jane Austen's richly ekphrastic novel *Emma*, which implicitly pleads for a correspondent theory of linguistic reference through the ekphrastic debates of Emma and Knightley, the most important of which concern Emma's idealizing portrait of Harriet Smith and Frank Churchill's conciliatory epistles. Like *Don Quixote*, the text posits an opposition between representational paradigms. The ekphrases seem to condemn representations that the Lockean empiricist paradigm describes as products of the fancy and to valorize those emanating from the understanding. On a textual level, Austen seems to support the valorized objectivity of the understanding; however, in subtextually revealing that this "objective" view of reality is grounded culturally not only in Lockean empiricism but also in British imperialism, the text's ekphrastic system offers alternative worldmaking and fancy as means of liberation. The debate also illustrates the limits of the Lockean episteme's attempt to find within the confines of sense and reflection an objective basis for knowledge and ethics. As in *Don Quixote*, the search for empirical accuracy leads to exposure of the constructed nature of the real, and in finding the binary opposition of fancy and understanding undecidable, the text then seeks a resolution through a conceptual and dramatic synthesis. Similarly, Leo Tolstoy, in *Anna Karenina*, contrasts Vronsky's conventionalized, ersatz Pre-Raphaelite portrait of Anna with the portrait of her by Mihailov, who reproduces sensory signs corresponding to her essential character. The ekphrases of the contrasting paintings establish terms by which Tolstoy dramatically renders an epistemological conflict between social and representational conventions and unmediated intuition. These terms are drawn from the conceptual vocabulary of the nineteenth-century Kantian romantic paradigm. For example, the artistic immediacy of Mihailov's portrait suggests a romantic desire for union with the external in nature, which can be achieved only when the medium of language or paint seems to disappear and the essential subject is revealed for sensual apprehension. These ekphrastic scenes, dramatizing the intuition of an essential reality, render the desire of the Kantian romantic tradition: to go beyond what can be revealed through representations to perceive the other in reality as thing-in-itself, or noumenon. Similarly, Tolstoy also attempts to go beyond medium and representations by using an effaced, deliberately unnoticeable style. Tolstoy, however, is aware of the necessarily conventional status of art and self-consciously reveals how even correspondences to essences are conventionally drawn.

The texts I examine from the twentieth century are more self-conscious of their dependence upon correspondence and coherence models of semiotic meaning and therefore foreground more explicitly the conceptual schemes and representational paradigms governing their language use. As a result, their ekphrases are more extended and more elaborately embedded within their narrative structures. In *Ulysses*, James Joyce's representational technique reflects a shift in the modernist paradigm from a scientistic early modernism, as seen in early Wittgenstein's atomistic theory of correspondence, to the coherentism of late modernism, as seen in the later Wittgenstein's theory of reality's social and linguistic construction. Joyce ekphrastically renders this conflict in several related ekphrases. For example, in "Scylla and Charybdis," the Aristotelian Stephen is paired against the Platonists Russell and Eglinton in a debate on *Hamlet* that presents the terms of this conflict, which in turn inform the structure of the novel. The first six chapters, which compose the "Telemachiad," and the last chapter, "Penelope," rest on a single style and the stable assumption of language's connections to the "here and now." The different styles of the middle chapters, however, from "Aeolus" to "Eumaeus," show that language is by nature polyphonic and the reality it evokes multiple. Joyce's novel, contemporaneous with the Einsteinian reinvention of the universe, shows reality as contingent upon our perceptual and linguistic capabilities. Thus, the entire novel, an encyclopedia of literary styles, catalogues the many worlds that men and women have linguistically made. The text's world-making through linguistic play reflects fictionally the later Wittgenstein's notion that language games and communities compose what we believe to be real, and of all examined novels, *Ulysses* most completely expresses the linguistic basis of reality, a belief central to the late modernist paradigm best revealed in the later works of Wittgenstein. However, in spite of the multiplicity of language and worlds within the text, Joyce, faithful to his "classical temper," achieves a synthesis of the real and the ideal, or the empirical and constructed worlds. He does so dramatically through the "fusion" of Stephen and Bloom and symbolically through an elaborate ekphrastic synthesis of oppositional representational modes—such as the musical fusion of tonic and dominant themes in a classical sonata. Also, the journey through the universe of discourses in *Ulysses* is ultimately brought home to "the hard rock of Ithaca" in the last chapter's celebration of Molly Bloom's sensuality, emblematic of the natural correspondence posited by early modernism. Finally, Thomas Pynchon, in *Gravity's Rainbow*, creates numerous ekphrases of popular films to problematize the notion of an extratextual reality to which representations can correspond. The effects of film show that what is thought of as reality is merely the product of culturally determinative representations, whose motives are often imprisonment and victimization. Pynchon's novel and his treatment of ekphrastic forms thus illustrate encyclopedically the postmodernist paradigm's analysis of discourse as ideologically motivated and of reality as constructed by coherentist schemes. However, in portraying the dangers of the constructed realities that imprison and victimize, *Gravity's Rainbow* nostalgically mourns the passing of a natural correspondence with the earth in the discourses of mythology and ritual.

Taken together, the consistent use of ekphrasis in these five novels reveals a regular pattern of literary conventional struggle between the conflicting correspondence and coherence paradigms of representation. However, in thematizing this struggle in order to establish truth-claims for a valorized paradigm of representation, the texts must represent both discourses, and this act of representation undermines any obvious attempt to deny the representational efficacy of the opposing paradigm. Each text implicitly recognizes the necessity of the oppositional other for its definitional status as well as its truth-conditions; therefore, denied the solution of erasure, it seeks to bring the other into the fold. Ultimately, in showing this binary opposition as false and undecidable, each strives, in the terms of its own historical discourse, to resolve the opposition through some dramatic synthesis. It is interesting to note how the first three texts, while supporting the guiding assumptions of a correspondence paradigm, generate ekphrases that defend coherence and discourse. The latter two, however, from the modern period, assume and support a coherentist theory of representation but generate correspondent ekphrases to expose the danger of language's drift from the world. Thus a realist text can be shown to have indeterminate allegiances to word and world.

Possible Worlds in Fiction

One way to read the mimetic discontinuity of an interpolated artifact with its frame narrative is as a conflict between an opposing representational paradigm portrayed within the text and the novel's own representational norm. Often this textual conflict is with an older paradigm whose mimetic norms now seem invalid. This literary parental rejection is most clearly evident in the novel because it is the most derivative of all genres. Rene Wellek and Austin Warren find artistic assimilation and refinement central to their positioning the novel's birth in eighteenth-century England: "The novel develops from the lineage of non-fictitious narrative forms—the letter, journal, the memoir or biography, the chronicle or history" (205). Considering the novel's late appearance in literary history and the extent to which it borrowed or assimilated conventions of other genres, it can legitimately be described as a late, hybrid form. A case just as convincing as Wellek and Warren's for the novel's heritage in nonfictional documents could be made for its heritage in the epic, dramatic tragedy or comedy, the romance, or pastoral. Friedrich Schlegel advances this hybrid theory: "The idea of the novel . . . is the idea of a romantic book . . . where all the forms and all the genres are mixed and interwoven" (Todorov 86). Individually, early novels clearly show their family resemblance to earlier literary genres. As *Don Quixote* is an outgrowth of the chivalric romance tradition and the novels of Samuel Richardson are heirs to the guides for familiar letter writing, so *Tom Jones* derives from the mock epic, *Robinson Crusoe* from the daily journal, and the *Castle of Otranto* from dramatic tragedy. In addition to these more obvious examples, many novels show a distant theoretical kinship with the aesthetics of nonliterary art forms. For example, the aesthetic doctrine of nineteenth-century literary realism borrowed freely from the representational theories of painting, and so, many novelists, particularly the French realists—Balzac, Stendahl, the Goncourt brothers, Burty, Rod, Zola, early Huysmans, and Duranty—reinforced the pictorial basis of their fictions with the interpolation of paintings and their creators.[9] And in like fashion, novels that are heirs of the fin de siècle symbolist movement—works by Joyce, Proust, and Huxley—display their allegiance to expressive artistic theories by interpolating musical works.[10]

9. See my appendix "Painting and the Nineteenth-Century Novel" for a fuller discussion of painting and novelistic realism. In addition to Wendy Steiner's work, another helpful study of the relation of painterly and literary representations is Francois Meltzer's *Salome and the Dance of Writing: Portraits of Mimesis in Literature.*
10. See my appendix "Symbolism and Music" for a fuller discussion of the role of music in the aesthetics of the late-nineteenth- and early-twentieth-century novel.

In the evolution of cultural as well as natural organisms, certain outmoded features of the parent or primitive ancestor are retained to remind, as does the navel, that (quoting *Ulysses*) "the cords of all link back." Similarly, novels often retain features of a parent genre, sometimes by portraying it graphically as an interpolated artifact to show how far the new form (faithful to its derivation from the Latin *novellus*, "new") has evolved from the older one. As M. M. Bakhtin remarks of genre, "Archaic elements preserved in a genre are not dead but eternally alive. . . . A genre lives in the present but always *remembers* its past, its beginning" (*Dostoevsky* 106). The motive for portraying these archaic elements is often one of repudiation, as Cervantes (author of the *Galatea*, an Arcadian romance) portrays in *Don Quixote* numerous romantic conventions avowedly to reject them. The novels of Jane Austen demonstrate a similarly discontinuous relation to an interpolated form from which they are derived. Many of her novels in early drafts imitated Richardsonian epistolary narratives, but with her discovery of a fuller, more penetrating technique of narration, the epistle becomes in *Emma*, her masterwork, an interpolated form used by charlatans for the purpose of falsification.[11] In another example, Gustave Flaubert's "Madame Bovary c'est moi" is widely interpreted as his exorcising the youthful Hugoesque sensibility that gave rise to early romantic narratives by making the sentimental novels interpolated within *Madame Bovary* a primary cause of his heroine's misfortunes. Flaubert's rejection is similar to Stendahl's, who illustrated his recanting of Rousseauian romanticism in the romantic novels of *Le rouge et le noir* that lead Julien Sorel to his fateful liaisons. And Thomas Hardy, in *Jude the Obscure*, records the passing of romanticism by transforming Jude's gothic-romantic paintings into the Christminster cakes he sells at a bazaar. In *Ulysses*, Joyce (author of *Dubliners* and *Stephen Hero*, both somewhat conventionally realistic narratives) calls the technique of his most conventional chapter, "Eumaeus," "Narrative (old)" and fills it with falsehoods, reinforced by the false stories within the story of Murphy the Sailor. And in the postmodernist *Gravity's Rainbow*, Pynchon treats the limitations of early modernist specificity and analytical philosophy's empirical exactness in his ekphrastic text *The Book*.

Most often ekphrastic discontinuity can be interpreted as juridically judging the novel's referential truth through contrast. By proving the discontinuous mode false, the text validates the truth-claims of that

11. For discussions of the epistolary mode in Austen, see Ian Jack, "The Epistolary Element in Jane Austen," and Norman Page, *The Language of Jane Austen*. See also my "Document of Falsimilitude: Frank's Epistles and Misinterpretation in *Emma*."

which is continuous. For example, the flat, wooden puppet knights of Cervantes' marionette theater emphasize the roundness of his flesh-and-blood knight Don Quixote. And the destructive liberties Emma and Frank Churchill take in judging character through their respective portrait and epistles give validity to Austen's implicit argument for referential stability in language. Another example of a contrastive ekphrasis used to reinforce referential stability is in *Little Dorrit*. Charles Dickens's false artist, Henry Gowan, describes his portrait of the arch-villain Blandois as "whatever you think he most looks like" (554). Dickens extends his argument against a work of art that can be anything into the realm of language by subtly criticizing the polysemous word used by Blandois's acquaintance Cavalleto: "Altro . . . a word being . . . a confirmation, a contradiction, an assertion, a denial, a taunt, a compliment, a joke, and fifty other things" (47).[12] In a significant nineteenth-century painterly novel, *L'Oeuvre*, Émile Zola also uses the discontinuous ekphrasis. The text tells of Claude Lantier, who, in his major painting, forsakes the representation of reality to conjure an ideal, an ethereal nude so unattainable that, crushed, he hangs himself in front of the painting, "gazing upon her with his fixed and lifeless eyes" (356). Lantier's painting confirms by contrast the truth-conditional validity of Zola's depiction of life.

In many novels, an ekphrastic description discontinuous with the referential norms of the novel is matched explicitly or implicitly with a continuous one in order to adjudicate between truth-claims: so Dickens sets Gowan's laxness in interpretation and meaning against the exactness of scientist William Doyce, who as inventor follows a creative doctrine similar to a realist novelist, and Zola pairs Lantier's idealism and subjectivism against the views of the fictional novelist Pierre Sandoz, whose aesthetic parallels that of Zola. Significantly, an interpolated artifact continuous with the referential system of the text that contains it can mirror the entire novelistic frame. An example of this is Vinteuil's little musical phrase in Marcel Proust's *A la recherche du temps perdu*. The protagonist Marcel's ambition in the last book of the series is to write a novel, conceivably the novel we are reading, which will evoke a response that the phrase had for himself and for Swann. Another painterly example that suggests such a synecdochical relation between the ekphrastic fragment and the novelistic frame is Tod Hackett's painting "The Burning of Los Angeles," which prophetically reveals the apocalyptic

---

12. I discuss the ekphrases in *Little Dorrit* more fully in my appendix on painting. A helpful discussion of art in general in this novel is Ira Nadel, " 'Wonderful Deception': Art and the Artist in *Little Dorrit*."

conclusion of Nathaniel West's *The Day of the Locust*. Similarly, when she concludes *To the Lighthouse* with a sentence describing the last stroke of Lily Briscoe's painting, Virginia Woolf ties the novel and the ekphrasis together as works that find a common answer to the problem of "subject and object and the nature of reality" (38). An even more challenging synecdochical relation between an ekphrasis and its frame narrative is in *Gravity's Rainbow*, where the ekphrastic use of film and an elaborate system of filmic codes make the entire text itself an imitation of a film. Most commonly, however, when ekphrasis is used for realistic self-definition, novels exhibit both continuous and discontinuous ekphrastic pairs.

The most significant way in which a discontinuous artifact is proven inadequate and false is by dramatizing the often tragic consequences that result when a character tries to construct a possible world within the terms of its limiting discourse. The tradition of possible-world fictional theory follows Saul Kripke's use of the Leibnizian possible-world concept in formal logic, which posits that "our actual world is surrounded by an infinity of other possible worlds" (Bradley and Swartz 2). Thus, according to this theory, fictional texts often present possible-world alternatives to the one deemed actual by consensus, to which they bear not a correspondent relation but rather one of coherence and logical fit. Joseph Margolis defines a possible world as "what is merely logically or conceptually compossible . . . with respect to the actual world" (163). As logical construct, a possible world is thus not expected to bear a correspondent relation to a consensual image of the actual world in terms of particulars; indeed, as Thomas Pavel indicates, "to require from possible worlds an inventory of beings identical to the inventory of the actual one is a position too restrictive for the representation of fictional ontologies" (47). Thus, because of the fictional creation of multiple possible worlds, the correspondence between the possible worlds within a fiction and the world deemed actual is complex and varied. Marie-Laure Ryan, in fact, creates a typology of fictional possible worlds, distinguishing the textual actual world (the textual image of the "actual" world) from textual alternative possible worlds, which she defines as "subworlds, created by the mental activity of characters" (5). I contend that these subworlds are not just the result of mental activity; they illustrate characters' worldmaking activities, which are metaphorized by the ekphrastic art forms with which the characters are identified; therefore, the mimetic function of these subworlds is to lay bare the device of world construction. Indeed, representing the construction of possible worlds within the text is a crucial means of validating the text's claim to realism. The evidence for such claims is not comparisons between the actual world and the possible world of fiction but instead between the several possible worlds constructed within the text through alternative theories of artistic and linguistic representation. However, the process by which rival realistic claims are made entails not simply creating a single fictional world that most clearly resembles the actual or real one; a realist text, instead, often displays several possible worlds implicitly to claim verisimilitude for a privileged one, continuous with the text's own mimetic norms, by showing its superiority over other false possible worlds that are textually represented as discontinuous with the text's mimesis. To use Leibniz's original terms for possible worlds: a privileged textual world displays truths that are necessary because they seem true for all possible worlds, as opposed to other, false textual worlds that display probable truths, true in only some worlds but manifestly untrue to some ontological, ethical, or epistemological standard that exists by consensual agreement in the stories we create about the "actual" world. It can be said, therefore, that the realist tradition in the novel is a search for necessary truth in possible worlds.

Novels that are centrally concerned with the issue of realism explicitly contrast alternative means and theories of creating art implicitly to contrast methods of worldmaking and the possible worlds that result. The ekphrastic pairs that exist in so many texts do not merely serve the purpose of matching the ekphrastic world model and the textual world model with a consensual image of the real world; they also contrast methods of worldmaking or world construal by alternative theories of artistic representation that presuppose alternative models of constructing worlds. By narrating the creation of art, the text, then, presents a variety of aesthetic models by which worlds are constructed. The represented artifacts thus, through a shared ontology and aesthetic, suggest the construal or creation of reality through language by the texts within which they are embedded. Many characters confirm the truth-conditions of the possible world affirmed as actuality by the text (the textual actual world) by tragically living out the ethical and ontological implications of the possible worlds created by false discourses. Conversely, characters living according to the realist assumptions of the discourse supported by the text often succeed in constructing a world view commensurate with the consensual standards of the textual actual world. These characters are shown capable of living in the world, as opposed to those who try to make an implacable reality yield to the discursive constructs of an aberrant imagination.

In the examples given above, the tragedies of Emma Bovary and Julien Sorel result because of their testing what the possible worlds of their romantic fictions offer. These ekphrastic fictions are discontinuous artifacts implying possible worlds that are discontinuous with the truth-conditions of the textual actual world. Similarly, Claude Lantier's suicide results from his inability to live in the "real" textual world while devoted to the illusory textual world of his painting. I discuss in greater depth similar dramatic implications for the novels I examine in the chapters ahead. For example, Cervantes renders both farcical and pathetic Don Quixote's attempts to live out the possible-world implications of the ekphrastic chivalric and pastoral romances. The novel, however, becomes tragic when, upon his deathbed, the Don relinquishes totally the notion of possibility through language. In *Emma*, the heroine's attempt to make caste relations conform to those posited by the ekphrases of her portrait and Frank's epistles ends in a nearly tragic loss. And the conventional overdetermining of Anna Karenina by the falsely sentimental stylization of Vronsky's portrait suggests the overwriting of her true nature by the false text and world of adulterous romance. In *Ulysses*, the characters of both Stephen and Bloom illustrate the dangers of assuming otherworldly views, which lead each to isolation. For Stephen, it is the rejection of the lived world in the name of aestheticism, and for Bloom, it is the rejection of the world in the form of intimate sexuality for the lure of an ideal world. In *Gravity's Rainbow*, false possible worlds are not so much chosen by characters as imposed from without by conceptual schemes whose primary purpose is to support a chosen few by means of suppressing all others.

The generic and world-testing characteristics of the realist novels I describe bear a similarity to Bakhtin's description of the menippean satire and its carnivalization of discourse. Although Bakhtin describes three roots for the novel—the epic, rhetorical, and carnivalistic—his descriptions of the modern novel are weighted heavily toward the carnivalistic and menippean. Like the menippea, the realist novel uses imaginary adventure "for the provoking and testing of a philosophical idea" (*Dostoevsky* 114); in the case of the realist novel, this idea is a paradigm's representational efficacy. However, for both the realist novel and the menippea, this philosophical testing is accomplished on a dramatic plane. The actions and motivations of characters serve as "moral-psychological experimentation" (116). Also important, the realist novel and the menippea are both characterized by "a wide use of inserted genres: novellas, letters, oratorical speeches, symposia and so on" (118). I widen these inserted genres to include nonliterary art forms, for artistic creation presumes a theory of representation and signification that has important implications for discourse.

The five novels I have chosen for extended discussion compose a great tradition within the genre and characterize how historical changes in mimetic paradigms are revealed rhetorically. These ekphrastic descriptions appear to be constative speech acts, utterances that describe a state of affairs, in this case an extratextual reality. But their real function is performative—more than representing a particular reality, they persuade readers to accept a particular *version* of reality by affirming it true through the illocutionary force of rhetorical appeal. It is through ekphrasis that a novel actually exhibits a dual mimesis—first to a fictionally constituted world presumed to have a metaphorical relation to reality and then to the rhetorical elements of the constituting activity. Riffaterre gives an interesting distinction between these two forms of referentiality by arguing that faulty interpretations of representational conventions are formed because of the assumption that "the reference on which the mimesis is based is from words to things, from the verbal to the nonverbal domain." His revisionary theory contends that verisimilitude is achieved by references "from words to words, or rather from texts to texts, and that intertextuality is the agent both of the mimesis and of the hermeneutic constructions on that mimesis" ("Intertextual" 142).[13] The ekphrastic forms in novels therefore refer less to an external reality than to the rhetorical operations of the texts themselves and the theory of language through which they were constructed.

Correspondence and Coherence

Ekphrasis can be considered a primary device of intertextual mimesis, but ironically it has been used to justify both correspondence and coherence theories of truth and reference. These two concepts—of language as externally correspondent to an external world or as an independent, coherent system for actively constructing a world—underlie any theory of representation, and all paradigms governed by a linguistic conceptual scheme fall into one of these categories. The latest paradigm shift in literary realism is then but the most recent turn of a continuing dialectic, similar to that posited by Tynjanov. Milton Munitz, basing *The Question of Reality* on this dialectic occurring throughout history, defines the first term as "the belief that insofar as reality is intelligible, it

13. "Intertextual Representation," first presented at the 1983 School of Criticism and Theory, is the best short introduction to Riffaterre's semiotic theory of mimesis. See also *Semiotics of Poetry*, particularly "The Poem's Significance." The essay "Syllepsis," in *Critical Inquiry*, and *Text Production* expand on his theory of intertextuality and verisimilitude. His most recent book, *Fictional Truth*, is most helpful in developing the rules of what he calls the "grammar of mimesis."

rests upon the extent to which some putatively objective set of inherent properties or structural patterns can be *discovered* as belonging to the *existents* that compose reality." The second "stresses the role human beings play in *constructing* and inventing various linguistic and conceptual schemes for rendering the materials of experience intelligible" (17). Language as correspondence implies a logical and empirical "match" between language and reality and that the truth-conditions of an assertion, or representation such as a novel, can be discovered by its correspondence with this independent reality. Rorty describes this epistemology as "not merely social but actual, springing from human nature itself, and made possible by a link between that part of nature and the rest of nature"; its adherents believe that this mode of rationality "*must* lead to the truth, to correspondence to reality, to the intrinsic nature of things" ("Solidarity or Objectivity" 5). In contrast, I use a comprehensive theory of coherence to describe the several noncorrespondence views that emphasize, not language's logical match with the world, but rather its coherence as a rational system containing analogical truths that fit the experiential world, not pointing toward some absolute notion of Truth or Reality. Instead of seeking a privileged vocabulary corresponding either divinely, empirically, or analytically with the essences of things in nature, a coherence theory of language explores the internal coherence of vocabularies allowing us to establish valid beliefs to construct a coherent map of the world. My use of a coherence theory of language borrows heavily from a coherence theory of truth, which is characterized by James O. Young as what "can be warranted by a system of beliefs" (467), or "the theory according to which the truth-conditions of sentences are *internal* to the system . . . of sentences speakers can be warranted in asserting" (468, my emphasis). Additionally, this coherence theory of language bears a relation to cognitive and constructivist epistemology, which Ernst von Glaserfeld defines as "a theory of knowledge [that] does not reflect an 'objective' ontological reality, but exclusively an ordering and organization of a world constituted by our experience" (201). Language's role is crucial in this construction and constitution. S. J. Schmidt's analysis of constructivism and realism emphasizes language as the primary tool of the human "system's constructional work," for "the status of reality, truth, meaning, and identity depends on conventions that determine what kind of rules are individually or socially accepted for the consensual *confirmation* of reality, truth, meaning, and identity" (263).

The linguistic theories of Edward Sapir and Benjamin Lee Whorf are especially relevant to a coherence theory of language. According to Sapir, "the 'real world' is to a large extent unconsciously built up on the language habits of the group" (Hoijer 92). Whorf concurs with Sapir in finding a concept of reality to be a product of linguistic habits and the constituting activity of the mind: "The categories and types that we isolate from the world of phenomena we do not find there because they stare every observer in the face; on the contrary, the world is presented in a kaleidoscopic flux of impressions which has to be organized by our minds—and this means largely by the linguistic systems in our minds" (213). What interests Sapir and Whorf is not how language mirrors the world but how it serves, in Nelson Goodman's terms, as an instrument of worldmaking. The early language theory of Wittgenstein in the *Tractatus* and his later one in the *Logical Investigations* contrast correspondence and coherence views. Wittgenstein writes of the earlier text, "In the *Tractatus*, I was unclear about 'logical analysis' and the clarification it suggests. At that time I thought it provided a 'connexion' between language and reality." But in his later work he phrases the question, "By what procedures do men *establish* links between language and the real world?" (Toulmin 62, 67). This argument has the following implication for realism: in texts governed by a correspondence paradigm the "connexion between language and reality" is given to the reader as an a priori, and as Barthes indicates, these texts often disguise the conventional nature of representation—whereas in texts governed by a coherence paradigm the *establishment* of links between the text and a postulated reality is given prominence, often by narratively playing with the conceptual schemes through which worlds are made. This practice is most clearly evident in the last two novels I describe—*Ulysses* and *Gravity's Rainbow*, exemplary novels presenting a coherentist view of reality. These novelistic examples of twentieth-century coherentist views play with the notion of worldmaking by proposing a number of possible worlds that are created by language. In summary, Wallace Martin implicitly describes the relevance of constructivist and coherentist epistemology when he writes that the "choice in life and literature is not between conventional practices and a truth or reality lying outside them, but between different conventional practices that make meaning possible" (71).

Modern aesthetic and literary theories have defined art and literature according to the polarities of correspondent and coherentist epistemologies. I want to examine this theoretical tradition to indicate its ingrained bias toward seeing correspondent language as the only way language works in the novel, which I contend has had an inhibiting effect on the study of novelistic discourse. Wilhelm Worringer's *Abstraction and Empathy* (1908) provided an early-twentieth-century aesthetic based roughly on correspondence and coherence views of language. Worringer describes correspondent aesthetics as an impulse toward empathy—the ability to identify with external forms and to derive aesthetic pleasure from sublimating self-interest. According to Worringer, the artistic practice of empathy is objective representation, and this aesthetic dominated classical, Renaissance, and indeed most European art until the early twentieth century. The opposing impulse is toward abstraction, evident in primitive, Egyptian, Byzantine, Romanesque, and most modern art. Worringer's aesthetic distinction provided what formalist and New Critical theorists perceived as formal principles underlying historical and generic changes.

Since the New Criticism, most theoreticians of the novel have interpreted these tendencies in generically definitive terms. For example, Robert Scholes and Robert Kellogg, in *The Nature of Narrative,* describe antithetical narrative types: out of the impulse Worringer calls empathy emerge "empirical" narratives, showing "allegiance to reality"; and out of abstraction emerge "fictional" narratives, showing "allegiance to the ideal" (13). David Goldknopf, in *The Life of the Novel,* locates the two impulses in the Cartesian opposition of inner and outer: a subjective, "psychological" form of narrative and an outer, "empirical" one (5–6). In *Character and the Novel,* W. J. Harvey, claiming Aristotelian imitation as the basis of novelistic realism, describes imitation as correspondence to reality and defines correspondence as an "angle of mimesis" (16). Representational texts, parallel to life, form a mimetic mode; idealistic texts, at wider mimetic angles, form an autonomous one.

An explanation why this dichotomy established a correspondent bias in modern novel theory can be found in one of the most influential New Critical studies of literary language—I. A. Richards's *Principles of Literary Criticism.* This is Richards's famous formulation of the dichotomy: "A statement may be used for the sake of reference, true or false, which it causes. This is the *scientific* use of language. But it may also be used for the sake of the effects in emotion and attitude produced by the reference it occasions. This is the *emotive* use of language" (267). According to this basic New Critical distinction, the scientific, or denotative, use of language—vehicle for the empathetic, mimetic, or empirical impulse—assumes a direct and unequivocal correspondence between a sign and referent. Emotive, or connotative, language is more affective and, aspiring less toward representation, calls attention to its autonomy. Consistently, critics of this era aligned emotive language with poetry, and scientific language with fiction. In the view of most New Critics, poetry in its purest form was considered autonomous artifact, whereas fiction achieved its essential state in a correspondent relation to an extratextual reality. For example, Ian Watt traces the origins of fictional language to "a prose which restricts itself almost entirely to a descriptive and denotative use" (29), and he characterizes realism in the novel as having "a more largely referential use of language than is common in other literary forms" (32). Watt further argues that the genre fulfills the correspondent function of language, since novelistic realism is "the correspondence between the literary work and the reality it imitates" (11). Marvin Mudrick writes that a novelist's allegiance to facts is so strong that his language must be unobtrusive to the point of being transparent. "In prose fiction," he writes, "the unit is not, as in poetry, the word, but the event" (205). Mudrick is close to F. W. Bateson, who writes, "If words are the media of poetry, what are the media of prose? . . . The answer would seem to be Ideas" (16). And Christopher Caudwell posits that "in the novel as opposed to poetry the emotional associations attach not to words but to the moving current of mock reality symbolized by the words" (226).

Ut Pictura Poesis, Space and Time

The New Critics' and formalists' predilection for valorizing poetic discourse over that of fiction is reflected also in their definition and use of ekphrasis. Most commonly their treatments are rooted in the tradition of *ut pictura poesis*—the search for a common aesthetic bond between poetry and the spatial arts.[14] As a result, most studies of ekphrasis are of poetry and define the convention narrowly as the description of a spatial art form. Jean Hagstrum's *Sister Arts* is both exemplary and influential in giving this narrower definition of ekphrasis for what Hagstrum calls iconic poetry. In defining ekphrasis as "literary descriptions of works of graphic art," Hagstrum distinguishes his theories from those of Julius Schlosser-Magnino, who uses the broader definition of the term as "any embedded description," saying, "I use the noun *ecphrasis* [sic] and the adjective 'ecphrastic' in a more limited sense to refer to that special quality of giving voice and language to the otherwise mute art object" (18n). Hagstrum and others use the convention to align themselves with the Horation tradition *ut pictura poesis* (as is the picture, so is the poem). As interest in this tradition grew in the eighteenth century, Gotthold Lessing, in *Laokoön*, derided it as sheer extravagance by posing the

---

14. The most thorough introduction to *ut pictura poesis* is Rensselaer W. Lee, "*Ut Pictura Poesis*: The Humanistic Theory of Painting." See also Hagstrum; William G. Howard, "*Ut Pictura Poesis*"; and Henryk Markiewicz, "*Ut Pictura Poesis*: A History of the Topos and the Problem."

question that has plagued the poetics of *ut pictura poesis*: how can poets create the illusion of spatial forms when poetic meaning is temporally apprehended?

Most New Critical and formalist studies of ekphrasis in literature oppose Lessing, aligning themselves with *ut pictura poesis* to find within the structure of poetic language a form or shape that transcends the flow of time—Eliot's "still point of the turning world" (119). For example, Cleanth Brooks, in *The Well-Wrought Urn*, focuses on the ekphrasis of the golden bird in Yeats's "Sailing to Byzantium" to show how the privileged temporal space of poetic language is thematized: "The golden bird whose bodily form the speaker will take in Byzantium will be withdrawn from the flux of the world of becoming. But so withdrawn it will sing of the world of becoming—'Of what is past, passing, or to come' " (190). Similarly, Leo Spitzer, examining Keats's urn, contends that the artifact provides a spatial metaphor of the poem's temporal structure.

The most ambitious and challenging formalist attempt to resolve the spatial-temporal dilemma posed by the ekphrastic text is in Murray Krieger's works. In an influential essay, "The Ekphrastic Principle and the Still Movement of Poetry; or *Laokoön* Revisited," Krieger argues that a poem achieves through imagery and image patterns a freedom from temporal flow. Krieger summarizes the purpose of ekphrasis from this perspective: "The object of imitation, as spatial work, becomes the metaphor for the temporal work that seeks to capture it in its temporality. The spatial work freezes the temporal work even as the latter seeks to free it from space" (107). Krieger argues that in privileged moments of poetic discourse, "whenever the poem takes on the 'still' element of plastic form which we normally attribute to the spatial arts" (106), space and time are not mutually exclusive categories. As he concludes in the penultimate sentence, "The poetic context can defy the apparently mutually exclusive categories of time and space to become fixed in the still movement of the Chinese jar that poets have summoned to their poetry as the emblem of its aesthetic" (127–28).[15]

Krieger further develops his theory of literary language in *Theory of Criticism* and *Ekphrasis: The Illusion of the Natural Sign*. These texts formulate more systematically several formalist and new critical perspectives and weigh them against the challenge of structuralism and poststructuralism. In the former text, he extends the empathy-abstraction

15. A good introduction to Krieger's use of ekphrasis in his developing literary theory is Gwen Raaberg's "*Ekphrasis* and the Temporal/Spatial Metaphor in Murray Kreiger's Critical Theory."

distinction by positing a representational scale ranging from the externally oriented imitative to the self-reflective and autotelic expressive. The
former, identified with existential reality, emphasizes the temporal flow
of narrative and life, and the latter uses those devices that stress the spatial
element, which he now more fully defines as the formal patterning that
can be imposed upon the existential and narrative flow of time, thus
separating the work self-consciously from empirical reality. Calling his
a humanist aesthetic, Krieger argues that it is through this form-making
ability that man transcends the material conditions of life and "transforms the nature and the time he suffers, and lives in the light of the
forms that work his inventive miracles" (*Theory* 244). While accepting
some of the structuralist and poststructuralist descriptions of ordinary
language as a system of differential relations, Krieger muses that "they
cannot confront the theoretical possibility that literary works are unique
and privileged systems" (*Theory* 215). Echoing the new critical claim of
a privileged and elite status for poetic and literary discourse, Krieger
argues that through the "frozen moment" we "bestow 'corporality' "
upon the poem and "accept the poem as present, as the present as *a*
present, a miraculous gift that seems to exclude all else . . . a 'now'
which never becomes a 'then' " (*Theory* 209). By arguing that literary
and poetic languages are elite and privileged forms evoking a unitary
"miraculous" presence out of the flow of time and otherness, Krieger is
most at odds with poststructuralist theory. Therein lies a significant
difference between his ekphrastic theory, based primarily upon poetic
texts, and the ekphrastic theory of fiction I develop. In his more recent
Ekphrasis, Krieger moderates his claims for the "presence" of the poetic
voice and consequently establishes an admirable middle ground between
correspondent and coherentist extremes. The privileged space for the
poem exists to satisfy the innate human feeling for language: "on the
one side . . . the semiotic desire for the natural sign and, on the other,
the rejection of any such claim to the 'natural,' for fear of the deprivation
it would impose on our freedom of internal movement, the freedom of
our imagination and its flow in its arbitrary signs" (10–11). While
reworking the concept of presence to that of the "natural sign," which
he concedes is an "illusion," Krieger attacks poststructuralism for denying the innate desire for natural correspondence that this sign represents.

Ekphrastic Presence and Absence

The literary and perceptual model of presence in Krieger's earlier writing, through which humans can transcend the temporal conditions of

material life, is related to the phenomenological *epochē*, the suspension of the natural standpoint as a foundation for perception. In his earliest work, Derrida attacks the notion of a privileged foundation for reflection as a nostalgic longing for absolute, undivided Being uncontaminated by the differential play of signification, a "dream" of "full presence, of reassuring foundation, of the origin and end of play" (*Writing* 292). Derrida argues that phenomenological reflection, in which the structured perception of bracketing and eidetic reduction create a moment that is anterior to discourse and time, what Edmund Husserl in his later works calls the "living present," is hardly the privileged unity it appears to be; it is, rather, like language, contaminated by the "play" of differences—the "now" contaminated by "was" and "to be." The apprehension of the word *and* experience depend as much on what is absent as what is present, for they operate through substitutions within differential relations, a signifying chain that allows for endless play, an infinite referring and deferring of meaning.[16] Every presence is therefore contaminated by absence, for meaning exists in consciousness as a presence only because of the phonemic, graphemic, perceptual, and conceptual differences between it and absent terms. Meaning is deferred because signs are not present or positive entities at all but rather effects of differences within signifying systems. This deferring of meaning as a signifying element working through the play of differences is implied in the Derridean term *différance*. Derrida writes that "the play of differences involves syntheses and referrals that prevent there from being at any moment or in any way a simple element that is present in and of itself . . . no element can function as a sign without relating to another element which itself is not simply present. This linkage means that each 'element'—phoneme or grapheme—is constituted with reference to the trace in it of the other elements of the sequence or system" (*Positions* 26).

Although Derrida elaborates his definition of the trace with reference to the general structure of the sign, he proposes that it relates to any philosophy of language or perception positing Being as presence: "All the names related to fundamentals, to principles, or to the center have always designated an invariable presence—*eidos*, *archē*, *telos*, *energeia*, *ousia* (essence, existence, substance, subject) *alētheia*, transcendality, consciousness, God, man, and so forth" (*Writing* 279–80). A foundation, presence, and privileged now outside of time are impossibilities because

16. One of Derrida's first published works, *"Speech and Phenomena" and Other Essays on Husserl's Theory of Signs*, attacks Husserl's idea of positing a foundation for knowledge in the unmediated data of consciousness. Other interesting encounters between Derridean thought and Husserlean phenomenology include " 'Genesis and Structure,' " in *Writing and Difference*, and *Edmund Husserl's "Origin of Geometry": An Introduction*.

meaning occurs by means of the play of differences, which depends upon temporal movement: "Without a retention in the minimal unit of temporal experience, without a trace retaining the other as other in the same, no difference would do its work and no meaning would appear. It is not the question of a constituted difference here, but rather, before all determination of the content, of the *pure* movement which produces difference. *The (pure) trace is différance*" (*Grammatology* 62). The not-now discomforting the now is the other to which the sign must refer for self-identity. Like the individual sign, the semiotic system of a novel achieves identity through differences, by the other leaving its trace in ekphrastic representations. Ekphrastic representations of the other often attempt by irony to confirm a privileged status for the referential system valorized by the text, but they ultimately problematize it. The ironic representations of the other, an alternative referential system, rather than confirm the supremacy and unity of a mimetic paradigm, show instead how it depends upon its opposite for definitional existence. Fictional realism, therefore, does not imply an unproblematic reference to an empirical world "out there"; realism achieves its status through the play of differences within a system of mimetic signs.

Don Quixote again provides the paradigm for this use of ekphrasis. Cervantes introduces several different types of narrators whom he describes as either poets or historians. For the poets, the sign's relations are between a chivalric and romantic code and the ideal essences of things; therefore, the ideal signifier "helmet of Mambrino" can miraculously transform the lowly signified "barber's basin." To the historians who anchor their language use upon evidential experience, a barber's basin is a barber's basin, nothing more. As a satire of chivalric romance, the text seems to valorize the historian's system of meaning. However, this valorization is problematized by the appearances of the other in ekphrastic scenes. In the example of Master Peter's puppet show, Cervantes brings to the stage numerous versions of poet and historian narrators, both textual and extratextual, and allows each to comment in his own manner. The result, a riotously humorous collision of interpretations, makes one of the most pointed statements in novelistic literature on the limitations of any system of language. As the narration is passed from narrative voice to narrative voice, poet or historian, novelistic discourse is defined as something transmitted, relayed through a chain of narrative signifiers. And the novel's theme, the search for the "original and true" history of Don Quixote, becomes an ironic statement on the impossibility of discovering the origin of this or any discourse.

The primary theme of *Emma* is its heroine's education in the proper and improper uses of language. This educative process serves to maintain social stability, for the typical plot of Austen's novels is the union of socially equal partners in marriage and the alignment of characters according to their proper caste. In *Emma*, Austen deliberately confuses the proper relationship of characters, their caste positions, and their moral values. By limiting herself for the greater part of the text to the erroneous point of view of her heroine, Austen draws her reader into the circle of deception and forces him or her to follow Emma's arduous education. The evidence of her education is her response to one of the novel's ekphrastic forms, Frank Churchill's epistles, which are circumlocutory distortions of the novel's primary values. What emerges as a norm for language use is a model radically redefining empirical correspondence as a social consensus regarding ethics and conduct. Subjective views such as Frank's, identified with Lockean fancy, are shown to be severely limiting in their selfish biases. On the other hand, objective views, identified with the understanding, are given primacy by being associated with such voices as the omniscient narrator's and Knightley's. These authoritative voices provide a realistic model for discourse by attempting to stabilize through social consensus the referential status of such crucial signifiers of conduct as "delicacy," "elegance," "duty," and "impropriety." However, the conflicting ekphrastic representations that would confirm this consensual system of meaning instead expose the artificiality of the naturalized social hierarchy. Eventually the textual artifacts representing the otherness of subjectivity reveal the ruthless arbitrariness of signifying practices in complicity with the workings of social power and domination.

In *Anna Karenina*, Tolstoy's ekphrastic portrait of Anna is an analogue of his literary portrait of her. The ekphrasis offers two portraits: Vronsky's and Mihailov's. The former is drawn from stale convention, and its maker's imagination distorts Anna's physical characteristics so that they conform to a stereotypical romantic ideal. The latter, on the other hand, so fully reveals Anna's physical being that the medium of oil and canvas seems to disappear and it becomes "not a picture but a living, lovely woman" (728–29). The language in Tolstoy's novel aspires toward a transparency similar to the painter Mihailov's medium. In such scenes as Levin mowing or Vronsky confessing to Anna during the snowstorm, Tolstoy attempts to remove the barrier of language so that readers respond to the scenes' physical contexts in much the same way as do the characters—through their senses. The novel's primary theme, connected with the character development of Levin, is the search for a transcendental vision of reality, one that can evade the distorting patterns of medium or discourse. And this theme appears prominently in the ekphrastic scene of painting. The perceptual model in both novelistic and painterly texts is one in which an essential reality of a character is revealed through the representation of an essentializing trait. Through this represented trait, the medium, both in word and in paint, seems to disappear, and in a moment of *alētheia* the inner reality of character is disclosed. This neo-Kantian theme of the innate purity of perception and representation, a striving for an ultimate correspondence with object or spirit, can be portrayed only textually; therefore, it achieves its privileged status through the intertextual references to other representational modes. The attempt to portray a spiritual empiricism linguistically causes this representation to enter the field of discourse and differential relations, where its identity exists in a system of signs, not extratextually in a spiritual or existential reality.[17] This striving to go beyond the word and toward the immediacy of the picture foreshadows Tolstoy's later rejection of literature for religious and prophetic writing.

Because of its encyclopedia of styles, the model of language and perception in *Ulysses* reveals the sign's dependence upon differential relations. Moreover, its linguistic relativism is one of the text's most significant innovations. As the Linati and Gilbert schemata indicate, Joyce viewed each episode from numerous artistic, technical, and symbolic perspectives, each implying a different style. By shifting emphases, Joyce illustrates the relationship between Stephen and Bloom alternately as that between Telemachus and Odysseus, Hamlet and Shakespeare (or Hamlet and Hamlet, Sr.), Don Giovanni and the Commendatore from Mozart's opera, tonic and dominant keys in a classical sonata, idealistic and realistic impulses, and father and son. By foregrounding the network of differential relations in which his characters achieve identity, Joyce questions whether the human subject can be considered from a unitary perspective. This multiformity of theme and character correlates with the carnivalesque mixing of discourses. The pastiches of literary styles in "Oxen of the Sun" suggest what Joyce has been engaged in throughout the novel, exploring the many ways language can be used to create possible worlds. As Joyce treats the coming together of Stephen and Bloom by illustrating many variations of the theme of consubstantiality, so does he thematize language use by depicting the spectrum of discourses that exist between the extremes of correspondent and coherentist expressions. Because of the multiple presentation of these different modes of rendering, the expressive values of *Ulysses* are close to those of *Don Quixote*, in which the Canon praises both romances and histories and in which the text disseminates narrative authority throughout a web

17. I treat Tolstoy's spiritual mimesis in my article "Tolstoy and the Conventions of Representation."

of textual and extratextual narrators, the poets and historians. In *Ulysses* there are many plays on the difference between referential and emotive, denotative and connotative, uses of language, which Cervantes treats by allowing his hero, by renaming, to transform an ordinary article of toiletry from a "barber's basin" to the "helmet of Mambrino." Stephen's ashplant, for example, is transformed from its ordinary use in "Telemachus" to the apocalyptic sword of Siegfried, Nothung, from Wagner's *Götterdämmerung*, when in "Circe" Stephen renames it and uses it in its symbolic function with apocalyptic effect: "Time's livid flame leaps with the ruin of all space" (583; 475). Both Joyce and Cervantes write paradigmatic menippean satires that explore the incommensurability of conceptual schemes due to the untranslatability of their discourses. And both emphasize what Donald Davidson claims to be the problematic nature of conceptualism: "Reality is relative to a scheme; what counts as real in one system may not be in another" (130).

The symbolic identities of Joyce's characters, themes, and situations are indeed multitudinous and splintered by difference; however, he seeks unity within this diversity by implying that the numerous forms exemplify the archetypal monomyth that underlies *Ulysses*, giving it shape and meaning. Thus, Joyce illustrates the dilemma of modernism that defined human reality as discontinuous and fragmented yet strove to repair its divisions by integrating them within the meaningful structure of an underlying myth. Joyce's Odyssean frame is a buried or implied ekphrasis. Other than in the title, it does not emerge by name, nor is it examined by the characters in any one specific scene; rather, it emerges in the very actions of the characters themselves as they conform to the epic's archetypal pattern. Several ekphrastic forms analogically duplicate an essential theme of Homer's epic: the consubstantiality of oppositional pairs—father and son, home and adventure. One of these is Shakespeare's *Hamlet*, which is introduced in a scene containing the typical elements of such ekphrastic debates as those between the Canon and the barber in *Don Quixote*, Emma and Knightley in *Emma*, and Vronsky and Mihailov in *Anna Karenina*. The oppositional impulses motivating Stephen and George Russell's debate on *Hamlet* are also expressed in other implicit or buried ekphrases in *Ulysses*—for instance, in the analogues of the Don and Commendatore in Mozart's *Don Giovanni* or the myth of Daedalus and Icarus. But I feel that formally the most significant ekphrastic treatments of consubstantiality are scenes textualizing this theme as the unification of tonic and dominant keys in a classical sonata.[18] These explicit and buried ekphrases provide unity to

---

18. Several studies speak metaphorically of a sonata structure in *Ulysses*. They include Ezra Pound's "James Joyce and Pécuchet" and Anthony Burgess's *ReJoyce*. The first study to treat seriously the novel's structure as a sonata is Robert Boyle's "*Ulysses* as Frustrated

an otherwise fragmented text not only by providing meaningful structure but also by providing the theme of unity through which Bloom and
Stephen are united with their oppositional others. The sonata structure
implied by the ekphrasis also provides a journey/home motif that mirrors the text's structure of the journey of various discourses from the
home of earthly correspondence, which is given in "Penelope," the coda
of *Ulysses*.

Similar to *Ulysses*, the encyclopedic form of *Gravity's Rainbow* presents
an intricate system of diametrically opposed ekphrastic artifacts presup-
posing different conceptual schemes and hence different realities. At one
extreme is purely empirical discourse, of which Pavlov's *Book* is the
clearest example. Devoted exclusively to the study of cause and effect,
The Book fulfills Hugh Kenner's definition of empirical narration as
"only the things an observer would have experienced . . . in the order in
which he would have experienced them" (*Joyce's* 4). *The Book* and
other empirical art forms are discontinuous with the mimetic norms of
Gravity's Rainbow. Counterbalancing *The Book*, Pynchon offers preverbal communication, Kabbalist myth, oral myth, and the unwritten songs
of the primitive Aqyn, about which Tchitcherine realizes: "soon someone
will come out and begin to write some of these down in the new Turkic
alphabet [. . .] and this is how they will be lost" (357). By refusing to
allow his narrative to be governed by the dictates of cause and effect,
Pynchon shows that his work's mimetic norms are more continuous
with the ekphrastic songs and myths of *Gravity's Rainbow*'s primitive
tribes, the Aqyn and Hereros. Through this identification, Pynchon
aligns himself against uses of language relying too rigidly upon the
grammatical and logical strictures of cause and effect. As opposed to the
verbal freedom of primitive forms, *The Book* and the Turkic alphabet
make language and its constituted reality deterministic and artificial.
Indeed, the major theme of *Gravity's Rainbow* is the conquest and
violation of natural forms by naturalized ones—from the rearrangement
of molecules in the invention of polymers to the imposition of artificial
linguistic systems over natural discourse. Pynchon shows that even the
sign's relation of signifier to signified is artificially imposed in order to
further the causes of manipulation and domination. The most extended
example, however, of an artificial form of causal design is the ekphrastic
use of film. The unalterable continuity of frames in a reel suggests the
causal rigidity of determinism. Pynchon makes *Gravity's Rainbow* a
parodic imitation of popular American and German expressionist films

---

Sonata Form." I argue against Boyle's rejection of sonata form in my "The Structural
Rhythm in *Ulysses*."

and illustrates their destructive effects by showing his characters either trapped by or escaping from the deterministic sequence of a reality created by film.[19]

Ekphrastic Systems

An individual scene that features an ekphrasis as a metaphor of a novel's mimetic norms is not an isolated unit; it usually forms part of a network of representational scenes, which I call the novel's ekphrastic system. An ekphrasis relates with other ekphrases in a novel to compose a systemic meaning of a text's formal and mimetic norms. Thus an ekphrasis is a sign that achieves meaning like any other sign—in a signifying system of similarities and differences. Riffaterre's definition of verisimilitude is relevant to my definition of ekphrastic system. According to Riffaterre, "truth in fiction rests on verisimilitude, a system of representations that seems to reflect a reality external to the text, but only because it conforms to a grammar" (*Fictional* xiii–xiv). The ekphrastic system is a vital component of the overall system of representations in a text that composes a grammar of mimesis. For example, the ekphrastic marionette show in *Don Quixote* can be understood only in the mimetic grammatical context of the Canon's and barber's debate on romances, the helmet of Mambrino, the song of Chrysostom, and the interpolated novelettes, such as "The Tale of the Foolish Curiosity." Frank Churchill's epistles compose the clearest sign of Austen's concern with the correspondent accuracy of language, but they achieve meaning only in their differential relations with other ekphrastic signs, such as Emma's portrait of Harriet Smith and, most important, the various verbal games in *Emma*—Mr. Elton's charade, Mr. Weston's conundrum, and Frank's letter puzzle. And in *Anna Karenina*, Mihailov's and Vronsky's portraits find meaning in the field of ekphrastic relations signifying Tolstoy's theory of art, a system that includes Mihailov's painting of Christ and Pilate, the French artist's illustrations to the Bible, the *King Lear* Fantasy for Orchestra that Levin criticizes, and the aborted works of Golenishchev.

19. Film is such a pervasive art form in *Gravity's Rainbow* that numerous studies have explored its implications for theme and structure. Some notable ones include Charles Clerc, "Film in *Gravity's Rainbow*"; Scott Simmon, "Beyond the Theater of War: *Gravity's Rainbow* as Film"; David Cowart, "Cinematic Auguries of the Third Reich in *Gravity's Rainbow*"; and Bertram Lippman, "The Reader of Movies: Thomas Pynchon's *Gravity's Rainbow*." I also treat the epistemological implications of *Gravity's Rainbow*'s use of film in my "Paracinematic Reality of *Gravity's Rainbow*."

In the context of ekphrastic systems, the fact that *Ulysses* and *Gravity's Rainbow* contain a multitude of artifacts is not in itself exceptional. What is exceptional is the degree of multiplicity. Like *Don Quixote*, these texts contain the multiplicity of inserted genres characteristic of the menippean satire. In *Ulysses* the coming together of Stephen and Bloom is portrayed ekphrastically as the resolution of tonic and dominant keys in a sonata, the discovery of Odysseus by Telemachus, the creation of Hamlet by Shakespeare, the subduing of Don Giovanni by the Commendatore, the return of Sinbad the Sailor, and many more. And in *Gravity's Rainbow*, the plots of literally dozens of popular films are given special significance by ekphrastic parallels with Rilke's *Duino Elegies*, Pavlov's *Book*, the myths of the Hereros, the songs of the Aqyn, and the music of Rossini and Beethoven. Written in a period of intellectual history in which language and truth are increasingly seen as coherent systems within conceptual schemes, *Ulysses* and *Gravity's Rainbow* provide more intricate networks of ekphrastic and intertextual relations to show a greater variety of conceptual schemes and their constituted realities. This theory of language and truth also relocates the act of reading from the level of extratextual reference to that of discourse.

The degree of complexity of ekphrastic systems within novelistic texts is one primary difference between how ekphrases are used in fiction and how they are used in poetry. An individual poem creates parallels between its discourse and the objectness of an isolated spatial artifact; a fictional narrative creates more complex relations between its discourse and its ekphrastic forms. Ekphrastic systems perform what Riffaterre calls the "transfer of a sign from one level of discourse to another" (*Semiotics* 4). Although Riffaterre calls this passage one from the mimetic level of reading to the semiotic, I would rather call this latter level the discursive, or rhetorical. It is the level of authorial argument and persuasion in the guise of unmotivated description.

I contend that this fictional use of the trope returns it to its classical origin. The Greek *ekphrazein* means "to speak out." Although Hagstrum uses this etymology to justify defining the convention as the speaking out loud of the mute art object, I argue that the speaking voice is that of the rhetor, or author, inserting a digressive description into the address or narrative to provide another level of appeal. Even the description of spatial forms in classical address has this rhetorical function. For example, in his panegyrical sermon delivered in 316 or 317 to honor Paulinus, bishop of Tyre, Eusebius embeds an elaborate description of the reconstruction of the destroyed church in Tyre. While the physical characteristics of the church are described in great detail, Eusebius's real motive is to persuade his audience to accept the principles of the invisible, spiritual church that are embedded in Christian practices (Kennedy 142). Similarly, in ekphrastic scenes that seem unmotivated narrative descriptions, the authorial voices "speak out" to persuade and move an audience to believe in the verisimilitude of a textual reality.[20]

Expressive and Mimetic Conflict

My textual examples are chosen not by virtue of their coincidental use of ekphrasis. They are texts I consider crucial to any theory of realism in the novel; that they all contain ekphrastic scenes is a testament to the convention's timeless relevance. The ekphrases in these novels reflect historical changes in literary realism's search for truth-values within novelistic discourse. What is interesting, however, is the way in which several of these novels seem explicitly to valorize a particular mimetic paradigm but yet, by seeking a form of synthesis, implicitly resolve its failure entirely to discredit the other. Cervantes' text is so exemplary for the novel because its realism stresses the limitations of all singular discursive paradigms. To show the absurdities of expressive, romantic signs corresponding to ideal essences, Cervantes creates the absurd figure of Alonso Quixada, who, gone mad from reading too many romantic fictions, ignores empirical correspondences and assigns himself the sign Don Quixote de la Mancha, the heir to the glory of Amadis of Gaul. However, Cervantes must have realized early the ironic potential of condemning fictions by creating one himself and chose to call his fictional text a history and attribute its composition primarily to a fictional historian—Cide Hamete Benengeli. A history is understood to be guided by empirical research, and Cervantes wanted to play with this illusion of historical verisimilitude. The conflict between correspondence theories in *Don Quixote* is then not between a fictional, ideal correspondence and a valorized extratextual and empirical one, but between *textual* versions of the ideal *and* the real. This paradox provided Cervantes with a self-conscious argument that generates much of the text's existential and linguistic play. By confusing the verisimilar claims of both idealistic poets and the empirical historians, by having the Canon find histories and romances equally true, by displaying a "true" puppet knight and a

---

20. Meltzer, in *Salome and the Dance of Writing,* enlarges Hagstrum's etymological definition of ekphrasis from the Greek meaning, "to speak out." She writes, "This does not mean that the character depicted need actually *speak* . . . but rather that the scene and/or character described is brought to life so vividly by the narration that the icon tells its own story, far beyond the static representation of its medium" (21).

"false" flesh-and-blood one, and finally by questioning both Don Quixote's romantic daydreaming and Sancho Panza's practical literalness,
Cervantes touches the heart of the realist dilemma. Because of its play
upon realism and worldmaking, *Don Quixote* is the exemplary realist
novel, a mean by which others can be defined. Fictional trends can be
measured by the direction they move from Cervantes' model.

In the nineteenth century the direction that the genre moves from
Cervantes' paradigm is further away from the expressive discourse of the
romance and closer to the illusion of empirical representation. In fact,
realism in the novel aligns itself so closely with the empirical impulse
that novelists of other inclinations, such as Hawthorne, Scott, Bulwer-
Lytton, and Poe, were compelled to distinguish their works from novels
by emphasizing their status as romances. Both of the novels of the
nineteenth century that I examine seek to find a correspondent relation
that will be a foundation for knowledge. Like Cervantes in *Don Quixote*,
Austen in *Emma* creates a quixotic protagonist, Emma, who is an
"imaginist." However, even more than Cervantes', Austen's text seems
unequivocal in dismissing romantic idealizing in favor of what seems
accurate and truthful observation. The ekphrastic forms in *Emma* illustrate the danger of representing a character idealistically, higher than his
or her proper correspondence in a world defined by rigid social caste.
Emma's ekphrastic portrait of Harriet Smith portrays this limited "natural daughter of somebody" (13) as a refined lady, and the result of this
false correspondence is very nearly disastrous for everyone concerned.
And Frank Churchill's ekphrastic epistles, which misrepresent himself
and his intentions, almost sabotage the two marriages that provide the
novel with a happy ending. Austen's novels create a kind of social
realism, one whose empirical impulse is based on an experience formed
not so much from an individual's sensory perceptions as from society's
collective agreement about the proper state of truth. Such agreement is
achieved by securing the referents of signs representing the caste system
valorized as reality. Implicitly, however, the novel's ekphrases expose
the limits of the Lockean paradigm, which seems grounded in a value-
free empiricism but is actually a discursive system naturalizing unequal
and artificially hierarchical social relations. And the union of Emma and
Knightley in marriage represents not just the subjugation of the fancy to
the understanding but rather a need to resolve the opposition with a
union, that of head and heart.

Tolstoy's novels, on the other hand, create a realism suggesting the
post-Kantian attempts to find correspondences between mind and sense,
noumenon and phenomenon. His texts attempt to ground both the
realist and romantic models of knowledge in the nineteenth century by

means of the transcendental experience of sensory phenomena. The analogues for such an experience are Mihailov's portraits, which reveal the physical characteristics of their subjects so accurately that their spiritual essences are also revealed. His portrait of Christ is significantly of "a man made God, and not God made man" (501). The revelation of Christ's divinity is through his human, physical characteristics. Similarly, Mihailov captures in paint the same physical features in Anna's expression that Tolstoy illustrates textually as embodying her essential self. In contrast to his treatment of Mihailov, Tolstoy rejects Vronsky's portrait of Anna, which is sketched according to the expressive conventions of a preconceived cultural ideal. His rejection of Vronsky's conventionalized portrait is also reflected in Levin's dismissal of the abstract speculations and theories of pseudoscientists, priests, metaphysicians, and spiritualists who attempt to find meaning in life within a transcendental reason not correspondent to the primal world of the senses. Levin discovers life's meaning instead by accepting the basic, seemingly paradoxical qualities of natural life—intuition, fatherhood, labor, and the instinctive understanding between lovers that circumvents verbal expression.

The direction that realism takes with Joyce's *Ulysses* is away from the correspondent biases of conventional nineteenth-century realism and closer to Cervantes' paradigm. Cervantes creates in *Don Quixote* a fiction balanced between reality and romance: it is a world that both poet and historian, Don Quixote and Sancho Panza, ideal and real, have a part in making. Cervantes' synthesis is reflected in Joyce's theory of consubstantiality. Joyce's polarities—Stephen and Bloom, son and father, Christ and God the Father, earth and sun, Telemachus and Odysseus, tonic and dominant—illustrate that meaning is not unitary or singular but rather multiple and contingent, ultimately depending upon a union of mimetic and expressive impulses. This view of meaning as dependent upon the converging parallax of multiple styles and conceptual schemes can be seen also in the formal characteristics of *Ulysses*. Aesthetically reminiscent of Joyce's realist period, in which he wrote *Dubliners* and *Stephen Hero*, the early sections of *Ulysses* are constructed upon a concrete realist framework in which the perspective is the mind's encounter with an external reality whose existence is unquestioned. From this base Joyce launches into rhetorical flights into different worlds constituted by the seemingly incommensurable vocabularies of different conceptual schemes.

The concept of realism as parody turns, from *Don Quixote* to *Ulysses*, a full circle. As I suggested earlier, realism began as parody, an ironic contrast of a supposedly false view of life with a supposedly truer one.

Cervantes' ironic position was to hold a clear, distinct mirror before the exaggerated distortions of chivalric romance in order to show the unreality of its vision, whereas Joyce held a quicksilvered, distorting reflector before the basic characters and conventions of conventional realism to show that its unitary view was too narrow and circumscribed to serve as medium for man's now more plural view of the natural and social world. The remedies Cervantes and Joyce prescribed established the direction of novelistic realism for their immediate successors. Cervantes' realistic perspective on romance turned fiction more in the direction of empirical observation, culminating finally in the fin de siècle movement of conventional realism. Joyce's liberating linguistic re-creation of everyday life turned a generation of writers away from traditional realist conventions to more experimental and expressive narrative techniques. Pynchon's *Gravity's Rainbow* signals this new direction of realism. Pynchon's parodic use of realist conventions, evidenced by the symbolic equivalents of realism in film, behaviorism, Pavlov's *Book*, and the Turkic alphabet, shows an abhorrence of cause and effect and hence a rejection of empiricism as primary epistemological tool. His use of spiritualism, magic, hallucination, and mythical analogy represents some of the other means that he believes are necessary supplements to causal and conventionally realist narrative. More than any other of the novelists examined, Pynchon foregrounds the political motivation behind valorizing any conceptual scheme as giving access to the real.

The Differential Play of Mimesis

The late work of Wittgenstein indicates that only by means of language games, which achieve coherence through a family resemblance of concepts, can a concept of reality ultimately be construed. In this sense realism is still a relational theory, but instead of postulating the relation as existing between words and external referents, a new theory finds the relation to be both intertextual and intersubjective. Realism, a practice and strategy of discourse, as opposed to an actual literary mode, can be intertextually defined as the lexicon of conventions denoting the real and intersubjectively defined as the actualization of those conventions to persuade and coerce a reader into accepting a text's model of reality. Texts defined by notions of realism as correspondence attempt to conceal these elements of discourse through naturalization—making them seem to originate from nature itself and not the artifice of language. These texts estrange the conventions of rival representational schemata by contrasting their artificial, and hence false, representations with their own, which would appear to be mirrors of nature. By contrast, realist texts governed by a discourse paradigm, though they attempt to discredit a rival representational mode, also show by means of perspectival shifts the variety of linguistic schemata through which a construal of reality can be achieved, thus undermining the claims for a single valorized one. However, once *any* text makes multiple worlds to establish truth-claims, the creating of fictional worlds argues against a single world model, either correspondent or coherentist.

An intertextual theory of realism precludes the possibility of extratextual denotative reference because the linguistic sign refers (or, following Derrida, *defers*) not to an external referent but to a connotative series of other signs. In the case of the novel, verisimilitude is not a function of corresponding structures of language and event. It is a correspondence *within* the system of language and literary conventions, a correspondence achieved by the rhetorical and discursive features of the text. By means of the rhetorical appeal of character debate, a text attempts to persuade a reader to accept a particular version of reality. Defining realism in intertextual terms actually inverts traditional realism/idealism, denotation/connotation, scientific/poetic language hierarchies. A text attempting to naturalize a single representation can do so only by representing it as an interpolated form within the text's own boundaries. Since it then admits that the world can only be known textually and relationally, a representation loses the juridical authority of a regulative outside as well as any claim that it might make for transcendental status.

Intertextual mimesis reveals not only the privileged unity of single meaning, it also reveals the play of differences that Derrida defines as *différance*—"the systematic play of differences of the spacing by which elements relate to one another" (*Positions* 27). Although Derrida's description of *différance* exists on the smallest unit of signification, the level of the individual sign, it can also be applied to the novel as a sign system. The text that would valorize a mimetic paradigm by claiming its transcendental correspondence to an extratextual reality, a regulative signified known as the real, must do so by transforming it into another signifier, an ekphrasis that is compared to other ekphrases. Thus, the correspondences are internal and potentially infinite. And by depending upon the difference between it and other models for the purpose of self-definition, a paradigm defers the legitimacy that the correspondence to a regulatory outside might give it. The path of deferring follows the endless re-presenting of contrastive representations, the paradigm of competing paradigms.

CHAPTER TWO

Chivalry Decoded:
Dialogistic and Perspectivist Voices
in *Don Quixote*

The Humanist-Scholastic Conflict

The early novel treating representation most problematically and thus
giving one of the first full portrayals of conflicting mimetic paradigms is
Miguel de Cervantes' *Don Quixote*. Dramatizing the problem of realism
as one of linguistic reference, Cervantes' novel thematizes the shift in
Renaissance linguistic paradigms from the scholastic view of referentiality, assuming a natural and even divine relation between words and
referents, to the nominalist and humanist one, interpreting reference as
a matter of convention and therefore as measure of man's freedom or
alienation from nature and divinity. However historically specific is
this conflict between scholasticism and humanism over referentiality, it
cannot be viewed as isolated and discrete but rather as one manifestation
of the perpetual opposition of correspondence and coherence views. In
fact, Nancy Streuver, in *The Language of History in the Renaissance*,
shows how the Renaissance argument emulates an earlier historical

manifestation of this struggle, the conflict between the Hellenistic Socratic philosophers and the Sophists.[1]

The Platonist elevation of the philosopher over the Sophist rhetor was
justified by a belief in a metaphysical truth existing independently of its
cultural representations, particularly the sullied medium of language.
Whereas the Sophists taught that truth was contingent upon situation
and human expressive capabilities, Socratic philosophy subordinated
these elements to final and universal ends. The scholasticism of the
medieval period conceptualized this Platonic-Aristotelian notion of the
Absolute as divine authority. In the cases of both classical philosophy
and medieval scholasticism, truth is seen as transcendent of human
reason and its medium, language. Rhetoric, the primary teaching of the
Sophists, thus becomes a source of error and illusion for both philosophy
and Christianity. On the other hand, the humanists share with the
Sophists an anthropocentric model—for both the primary epistemological measure is human. The classical ideals of *techné* and *kairos* conjoin
with the Renaissance humanist notion of *virtù*, and human artifice,
instead of being seen as illusion, is viewed as the primary method of
communicating truth. The humanist revival of classical learning brought
an increased appreciation for rhetoric, particularly by rediscovering
Cicero, and it also presented a focus for truth that was intertextual,
through the monuments of human learning, rather than extratextual,
through divine revelation.

Both the Platonists and the scholastics developed a referential theory
anchored by the metaphysical presence of an extratextual authority.
Contrastingly, the Sophists and humanists celebrated the human capabilities for authorship and found authority in the edifices of language and
tradition. However, the humanists did not entirely advocate freeing
language and imagination from all foundational constraints, and this
search for a foundation for linguistic play can be seen in their attempt to
resolve this paradigmatic opposition by a synthesis of creativity with
tradition. The crisis manifest in the revolutionary shift of linguistic
paradigms caused a reexamining and moderating of the extremes of the

1. Nancy Streuver, in *The Language of History in the Renaissance*, argues that "the
tension between philosophy and rhetoric is the dynamic of the history of language theory
in antiquity" (7), and she traces this tension to its later manifestation in medieval
scholasticism and Renaissance humanism. She identifies rhetoric as the basis of sophism
and humanism and, quoting Barthes, implies that contemporary structuralism shares this
paradigmatic formulation (15). Rhetoric's valorizing human linguistic abilities, a form of
techné, rather than any divine or philosophic access to extralinguistic truth, reveals an
anthropocentrism that is compatible with much postanalytical philosophy.

newer model. For example, Elias Rivers argues that from its origins in the attempt to establish classical Latin as the accepted language for formal writing, the humanist idealization of classical learning was manifest in the numerous linguistic commentaries that advocated applying the regularities of Latin grammar as templates over the syntax of emerging vernacular languages.[2] The impulse of the humanists to synthesize classical form with vitally growing and new written languages was a significant factor in the sudden explosion of vernacular literary achievements, as seen in the works of Castiglione, Dante, Petrarch, and Boccaccio. In fact, in all the major European languages—Provençal, French, Italian, Portuguese, and German—this dialectical synthesis of traditional form and novel expression influenced literary creativity. In Spain, as Rivers shows, Garcilaso and Boscán successfully mediated a Spanish literary vernacular with classical form. According to Rivers, "the real linguistic revolution turned out to be, not the pan-European humanists' restoration of Classical Latin, but the national vernacular writers' invention of neoclassical styles in the modern European languages" (25). Showing how many Renaissance writers viewed the combining of the "vox populi" with Latinate grammar as an ideal synthesis of classical and Christian elements, Rivers comments that Cervantes in *La Galatea* attempted a similar synthesis in his Spanish Renaissance modernization of the classical pastoral. However, Cervantes' treatment of this paradigmatic conflict and synthesis changed from the relatively simple *Galatea* to the much more complex *Quixote*. In his masterwork, Cervantes explores more fully the dangers of both correspondent and coherentist extremes. He uses the Don to parody views of language as correspondent to ideal, essential realities. But he also gives the voice of humanist grammatical remediation to the deluded Don, whose corrections to

---

2. In his "Cervantes and the Question of Language," Elias L. Rivers says that the humanists' motivation for attempting to restore Latin was to return to the common basis of European culture, which would encourage its rebirth. The divisions between classical Latin, vulgar Latin, and emerging European dialects created social and cultural divisions that hindered what the humanists perceived as literary progress. Unable to delay the dissemination of modern European dialects, the humanists nonetheless were able to encourage the adoption of neoclassical styles. Boscán's translation of Castiglione's *Cortesano* (1534) and Garcilaso's poetry (1543), cited as ideal Spanish syntheses of classical style and modern language, were well known in Cervantes' age and were given as models of a Christian and classical synthesis. Rivers argues that the parallels between Cervantes' *La Galatea* and Garcilaso's poetry are numerous. But the shift from the *Galatea* and the *Quixote* is marked, and it "seems to correspond to something akin to what Hiram Haydn has called the 'Counter-Renaissance,' the skeptical disintegration of that early optimistic synthesis reflected in a classical style of language" (28).

Sancho, a band of goatherds, or such dubious listeners as Don Diego de Miranda are farcical and inappropriate. Moreover, the unity of style idealized in the classical-Christian synthesis disappears in the stylistic variety of the text's many represented conversations and monologues. Throughout the text, the oppositional conflict between these paradigms appears central, but Cervantes here emphasizes its undecidable character.

In fact, the aspect of the humanist-scholastic paradigmatic debate concerning language that appeared in Cervantine Spain and more than likely influenced Cervantes directly in composing *Don Quixote* was its undecidability. A good example of how the undecidable nature of the conflict was manifest is in the work of Juan Huarte, whose *Examen de ingenios para las ciencias* (1575) is credited by Malcolm Read as having at least indirectly influenced Cervantes' ideas on language.[3] As interpreted by Read, certain portions of the *Examen* present an argument for "the conventional status of the word as a condition of human freedom in the sense that language itself is a product of human ingenuity" (272). Exhibiting progressivist and humanist tendencies in these sections of his text, Huarte cites the diversity of languages as evidence of linguistic progress and evolution. Discomfited, though, by a seemingly unbridgeable gap between words and referents, Huarte also reveals a basic conservatism by arguing elsewhere for a radical empiricism in scientific language use, urging scientists to trust only phenomena and sensory perception (Read 274). As further evidence of how problematic this debate over referentiality had become to Renaissance humanists, Huarte later in the *Examen* reverses his conventionalist position by postulating a Platonic view of language, perhaps best expressed in the work of a

3. Read's article "Language Adrift: A Re-appraisal of the Theme of Linguistic Perspectivism in *Don Quijote*" relates the general pan-European conflict between the humanist and scholastic views of language to its manifestation in Renaissance Spain. Read writes, "The Scholastic view of language rested upon a 'moderate realism' and 'naturalism' to the extent that it assumed a large measure of correspondence between words (symbols), thought (reference), and things (referents)" (271). He suggests that "it was from a nominalistic, 'conventionalist' basis that the early humanists assailed the scholastic edifice. For the first time these scholars seriously considered the possibility that language may condition thought by interposing a disturbing grid between man's inward nature and the outside world" (271–72). Read notes that scholars have often cited Huarte as a source for Cervantes on the subject of madness, but rarely on language, where they share parallel contradictory attitudes. Cervantes shares Huarte's enthusiasm for language's progressivist and expressive capabilities—signs of human evolution toward an ideal. But Huarte, a nominalist, doubted language's reliability, and his work "anticipates the conviction . . . in the seventeenth century that language does not adequately reflect reality" (274). Read concludes, "It was precisely the distance between the *significant* and *signifié* in language that Cervantes explored artistically in his work" (275).

contemporary, Francisco Sanchez de las Brozas, who in 1587 published *Minerva*, a grammar of Latin. In this work, de las Brozas, citing the near perfection of Latin, argues against linguistic progress by postulating a lost natural basis for correspondent signification in man's first signifying system, the lost language of Adam, in which the relation between word and referent was sanctioned by divine authority (Read 278–79). The late-Renaissance crisis over language, then, was sparked by an inability completely to resolve the significant issues raised by this conflict—the nominalist and scholastic belief in the correspondence of words to divine essences, the empiricist trust in words' correspondences to objects of nature, and, finally, the fear underlying the humanist celebration of language as artifact, raising doubt over language's connection with anything other than its own coherent system.

Huarte's—and the age's—paradoxical attitude toward language is also reflected in *Don Quixote*. On the one hand, Cervantes postulates a conservative language theory. This position is summarized by Leo Spitzer, who argues in his classic linguistic work on *Don Quixote* that the novel is "an indictment of the bookish side of humanism . . . [in which] . . . writers of the Renaissance were able to build up their word-worlds out of sheer exuberance, free to play linguistically"(52).[4] Critics such as Spitzer, who view the novel as critiquing the linguistic excesses of humanism, represent a traditional critical approach describing the work as satirizing any human language that misrepresents the reality of the empirical world. Writing also from this perspective, Harry Levin calls *Don Quixote* the first example of realism in the novel because "realism . . . has originated in parody," and in parodying the excesses of chivalric romance *Don Quixote* establishes the terms for a modal description (*Gates* 47), one that implies a pattern of parody and correction. This traditional approach, though compelling, is undermined by the model of language posited in the novel. While it is true that in thematizing representation Cervantes satirizes the humanist theory of language for lacking an essentially divine or necessarily empirical correspondence, the novel's narrative strategies, particularly its use of ekphrasis, reveal a much more problematic stance and place the novel at the center of the Renaissance crisis over the authority of representations, a crisis in which

4. Spitzer, in "The 'Ode on a Grecian Urn' or Content vs. Metagrammar," argues that Cervantes was aware of implicit constraints upon the wordplay that he defines as perspectivism. It was necessary for Cervantes to recognize "a realm of the absolute—which was, in his case that of Spanish Catholicism. Cervantes, while glorifying in his role of the artist who can stay aloof from the '*engaños a los ojos*,' the '*sueños*' of the world, and create his own, always sees himself as overshadowed by supernal forces: the artist never denies God, or His institutions, the King and the State" (61).

ultimately the privileging of any correspondent relation is questioned. Also, the many debates on language, particularly those that attempt to define a proper or correct language by calling attention to the inadequate correspondence of others, are undercut by the exuberance of stylistic invention in *Don Quixote*.

Commenting on this multiplicity of styles, Bakhtin writes that the best example of heteroglossia, or the inherent conflict arising from the social diversity of languages, is "*Don Quixote*, which realizes in itself, in extraordinary depth and breadth, all the artistic possibilities of heteroglot and internally dialogized novelistic discourse" (*Dialogical* 324). The representation of various literary and nonliterary styles in the novel problematizes the valorizing of a privileged discourse, regardless of whether it claims extraliterary correspondent authority or whether, in attempting to synthesize Christian and classical elements, it claims a traditional one. As in the cases of other exemplary realist novels, the representation of other discourses problematizes the unitariness of the present sign. Spitzer's term for the novel's polyphony is "linguistic perspectivism," and he acknowledges that such stylistic diversity undercuts the humanist desire for unity. He writes, "Whereas, to Dante, all dialects appeared as inferior . . . realizations of a Platonic–Christian ideal pattern of language, as embodied in the *vulgare illustre*, Cervantes saw them as ways of speech which exist as individual realities and which have justification in themselves" (21). Cervantes' perspectivism emphasizes language's instability by showing how linguistic signs drift from referential anchors, whether correspondent referents or intertextual conventions.

When considering the stylistic perspectivism and use of ekphrases in *Don Quixote*, one must acknowledge that a primary characteristic of the art of the seventeenth and eighteenth centuries is its ekphrastic richness, the creation of multiple perspectives by means of internally shifting modes of representation. Such shifts are created by Shakespeare's placing a play within the play *Hamlet*, Vermeer's painting an artist painting a subject in *The Studio*, and Lope de Vega's writing about a sonnet in his "Soneto de repente" or about literature in general in *La Dorotea*.[5] Michel Foucault's famous interpretation of Velázquez's *Las Meninas* in *The Order of Things* shows that the impulse behind such internal mirroring was the period's desire to represent representation, thus mirroring and confirming its authority. But Foucault indicates that even though the painting (of a painter painting a subject reflected in a mirror) can encompass the

---

5. For a discussion of this aspect of baroque art and literature, see Americo Castro, "The Baroque as a Literary Style," in *An Idea of History: Selected Essays of Americo Castro*.

basic aspects of representation, as defined by Dreyfus and Rabinow—
"the producing of the representation (the painter), the object represented
(the models and their gaze), and the viewing of the representation (the
spectator)" (25)—it cannot represent the act of representation itself, the
immediately temporal creation of artistic meaning. This painterly symbol of the age's desire to confirm an authority for representation by
allowing it to portray itself and hence its capability for establishing truth-
conditions ultimately confirms only the limits of representational truth.

The Interpolated Authors

A more exemplary model of the age's concern for representational
authority than *Las Meninas* is *Don Quixote*. Even in the age of the
baroque, few works of literature exhibit the perspectival intricacy of *Don
Quixote* and its sheer variety of ekphrastic scenes that portray the reading,
creating, or performing of fictions. As menippean satire, the text produces this variety of discourses to test their efficacy in dramatic situations. This, in fact, is the importance of several of the ekphrases—they
dramatize the text's major theme of the relation between word and world
as well as duplicate and comment upon the narrative structure. The
ekphrastic system of *Don Quixote* generates numerous examples of the
motif of representational authority, ranging from the five interpolated
novelles of book 1, which appear superficially independent of the primary
story, to the more reflexive tales of book 2 (such as the puppet show,
the elaborate Trifaldi play of the Duke and Duchess, Don Quixote's
vision in the Cave of Montesinos), which comment more directly upon
their fictional frame. Cervantes redoubles his representational theme
numerous times by creating a series of characters as authors of the
novel within the novel. When most of these author-characters seem to
converge upon the stage at once—upon the literal ekphrastic stage, as I
discuss later, of Master Peter's puppet play—the reader is afforded a
perspective from which the narrative can be viewed as though transmitted by a series of author-characters identified implicitly or explicitly as
authoritative narrators of the novel *Don Quixote*. This important ekphrastic scene of representation, rather than confirm a representational
authority, reveals conflicting authorial agents who call all authority into
doubt. The collision of these other discourses makes it impossible to
speak of a valorized, unitary discourse as foundation.

Simply, this central ekphrastic episode narrates Don Quixote and
Sancho's attending the marionette theater of Master Peter, itinerant

showman. The puppet show consists of an assistant, who narrates the story and indicates significant action with a pointing stick, and Master Peter, who works the puppet's strings from behind the stage. The story performed, the liberation of Melisandra from Moorish imprisonment by her knight-errant husband, Sir Gaiferos, is a chivalric legend from French and Spanish ballads. Easily deluded by the artistic illusion into believing the play real, Don Quixote leaps upon the stage and attacks the Moorish villains with his sword, smashing the puppets to bits. Through Don Quixote's farcical action, Cervantes uses the ekphrastic puppet show humorously to dramatize the consequences of his character's attempt to live his life within the possible world created by a limiting discourse. This simple description, however, belies the episode's contribution to the narrative intricacy of the text, as well as its depiction of the crisis in the humanist paradigm's search for linguistic authority.

George Haley and Ruth El Saffar show in their respective studies of the narrative of *Don Quixote* that if the voices of the characters narrating the play are considered with the still resonant voices of other narrators who speak throughout the text, a complex pattern emerges.[6] Moreover, the discursive pattern in this ekphrasis emulates and calls attention to that of the entire text, shedding light upon its own theory of representation. The fictional authors within the text narrate their versions of the story of Don Quixote after it has been narrated to them by their predecessors and alter it according to their different views of language, which are, writes Spitzer, "different reflections of reality" (55), creating conflicting possible textual worlds. A brief overview of the narrative voices reveals the complexity of discourse in the text itself as well as in certain ekphrastic scenes. It also reveals that the narration generates so many incommensurable textual worlds that it problematizes the typology of possible worlds in narratological theory. According to Marie-Laure Ryan, there are two kinds of possible worlds in texts—the first, the "textual reference or actual world," is one "for which the text claims facts; the world in which the propositions asserted by the text are to be valued . . . the center of a system of reality," roughly equivalent to "the actual world, our system of reality"; and the second, the "textual alternative possible world," is composed of "mental constructs formed by the inhabitants of the textual actual [reference] world" (glossary). *Don Quixote* and other realist novels show that characters often attempt

6. On the subject of the narrators of *Don Quixote* and the narrative texture of the episode dealing with Master Peter's puppet show, I am indebted to two classic works on the subject—Ruth El Saffar's *Distance and Control in Don Quixote: A Study in Narrative Technique* and George Haley's "The Narrator in *Don Quijote*: Maese Pedro's Puppet Show." Another interesting discussion of the scene is in Robert Alter's *Partial Magic*.

to make the possible worlds that are "mental constructs" into actuality, especially if one believes the constructivist notion that reality itself is a mental construct. Also, while *Don Quixote* satirizes the possible world constructed by the Don, it creates so many possible worlds claiming actuality or reference that no world can serve as an unquestioned foundation.

Before understanding how the ekphrasis tests the existential ramifications of each narrative discourse, it is necessary to evaluate fully each narrative voice, including Don Quixote's. First there is the original narrative voice, who speaks from the novel's opening page and displays himself as a historian, scrupulously compiling written facts concerning Don Quixote. But since the documented sources of this First Author fail him while narrating one of the knight's early adventures, he leaves the story unfinished. Then the Second Author, emerging mysteriously in the ninth chapter of book 1, speaks to readers in the first person as a fellow reader whose frustration with the First Author's failure to complete his story motivates him to search throughout Spain for the document containing the conclusion. By accident, he discovers an obscure Arabic manuscript that is the complete history of Don Quixote, and the rest of the novel, from the unfinished adventure to the end, is purportedly the impartial rendering of this authentic document. The Second Author, however, intrudes into the narrative on numerous occasions to defend Don Quixote's humanistic vision and must hire a Spanish-speaking Moor to translate the manuscript. This translator uses the poetic license of a Third Author to question and sometimes alter the facts given in the original account. Needless to say, these intrusions and qualifications tend to diffuse the claim of authenticity for this "original, true history" composed by the Fourth Author, supposedly the ultimate one—Cide Hamete Benengeli, Arabic historian.

This system of fictionalized narrators disseminating the authority for the story through a labyrinthine web of voices is made even more complicated by the number of "extratextual" narrators who are introduced in other ekphrases.[7] The first is the fictionalized author of the actual text we are reading, the prologuist who, in an ekphrasis, introduces the text with the problem of finding authority for his "history."

7. Ralph Flores, whose ideas have influenced my own concerning the narrators of *Don Quixote*, provides a very interesting discussion of the poststructuralist implications of the fragmenting of the narrative into separate voices in his "Deconstructing Authors: *Don Quixote*." Beginning his article with an analysis of the prologuist's attempt to master his text by claiming genealogical authority, fathering, Flores notes how the successive narrators undercut this claim: "No mastery, least of all by authors, seems possible over such endless mimetic proliferation" (100).

In the dramatized composition of the ekphrastic prologue, the prologuist complains to a friend that his text will not have the authority of other histories: ". . . other works . . . so full of sentences from Aristotle, Plato and the whole herd of philosophers. . . . My book will lack all this; for I have nothing to quote in the margin or to note at the end" (26). The friend offers an ingenious solution to the prologuist's dilemma, for he calls attention to the complete fictionality and illusion of all extratextual authority. He advises the prologuist to invent the lacking authority; the problem of "the sonnets, epigrams and eulogies . . . can be got over by your taking a little trouble and writing them yourself. Afterwards you can baptise them and give them any names you like" (27). By convincing the prologuist that the authority of discourse is entirely textual, fictional, having no recourse to an extratextual reality, the friend gives him license to suspend the relation of textual sign to extratextual referent, granting him the freedom to construct relations and a world as arbitrarily as the Don reconstructs the world's signs within his system of chivalric codes to create the possible world of romance.[8] The friend's solution also problematizes the humanist mission of using tradition as foundation for signifying practices.

A further complication of the narration is invented when, in passing, the text questions its own authority by commenting on other texts about Don Quixote. Ralph Flores shows that the Second Author's voice, hovering over Cide Hamete's text, comments on several occasions on other "histories," undramatized ekphrases that, though compared invidiously with Cide Hamete's, offer alternative versions and worlds. Although some of these "histories" "give us so short and skimped an account of events that we scarcely taste them" (Cervantes 121), they suggest other treatments mediating between "the original true history" we are reading. In addition to these accounts are other "extratextual" voices emerging from ekphrases to indicate the text's transmitted status. John Weiger comments on references to commentaries on Cide Hamete that further mediate the transmission of "the original, true history." These include marginalia in the lost manuscript that refer to a "them" who say that Dulcinea "was the best hand at salting pork . . . in La

8. See Ramon Salvidar, "Don Quijote's Metaphors and the Grammar of Proper Language," for an interesting discussion of how the prologue establishes the terms for Cervantes' transformation of the narrative into supplementary voices and for Don Quixote's transformation of the world through renaming. Salvidar writes that Don Quixote's search for a proper language to express his chivalric mission is matched by the text, in which "the author and his fictional voices establish this dialogue of contradictions concerning the nature of literary language in general, and concerning the manner in which to create a proper language for the expression of Don Quijote in particular" (257).

Mancha" (76) and other references to a "they" who claim that the translator did not accurately relate a subsequent passage (745).[9]

Don Quixote presents an extremely complicated narrative structure because of its narrative redoubling and extensive series of narrators within each ekphrastic story. However, even within this complex ekphrastic system, Master Peter's puppet show is one of the richest ekphrases because it, according to Haley, "reproduces on a miniature scale the same basic relationships among storyteller, story, and audience that are discernible in the novel's overall theme" (147). It is, then, an ekphrasis continuous with both the novel's narrative and discourse and therefore deserves greater attention within the ekphrastic system of *Don Quixote*. Like many ekphrases, it creates an alternative textual world that comments upon the frame world. Additionally, in this ekphrasis the types of author-characters within the frame narrative are dramatized by characters narrating the interpolated tale. Thus, the puppet show has an intrusive narrator, the "boy-assistant," an "interpreter and announcer" (638) calling himself a historian, telling a "true story . . . taken word for word from the French chronicles and the Spanish ballads" (638). Master Peter, invisibly controlling the actions of the puppets by means of strings, gives the appearance of an effaced narrator who, like Flaubert's, is "present everywhere but visible nowhere." Yet by playing with his doll-characters, Master Peter resembles a Thackerayan self-conscious voice that stresses the artificiality of fiction. In these dual roles, Master Peter embodies the ambivalent roles of the narrative voices in *Don Quixote*. Finally, Don Quixote interprets the chivalric signs of the puppet show as he interprets all of the signs that bear a correlative relation to chivalry—by assigning them to referents within his own fictional world, a possible world he carries, writes Marthe Robert, "inside himself like an incurable wound" (17). Thus, the Master Peter ekphrasis heightens readers' awareness of not just the story before them but also what David Thorburn calls "the drama of the telling" (437), the struggle of several different narrators to interpret and relay the story through different mimetic paradigms.

Poets and Historians

The puppet show ekphrasis is also important because it foregrounds Cervantes' typology of narrators. Two opposing groups of artist-

---

9. John G. Weiger provides a helpful discussion of the extratextual voices that appear in the margin of the text that the implied reader has been given by the Second Author. See his "Prologuist: The Extratextual Authorial Voice in *Don Quixote*." The implications of his argument are explored more fully in his more recent *In the Margins of Cervantes*.

characters, called poets and historians, thematize the opposition between correspondence and coherence theories of referentiality and its historical manifestation in the scholastic and humanist paradigmatic conflict. Of these internal narrators in *Don Quixote* Scholes and Kellogg write, "As the entire narrative turns on the interplay between a realistic and an idealistic view of life, the opposition between poet and historian is a crucial one to the whole conception of the book" (253). The text dramatizes the opposition between poet and historian in their differing approaches to nature and reality. They thus reflect the argument of linguists in the seventeenth century over correspondence, as described by Murray Cohen: "Some linguists . . . see the goal of their language work as the *recovery*, in the shapes and sounds of linguistic elements, of the *essences of things in nature*; others tend to define their work as *reproducing*, through mostly arbitrary symbols, *the composition and coherence of things in nature*. Linguists of the first group associate their plans with . . . *Adamic naming*. . . . The other linguists associate their proposals with those of the *empiricists*" (21) (my emphasis). Cohen defines both linguistic views as aspiring toward correspondence—the former to an essential reality, the latter to an empirical one. However, through numerous textual examples, the distinction between these artist-characters becomes clear. The historian is an empiricist who, through careful documentation and sensory proof, seeks to anchor the arbitrary play of signs to empirical reality. On the other hand, the poet, not limited solely by empirical fact, strives to construct a reality according to the essences of things within the coherence of the conventional signs of an ideal world. Paradoxically, on the level of theme, this fragmenting of the narrative into several distinct voices reinforces a view of signification in which the relation between word and thing is necessarily determined by external referential anchors, for most of the voices join to defend empirically correspondent signifying relations; however, on the level of reading, this fragmentation also ironically subverts *any* theory of language implying a fixed relation between word and referent, whether essential or empirical. Treating the Don as the intentional object of a series of interpreters, the text defines individual perception and communication as acts bordered by the undefinable and capable of endless supplementation. The form this supplementation takes is the dissemination of the narrative into strands of contradiction and correction. Ralph Flores calls a reading of *Don Quixote* as indeterminate text one that is "framed by supplementarity" (102). What results defamiliarizes a view of fiction as history—the representation of a world corresponding to the sign system through which it is known.

In a novel so concerned with the unrelatedness of idealistic fiction and reality, the opposition between poet and historian seems to valorize the historians' perspective. However, as each narrator imposes a perceptual schema, or grid, around the object (Don Quixote) to provide a representation free from doubt, the various narrative perspectives accentuate the presence of an unlimited margin of corrective commentary. In the end, this marginality proves unstable any extratextual referential relation. Ironically, in a novel also so concerned with naming and accuracy, the narrative proves futile any attempt at matching signifier with signified. The title *Don Quixote* deceptively points toward a signified, the *"true history of Don Quixote de la Mancha,"* but as the narrative is passed from voice to voice, the promise of ultimate denotation is subverted by endlessly repeated signifiers pointing toward nothing but marginality. For Alonso Quixada, the gap in signifying relations is both comic and tragic as the narrative traces dramatically his disastrous attempts to make his self-designated signifier, Don Quixote, match the signified of chivalric knight. In spite of the obvious farce throughout the text, his tragedy is manifest not only in his suffering, his painful inability to bridge the nominal gap, but also existentially, in his becoming, in Foucault's words, "a sign wandering through a world that [does] not recognize him" (*Order of Things* 48). In book 2 of the novel, when discussing various treatments of himself as fictional character, the Don discovers that he has lost his sought-after identity and has become a repeatedly transmitted signifier in the sign representing himself within the works of Cide Hamete, Cervantes, and Avellaneda, the author of the unauthorized sequel to *Don Quixote*, which is another alternative textual world.

Bruce W. Wardropper shows that the conflict between poetic and historical visions in *Don Quixote* is connected to another Renaissance manifestation of the correspondence-coherence linguistic conflict. Beginning with the Aristotelian differentiation between history as "what has happened" and poetry (or fiction) as "what might happen" (80), Wardropper illustrates how Cervantes calls attention to the artificial distinction between the two categories. Cervantes called his work an *historia*, a term that embraces both fiction and history in Renaissance Spain. In fact, as Wardropper indicates, English is the only Indo-European language using different words to distinguish between fiction and history as narrations of different kinds of events. Eventually though, a bifurcation of the concept occurred late in this period, with the consignment of separate literary genres for each mode: prose became the vehicle for history and verse that for imagined or fictional events. However, a crisis occurred over the legitimacy of this distinction when such prose histories as the *Cronica sarracina* (1430), the *Libros plumbeos* (or the "Leaden Books," discovered between 1588 and 1595), and the chronicles known as the *falsos cronicones* (printed in 1610) were shown to be fictional. Wardropper's reading allows one to see that history (or at least the false histories that scandalized the learned world) is as likely an object of falsification and error as are chivalric romances. This creation of a false authority in a contrived history is a likely object of parody in the prologue ekphrasis.

Ekphrastic Questionings of History

Two early ekphrases in the text show how the poet-and-historian conflict is undecidable. Thus, these elements of the novel's ekphrastic system reinforce the referential claims by the puppet show. The first is an important ekphrastic scene in which the Canon of Toledo and the village priest engage in a debate over a number of specific fictional works as well as the general merits of such fictions.[10] This scene is important in the way it frames the correspondence-and-coherence conflict in terms of a character debate over an ekphrastic form, similar to those in *Emma*, *Anna Karenina*, *Ulysses*, and *Gravity's Rainbow*. The Canon describes two kinds of fictions; of one, he says:

> the more it resembles the truth the better the fiction, and the more probable and possible it is, the better it pleases. Fictions have to match the minds of their readers, and to be written in such a way that, by tempering the impossibilities, moderating excesses, and keeping judgement in the balance, they may so astonish, hold, excite, and entertain, that wonder and pleasure go hand in hand. None of this can be achieved by anyone departing from verisimilitude, or from that imitation of nature in which lies the perfection of all that is written. (425)

The Canon's description of fiction as history presents the basic elements of the correspondence theory of reference and a mimetic theory of literature, which, derived from Aristotle, extend through the empirical impulses of the Enlightenment and neoclassicism to the fin de siècle forms of realism and naturalism. Milton Munitz sees the philosophical

10. I am indebted to Terrence Doody, "*Don Quixote*, *Ulysses*, and the Idea of Realism," for the idea that the Canon's divided argument, descriptive of *Don Quixote*'s dual allegiance, is also descriptive of divergent views of realism that come together again in *Ulysses*.

foundation of this realism as a "fundamental and unquestioned belief in the existence of an independent reality . . . made up of its own component entities," which forms the basis of "a wide range of epistemological approaches—for example, empiricist, rationalist, revelationist, fidest, mystical" (27). Appearing to agree with his character the Canon, Cervantes throughout *Don Quixote* uses the external world as touchstone to show that the signs of chivalric romance fail as elements of a mimetic paradigm because they lack a necessarily correspondent relation to reality. The Canon, however, admits that he has had a secret admiration for such romances and has even attempted to write one himself (adding himself to the list of author-characters within the text), and he ultimately argues both sides of the ekphrastic debate, defending idealist fiction with nearly equal conviction: "For all that he had said against such books, he found one good thing in them: the fact that they offered a good intellect a chance to display itself. For they presented a broad and spacious field through which the pen could run without let or hindrance. . . . Sometimes the writer might show his knowledge of astrology, or his excellence at cosmography or as a musician, or in his wisdom in affairs of state, and he might even have an opportunity of showing his skill at necromancy" (426). In emphasizing the individual artist's ability to imagine details of the story, "without let or hindrance" from empirical necessity, the Canon now suggests what amounts to a coherence view of language and literature, postulating that the imagination of the artist should not be subject to empirical constraints. In being unable to decide finally between the narrative roles of the poet and historian in creating fiction, the Canon reflects Cervantes' own indecision in valorizing a particular representational mode.

Cervantes' indecision over the correspondence-and-coherence dilemma, which is manifest in his characterizations of poets and historians, is also reflected in another important ekphrasis within the ekphrastic system—the prologue. Cervantes thematizes the importance of establishing authority for the discourse of the text by creating the prologuist, who speaks directly to the reader, thus establishing the immediacy of unmediated dialogue.[11] In describing his work as progeny that he has fathered (or stepfathered), the prologuist uses genetic metaphors to suggest a necessary and correspondent relation between himself and the

11. I agree with Weiger when he argues against most other critics who identify the Second Author and the prologuist with Cervantes. Weiger comments upon Cervantes' parodic treatments of historians elsewhere and notes that the prologuist has named his work "the history of Don Quixote," not *The Ingenious Gentleman Don Quixote de la Mancha*, as Cervantes, the fictionalist, names it in his signed dedication. He identifies the prologuist as another one of the extratextual voices that emerge from the text.

literary sign he creates. But in spite of this immediate discourse as present to the reader, the prologuist admits to great difficulty in writing the preface: "Many times I took up my pen to write it, and many times put it down, not knowing what to say" (26). His difficulty is that his "child," "naked and unadorned" (26), cannot have an identity as sign until it enters the intertextual relations of similarities and differences that a generic model can provide. Further, the authority of any communicative act can be inscribed only within a system of codes, into which the author's "child," like a presocial adolescent, has not yet been admitted. The prologuist's mistake is to assume, as a historian might, that such intertextual authority must also be necessary and correspondent, and because of his "inadequacy and scanty learning" (27), the prologuist is tempted to consign his manuscript to oblivion. The friend who interrupts the prologuist at the point of this dilemma educates him as to the fictional basis of intertextual definition by suggesting fictional or fabricated solutions to each of his concerns. Ramon Salvidar, writing on the prologue, comments, "The friend's refusal of textual authority and traditional expressions of empirical truth is in effect a refusal of the authority of referential language. For him that authority can always be produced from the resources available to literary discourse and the artistic imagination" ("Don Quijote" 256). As the novel progresses, Cervantes proceeds to show how, if authority can be fictionalized, it can be repeatedly fictionalized, as in the example of the series of character-authors. By problematizing the role of the producer of the discourse, Cervantes also problematizes the status of the sign by showing its authority as fictional, capable of repeated re-creations. By establishing no true presence for discourse, no true history corresponding to an extratextual reality either divinely or empirically, Cervantes implicitly endorses a coherence view of truth, in spite of the empirical corrections of Don Quixote's vision. The collision of competing "correspondent" relations casts doubt on truth as absolute correspondence and shows instead the incommensurability of different conceptual schemes.

Don Quixote as Author

Don Quixote is the author-character whose use of literary signs most highlights the dilemma revealed in these ekphrases; therefore, it is necessary to characterize his authorial role. Part of the novel's parodic intention is to portray him both as reader of chivalric romances, in his responses to the ekphrastic art forms, and as author, a fictionalist in his transformation of the "real" textual world into the "fictive" textual one in which he is chivalric hero. He creates a possible world in which the "true" correspondence of words are with the essences of objects as defined by the idealist myth of a Golden Age. One could argue that his tragedy begins when he assumes the role of poet and attempts to make the world conform to his version of correspondence by a process of language—renaming. In so doing, he confirms the linguistic basis of worldmaking. Of all the Don's initial attempts to "translate his desires into actions" (33), the one to which he gives most effort is exchanging original, mundane names for ideal, chivalric ones. Inspecting his hack, he decides that "it would be wrong for the horse of so famous a knight . . . to be without a famous name," so he "spent four days pondering what name to give him" (34). The name he finally decides to use, Rocinante, indicates etymologically the process of transformation that has just taken place. *Rocin*, "a hack," and *ante*, "before," show that what was once a hack is now, through renaming, the noble mount of a knight-errant. Four days may be sufficient to rename a horse, but it takes Alonso Quixada eight days of deliberation to rename himself Don Quixote de la Mancha.

Beginning with these two transformations through renaming, attaching signifiers of a chivalric alternative world to signifieds consensually authorized to describe a textual version of actuality, Don Quixote attempts to re-create nearly the entirety of this consensually acknowledged actual world by renaming: the farm girl Aldonza Lorenzo becomes Dulcinea del Toboso, inns become castles, windmills become giants, two flocks of sheep become the armies of Laurcalco and Timonel of Carcajona, and a barber's basin becomes the helmet of Mambrino.[12] In fact, the adventure of the novel could be interpreted as the Don's heroic attempts to restore the "real" signifieds, within his alternative possible world, of the signifiers Don Quixote, Dulcinea, castles, giants, and threatening armies from their transfigured states, within the textual "real" world, as the signifieds Alonso Quixada, Aldonza Lorenzo, inns, windmills, and flocks of sheep. Restored to their "untransfigured" states, these signs assume meaning within the coherent, intertextual pattern of his chivalric model of reality, which has been derived from the myth of the Golden Age. His various adventures are, in fact, struggles against the movement of these signs to the supposedly empirical meanings assigned

12. Jorge Luis Borges, whose themes constantly touch upon Cervantes', has written the definitive postmodernist story that deals with the linguistic transformation of reality— "Tlön, Uqbar, Orbis Tertius." In this story, signifiers generate their own signifieds, reversing the process of naming and creation.

to them by society. That his restorations are totally subjective, Cervantes makes clear time after time. Yet in addition to portraying his protagonist ironically as a madman deluded into believing that things are what they cannot be, Cervantes also portrays him sympathetically as a poet, envisioning things according to how Aristotle defines the poet's task, which is "not . . . to tell what happened, but the kind of things that would happen—what is possible according to possibility and necessity" (*Poetics* IX.2). He is often shown as a self-willed, conscious creator aware simultaneously of the transformed and untransformed states of the signifieds he has altered. When reminded by the barber of his true identity, Alonso Quixada, Don Quixote replies, "I know who I am . . . and I know, too, that I am capable of being not only the characters I have named, but all the Twelve Peers of France and all the Nine Worthies as well" (54). And when the Don tells Sancho that Dulcinea is really Aldonza Lorenzo, he answers his squire's protests by saying, "I imagine all I say to be true, neither more nor less, and in my imagination I draw her as I would have her be" (210).

In spite of its apparent ludicrousness, Don Quixote's idealism manifests itself in one form of possibility—the belief in the perfectibility of man. For example, Erich Auerbach suggests that through his madness the Don attempts to break out of the paralyzing conditions of his social position and advanced age (348). The madness can thus illustrate not only the danger but also the promise of exploring language's ultimate potential to transfigure. In the end, Don Quixote's belief in the transcendental power to re-create himself and the world according to possibility has infected even hard-minded Sancho, who professes, "Every man's the son of his own deeds; and since I'm a man, I can become pope, let alone governor of an isle" (423). And Sancho proves his belief by actually becoming a governor and by succeeding in his new role quite well.

What Don Quixote lacks to authorize him as a transfiguring fictionalist is an audience, a consensus, and his missions can be seen as attempts to create an audience of believers. He seeks to verify his fiction by testing to see if it (using the Canon's words) "matches the minds" of those who participate in it. But when the Don's friends and captors conspire with playful trickery to agree with him that the basin is really the helmet of Mambrino, they cruelly mimic a believing audience's response. By pretending to believe in Don Quixote's renaming and transfiguring the basin, the group of characters establishes a paradigm for almost all the other characters who participate in his transformations of the world through language. Dorothea is renamed Princess Micomicona; Samson Carrasco becomes the Knight of the Mirrors; a maiden of the Duchess is transformed into the Countess Trifaldi—all to fool Don Quixote.

Similarly, the elaborate masquerades and plays the Duke and Duchess invent at Don Quixote's expense are antithetical examples of the knight's purpose as fictionalist. As fictionalists, the Duke and Duchess are concerned with no more than having fun with the Don's madness, playing along with his world in order to laugh silently at his absurdities. Thus, they represent what the implied author of *Don Quixote* might have been like had he not tempered his ironic vision with sincere sympathy for his hero. Don Quixote's search for a believing audience leads him to be manipulated by the traps set for him by characters like the Duke and Duchess, but their cruel traps also serve to contrast with his purely altruistic mission. He most directly expresses his goal of finding a world of believers in his speech to Don Lorenzo when, after enumerating the virtues of the conventions of knight-errantry, he concludes that he would like to "make you see how beneficial and necessary knights-errant were to the world in past ages, and how useful they would be in the present, if they were in fashion. But now, for the peoples' sins, sloth, idleness, gluttony and luxury triumph" (583). In spite of the farcical situations in which Don Quixote's lexical madness places him, Cervantes allows him here to say something important about truth-conditions in discourse— that they are dependent upon the sincerity of motivation. Mario Valdés's description of the literary truth-claim has a similar pragmatic focus: "The subject matter of truth-claims is . . . not the physical data of the world that corresponds to the statement, but rather the reader's degree of accessibility and relationship to that data within the lived world of language" (4–5). Thomas Pavel defines the accessibility of possible worlds in such a manner: "Accessibility and alternativeness formally represent the intuition that some states of affairs are possible relative to the real ones while others are not" (45). *Don Quixote* indicates that accessibility has a moral dimension and is dependent upon the motivation of the enunciator and its recognition by listeners and readers. On the one hand, Don Quixote's failure to find an audience of believers represents a rational failure on the part of characters to find accessible a world in which violations of empirical truth, such as windmills as giants, abound. However, the text asks us to consider morally the alternative possible world created by the Duke and Duchess. In acknowledging its artificiality, they sustain our conventions of verisimilitude; however, they do so while violating our conventions of decency or understanding of truth as a function of minimizing self-interest. The text asks us to judge which world is more accessible to both standards of truth, moral and empirical.

However, when his idealistic mission becomes solipsistic nightmare, Don Quixote gradually withdraws from reality, a withdrawal perhaps precipitated by his experience in the Cave of Montesinos, called by Gethin Hughes "an intimate moment when we are permitted to penetrate the inner recesses of his mind" (112). Like his earlier idealistic imaginings, this unearthly vision or dream is unverifiable, and he is unable to convince any of the other characters of its reality.[13] What is remarkable in this case, however, is the despair attendant upon his failure. In desperation, he becomes obsessed with proving the experience true, asking such unreliable sources as the magician in the Trifaldi masquerade and Master Peter's soothsaying ape if it actually occurred. Don Quixote's failure to persuade anyone to believe his story of the Cave of Montesinos reflects his ultimate failure to find an audience of believers in the correspondence of chivalric signs to the ideal world of the Golden Age, and this failure is a dramatic transition within the narrative to the abandonment of his mission and finally his death.

Don Quixote's failure to sustain his vision can be interpreted as being rooted both in the nature of his vision *and* in the consensual world. The Don establishes the relation between word and thing, not through a consensus supported by empirical logic, but through an act of faith. As the primary symbol of the poet, Don Quixote requires that his audience share his poetic belief in his vision, and thus he would establish a consensus not from the empirical correspondence of signs within his discourse but rather from the integrity of its motivation. For example, when the merchants from Toledo complain they cannot declare Dulcinea the most beautiful woman in the world, simply because they have not seen her, the Don replies, "If I were to show her to you . . . what merit would there be in your confessing so obvious a truth? The essence of the matter is that you must believe, confess, affirm, swear and maintain it without seeing her" (51). The Don asks the merchants to believe in the essence of Dulcinea's existence, as signified by her ideal name and the illocutionary force of his naming, rather than trust their sullied senses. The absence of faith Don Quixote continually discovers in the world about him is treated humorously here, but Cervantes shows its more dramatically serious implications in the closing chapters when Sancho refuses to carry out the cruel, ridiculous penance of self-flagellation the Duke and Duchess mischievously prescribe for the disenchantment of Dulcinea. Disregarding the foolishness of the penance, the disillusioned

13. Cervantes desired to stress the solipsistic and subjective nature of the Montesinos episode by distancing Cide Hamete from the narration. In the chapter following the narrative of the adventure is an intrusion by the translator of Cide Hamete's text, who reads a note "in the margin in the hand of this same Hamete" (624), which casts doubt on the authenticity of the knight's story and notes that Don Quixote retracted it on his deathbed.

knight can only resign himself to a refusal from his squire that earlier would have instantaneously aroused his indignation.

Don Quixote's humanistic faith is manifest in his desire to be constant to the ideal names and chivalric world to which they correspond. His insistence on believing in the identities he has given objects by renaming, in spite of the contrary proof of his senses, is the source of humor for many sequences in the text. However, his insistence on the precise use of language throughout the story reveals his innate sense of how his chivalric world depends on his language use becoming a coherent structural system. Don Quixote is a veritable semanticist in correcting the goatherd Peter's and Sancho's malapropisms as well as the other characters' improper use of chivalric names. He frequently rails against Sancho's using an inappropriate proverb to provide commentary for the situation at hand. He scolds his squire: "I do not find fault with a proverb aptly introduced, but to load and string on proverbs higgeldy-piggeldy makes your speech mean and vulgar" (742). This echoes his constant refrain: "What have all these proverbs to do with the matter we are discussing?" (201). Lacking consensual proof for his chivalric world, the Don struggles to maintain its identity by guarding its linguistic coherence.

However, the chronology of the text traces the progressive correction of Don Quixote's linguistic vision. A proper gauge of his miscalculations and their eventual rectification is the change in the name he applies to himself throughout the text. The leap from Alonso Quixada to Don Quixote de la Mancha is, in socially consensual terms, totally irrational, born from madness and based on no other criterion than desire. When he assumes the name Sancho invents, "The Knight of the Sad Countenance," his reasons are partly understandable, for in appealing to the authority of the chivalric intertext, his primary justification is that it is "right for me to take some title, as all knights did in the olden days" (147). But his reasons can also be justified empirically, for the name indicates the suffering he has endured. His next title, "The Knight of the Lions," is, on the other hand, more suitable than any of the others because it bears some correspondence to an actual event he has experienced—his display of courage before an uncaged lion. This last title serves him until his chivalric vision begins to disappear. He then creates an ideal vision of the world almost as irrational as the preceding one. The possible world of the pastoral romance he envisions is a recompense summoned by necessity in order to endure the painful loss of his chivalric ideal, and it is created by the same process, renaming:

> He told them also how he intended to turn shepherd for the year, and pass his time in the solitude of the fields, where he

could give free rein to his amorous thoughts, whilst occupying
himself in that pastoral and virtuous calling. He begged them to
be his companions, if they had not much to do and were not
prevented by more important business, and said he would buy
sufficient sheep and stock to give them the name of shepherds.
But, he informed them, the principal part of the business was
already done, for he had fixed on names for them which would
fit them to a T. The priest asked him for them, and Don Quixote
replied that he was to call himself the shepherd Quixotiz,
the Bachelor the shepherd Carrascon, the priest the shepherd
Curiambro and Sancho Panza the shepherd Panzino. (932)

In this summons to his friends, Don Quixote invokes an ideal world
similar to his previous one. The world could be conjured as before—by
a transformation in language, renaming. But as before, the names or
signs cannot be proven to correspond empirically to their objects. Nor
would his appeal for an audience, his request that his friends join him, be
any more successful than it was earlier. When he recants his belief in
knight-errantry on his deathbed, he recants his belief in the pastoral
romance as well; Cervantes dramatizes the pastoral ideal, as a lure for his
protagonist to refuse, in order to prove him cured from addictive, idealist
visions. Then he chooses a name by which to be remembered that truly
befits his character, Alonso Quixano the Good, one that coincides
empirically with the consensus of all his friends and acquaintances, his
true audience of believers: "He was always of an amiable disposition and
kind in his behaviour, so that he was well beloved not only by his own
household but by everyone who knew him" (937).[14] However, I am not
alone in finding the conclusion of the novel partly tragic, less because of
Don Quixote's death than his loss of sustaining ideals, which leads to his
withdrawal from the world.

The Puppet Show

In spite of Cervantes' later sympathy for Don Quixote's vision, the text,
for the most part, cruelly satirizes it. The flaw in his chivalric ideal is

14. Howard Mancing, in *The Chivalric World of Don Quijote: Style, Structure, and Narrative
Technique*, analyzes the speeches, allusions, references, and vocabulary of the successive
chapters of the text and notes a continuing decline in the emphasis given chivalry. He
writes that "never in part II does Don Quijote even come close to displaying the degree of
dedication to and enthusiasm for knight-errantry that was characteristic of . . . the first
half of part I" (170).

made ludicrously apparent during the ekphrasis of the puppet show. At the end of the episode, Don Quixote is surrounded by broken bits of puppets and realizes that he has mistaken them for real people. For once, he is forced from his alternative world into the actual one. He explains apologetically, "I assure you gentlemen that all that has passed here seemed to me a real occurrence. Melisandra was Melisandra; Sir Gaiferos, Sir Gaiferos; Marsilio, Marsilio; and Charlemagne, Charlemagne" (643). Unlike those moments of occasional lucidity in which he sees clearly both the altered and unaltered states of the objects he has renamed, when the Don is lost in his idée fixe, he allows the given name of an object to bear the full weight of significance, disregarding the proof of his senses. Thus, the sign "Sir Gaiferos" is so resonant in meaning for the knight that it is inconsequential that its referent is a puppet. For Don Quixote, the signified, the mental representation of Sir Gaiferos, is commensurate with its chivalric signifier, regardless of its discrepant relation to an external referent. What surprises is that Don Quixote, emerging momentarily from his delusion, admits that the external referents for the chivalric signs are puppets, not stubbornly insisting, as with the windmills / giants or barber's basin / helmet of Mambrino, on believing that the signifiers bear the full weight of signification.

However, a close examination of this ekphrasis calls into question the existence of a foundational discourse, which makes the Don's signifying error seem less egregious on a discursive, if not existential, level. Each author-character—from Don Quixote to the boy-narrator, Master Peter, Cide Hamete, the translator, the Second Author, and finally the First Author—handles the nature of illusion through language in a different manner; and the appearance of each as a supplement to another undercuts the claim any might have to final authority. A progression of narrators, beginning with the most deluded, implies a corrective pattern, but the correction does not necessarily unfold as a series of speakers with successively greater authority. The pattern of correction is circular. Each one is corrected by another, undermining each of their singular views.

Don Quixote is invited by Master Peter's assistant to believe in the truth behind the story of the puppet show; the boy-narrator declares, "This true story, here presented to your worships, is taken word for word from the French chronicles and the Spanish ballads" (638). His claim of intertextual accuracy, of the story as history, echoes the First Author's claim for his story, "that we do not depart by so much as an inch from the truth in the telling of it" (31). In fact, one possible reason the Don reacts so violently is that the story of the puppet show, both in popular legend and in the boy-narrator's version of it, echoes the story of *Don Quixote*. Telling of Sir Gaiferos's rescue of his wife Melisandra from bondage in a Moorish castle, the narrative reflects Don Quixote's mission to recover the "true," essential nature of things from bondage, their quotidian states invoked by the spells of evil enchanters. His most consistent adversaries are these enchanters, sages, and magicians who, from his point of view, disguise the true referents for his chivalric signs so that giants appear to be windmills, armies to be sheep, and the incomparable Dulcinea to be a foul-smelling peasant. He instructs Sancho that "spells transform all things and change them from their natural shapes. I do not mean that they actually change them, but they appear to, as we learnt by experience in the transformation of Dulcinea, sole refuge of my hopes" (660–61). The rescue of Dulcinea from her bondage in a spell becomes the central focus of Don Quixote's life. In restoring the "proper" signified to the signifier Dulcinea, the Don would be able to accomplish an alignment of language around the coherent paradigm of chivalry, thus stabilizing the referential drift caused by the "enchanters" who create the everyday.[15] However, Cervantes shows that such stability is impossible in language, which is always susceptible to substitution on the level of the signifier.

The enchanters' transformations are antitheses of Don Quixote's transformations through language. Whereas he identifies common signifieds with ideal, chivalric signifiers, the enchanters, on the other hand, identify them with signifiers belonging to the mundane, the quotidian. After having first identified the enchanter as Freston, the evil magician, Don Quixote confesses apprehensively to Sancho, "I am afraid that if the author of that history of my exploits, which they say is now in print, chanced to be some enchanter hostile to me, he has probably changed one thing into another, mingling a thousand lies with one truth, and digressed to narrate actions out of the sequence proper to a faithful history" (516). Thus, Don Quixote conjectures that the narrator of his history is an evil enchanter who has presented a false, parodic version of his real state. The Don's fears concerning the narrator of his story parallel his criticism of the boy-narrator's story of Sir Gaiferos. Indeed, the boy-narrator is a humorous version of an "evil enchanter" who has transformed an ideal, chivalric story into a more common one. Don Quixote worries that his "history" will be marred by digressions that are unfaithful to the true sequence of events. His first criticism of the

15. Ramon Salvidar argues convincingly that Don Quixote sees the foundation of his quest as the restoration of the signifier Dulcinea to her transcendent state as chivalric signified. As "organizing symbol" for his ideal, Dulcinea might give coherence to his mission; however, "the narrative poses the distinct possibility that this symbolic entity is not a sign of a transcendental truth, but is simply a metaphor of a metaphor" ("Don Quixote's Metaphors" 273).

boy-narrator is over a digression; he says, "Boy, boy . . . go straight ahead with your story and do not go curving off at a tangent; for it requires much proof and corroboration to bring a truth to light" (639–40). And the knight's fears that the evil enchanter will mix lies with truth are expressed in his criticism of the boy's use of detail—his portrayal of Moorish bells instead of kettledrums and a clarion.

As it turns out, Don Quixote's criticisms are somewhat justified, for the boy's story, though called verisimilar, deliberately falsifies the original version found in ballad and legend. He portrays Sir Gaiferos as an idler, playing backgammon while his wife is kidnapped. And his description of the escape, with Melisandra hanging in midair with her skirt caught on the balcony, is a Punch-and-Judy routine, not the relation of heroism. The boy-narrator, transforming the chivalric ideal into farce, translates the language of chivalry into the discourse of clowns. By manipulating the story with puppets for the purpose of ridicule, the boy-narrator foreshadows the manipulation of Don Quixote by the Duke and Duchess of Trifaldi, who use the lexicon of the knight's ideal world to debase and mock him. The boy-narrator also suggests what *Don Quixote* would have been like had Cervantes viewed his hero as clown, without the noble stature he gains progressively in the temporal course of the narrative. The boy's attitude toward fiction, opposing Don Quixote's, is to admit freely its illusion. His physical position on the stage highlights this strategy. With one foot in the real world and another on the fictional world of the stage and with a pointing stick to guide the audience's responses to the characters, he parodies the intrusive author. And he serves as a reversing mirror to reflect the self-consciousness of *Don Quixote*'s implied author. The boy-narrator shows that a narrative stance not motivated by understanding, poetic faith, and honesty inevitably leads to a kind of callousness toward character. Characters are not real, hence they are dolls, objects of farcical manipulation.

However, the boy is not the ultimate authority as fictionalist in the puppet show. Behind him is Master Peter, the actual author of the play and invisible manipulator of the puppets' strings. In choosing one of the most artificial of artistic media, he parodies verisimilitude in art with the ironic relation he establishes between chivalric names and wooden-doll referents. Even more than his assistant, Master Peter openly admits the illusion of the artifice: not content to remain invisible behind the stage, he continually intrudes to provide apparently truthful commentary, criticism of the boy's narration, and defense of himself as narrator. Master Peter's free admission of the fictional illusion gives the appearance of complete honesty. Unlike the Duke and Duchess, his fiction is presented to fool no one into believing it real. Don Quixote is fooled only because of his mad fixation, and even he cannot sustain his irrational vision when the only evidence of his battle with the Moors is a scattered heap of broken wood. Master Peter defends his theory of fiction in response to Don Quixote's criticism of his play's verisimilitude: "Don't they perform countless comedies in these parts almost every day, full of innumerable improbabilities and absurdities? But, for all that, they have a successful run and are greeted, not only with applause but with admiration and all . . . so long as I fill my bag they can act as many improbabilities as there are motes in the sun" (641). Though his real ambition is to "fill my bag," Master Peter ironically echoes the part of the Canon's two-sided argument that defends idealist fiction and gives the artist full privilege to abandon verisimilitude when it hinders the creative freedom of his imagination. But more important, Master Peter's attitude toward the illusion of his artifice represents a shift of perspective from that of his assistant. The boy has one foot constantly upon the stage, and with his pointing stick and incessant commentary, he continually guides and shapes the audience's responses. Master Peter, on the other hand, has resolved to tell the story by "deeds, not words" (638), but no sooner has the dramatization started than he steps from behind the stage and reverts to words in his telling, effectively destroying any sense of empirical actuality. Master Peter's comments on fiction and his actions as narrator reveal a narrative stance realistic in one respect. By building and destroying illusions and by addressing his audience directly, he implicitly admits that art is illusory and desires only to share this knowledge with his audience so that the boundary between art and life can be maintained. By not deluding the viewer into believing that he or she is witnessing an unfolding reality, Master Peter can present art as play, a game motivated by self-interest. Moreover, his comic stance of undisguised intrusions, anticipating the authorial roles of Sterne, Joyce, and Barth, is another parodic mirror of Cervantes' role. Master Peter establishes his narrative authority in this appeal for sympathy by sharing the secrets of his illusions. Thus, because of his apparent honesty, the rest of the audience of the puppet show and the readers of the novel sympathize with Master Peter when he laments the loss of his kingdom due to Don Quixote's inability to discriminate between art and life. Even the deluded knight comes to his senses and pays this honest author a large sum for his loss.

But wait. After Master Peter has pocketed Don Quixote's money and has left the scene, the reader learns that the guileless puppet master is none other than Gines de Pasamonte, the leader of the ungrateful galley slaves Don Quixote freed in an earlier adventure, the same rogue who later stones his liberator and steals Dapple, Sancho's ass. He is also another author-character, the author of *The Life of Gines de Pasamonte*, an autobiography remaining unfinished until his life is over. The revelation for the reader (withheld from the other characters) is that this artist who had won his audience's confidence by sharing the secret of his art's illusion had been himself hiding behind an illusion and a false reference—an eyepatch and the name Master Peter. Thus, the reader has been taken in by an illusion this intrusive author had prepared after having gained credibility by divulging the mechanics of another illusion. However, now, after having been duped as surely as the deluded knight he or she had just earlier found so comical, the reader can readjust perspectives to assume once again a privileged position in relation to the characters of the novel.

But wait again. The information concerning Master Peter's true identity has come to the reader through an authorial intrusion by Cide Hamete Benengeli, one of the most ubiquitous of the narrators of *Don Quixote*, appearing in at least twenty-five separate intrusions.[16] Paradoxically, the reader must have faith in an authorial intrusion warning against the deceit practiced by another intruding author. Yet Cide Hamete, presented throughout not as an illusionary artist but as an objective historian, is meant to represent the first of the Canon's two-sided argument, judging fiction true according to how verisimilitude and detail can provide a perfect imitation of nature. Cide Hamete's role is further defined when Don Quixote and Samson Carrasco discuss the book concerning the knight's adventures that the Moor has just published. Don Quixote complains that Cide Hamete should have left out many of the unflattering things that had happened to Sancho and himself in order to have composed a more entertaining story. The bachelor corrects him by repeating the Aristotelian distinction between fiction and poetry: "It is one thing to write as a poet and another as a historian. The poet can relate things, not as they were, but as they should have been" (488). The implication is that Cide Hamete, portraying things just as they were, has written according to necessity and composed a realistic account of the knight's adventures.

The statements of the Second Author on the work by Cide Hamete support its claim to authenticity. The title of the parchment he discovers by accident is "*The History of Don Quixote de la Mancha*, written by Cide Hamete Benengeli, Arabic Historian" (77).[17] Later he describes the

16. For a discussion of the appearances of Cide Hamete, see Ruth El Saffar's *Distance and Control in Don Quixote*, 102.

17. Just as the title invalidates the claim that the prologuist is Cervantes, so does this title invalidate identifications of the Second Author as the author of *The Ingenious Gentleman Don Quixote de la Mancha*.

practice of historians in general as "exact, truthful, and absolutely unprejudicial" (78), and more specifically, "Cide Hamete Benengeli was a very exact historian and very precise in all his details, as can be seen by his not passing over these various points, trivial and petty though they may be" (121). As historian, Cide Hamete is thus presented as compiler and chronicler of all truthful facts concerning Don Quixote. His intrusions, as Ruth El Saffar points out, generally serve to reveal the truth behind an artifice used by other author-characters to trick Don Quixote (102). Armed with "true facts," Cide Hamete is able several times to shatter illusions presented by these other authors. But Haley indicates that in spite of the instructive service Cide Hamete performs for the reader, he too engages in deception (160). In relating the stories of the interior fictions, the illusions that deceive Don Quixote, he withholds the secret of the illusion until the end. Able to reveal the identity of Master Peter at the beginning of that episode, he instead allows readers to be deceived along with the characters. The chronology by which he relates this story prejudices the reader against Don Quixote and confirms the knight's suspicions that the sage enchanter who would author his story might "narrate actions out of sequence proper to a faithful history" (516) in order to misrepresent what really happened.

The chapter in which Cide Hamete reveals the identity of Master Peter opens with the Moorish author swearing that what he will relate is now the truth. However, an appeal this fervent seems both an apology for the earlier falsification and a protest that he will no longer deceive. This passage is a unique one in which three of the four narrators speak at once:

> Cide Hamete, the chronicler of this great history, introduces the present chapter with these words: *"I swear as a Catholic Christian,"* on which his translator observes that Cide Hamete's swearing as a Catholic Christian, he being a Moor, as doubtless he was, meant only that as a Catholic Christian, when he swears, swears, or would swear the truth, and observe it in all he says, so he should tell the truth, as if he had sworn like a Catholic Christian, in writing of Don Quixote; especially in his statement regarding who Master Peter was, and about his ape that amazed the whole countryside with its prophesyings. (646)

Cervantes stresses the difficulty of verifying truth-claims by purposefully confusing the syntax. Three voices and three views, intermingling and colliding, call into question not only the possibility of ultimate denotation, free from connotative play, but also an ultimate origin for discourse.

By intruding into Cide Hamete's intrusion, the translator undermines the historian's claim of ultimate authority. The translator shatters Cide Hamete's illusion of historicity by constantly pointing out discrepancies in the narrative. Here, the translator, a Moor himself, clarifies the fallacy of the Moorish author giving a Christian oath. Elsewhere, he omits dubious passages and declares others apocryphal. The presence of the translator serves to remind that this history is not given firsthand but is transmitted, and the Second Author's initial doubts about the veracity of a Moorish author are doubled by having a Moorish translator. The text is seen, writes Harry Levin, at "three removes," containing "afterthoughts like a palimpsest" ("Example" 46).

The Second Author as Ideal Reader

The ekphrastic Master Peter episode serves as a stage for Cervantes to exhibit several narrators, each presenting a version of fictional truth. The series of narrators could follow a pattern of correction, with the last one revealing a final referential truth, but this is not the case. Establishing such an ultimate authority would arrest the confusing dissemination of the signifier Don Quixote and privilege a unitary signified for him, whether as idealistic dreamer, fool, or humanistic reformer. But as the narrative passes from Don Quixote to the boy-narrator, Master Peter, Cide Hamete, the translator, the First Author, and the Second Author, each undercuts the other's authority. Does Cervantes imply, then, that all narrators are equally untrustworthy? The Second Author provides a possible answer. Throughout the text the changing relation of the Second Author to Cide Hamete is one of the most interesting of the character-author relations. It is the Second Author's intrusion into the narrative begun by the First Author in chapter 9 of book 1 that first makes the reader aware of the perspective of multiple narrators. In that chapter, after the original author has carried his description of Don Quixote's confrontation with the Basque through to mid-battle, a mysterious second voice picks up the narration: "At this critical point our delightful history stopped short and remained mutilated, our author failing to inform us where to find the missing part. This caused me great annoyance, for my pleasure from the little I had read turned to displeasure at the thought of the small chance there was of finding the rest of this delightful story" (75). The remainder of the chapter details the Second Author's search for the conclusion, his discovery of the Arabic manuscript, and his hiring of the Moorish translator.

Significantly, the Second Author is portrayed as having abandoned his role as a reader of the First Author to become a reader of Cide Hamete. Equally significant is that as reader the Second Author is similar to another reader—Don Quixote. Both the Second Author and the deluded knight, surrendering themselves to a belief in the fictions they are reading, attempt to transform their beliefs into reality. They thus represent a coherence view of truth, defined by James Young as "what can be warranted by a system of beliefs" (467), as opposed to correspondence theories, in which truth-conditions are those that "correspond to reality" (468). The Second Author's quixotic goal is to bring to light the suppressed history of Don Quixote; and, as he reminds the reader, if it were not for him, the novel would never have been read. His quest, he tells, grew out of his faith in the reality of Don Quixote's existence and a belief in the ideals for which he stands. He describes himself as "anxious and eager for real and authentic knowledge of the whole life and marvels of our famous Spaniard, Don Quixote de la Mancha, the light and mirror of Manchegan chivalry, and the first man of our times, of these calamitous times of ours, to devote himself to the toils and exercise of knight errantry" (75–76). In the Second Author, Don Quixote finds a believing audience; and his mission, as described to Don Lorenzo, to "make you see how beneficial and necessary knights-errant were to the world in past ages, and how useful they would be in the present" (583), is fulfilled.

The Second Author, then, begins his reading experience from a position of belief in the story; what he suspects at first is the originator of the discourse. In the beginning of his account, he tells the reader, "In this history I know that you will find all the entertainment you can desire; and if any good quality is missing, I am certain that it is the fault of its dog of an author rather than any default in the subject" (78). But after these early criticisms, the Second Author is increasingly drawn to praise the Moorish historian, culminating in the extolling apostrophe opening chapter 40 of book 2: "All who enjoy stories like this should show their gratitude to Cide Hamete, its first author, for his meticulousness in recording its minutest details, leaving nothing, however trivial, which he does not bring clearly to light. He depicts thoughts, reveals intentions, answers unspoken questions, clears up doubts, resolves objections; in fact, elucidates the slightest points the most captious critic could raise. O most renowned author!" (721). What has convinced the Second Author that Cide Hamete, whom he had earlier characterized as a "dog of an author," is now a perfect historian? Using the criteria provided by several characters on the necessary qualities of a historian, Cide Hamete is a failure, for he gives few indications of his sources, of where he uncovered his detail; nor does he present his story in the sequential order Don Quixote expects of histories. Clearly, then, the final belief of the Second Author in the veracity of Cide Hamete is an act of faith, based on his belief in the motivational sincerity and illocutionary force of the Moor's discourse. It is similar to what Don Quixote requires of the merchants—to believe, in spite of the lack of sensory proof.

An alternative to the failed historian Cide Hamete is the novel's truest historian—the First Author. He provides more descriptive and biographical detail than any other of the narrators, offering, indeed, a compendious catalogue of Don Quixote's readings in chivalric romance. He gives verifiable sources for his information and indicates when these sources are inadequate. Of Don Quixote's original name, for example, he writes, "They say that his surname was Quixada or Quesada—for there is some difference of opinion amongst authors on this point" (31). And he writes of Don Quixote's first expedition, "There are authors who say that the first adventure he met was that of the pass of Lapice. Others say it was the windmills. But what I have been able to discover of the matter and what I have found written in the annals of La Mancha, is that he rode all that day, and that at nightfall his horse and he were weary and dying of hunger" (37). This reference to the number of other histories of Don Quixote indicates that the First Author's sources were these other written accounts, an intertextual link to an identity he supposedly attempts to verify by factual proof. As historian, he does not go beyond what he can find in research and refuses to create imaginatively adventures for which there are no sources. He qualifies, therefore, to be the historian described by the Second Author, the Canon, Samson Carrasco, and Don Quixote—the chronicler of reality that Cide Hamete is in theory but not in practice.

However, Cervantes indicates that there are flaws in the First Author's approach. In the very first sentence of the text, he betrays an arbitrariness about language that renders suspect his account in spite of its use of "objective" detail: "In a certain village in La Mancha, which I do not wish to name . . ." (31). The First Author as historian suggests those linguists Cohen defines as approaching reference empirically, matching "arbitrary symbols" with "things in nature" (21). Whatever are his reasons for concealing the name of the village, the arbitrary manner in which he dismisses the importance of linguistic signs reminds us that no matter how numerous his facts, this author's method conceals more than reveals the text's true referents. Also, the sources the First Author has for these referents taken as facts are no more than other books, an intertextual link to a reality existing only in writing. At some point, each historian has to adopt the technique of the poet: he must imaginatively create a world by establishing a coherent vision through language. The First Author, failing to recognize this, arrives at an impasse near the beginning of the novel: "The author of this history left the battle in suspense at this critical point, with the excuse that he could find no more records of Don Quixote's exploits than those related here" (74). The impasse created by the First Author's adherence to facts motivates the creation of the Second Author, an ideal reader surrendering himself, through belief and imagination, to the coherent model of the world implied by the language of chivalry. Implicitly, the Second Author is moved by the power of Cide Hamete's discourse and is convinced in the integrity of his motivation. Unlike the boy-narrator and Master Peter, who tell chivalric stories for the purpose of ridicule and fraud, Cide Hamete invents Don Quixote for a moral purpose, presenting him as a paragon of virtue, knightly or otherwise. Cide Hamete's devotion to his character and what he represents is clearly evident in the novel's conclusion, where he writes, "For me alone Don Quixote was born and I for him" (940). Poetic belief is just reward for such devotion.

Realism as Performative Statement

As each author-character posits a theory of realism according to a conception of language and illusion, an interesting contrast forms between the two extremes. The poet Don Quixote believes that the name, word, or symbol reveals an object's reality. The First Author, on the other hand, casually tells that he does not care to relate the name of the village where his hero lives and does not even bother to clear up an ambiguity in the protagonist's proper name because "this does not much concern our story" (31). The movement from Don Quixote's idealism to the First Author's empirical realism consists in a devaluing of language in favor of the thing, a valorizing of the signified over the reproducible signifier. It is a devaluation that Dickens would parody in *Hard Times*, where Mr. Bounderby says, "You must discard the word Fancy altogether" (5). It would find expression in William Carlos Williams's "Say it! No ideas but in things" (14). And it would motivate Hemingway to write, "There were many words that you could not stand to hear and finally only the names of places had dignity. . . . Abstract words such as glory, honor, courage, or hollow were obscene beside the concrete names of villages" (185). The derivation of realism from the Latin *res*, "thing," betrays this prejudice.

The movement from Don Quixote's nominalist idealism to the First

Author's empirical realism consists in this devaluing of signs in favor of referents, of coherence in favor of correspondence. Robert Alter writes, "The novel begins out of an erosion of belief in the authority of the written word and it begins with Cervantes" (3). This erosion of belief, dramatized in the figure of Don Quixote, propels the novel toward restoring signs to a correspondent relation to natural referents. The Don, using language emotively, expects the attitudinal effect of such signifiers as "the helmet of Mambrino," "Dulcinea," and (what is most important) "Chivalry" to be so powerful as to alter transcendentally not only their signifieds but also their external referents. But by parodying fictions of knight-errantry in emphasizing their lack of correspondence with reality, Cervantes shows Don Quixote, "imitating the language of his books" (37), call a puppet Sir Gaiferos. This contrast creates a tension that cannot be relieved until the puppet is called a puppet once more. The sign has been adjusted to suit its referent, and the adjustment is downward in scale. Here Cervantes' realism is deflationary; language serves the world by reflecting it literally. Yet paradoxically Cervantes allows the series of empirical investigators into the ludicrous ideals of Don Quixote to culminate in a reader and author who finally confirm those ideals—ideals that create the novelistic reality we are reading.

By creating numerous author-characters, Cervantes also creates numerous conceptual schemes by which these characters organize the signifying relations of sign and referent, signifier and signified, language and world. Through the admission of the possibility of numerous perspectives, Cervantes ultimately denies the possibility of any one system being grounded in an absolute correspondence. Rather than make the false, absent signifiers present to confirm the presence and claims of a "true" valorized one that denotatively points to an extratextual signified, the text instead questions even the possibility of extratextual reference. Not proving the insufficiency of one system in favor of another that is empirically correspondent, Cervantes proves, rather, through the method of validating truth-claims by a process of falsifiability, that all systems of understanding are epistemologically incommensurable and untranslatable yet intertextually dependent upon each other. There can be no appeal to an ultimate authority within a discourse by pointing to the sanction of the ultimate referent, signified, or thing. Anthony Cascardi writes that the novel does not, as commonly interpreted, explode the idea of the unrelatedness of signs to chivalric ideals, but rather, "it is precisely the idea of knowledge as some sort of correspondence of ideas or language to facts, outside of human judgment and culture, which Cervantes explodes in the *Quixote*; indeed, it is only because the discovery of human knowledge is also a discovery of human contingency that it counts for anything at all" (167).[18] In suggesting that all knowledge is contingent upon the conceptual schemes and languages that organize our information about the world, Cervantes indicates that if there is any sanctioning authority in discourse, it resides in faith and motivation and exists in the conventions that give meaning to our lives. Why the novel ceases to be comic and has the tone of tragedy at its end is that it dramatizes the character's loss of sustaining faith in a fictional world of possibility, a loss of illusion that leads to his disillusionment with the world of necessity and ultimately to his death. While the novel tests the discourse that Don Quixote uses to describe the empirical world and finds it lacking, it confirms his procedure of worldmaking through discourse by validating its dependency upon motivation.

Thematized, the reading experience of Cervantes' novel implies a definition of realism different from the one foregrounded in the plot. The narrative structure indicates that realism is largely a matter of rhetoric, discourse, and not accurate correspondence. With this perspective, Douglas Hewitt's description of realism holds true: "Realistic novels, in short, do not affect us as being like life; they are the experience of being told about life by someone whom we trust" (55). The motivation for the production of numerous author-characters is the search for such an authenticating rhetoric as described by Hewitt. The effect of this production is to separate the discourse of the novel from its story, for the reader's attention is constantly drawn away from the knight's struggle (to make reality correspond to his verbally created ideal) to the author-characters' struggle (to make this story into a book). On the level of story, Cervantes seems to expose as false a coherence view of truth by applying proper correspondence as corrective. But on the level of reading, truth is authenticated not by a correspondent signifying system but by a discourse that elicits belief because of the integrity of its motivation. In giving disproportionate emphasis neither to correspondence nor to coherence theories of reference, and rather in emphasizing their relations in manifold ways, *Don Quixote* is the exemplary realistic novel, the means by which others can be defined.

18. Anthony J. Cascardi, in "Perspectivism and the Conflict of Values in *Don Quijote*," argues that the theory of ethics evolving from the text is one that denies the possibility of truth existing apart from conceptual schemes by which we know the world.

CHAPTER THREE

Fancy and Understanding and the Ekphrastic Riddles of *Emma*

The Lockean Episteme

Paradigm shifts in novelistic realism are represented in revolutionary texts as struggles between contrasting paradigmatic views of linguistic reference. Key novels appearing near the end of traditional or the beginning of newer paradigms thematize this struggle through ekphrastic topoi containing the same elements and form as the ekphrases of novels that explored the discursive limits of earlier paradigms. Thus, in spite of historical changes in epistemological and linguistic views, ekphrases of novels in transitional periods share similar revolutionary functions. Although these revolutionary texts use methodologies commensurate with the culturally determined boundaries of their epistemological horizons, their ekphrastic systems consistently reflect the terms by which the historical period reinterprets or defends the relations of word, idea, and thing. In this basic structural sense, ekphrases of significant texts represent the changes in broader paradigms of knowledge, the epistemes of Foucault, which he calls "the total set of relations that unite, at a given period, the discursive practices that give rise to epistemological

figures, sciences, and possibly formalized systems of knowledge"
(*Archaeology* 191). What count as significant texts are those that explore
a discursive mode (and its correspondent episteme) to its margin of
understandability and hence imply what will replace it. However, I have
shown in *Don Quixote* and further illustrate in subsequent analyses that
the procedures for thematizing representation not only reveal the margins of understandability of a dominant and fading realistic paradigm
but also imply the limits of the valorized one. Quite simply, a realist text
cannot maintain a true-false dichotomy in exploring the capabilities of
correspondence and coherence without betraying its conflicting allegiances to word and world.

By interpreting the ekphrastic scenes of *Don Quixote* in the historical
terms of the scholastic-humanist and nominalist-empiricist debate on
language, I am not merely showing how these influenced Cervantes'
views on language but rather describing the conceptual vocabulary
within which he could challenge and erect theories of realistic representation. Cervantes' revolutionary example shows how parody and a surplus
of representations troubled the rules of both the fading medieval and the
emerging rationalist paradigms that attempted to regulate the signifying
relations of word–idea–thing. By parodying the Don's interpreting signs
as emblems of a romantic, spiritual reality, Cervantes undercuts the
scholastic claims of transcendental signification. But the text also implies
that the emerging paradigm, with its humanist faith in reason and its
emphasis on signifying processes themselves, fails to provide a foundation equivalent to medieval religiosity. Like the contemporary example
that Foucault explicates, Velázquez's *Las Meninas*, the numerous representations in *Don Quixote* of representation itself serve only to exhibit
the gap between discourse and world, a gap that Adamic theories of
language attempted to elide.

I would like now to examine a subsequent shift in paradigms and
illustrate how an exemplary text uses ekphrasis both to defend its
dominant assumptions and to reveal its limitations. The historical shift
from not only Adamic but also rationalist theories of linguistic meaning
was epitomized by the publication of John Locke's *An Essay Concerning
Human Understanding* in 1690 and reflected in Jane Austen's masterwork
Emma. In the *Essay* Locke directly attacks the essentialist foundation of
Adamic and rationalist views by positing a theory of language that
proposes an arbitrary connection between word and idea, or signifier
and signified. He writes, "The same liberty also that *Adam* had of
affixing any new name to any *idea*, the same has anyone still" (III.4.51).
From the standpoint of modern semiotics, Locke's theory of language is
revolutionary, since it embodies many key principles of Saussurean

linguistics. In addition, his influence upon contemporaries was so pervasive that it allows theorists to speak of a "Lockean episteme" because, according to Gabriele Bernhard Jackson, "Locke's great work, like Freud's, painted a new portrait of the human subject from within [and] modified contemporary understanding of all intellectual and emotional phenomena. Education, ethics, political doctrine, sociology, aesthetic theory, analysis of language—all were inevitably affected" (29).[1] Although Foucault places Locke historically in his Classical Age, a closer view of his work shows that his paradigm of knowledge is perhaps transitional, bridging the former's Classical with his modern age, which he calls the Age of Man.[2] One significance of Locke's work is that his materialist theory of knowledge culminates Newtonian and natural philosophy's questioning of metaphysics. According to Robert L. Armstrong, Locke's work contributed to a late-seventeenth- and eighteenth-century conception of metaphysics as "a catch-all label for almost any kind of discredited subject or discipline" (369). Thus, as rationalism and humanism drove a wedge between the divine correspondence of words and things in nominalism and Adamicism, Locke's materialist empiricism questioned the rationalist notion of equivalence between things and the ideas of reason.[3]

The *Essay* divides human knowledge into three sciences. The first science, "natural philosophy," concerns "the knowledge of things, as they are in their own proper beings" (IV.21.1). The second, "ethics," is

1. A detailed analysis of a Lockean episteme and its influence on the period is Gabriele Bernhard Jackson's "From Essence to Accident: Locke and the Language of Poetry in the Eighteenth Century." Paralleling many of Hans Aarsleff's findings on Locke's influence, Jackson argues that Locke's main contribution in the *Essay* was to overthrow the essentialist notions of Adamicism. The shift in poetry of the period can be seen in a movement away from essentialist literary techniques such as a Neoplatonic categorizing of forms, qualities, and substances. The new poetry, characterized by the work of Gray, Thompson, and Johnson, emphasizes instead the mind's capacity to name and organize objects apart from a priori forms.

2. Locke's theories of language call into question Foucault's definition of discourse in his Classical Age. According to Foucault, "Classical language [is] the *common discourse* of representation and things . . . the place within which nature and human nature intersect" (310). The "profound upheaval," the "archaeological permutation," occurred when the rationalist equivalence between mind and nature disappeared, and discourse achieved the opacity that Locke feared.

3. In "John Locke's 'Doctrine of Signs': A New Metaphysics," Robert L. Armstrong interprets Locke as central to the antimetaphysical, materialist epistemology that evolved from Newtonian natural philosophy. Armstrong notes that most references to metaphysics in the *Essay* are disparaging: "He speaks of metaphysics as . . . reasoning from maxims or principles supposedly self-evident or indisputable. Correct thinking, he argues, must depend upon having clear and distinct ideas in mind, words being meaningless unless they stand for such ideas" (370).

"the seeking out of those rules and measures of human actions, which lead to happiness, and the means to practice them" (IV.21.3). The last science is the "doctrine of signs," the function of which is

> to consider the nature of signs the mind makes use of for the understanding of things, or conveying its knowledge to others. For since the things the mind contemplates are none of them, besides itself, present to the understanding, it is necessary that something else, as a sign or representation of the thing it considers, should be present to it; and these are *ideas*. And because the scene of ideas that makes one man's thoughts cannot be laid open to the immediate view of another, nor laid up anywhere but in the memory . . . therefore, to communicate our thoughts to another, as well as to record them for our own use, signs of our ideas are also necessary. (IV.21.4)

Locke, prophetically calling his doctrine of signs *sēmeiōtikē* (IV.21.4), most fully elaborates it in chapter 3 of the *Essay*, "On Words." There he attacks the Platonic and Aristotelian foundations of both Adamicism and rationalism, which is the essentialist notion that the relation between ideas (as well as signs) and things is one of identity, that ideas share an essential form with their referents in the external world. Locke challenges the notion of identity in signifying, regardless of whether this identity comes from a medieval conception of spirituality or a rationalist notion of mind. To illustrate the discontinuity between ideas or signs and external referents, Locke uses the terms "nominal essence" and "real essence." The nominal essence is the mental representation of a few empirical qualities given a name or word to signify an object. The object's real essence, its inner makeup, remains unknowable and exists only as the external cause of ideas and their signs. Locke emphasizes that the attachment of names to nominal essences representing these selective qualities is arbitrary; nominal essences "have for the most part, in all languages, received their birth and signification, from ignorant and illiterate people, who sorted and denominated things by those sensible qualities they found in them"; and the assortment and denomination of these attributes, as well as the selection of details to represent the whole, are "almost infinite" (III.9.12) because "there is scarce any particular thing existing, which, in some of its simple *ideas*, does not communicate with a greater, and in others a less number of particular beings: Who shall determine in this case, which are those that are to make up the precise collection, that is to be signified by the specific name?" (III.9.14).

It is not difficult to translate Locke's notion of the sign as existing in the relation of word–idea–thing to the Peircean triad of sign–interpret-ant–object. Nor is it difficult to find the Saussurean concept of the arbitrary relation of signifier and signified in the Lockean sign. As Locke says specifically, "*Words* . . . come to be made use of by Men as *the signs of* their *ideas*; not by any natural connection . . . but by a voluntary imposition, whereby such a word is made arbitrarily the mark of such an *idea*" (III.2.1) (my emphasis). But before finding easy equivalents between Locke and modern semiotics, one should consider the uses Locke made of his theory.[4] Unlike some disciples of Saussure, Locke hardly celebrates the liberation of linguistic signs from determining external referents. An empiricist, he reveals a basic distrust of language, particularly those words not derived from what he calls "sensible ideas" and therefore existing at a higher level of abstraction than those that can be empirically validated. According to his real-nominal essence distinction, actual truth bears some relation between idea and thing; on the other hand, metaphysical truth, composed of abstract ideas, is merely the relation of idea to idea and is therefore completely cut off from the world of sense and meaning. Of abstract words particularly, Locke says, "*General* and *universal* belong not to the real existence of things; but *are the inventions* and *creatures of the understanding*" (III.3.11) (my emphasis). The concern of so much of the *Essay* is signification and language because Locke wanted to reveal "the cheat and abuse" of words (III.10.5). In the "Epistle to the Reader," he warns that "vague and insignificant forms of speech, and abuse of language, have so long passed for mysteries of science . . . that it will not be easy to persuade, either those who speak, or those that hear them, that they are but the covers of ignorance, and hindrance of true knowledge." True and irrefutable knowledge to Locke would be the knowledge of things; but as Locke says later in the *Essay*, "Because men would not be thought to talk barely of their own imagination, but of things as really they are; therefore they *often suppose their words to stand also for the reality of things*" (III.2.5).

It is ironic that an epistemology such as Lockean empiricism, so grounded in a correspondence theory of knowledge, would develop a

4. Hans Aarsleff's works have done much to show the relevance of Locke to twentieth-century theories of language. See *The Study of Language in England, 1780–1860*, and particularly *From Locke to Saussure*. Aarsleff argues that though Locke and Condillac never used the terms, they consistently spoke of language as a social institution. In his emphasis on the arbitrary relation of sign and thing and the subjective languages this implies, Locke predates Wilhelm von Humboldt's use of these concepts. Aarsleff places Locke in a central position as the originator of many key concepts of modern semiotics and credits Condillac with carrying Locke's ideas to their logical conclusions. Condillac's contribution is most evident in his positing a linguistic basis for all knowledge and ideas. See especially "Leibniz on Locke and Language," in *From Locke to Saussure*.

view of language fundamentally coherentist. In rejecting the essentialist positions of Adamicism and rationalism, Locke implies that language is a social institution reflecting not the world at large but rather the social world of the people who invented it. And as "creatures of the understanding," the invention and denomination of abstract words should more clearly epitomize the social rather than the empirical context. However, the Lockean paradigm could not develop fully a social theory of knowledge without threatening its empirical basis. The empiricist attempts to accommodate the social and the empirical, evolving from the ethics of Shaftesbury and Hutcheson to the skepticism of Hume, define the epistemological boundaries of this paradigm and carry its conclusions to a point of undecidability.[5]

Knightley and Emma's Debate

The Lockean skepticism concerning language is ekphrastically thematized in several novels of the period. Indeed, as the example of *Don Quixote* indicates, the discursive patterns of an episteme appear in texts not just as an external, regulative norm; they are also portrayed internally in scenes representing discourse. One of the best examples is in Jane Austen's *Emma*. In *The Rise of the Novel* Ian Watt calls the novels of Austen the apotheosis of the eighteenth-century novel and, as such, literary exemplars of the Lockean episteme. Moreover, like *Don Quixote*, their ekphrastic representations explore the range and boundaries of the realistic paradigm that evolved from an epistemic social foundation. And like *Don Quixote*, the ekphrases of *Emma* reveal that a major concern of the text's realism is the referential status of the sign. According to Watt, Austen stands at the end of a tradition of eighteenth-century novelists who were influenced by Locke's theories of language. Watt defines this tradition as a break with the previous one, which "was not primarily concerned with the correspondence of words to things, but rather with the extrinsic beauties which could be bestowed upon description and

5. Empiricist theories of meaning sought to reconcile a materialist explanation of knowledge with ethics. Both Hutcheson and Shaftesbury posited a moral sense, a common body of ethical knowledge that all humans have access to, regardless of their stages of development. Unexplained aspects of their ethics—such as how this "sense" is acquired and why only humans have it—pointed inevitably to the contrary and irreconcilable directions of a social theory of meaning or the idealist skepticism of Hume.

action by the use of rhetoric" (28).[6] Locke, attacking rhetoric, states that "eloquence, like the fair sex" (III.10.33–34) deceives by means of pleasure. Thus, Locke returns to an early manifestation of the correspondence-coherence debate by contrasting foundational truth with rhetoric, echoing the Platonist-Sophist argument and its scholastic-humanist repetition outlined in the previous chapter.

Paralleling Locke's critique of rhetoric, Austen, near the beginning and the end of *Emma*, dramatizes ekphrastic debates between Emma Woodhouse and Mr. Knightley on the character of Frank Churchill as revealed by two eloquent and deceiving letters of apology that he sends to avoid censure for apparent breaches in social decorum. This debate then follows the familiar ekphrastic topos of character debate over a representational form, similar to that engaged in by the Canon in *Don Quixote*. Frank's first epistle is addressed to Mrs. Weston, whose marriage to his father he neglected to attend; although the unquoted letter announces his further delay in coming to Highbury, its tone, like an earlier one thought by all a "handsome letter" (18), is so conciliatory that Emma shifts the blame for the delay from Frank to Mrs. Churchill, the young man's rich and querulous aunt. Knightley, however, is harsh in judging Frank for what he interprets as rhetorical equivocation and declares, "He can sit down and write a fine flourishing letter, full of professions and falsehoods, and persuade himself that he has hit upon the very best method in the world of preserving peace at home and preventing his father's having any right to complain. His letters disgust me. . . . No, Emma, your amiable young man can be amiable only in French, not in English. He may be very 'amiable,' have very good manners, and be very agreeable; but he can have no English delicacy towards the feelings of other people" (148–49). Although Emma knows Frank only through his letters, she defends him against Knightley's charges and defines what Knightley calls equivocation as versatility and agreeableness: "He can adapt his conversation to the taste of every body, and has the power as well as the wish of being universally agreeable. To you, he will talk of farming; to me, of drawing or music; and so on to every body, having that general information on all subjects which will enable him to follow the lead, or take the lead, just as propriety may require, and to speak extremely well on each" (150). The format of this debate is repeated in the last book of the novel by Emma's and Knight-

6. In *The Rise of the Novel*, Watt argues that realism in the novel grew from the skepticism regarding language that was reflected by the writings of Locke. If words did not stand directly for things, then great care had to be taken to nurture whatever correspondence could be achieved. Watt writes that both Defoe and Richardson sought to achieve "the immediacy and closeness of the text to what is being described" (29).

ley's discussion of another epistolary exercise in ingratiation: Frank's apology to those affected by the concealment of his engagement to Jane Fairfax. Although the implications of the first debate are expanded significantly in its repetition, the initial argument between Emma and Knightley over Frank's use of rhetoric can be viewed as a nucleus around which the moral and perceptual oppositions of the novel revolve.[7]

As revealed through these debates, Emma's and Knightley's worldviews contrast different codes of conduct and different concepts of perception and communication. Through dramatic action, Austen explicitly reveals the apparent flaws of Emma's perceiving the world through the discursive truth defined by this ekphrasis. The debates also define the limits of the authorized discourse by contrasting a socially sanctioned view with an apparently aberrant one. According to the social code reflected in the narrative surface of the novel, Frank's letters are elaborate attempts to define (or, in his case, excuse) behavior through persuasive, polished, and ultimately falsifying language. With the epistle as interpolated artifact, the text defines moral values by varying Cervantes' method of providing an implicit, self-reflexive argument on linguistic correspondence and correct and incorrect naming. The linguistic debates between Emma and Knightley concern not only the motivation of the writer but also the use of a "proper" discourse and the sanctioned referents of such key moral abstractions as "delicacy" and "elegance." As in Don Quixote, the argument is underscored by numerous other ekphrastic variations, such as Jane's letters, Elton's letter and charade, Emma's portrait of Harriet, and the word puzzle that Frank uses to reveal his "blunder." Thus, while not fulfilling as fully the generic description of the menippea as Don Quixote, Emma nonetheless replicates one of its most important realist patterns—the embedding of numerous ekphrastic forms that serve to test the efficacy of a discourse. But in moving from Don Quixote to Emma, the empirical-idealist philosophic debate shifts from an existential to a social level, and it is appropriate that the terms be expressed not by the interpolation of a form of the romance, which transcends the ordinary, but rather by the epistle—the "occasional art" of everyday social intercourse. Reflecting this social, rather than existential, emphasis, debates over reference do not concern the signifying relations of objects such as windmills and giants but rather character and moral abstractions. Thus, Frank's letters (as well as other ekphrases), concealing the truth of his own character and the proper relations of other characters (such as his engagement to Jane and his and

7. In my analyses of Frank's letter writing, I am indebted to U. C. Knoepflmacher, "The Importance of Being Frank: Character and Letter-Writing in Emma."

Emma's infatuation), highlight the potential instability of all "letters," graphic inscriptions removed from external referents.[8]

Fancy and Understanding

Emma's defense of Frank's first letter echoes the Canon's defense of the romancer, who, unrestrained by the limitations of the everyday, can tell of any real or imagined event that would delight the reader, "describing shipwrecks, tempests, encounters and battles . . . now depicting a tragic and lamentable incident, now a joyful and unexpected event" (426). Emma admires and defends Frank, as he is seen through his letters, because "he can adapt his conversation to the taste of every body. . . . To you, he will talk of farming; to me, of drawing and music . . . having that general information on all subjects" (150). As I indicate later, the episteme in which the text is produced cannot tolerate the linguistic relativism characterized by Frank's "adapting his conversation to the taste of every body." Not to conform to a consensually approved model of language is an exercise of unrestrained subjectivity, or, in Lockean terms, the use of fancy, exhibited by both Emma and Frank. The ethical norms of the age condemned a subjectivity that could lead to relativism in social communication. Without contextual determinants to supply an objective standard, individual views might be no more than self-serving statements. When Locke wrote that "words . . . signify nothing but the ideas that are in the mind" (III.2.1), he expressed a fear of the linguistic and moral relativism inherent in the private language of subjectivity. Thus, in the *Essay* he contrasts wit, the faculty of the fancy, with judgment, the faculty of the understanding.

As opposed to the fancy, the understanding, as the operations of the mind, can only be expressed by "clear and distinct ideas" ("Epistle"). Condemning fancy, or wit, as a "court-dresser," a sycophant "that studies but to please," Locke identifies its operations in the tropology of rhetoric, "wherein for the most part lies that entertainment and pleasantries of wit, which strikes so lively on the fancy . . . because its beauty appears at first sight, and there is required no labor of thought to examine what truth or reason there is in it" (II.11.2). Echoing Locke's

8. My discussion of the figurality of language counters Catherine Belsey's notion of *Emma* as a "classic realist text" with which "nothing can be done" (*Critical Practice* 79). An interesting overview of various theoretical approaches to *Emma* is in Edward Neill's "Between Deference and Destruction: 'Situations' of Recent Critical Theory and Jane Austen's *Emma*."

sentiments, Knightley condemns the embodiment of fancy, Frank: "He can sit down and write a fine flourishing letter, full of professions and falsehoods, and persuade himself that he has hit upon the very best method in the world of preserving peace at home and preventing his father's having any right to complain" (148–49). The rhetorical disguise inherent in Frank's letters represents a delay in the proper matching of signifying terms, a delay motivated by purely selfish ends. If the main theme of the novel is a uniting of the proper characters in marriage, then the unifying of subjects with objects of desire could exemplify the episteme's obsessive concern with discovering the proper correspondence between sign and referent. In delaying the discovery of a proper correspondence, Frank's letters conceal more than reveal and illustrate the abuses of subjectivity. What is important, this and other ekphrases in *Emma* are used to prove a paradigm true by giving illustrations, through interpolated forms, of the falsity of its opposite.

The obverse of fancy is, of course, understanding, which, as I shall illustrate more fully, finds an exemplar in Knightley. Locke defines understanding, or judgment, in communication as the expression, not of a priori or innate ideas, but rather of ideas forged out of the hearth of experience and molded by both the mind's relational powers and by normative social conventions. Within unitary social and empirical contexts, the faculty allows one to speak "clearly and distinctly" to his or her listeners so that they will not be misled. Since Frank's letters relativistically reflect personal, rather than social or empirical, standards, he is censured by Knightley as having no "delicacy towards the feelings of other people" (149). The role of understanding in the text is to translate the hidden, private, and subjective into open and public terms. And the disclosure of the proper relations of characters, which Frank's texts conceal, represents the triumph of social understanding.[9]

The kind of truth that Knightley seeks to uncover in Frank's letter, moral truth, is the second of Locke's three sciences, which he defines as speaking of things "according to the persuasion of our own minds, though the propositions we speak agree not to the reality of things" (IV.21.1). Agreeing not at all with the reality of things but rather with the reality of minds, ethics depends even more than the other sciences

9. John P. McGowan, in "Knowledge/Power and Jane Austen's Radicalism," argues that *Emma* is a central text illustrative of a shift from the Foucaultian Classical Age to the modern one, which he defines as Romanticism. McGowan traces the contradictory pattern of the narrative, which on the surface confirms a "classical world of public meanings" while subtextually validating a romantic world that "searches out hidden facts and meanings" (6). I agree that this contradiction between theme and narrative strategy is central to the text of *Emma*.

upon finding a regulative norm. Of his second science, Locke says that "*ethics* . . . is the seeking out of those rules and measures of human actions, which lead to happiness and the means to practice them. The end of this is not bare speculation and the knowledge of truth; but right, and a conduct suitable to it" (IV.21.3). *Emma* illustrates the social process of "seeking out rules and measures" guiding conduct, and like Locke's *Essay* it concentrates on the linguistic foundation of this knowledge. Emma's moral education in the course of the novel is traditionally interpreted as the rectification of her private language, developed too entirely by subjectivity and fancy, and her acceptance of the language of social consensus. Knightley's early condemnation of Emma is seen to exemplify the text's evaluation of her: "She will never submit to any thing requiring industry and patience, and a subjection of the fancy to the understanding" (37). Thus, one of Emma's roles in the text is to prove the truth of the understanding through the mistakes that her fancy leads her to make. The dramatic course of the novel traces the near tragedy that results from her constructing a world from the coherence established by the false terms of her, and Frank's, fancy.

One of Locke's concerns regarding ethics and human knowledge in general, and one that is embodied in *Emma*, is the truthful relation of the individual mind and the minds of others, a principal way of perceiving the distinction between fancy and understanding. Throughout the *Essay*, Locke makes clear that the norm to which individual views or fancy must conform is not a transcendental form of the understanding but rather its much more limited social and empirical form. In empirical terms, the understanding is the translation of the sensual into the consensual. Locke confirms the social basis of the understanding in this description of the *Essay*: "Our business here is not to know all things, but those which concern our conduct" (I.1.6). In his essay on Leibniz's response to Locke, Hans Aarsleff points out that the German philosopher, writing from an idealist-transcendental tradition, fundamentally misunderstood Locke's more limited use of the term "understanding." Underlying the *Essay*'s empirical theory of knowledge is a social theory of human conduct recognizing the problematic role of language. The private languages of Frank and Emma are open to criticism because they are too subjective to incorporate the subjectivities of others. Albeit it is her desire to make the world conform to her subjective view of it, Emma ultimately fails because of the solipsistic nature of her knowledge, thus textually dramatizing the dangers of a world created through fancy.

Reflecting Locke's concerns, the ekphrastic debates in *Emma* over fancy and understanding, subjectivity and objectivity, and imagination and consensus thematize the period's realization of language's ultimately figural nature. Austen's novel appears at the time Foucault marks as the collapse of the classical episteme, a period in which it was hoped that representation and discourse could, like sense organs, naturally reflect elements in the external world. The new age, the Age of Man, is characterized by a theory of discourse and language that acknowledges the opacity and artificiality of signs. Foucault writes in *The Birth of the Clinic* of this transitional period: "At the end of the eighteenth century . . . seeing consists in leaving to experience its greatest corporal opacity; the solidity, the obscurity, the density of things closed in upon themselves, have powers of truth that they owe not to light" (xiii). In *The Order of Things* Foucault argues that scientific and prescriptive views of language of the earlier period were attempts to discover a regulative norm outside of and governing discourse, and their failures foreshadowed a a later shift. He describes them as

> the fundamental nominalism of philosophy from Hobbes to Ideology, a nominalism that is inseparable from a critique of language and from all that mistrust with regard to general and abstract words that we find in Malebranche, Berkeley, Condillac, and Hume; the great utopia of a perfectly transparent language in which things themselves could be named without any penumbra of confusion, either by a totally arbitrary but precisely thought-out system (artificial language), or by a language so natural that it would translate thought like a face expressing a passion. (117)

If language corresponds neither to an empirical view of things nor to the light of rationalism, then stability must be sought elsewhere, and *Emma* appears to find it in a social norm. The many ekphrases in the novel, particularly the epistolary ones, are positioned to illustrate the potential instability of signs that are produced and received outside the authority of a sanctioned discourse. In addition to thematizing the authoritarian discourse's taming of figurality through numerous ekphrastic scenes, the text also embodies it in the dramatic actions of characters and in the narration. But like *Don Quixote*, *Emma* ultimately explores the limitations of the discursive paradigm by showing it finally unable to control language's figurality.

Austen and the Epistolary Mode

Of the numerous ekphrases in the novel, I contend that the epistle thematizes the moral and intellectual nucleus of *Emma* not only because it was a primary means of communication in Austen's world and symbolizes the subversive and figural play of the grapheme, but also because it represented a convention of the novel that she attempted to outgrow. Thus, this ekphrasis, like the ekphrases of the romance in *Don Quixote*, illustrates both the epistemological paradigm and the specific generic model that the text seeks to overthrow through parody.

According to Watt, the works of Jane Austen are the apotheosis of the eighteenth-century novel because they successfully resolve the conflict of inner and outer presentation highlighted by the contrasting styles of Richardson and Fielding. Writes Watt, "[Austen] was able to combine into a harmonious unity the advantages both of realism of presentation and realism of assessment, of the internal and of the external approaches to character" (297). However, Watt describes Austen's novels as more Richardsonian in nature: "In her novels, there is usually one character whose consciousness is tacitly accorded a privileged status, and whose mental life is rendered more completely than that of the other characters" (297). This describes the strategy of *Pamela* and *Clarissa*, as well as *Emma*. But the technique by which Austen renders the subjectivity of her heroine is different from that employed by Richardson. Richardson conceived of his novels as a series of epistolary soliloquies—a collection of unmodified subjective views. Austen, on the other hand, mixes Emma's inside views with direct and indirect authorial commentary. From the first sentence of the novel, in which "seemed to unite" subtly qualifies the enumeration of Emma's blessings, to the climax of her revelations, in which she realizes "the blunders, the blindness of her own head and heart" (411–12), our views of Emma's interior vision are mediated by an authoritative narrative voice that embodies the moral code of the novel and Austen's society. By so using narrative authority, Austen appears to provide the reader with an objective standard showing how Emma's subjective view of herself in society moves from a position that "seemed to unite some of the best blessings of existence" (5) to one that, at the end of the novel, is indeed "the perfect happiness of the union" (325).[10]

Wayne Booth indicates that Austen limits inside views to Emma and, to a lesser extent, Knightley, because the other two major characters, Jane and Frank, must be viewed always from an external vantage point—penetrating either of their thoughts would shatter a central mystery of

10. Wayne C. Booth, in *The Rhetoric of Fiction*, illustrates narrative distance with an analysis of *Emma* because Austen is "one of the unquestionable masters of the rhetoric of fiction" (244). Booth felt that Austen's main problem was manipulating readerly access to Emma's inside views to maintain sympathy for a character she felt "no one but myself will much like."

the novel, their secret engagement (254). However, both Jane and Frank present subjectivity through letters, the form it takes in the novels of Richardson and his imitators. Austen uses the subjectivity of personal letters as examples of false subjectivities to show, by contrast, the truth of the inside views supported by the moral authority of the omniscient narrative voice. Ian Jack notices that generally in her novels, "Jane Austen is always less willing to give us a letter which is evidence of a good character than a letter which reveals a bad one" (181). And in his specific discussion of letter writing in *Emma*, U. C. Knoepflmacher notes that "Frank's elliptical behavior and Jane's enforced reserve are connected by Jane Austen to the practice of writing letters which can mask the true sentiments of the writer" (640).

As Cervantes progressed from writing a romance, the *Galatea*, to what some critics refer to as an "anti-romance," *Don Quixote*, so Austen progressed from the epistolary novel to a more complete form using the epistle to define, by parodic contrast, a newer, fuller medium. A number of scholars have written on Austen's early use and later abandonment of the epistolary form. Ian Jack claims that "it was from Richardson and Fanny Burney that she learnt her art" (174). Norman Page, however, provides the most helpful discussion of Austen's use of the epistolary form by chronicling her movement away from the convention (167–86). Her first exercises in the form were the epistolary novels *Love and Friendship* and *Lesley Castle* (dated 1790–92). There is also evidence to indicate that several of Austen's later novels were revisions of earlier epistolary ones. Although the manuscript of the epistolary novel *Elinor and Marianne* has not survived, B. C. Southam, in *Jane Austen's Literary Manuscripts*, cites both external and internal evidence that indicates it was an epistolary draft of *Sense and Sensibility* (55–57). The case is similar with the lost *First Impressions*. Although there is none of the external evidence for epistolary form that there is for *Elinor and Marianne*, Southam convincingly argues that it was also a novel in letters whose vestigial form can be seen in the forty-four uses of letters in *Pride and Prejudice*, which seems a recasting of the earlier manuscript (62). Q. D. Leavis argues less convincingly that a later epistolary version of *Lady Susan* formed the basis of *Mansfield Park* (114–42). To accept Leavis's theory, one would have to assume that Austen returned to the epistolary form at about 1808–9. However, Austen's revising *First Impressions* and *Elinor and Marianne* from epistolary to conventional narratives and her writing *Northanger Abbey* in conventional form between the years 1796 and 1799 indicate that in this period she matured beyond the novel of letters. Agreeing with this assessment, Page concludes, "The history of her relationship with the epistolary mode is, therefore, a record of its early use and gradual abandonment in favor of other narrative techniques, though important traces remain even in the later novels" (172). In *Emma* the epistle remains primarily as a parodic form, a device of falsification for untrustworthy characters.

Watt writes that Richardson uses the letter as a "short cut . . . to the heart" (195). This direct approach to subjectivity in point of view ultimately led to such sentimental excesses in the eighteenth-century novel that it created a conventional heroine, who, according to Dorothy Van Ghent, can be characterized by her "debility" (50) and who constantly apologized for the tears staining lachrymose correspondences. But many of *Pamela*'s readers felt that her letters masked her true motives, and Fielding took advantage of such a view by having Shamela write, "I thought once of making a little Fortune by my Person. I now intend to make a great one by my Vartue" (53). In *Emma*, Austen uses the letter as an ekphrasis to show that it can disguise, as well as give direct views, of the heart's true feelings. For the reader, the novel unfolds like a mystery in which he or she is to discover gradually through a series of revelations the actual feelings and relations of characters, and letters are used to serve this end. Letters are summarized, anticipated, praised, criticized, and remarked upon throughout the novel, and the reader must concentrate on the recipient's responses for clues to the letter writer's character. Not until the end of the last volume is a letter (Frank's final one) quoted in full, and by then most of the major mysteries have been revealed. At this point the reader is finally in a position to compare the truth of fact with the truth in letter, a comparison revealing Frank's and his interpreters' true characters. The disclosure of Frank's letter parallels the disclosure of character relations and completes the text's progress from the hidden and private to the open and social.

However, Austen uses the letter for larger purposes than just revelation of character. *Emma*'s obsessive concern with epistles and its subtle rejection of the epistolary mode in fiction represent Austen's self-conscious attempt to transcend an outworn narrative technique by revealing its potential for falsification. The text also posits that for subjective views, the stimulus of fancy, to be considered trustworthy by readers, they must be supported by different forms of the social standard of understanding. The trustworthy, dependable Knightley is one of such forms. But the ultimate external standard the reader is expected to trust is, of course, the voice of the intrusive author, which Watt defines as an "august and impersonal spirit of social and psychological understanding" (297). By exemplifying the moral and intellectual values of community, the author's voice embodies the authority of social consensus. But rising above the role of consensual voice, Austen's omniscient narrator is described by Wayne Booth as being nothing less than "a perfect human being, within the concept of perfection defined by the book" (265). Her omniscience, then, reveals the range and limitations of social knowledge. Obviously, to maintain any sense of mystery for the reader, or any joy of surprise or sudden elucidation, the text must limit use of complete omniscience in order to create a sense of doubt about the honesty and reliability of certain characters, particularly Frank. By so restricting omniscient narration, an implicit debate on the proper and improper use of language can evolve throughout the novel, focusing primarily on characters' subjective and objective judgments of Frank's epistles. These judgments serve as partial movements of the debate that appears to be resolved, first, by the extended ekphrastic debate between Emma and Knightley on Frank's final letter and, last, by the omniscient author's final summation.

English Delicacy

The ekphrases in the text not only thematize the oppositional terms of fancy and understanding but also the key moral abstractions whose meanings the text seeks to secure by showing dramatically the consequences of their misunderstanding. Returning to the ekphrasis of Frank's first letter and Emma's remark—"he can adapt his conversation to the taste of every body"—readers might be reminded of *Northanger Abbey* and Henry Tilney's criticism of Catherine's use of the word "nice": " 'Very true,' said Henry, 'and this is a very nice day, and we are taking a very nice walk, and you are very nice young ladies. Oh! it is a very nice word indeed!—it does for every thing. Originally perhaps it was applied only to express neatness, propriety, delicacy, or refinement;—people were nice in their dress, in their sentiments, or in their choice. But now every commendation on every subject is comprised in that one word' " (77). A speaker or a writer like Frank, who uses language "to the taste of every body," is like a word that "does for everything"; neither can have any real value in the Austenian world, the standards of which are maintained by a discourse with relatively fixed and precise meanings that should not be altered to suit equivocal and subjective views. Arnold Kettle writes, "The precision of her standards emerges in her style. Each word—'elegance,' 'humour,' 'temper,' 'ease'—has a precise, unambiguous meaning based on a social usage at once subtle and stable" (115). C. S. Lewis writes also of Austen's propensity for using words signifying moral values that have lost their once stable meanings due to the modern age's linguistic and moral relativism: "The great abstract nouns of the classical English moralists are unblushingly and uncompromisingly used: 'good sense,' 'courage,' 'contentment,' 'fortitude,' 'some duty neglected, some failing indulged,' 'impropriety,' 'indelicacy,' 'generous candour,' 'blamable trust,' 'just humiliation,' 'vanity,' 'folly,' 'ignorance,' 'reason.' These are the concepts by which Jane Austen grasps the world. . . . All is hard, clear, definable" (28). Austen's treatment of these abstractions is guided by a Johnsonian impulse toward clarification and the unproblematic. Clarifying the referents of such ethical abstractions would make these social representations as easily demonstrable as natural ones, and a mimesis of social conduct would be analogous to those that are empirically verisimilar. This clarification, serving to anchor the referential drift of signifiers from socially approved signifieds, resembles the empirical correction of Don Quixote's language use. But while the texts attempt to sustain a unitary and unproblematic signification for ethics, they also reveal the episteme's constraints. These constraints are noted by Mark Schorer, who, along with Lewis and Kettle, comments upon Austen's use of abstractions, which he describes as "buried or dead metaphors" (99). But Schorer emphasizes that the connotative metaphorical values of many of these abstractions suggest commerce and property in the Austenian world. One might argue further that words expressing moral values have a commercial basis because the moral code of the age was tied to a mercantile ideology. Securing these signifiers to socially approved signifieds would have the effect of codifying a capitalistic and patriarchal discourse, whose power is disguised as morality.[11]

One of the text's narrative strategies is to use authoritative narrative voices to sanction the consensually approved signifieds for these moral signs. Graham Hough points out that the normative style described by Kettle and Lewis should be identified with the omniscient narrator's voice, which is "general, abstract, evaluative, and formally correct" (55). He explains further, "It is general because common knowledge is assumed. . . . It is abstract because the appeal is not merely to a shared sentiment, but to an explicit, formulated code of values, of which the abstract nouns are a sufficient sign. It is evaluative because the highest human faculty is to make right judgements" (56). Hough contends that this voice represents the ultimate of human truth in Austen's world, a truth limited, admittedly, to a narrowly social and not natural world,

---

11. In "Community and Morality: Towards Reading Jane Austen," David Aers discusses the extent to which the ethical values in Austen's novels are embedded in the Tory ideology of nineteenth-century agrarian England.

hence "the truth-values of Jane Austen are more readily explained on a coherence theory of truth than on a correspondence theory" (78). In spite of the empirical tenor of the age's philosophical paradigm, the truth-values cohere to a system of beliefs rather than correspond to external facts. As in *Don Quixote*, truth is a measure of illocutionary force; but more so than Cervantes' text, Austen's implicitly questions the ulterior motivations that are revealed through connotation. Truth in *Emma* is epitomized by the authorial voice, and deviations from this truth are signaled by stylistic deviations from the narrative norm. Thus, writes Hough, "characters we are to approve assimilate their speech to the objective narrative . . . as the characters [who] diverge from this norm . . . are ridiculous or bad" (70). Knightley, "who is never wrong" (69), is increasingly identified with the omniscient voice, and his judgments give early clues to Frank's "real" character. His ekphrastic debates with Emma on proper and improper naming are not merely debates on style; they are ethical debates on the stability of reference of the moral abstractions on which the class ideology depends. Moreover, the debates reflect the episteme's struggle to find a foundation for identifying, naming, and understanding such moral abstractions. His ultimate rhetorical victory illustrates the constraints that the dominant discourse places upon signification, restraining the connotative play of signifiers so that the relation of knowledge and power is concealed.

It should be noted that nearly all of Austen's novels thematize the conflict of moral abstractions. As Gilbert Ryle indicates, the titles of three of her novels are derived from moral abstractions—*Sense and Sensibility*, *Pride and Prejudice*, and *Persuasion*. The theme of each of these novels is the conflict of abstractions that are descriptive of moral conduct. And like many realist texts, the truth of the approved term is validated by proving its opposite false. As Ryle indicates, the dramatic conflict of all her novels emanates from the action of characters embodying qualities that are comparative and contrastive with a key moral abstraction. *Emma*, for example, might have been titled *Influence and Interference*. While Ryle is correct about Austen's nearly allegorical use of character and her predilection for portraying key abstractions, it would be more correct to say that although a single abstraction may be used as nucleus, the texts are motivated by a desire to stabilize the referents of a whole range of moral terms.[12] This, indeed, is the primary purpose of the ekphrases of *Emma*.

12. Ryle's classic essay "Jane Austen and the Moralists" also finds Austen's works pivotal in an epistemic shift. He argues that her novels illustrate a transition from a Calvinist ethic, which defines human conduct in terms of absolute definitions of morality. This is a bipolar ethics in which individuals are saints or sinners, influenced by body or spirit, and are irrevocably saved or damned. Austen's ethics, acquired from Shaftesbury, finds humanity

Fancy and understanding are two key abstractions that I have detailed, but the ekphrases reveal others that are also significant. For example, Stuart Tave has written that "delicacy" and "elegance" are words used frequently as moral touchstones in *Emma*; they are two of the "great abstract nouns of the classical English moralists," of which Lewis writes.[13] "Delicacy," a moral metonym of "elegance," is requisite for all characters called elegant, truly or falsely, throughout the novel. As noted by the *OED*, "elegance" signifies "refined grace or propriety"—outward manifestations of cultivation and taste. But a primary eighteenth-century usage for "delicacy" is "delicate regard for the feelings of others," a psychological manifestation of elegance, and a drastic shift from its primary meaning in the sixteenth century as "soft, tender beauty." In spite of the critical emphasis on "elegance" as the primary social quality in *Emma*, "delicacy" is closer to the novel's moral center. It is the quality that Emma, who is "handsome, clever, and rich," lacks in order to "unite . . . the best blessings of existence"; and according to conventional interpretations of the novel, it is through Knightley that she acquires this quality necessary to her perfection. And it is through their paradigmatic ekphrastic debate that this process begins.

The most severe charge Knightley levels against Frank in response to his first letter is that "he can have no English delicacy towards the feelings of other people." To clarify what is meant by delicacy, Austen purposely contrasts two ekphrases: Frank's letter with Robert Martin's, which contains his proposal to Harriet Smith. In spite of the fact that Emma has dismissed Martin as "a completely gross, vulgar farmer" (33), she grudgingly credits him with having written a decent letter: "The style . . . was much above her expectation. There were not merely no grammatical errors, but as a composition it would not have disgraced a gentleman; the language, though plain, was strong and unaffected, and the sentiments it conveyed very much to the credit of the writer. It was short, but expressed good sense, warm attachment, liberality, propriety, even delicacy of feeling" (50–51). Emma can admire delicacy in others even though she lacks it herself. Her lack of this quality is highlighted by how Knightley implicitly defines it. By showing "English delicacy," Knightley observes the class distinctions in this very caste-oriented world

---

neither purely good nor purely bad but rather composed of numerous attributes that evolve according to individual experience. Her novels trace the evolution of characters' moral traits toward states of relative perfection.

13. I am indebted to Stuart Tave's *Some Words of Jane Austen* for a recognition of the centrality of the words "delicacy" and "elegance." Tave's work is important in its concentration upon the linguistic dimension of Austen's epistemology. He traces the pattern of words in the several novels that serve the mediation of the individual with the social.

while seeming to show regard for those existing in lower levels. A novel written about and for the landed gentry illustrates that they should show "delicacy" toward the conditions of those in lower social strata. It is this form of delicacy that allows us to regard Knightley as the text's paragon of virtue, and Emma's lack of it seemingly exposes her as a snob. Lacking delicacy, Emma's imagination goes unchecked because she feels that her privilege entitles her not to have to take into account others' subjectivities. As Susan Morgan writes, "Truth, in this novel, is that individuals have an inner life apart from other people's wish for them, an inner life that cannot be experienced by someone else but must be honored nonetheless" (38).[14] However misguided, Emma grudgingly repeats her favorable evaluation of Robert Martin when Harriet relates her meeting with him after she has sent her letter of rejection. Emma observes, "The young man's conduct, and his sister's, seemed the result of real feeling, and she could not but pity them. As Harriet described it, there had been an interesting mixture of wounded affection and genuine delicacy in their behavior" (179). Ironically, though Emma recognizes the virtue of delicacy in Robert Martin's letter and conversation, she dismisses her lack of it as social privilege. After complimenting the genuine feeling in Martin's letter of proposal, she instructs Harriet, "You need not be prompted to write with the appearance of sorrow for his disappointment" (52). Tave comments upon Emma's hypocritical recognition of delicacy in others' actions while ignoring her own indelicate behavior: "Robert Martin is delicate but Emma Woodhouse is not . . . because the needs of her imagination make her own mind improper and indelicate" (221).

Knightley, the text's embodiment of delicacy, offers another definition of the virtue in describing Robert Martin: "He always speaks to the purpose; open, straight forward, and very well judging" (59). Later, Knightley criticizes Jane Fairfax for her reserve by saying, "I love an open temper" (289). In the world of *Emma*, delicacy also implies that genuine feeling for others calls for direct, unequivocal converse in speech and letters. It should be a discourse recognizing that falsification upsets a careful social equilibrium, which only delicacy can maintain. Delicacy in conversation or writing calls for the speaker to use words in a clearly

14. Morgan's *In the Meantime: Character and Perception in Jane Austen's Fiction* places Austen in a central position in the evolution of characterization in the novel. Echoing Ryle, Morgan contrasts the flawed but morally redeemable Emma Woodhouse with the perfect but changeless Clarrisa Harlowe. Emma's instruction regarding the subjectivities of others is carried out on a social and empirical level. Unlike Clarrisa, Emma lives in a morally relative world and has a modern consciousness, shaped by experience. These features allow for character change and education, key aspects of later novels of the nineteenth century.

referential relation to objects or qualities, a relation agreed upon by social consensus. The lack of this quality problematizes communication and all other social relations. "Gallant," the epithet most often used to describe Frank, implies a moral conduct that exhibits only the superficial exterior of English delicacy—a going through the motions that makes him, according to Knightley, "amiable only in French."

Emma's movement from her contrived infatuation with Frank to her real love for Knightley represents the course of her education in "English delicacy" and the prescribed social discourse. At the novel's beginning, she is, with Frank, at an extreme moral distance from Knightley. The text's dilemma is to maintain readerly sympathies for Emma while dramatizing moral values that show her at fault. A related problem is the didactic narrative voice, which, in identifying with Knightley and his avuncular criticism of Emma, directly tells the reader of Emma's faults on the novel's opening page: "The real evils indeed of Emma's situation were the power of having rather too much her own way, and a disposition to think a little too well of herself; these were the disadvantages which threatened alloy to her many enjoyments" (5–6). The text overcomes these problems by relying less and less on the omniscient authorial voice as the narrative progresses, which forces readers to identify with Emma's view of the world. As Adena Rosmarin indicates, Emma's role in the novel increasingly becomes that of an interpreter of ekphrases, various word puzzles, charades, and letters that contain clues to the central mysteries of the novel. Rosmarin writes that "the growing subtlety of Emma's misreadings increasingly challenges and thus develops our reading competence, our misreadings and Emma's becoming increasingly alike, both in kind and degree, till our reading of Churchill's letter shows them to be one" (325).[15] In many of these ekphrastic scenes, debates pairing Emma's "incorrect" readings against Knightley's "correct" ones occur, and their identification with the heroine locates readers outside the moral views of the episteme. But I contend that although Knightley's correct reading of Frank's letter and the reappearance of the authorial voice near the novel's end confirm the authority of the dominant discourse, our lengthy identification with Emma provides

15. In " 'Misreading' *Emma*: The Powers and Perfidies of Interpretive History," Adena Rosmarin applies an affective model of interpretation to study the narrative of *Emma* and concludes that the text uses the strategies of revelation and disguise to complicate easy notions of the text's mirroring a unitary truth. While contending that certain narrative strategies "help the novel approximate the mimetic ideal of accurate representation, of a transparently envisioned content," Rosmarin contradictorily maintains that "the mimetic model is self-supporting and exclusive, eager to constitute some textual 'facts' but blind to others" (317).

us with a position from which to critique this social norm. First, the text itself allows for such an interpretation, for while valorizing open and clear discourse, it is itself successful as a dramatic narrative because it maneuvers and fails to disclose. But more important, since Knightley is the character most identified with truth, his elevation can only come through the appearance of his opposite, Emma. And our lengthy identification with Emma as oppositional other, during which we subtly become aware of the virtues of her fancy as well as its faults, forces us to call into question the binary opposition elevating Knightley and understanding.

Emma as Imaginist

On the narrative surface, the text explicitly condemns the world Emma creates by showing her inappropriate interpretation of numerous ekphrases, even though, on a subtextual level, her readings and creations can be viewed in a somewhat more favorable light. The text apparently provides an early clue to what seems to be Emma's moral weakness: her underestimating Robert Martin's value while overestimating Mr. Elton's. As Martin's delicacy early in the novel mirrors Knightley's virtues, so Elton's flaws mirror Frank's (and, at this point, Emma's). During the same conversation in which she calls Martin a "gross, vulgar farmer," ignoring the delicacy of his letter, she recommends Elton above all suitable bachelors: "I think a young man might be very safely recommended to take Mr. Elton as a model. Mr. Elton is good humoured, cheerful, obliging, and gentle" (34). And later she calls him "a most valuable, amiable, pleasing young man" (111). In spite of realizing of Elton that "for with all his good and agreeable qualities, there was a sort of parade in his speeches which was very apt to make her laugh" (82), she is fooled by his endless compliments, flattering language, and ingratiating speeches into believing that he is courting Harriet and not herself. But when the reality of Elton's motives is asserted physically and violently, she is forced to conclude, "There had been no real affection either in his language or manners. Sighs and fine words had been given in abundance; but she could hardly devise any set of expressions, or fancy any tone of voice, less allied with real love" (135). And appropriately, when the rejected Elton departs from Highbury, he leaves a "long, civil, ceremonious note" (140) that falsifies his true motives, as Martin's short, direct letter does not. Emma's misreading of characters is analogous to her misreading of these ekphrastic texts—in both cases her subjective reading fails to take into account the wholly disparate subjectivities of others.

Elton's equivocation and his indirect use of language anticipate Frank Churchill's similar behavior, but these clues are insufficient for Emma. As a kind of mirror of her faults, Elton is misinterpreted by Emma, much as she misreads the ekphrastic forms. Moreover, she is unable to learn a lasting lesson from Elton's flaws because of her unknowing possession of many of them. For one, in rejecting Harriet, Elton exhibits the same motive as Emma in dismissing Robert Martin—pure snobbery. He complains, "Miss Smith is a very good sort of girl; and I should be happy to see her respectably settled . . . no doubt, there are men who might not object to—Every body has their level: but as for myself . . . I need not so totally despair of an equal alliance as to be addressing myself to Miss Smith!" (132). Thus, both Emma and Elton exhibit a lack of delicacy in their using class status to dismiss the feelings of others. But more important, Emma shares with Elton a tendency to misrepresent herself and life through ploys and disguises. Elton's "charade," an important ekphrastic word game that offers its meaning only as a puzzle to be solved, is another contrast to the simple, direct, and truthful language of Robert Martin. Its equivocal form shows language at its most figural:

> My first displays the wealth and pomp of kings,
>   Lords of the earth! their luxury and ease.
> Another view of man, my second brings,
>   Behold him there, the monarch of the seas!
>
> But, ah! united what reverse we have!
>   Man's boasted power and freedom, all are flown;
> Lord of the earth and sea, he bends a slave,
>   And woman, lovely woman, reigns alone.
>
> Thy ready wit the word will soon supply,
> May its approval beam in that soft eye!
>
> (71)

In the terminology of Harold Bloom, Emma provides a strong misreading of the charade, a poem whose two quatrains suggest, as she correctly reads, "courtship"; but in failing to see that the charade is meant for herself and not Harriet, she shows the limits of her imagination. However, both Paul H. Fry and Joseph Litvak show how the answers to the charade, "court" and "ship," are implicated in the dominant social discourse, since they imply royalist power and mercantile ownership. Litvak suggests that Emma's strong misreading could be a willful one in which she refuses to see herself represented as property. According to Litvak, Emma's misreading might oppose the text's and discourse's moral norm, which sees women as property, and introduce a subtextual ethic that subverts textual and social authority.[16] This ekphrasis thematizes how the reader's identification with Emma as other, through limited omniscience, problematizes the truth-claims of the valorized present term in the discourse of power.

For the most part, the text indicates that Emma's misrepresentations, though not as blatant as Elton's, are perhaps more insidious because of the real and potential havoc they wreak on herself and others. Thus, the dramatic testing of her discourse and world explicitly proves them false. However, her motivations are portrayed differently and to some extent more favorably. For example, one reason she misrepresents the world is because she cannot accept its imperfections. David Minter suggests a reason for this "flaw": "Emma allows her fancy and imagination to shape and distort her perception of reality; and because she demands a harmony and symmetry life cannot attain, she permits herself to meddle and interfere with the lives of other people" (51). Emma's motivations, then, are close to those of an artist, even though she suffers and brings suffering upon others in trying to make reality conform to her aesthetic vision. Emma's painting of Harriet, another of the text's numerous ekphrases, parodies the Pygmalion theme in that she tries to make the real Harriet into the ideal Harriet she portrays on canvas: "As she meant to throw in a little improvement to the figure, to give a little more height, and considerably more elegance, she had great confidence of its being in every way a pretty drawing at last" (47). Knightley's reminder, "You have made her too tall, Emma" (48), has the effect of Sancho's "What's giants?" when Don Quixote attacks the windmills; it deflates Emma's aggrandizement of Harriet's character. Even Mrs. Weston notices, "Miss Smith has not those eye-brows and eye-lashes. It is the fault of the face she has them not" (48). Only the falsifier Elton approves of Emma's falsifications. Emma's notion that she could "give . . . considerably more elegance" to the real Harriet as easily as applying another brushstroke signifies her ignorance of that quality. Emma, blind to her

16. Litvak, in "Reading Characters: Self, Society, and Text in *Emma*," argues that the figurality of language is associated with a subversive feminine psychology that attempts to problematize the unitary signifying practices of patriarchal discourse. He contends that the conventional interpretations of *Emma* as a novel of education ignore the subtextual elements celebrating free play and the imagination. He argues against critical views that see Austen's texts as entirely supportive of the dominant discourse.

own lack of elegance, believes she can bestow it upon whomever she pleases. In attempting to make the word "elegance" transform the inelegant Harriet, Emma reflects Don Quixote's use of language when he, for example, tries to transform the vulgar Aldonza Lorenzo into a beautiful damsel by applying the *nomen* Dulcinea del Toboso. The portrait of Harriet is a sign, or signifier, of elegance that does not correspond to a designated signified. Like Don Quixote with his ideal names, Emma, following her subjective ideal, tries to re-create the world by questioning and problematizing social views of it. Additionally, her signs or symbols of transformation come from as romantic a conception of the world as the Don's. Her romanticism is derived, as is his, from a kind of solipsism—a vision of the world in which she is creative center. And Emma's attempts to make the world conform to what she calls it (the portrait, for example, as a sign of elegance signifying the inelegant Harriet) are shown to be as much failures as are his.

The ekphrasis of Harriet's portrait is the most concrete example of Emma's casting the world into a mold preconceived by her imagination. It is a product of her cleverness and her fancy, virtues that isolate her both favorably and unfavorably from others. She smugly evaluates her talents while waiting for Harriet at Ford's: "A mind lively and at ease, can do with seeing nothing, and can see nothing that does not answer" (233). Emma's mind is a creator's, and she sees a world rich in potential and variety. Similarly, Emma makes another flattering evaluation of her cleverness when she concocts a romantic intrigue between Harriet and Frank, who has saved her little protégée from a band of discourteous "gipsies": "Could a linguist, could a grammarian, could even a mathematician have seen what she did, have witnessed their appearance together . . . without feeling the circumstances had been at work to make them peculiarly interesting to each other?—How much more must an imaginist, like herself, be on fire with speculation and foresight!" (335). Unlike linguists, grammarians, and mathematicians, whose methods limit them to exact and precise interpretations, Emma can use appearances as the groundwork for speculation and foresight. An imaginist, indeed a worldmaker, Emma creates (rather than accepts unquestioningly) the social world in which she lives. The world Emma tries to create is derived from fictive materials similar to those used by Don Quixote—the language of romantic fiction. But instead of using chivalric romances as a model, Emma looks to the conventions of the gothic romance. From the very beginning, the reader sees Emma trying to make the world a romantic one in which the orphaned Harriet, discovered to be the daughter of a nobleman, is molded into the elegant bride of Mr. Elton; in which she, Emma, receives and refuses the blind devotion of Frank, who then becomes the courageous hero-lover of Harriet after saving her from "gipsies"; in which Jane Fairfax is secretly admired by the married Mr. Dixon. And most important, Emma tries to create a world in which she herself remains unmatched and unequaled in elegance. However, Emma's romantic vision is as much restricted by the world as is the Don's, for her freedom to imagine is limited by the dominant class ideology, which, as the novel progresses, restricts it further along lines of caste and gender.

The Limits of the Imagination

During the course of the novel, the possible world created by Emma is shown, like Don Quixote's, to collide with a textual version of actuality, in this case a social, rather than empirical, one. Ultimately, the world Emma attempts to create is shattered when she recognizes the indelicacy of her behavior, which makes her, in social terms, anything but elegant. Her acceptance of the true signifieds for these signifiers of self reflects Don Quixote's eventual acceptance of Alonso Quixada as name. By his actions and his evaluations of Martin, Knightley defines the meaning of delicacy and elegance according to a standard of verisimilitude agreed upon by a consensus of those in his, and Austen's, social class. Emma's gradual acceptance of the objective signifieds for these signifiers, which contradict her subjective view of them, is a measure of her education. At the novel's beginning, the world of Highbury offers Emma no feminine companion with whom she can compare her own perceived elegance. But when Jane Fairfax enters the scene, Emma, comparing the young girl with herself, discovers that her own qualities are matched and in many ways exceeded: "Jane Fairfax was elegant, remarkably elegant; and she had herself the highest value for elegance. Her height was pretty, just such as almost everybody would think tall, and nobody would think very tall; her figure particularly graceful. . . . It was a style of beauty, of which elegance was the reigning character, and as such, she must, in honour, by all principles admire it:—elegance, which, whether of person or of mind, she saw so little in Highbury" (167). Emma, uncomfortable around Jane, is annoyed by Miss Bates's constant adulation of her niece because she suspects that she may have found someone superior to herself, representing a new standard of reference for elegance in Highbury. Emma's smugness is threatened once again by Mrs. Elton, who defines elegance in reverse; in this woman, who blatantly demands that others accept her as superior and who claims the right to meddle in

Jane's life as a matchmaker much in the same way Emma does in Harriet's, Emma should be able to see herself. Like Emma, who is introduced initially as "handsome, clever, and rich" (5), Augusta Hawkins, soon to be Mrs. Elton, is announced as "handsome, elegant, highly accomplished, and perfectly amiable" (181), but Emma can recognize her false elegance: "She would not be in a hurry to find fault, but she suspected there was no elegance;—ease but not elegance.—She was almost sure that for a young woman, a stranger, a bride, there was too much ease. Her person was rather good; her face not unpretty; but neither feature, nor air, nor voice, nor manner, were elegant" (270).

With all the other characters whose elegance is exposed as pretense— Frank, Mr. Elton, Mr. Weston, and Emma herself—Mrs. Elton shares a single, consistent quality: smooth, flattering, rhetorical verbosity. Illustrating Locke's fear of linguistic distortion, they create merely a veneer of elegance through an excessive overlay of external stylistic refinement. They falsify themselves through words that disguise their lack of delicacy in a manner similar to Emma's falsifying the true character of Harriet through the idealized portrait. As Frank Bradbrook notes, "Great conversationalists are usually insincere as well as incorrect in their use of language, and reading a novel of Jane Austen is largely a matter of distinguishing between 'the usual rate of conversation' " (41).

Emma, able to see through Mrs. Elton's vulgar opulence to the true indelicacy within, cannot see through Frank because the young man has ready allies for his falsifications—Emma's vanity and imagination. Indeed, along with Mr. and Mrs. Elton and Mr. Weston, he serves to mirror the flaws in Emma's world, much like Cervantes provides false knights, such as Samson Carrasco, to reflect upon Don Quixote's. Frank pretends to court Emma, of course, only to disguise his engagement to Jane, but the false courtship holds many charms for Emma—she is able to fabricate a romantic adventure for herself and (with Frank's aid) for Jane with Mr. Dixon. Frank has an intoxicating influence on Emma. Because of his callous machinations, she actually begins to lose control of herself, allowing her flaws (enhanced by Frank's flattery) to dominate her. It is, in fact, through those scenes involving Frank that the text most severely tests the possible world created by Emma's discourse. All that society finds wrong with Frank and Emma and with the alternative world they try to create becomes apparent at the disastrous party at Box Hill. When Frank playfully announces to the gathering, "I am ordered by Miss Woodhouse . . . to say, that she desires to know what you are all thinking of" (369), he, in essence, gives voice to Emma's deepest desire—to know everyone's thoughts and be able to manipulate their lives because of such a privilege. As a creator, an imaginist, she demands her own form of omniscience. Later, when Frank moderates his request, speaking for Emma—"she only demands from you either one thing very clever . . . or three things very dull indeed" (370)—he gives expression to a more admirable aspect of Emma's imagination, its demand that the world be more entertaining, rich, and varied. Lionel Trilling calls this "a poet's demand" (xvi). In fact, because of this quality the modern reader may find Emma a much more sympathetic character than the one Austen was afraid "no one but myself will much like." Although socially unsanctioned, her imagination and liveliness stand her apart from those characters who are approved. Even Knightley seems by modern sensibilities too didactic and authoritarian to be as interesting as the fallible Emma. This is one of the several ways in which the other world created by Emma problematizes that which is sanctioned.

However, at Box Hill, Frank's presumptions on the part of her omniscience and privilege make Emma nearly giddy with her own power. Whereas before she harmed others innocently with her cleverness and imagination, now Frank encourages the darker side of her self. When Miss Bates tries to add to the levity by making fun of her own ability to say dull things, Emma insults her: "Ah! ma'am, but there may be a difficulty. Pardon me—but you will be limited as to number—only three at once" (370). This insult is particularly devastating because it is given to Miss Bates, who, as the most pitiable character in the novel, is, according to Bradbrook, "a test of other people's chivalry, forebearance, and charity" (54), and, one might add, delicacy. Emma's indelicacy represents the furthest reach of her world of imagination from the world of social responsibility. Showing how far she has departed from the sanctioned discourse, it evokes the strongest reaction from Knightley, who again reminds her of the limitations of imagination. "I will tell you truths while I can" (375), he says in Locke's "clear and distinct" language, blunting not a whit the full force of censure: "Were she a woman of fortune, I would leave every harmless absurdity to take its chance. I would not quarrel with you for any liberties of manner. Were she your equal in situation—but, Emma, consider how far this is from being the case. She is poor; she has sunk from the comforts she was born to; and, if she live to old age, must probably sink to more. Her situation should secure your compassion" (375). Another ekphrasis, Mr. Weston's conundrum ("What two words . . . express perfection . . . M. and A.—Em-ma"), coming at the heels of Emma's disgraceful action, not only emphasizes how far the heroine is from a perfect state, but, as word game, it also contrasts with Knightley's direct honesty: "I will tell you truths." Mr. Weston's inappropriate use of perfection in reference to Emma echoes Emma's own mismatching of elegance with Harriet. Both the conundrum and the portrait are ekphrastic metaphors of language discontinuous with the social linguistic code. Like father, like son; Mr. Weston is a falsifier, an eloquent, charming misrepresenter of events. Emma has already perceived some of this when she thinks of Weston, "To be the favourite and intimate of a man who had so many intimates and confidants, was not the first distinction in the scale of vanity" (320). When Emma leaves Box Hill, she retains Knightley's true, and not Weston's false, representation of herself, and her acceptance of this truth is the climax, the turning point of the novel, the point at which she is able to confront fully the sanctioned truths soon to be revealed: "Never had she felt so agitated, mortified, grieved at any circumstance in her life. . . . The truth of his representation there was no denying. . . . How could she have been so brutal, so cruel to Miss Bates!—How could she have exposed herself to such ill opinion in anyone she valued! And how suffer him to leave her without saying one word of gratitude, of concurrence, of common kindness" (376).

The Education of Emma

"I will tell you truths while I can"—*Emma* is a novel about truth-values and the social means by which they are validated: by proving the oppositional terms false. At the party at Box Hill, the text introduces the patrons of falsification—unrestrained imagination, flattery, insincere verbosity, and vulgar opulence. And afterward Emma is positioned to see the workings of social truth. Following her difficult admission of wrongdoing, Emma is soon allowed to see truly. When Mr. Woodhouse informs Knightley of Emma's repentant visits to Miss and Mrs. Bates, she is praised for her attentiveness: "Emma's colour was heightened by this unjust praise; . . . It seemed as if there were an instantaneous impression in her favour, as if his eyes received the truth from her's, and all that had passed of good in her feelings were at once caught and honoured" (385). Here Emma receives a hint of the kind of truth that will soon be revealed—a kind communicated instantaneously, through impressions and not words. But before she can see this truth completely, she must be instructed again. Her next "lesson" comes with another ekphrasis, Frank's letter to the Westons that announces his secret engagement to Jane and discloses his disguise. With her new moral knowledge, Emma condemns Frank harshly: "Impropriety! . . . is too calm a censure. Much, much beyond impropriety!—It has sunk him, I cannot say how it has sunk him in my opinion. So unlike what a man should be!—None of that upright integrity, that strict adherence to truth and principle, that disdain of trick and littleness, which a man should display in every transaction of his life" (397). The standard for manhood Emma evokes is, of course, Knightley's. It is the same standard that Knightley had insisted upon when he discussed with Emma his view of Frank through the first letter: "There is one thing, Emma, which a man can always do, and that is, his duty; not by maneuvering and finessing, but by vigour and resolution" (146). Frank's rhetorical "tricks" and "maneuvering" contrast with Knightley's "strict adherence" to social truth.

The text disguises the source of social truth by presenting it more as an a priori intuitive realization than as an external code. It shows that through words, the abstractive tools of rhetoric, truth can be disguised. All the characters of *Emma* who are most proficient and skilled in language use it excessively to compensate for their lack of truth. The text implies that when truth is there, it can be exchanged, as by Knightley and Emma, through a sensible glance. Emma's revelation of "the blindness of her head and heart" (411–12) leads her to realize that "to understand, thoroughly understand her own heart, was the first endeavor" (412). The process by which she understands her own heart is, ironically, by gradually losing her subjectivity to the authoritative worldview of Knightley, which is considered objective. Her new emotional awareness allows her to recognize the central truth of the novel— her love for Knightley as well as the stable social vision he represents. In contrast with all the other mellifluously eloquent lovers, Knightley declares himself by saying, "I cannot make speeches, Emma. . . . If I loved you less, I might be able to talk about it more. But you know what I am.—You hear nothing but truth from me" (430).

After this short opening declaration by Knightley, the text makes its famous withdrawal from dramatized scene, summarizing what Knightley and Emma say to each other not, as popularly conceived, out of discretion, but rather as a final testament to the relative unimportance of words in the communication of truth. The true proposal by Knightley is undramatized, whereas Elton's false one is quoted verbatim. Here, only the narrative voice must speak: "Seldom, very seldom does complete truth belong to any human disclosure; seldom can it happen that something is not a little disguised, or a little mistaken; but where, as in this case, the feelings are not, it may not be very material" (431). The omniscient narrative voice gives the novel's final statement on the proper communication of truth. Granting that disguise and mistake are inherent in any discourse, it affirms that when true feeling motivates the communication, such interferences can be overcome. But when the medium bears most or all of the weight of signification, as do Emma's portrait and Frank's epistles, the possibility of falsification is much greater. Of course, Knightley has told Emma all these things before, but it is entirely appropriate that his speech be given by the omniscient narrator. As Hough indicates, Knightley, like the omniscient voice, is "the foe of unregulated fancy," and the "acutest passages of moral and psychological understanding are accorded him" (69). In their command of moral abstractions and the authority given their discourse, the narrative voice and Knightley are identified with each other. Both utter the key moral abstractions of the novel with a proprietary tone. And though the narrator's commentary on other characters generally is ironic, when applied to Knightley it has a sanctioning effect. The omniscient narrator's assumption of his voice represents the final synthesis of their authorities.[17]

It is no coincidence that the next chapter does not reveal more about Knightley and Emma but instead gives a verbatim quote of Frank's final letter, the text's most extensive ekphrasis, with several characters' reaction to it. This ekphrasis encapsulates the text's positioning of rhetoric against truth. Knoepflmacher calls the letter "an epistolary masterpiece worthy of Lord Chesterfield's *Letters to His Son*" (654), but the reader, by this time, has been put on guard against extended, florid speeches. As before, Frank is shown trying to evade responsibility for his misconduct by a verbose, polished, circumlocutory apology. Verbosity is needed here because his conduct, if described simply and directly, would be judged inexcusable by those he has offended; it must be viewed through the distorting circumlocutions to be judged anything else. Frank himself shows he is aware that the length of his apology makes it suspect when he writes, "this letter, which will be longer than I foresaw" (439), and, later, "I must still add to this long letter" (440). In seeking Emma's good graces once again, Frank resorts to his old weapon—flattery—with predictable results. Emma is lulled by his deceptive pleasantries into a state of admiration: "Every line relating to herself was interesting, and almost every line agreeable" (444). She has not learned completely the lesson taught by Knightley and must be reeducated. In reading Frank's letter, Emma unknowingly accepts rhetorical conventions for true feelings. Thus, she falls victim to the tropes of rhetoric that Locke warns can falsify by means of pleasure and beauty. As the "Aeolus" chapter of

17. In "*Emma*: A Study in Textual Strategies," Thorell Tsomondo argues against critical interpretations that see Knightley and his discourse as monolithically and univocally truthful. He notes the several ways that Austen distances from him her own implied views and the voice of the omniscient narrator.

Ulysses presents an encyclopedia of rhetorical devices, so Frank's letter in *Emma* is a single volume in an encyclopedia of rhetoric detailing the tropes of emotional appeal; *anacoenōsis, apostrophē, comprobatio, donysis, encomium, erōtēsis, eucharistia, paeonismus, onedismus, philophronēsis, eulogia, exuscitatio, apoplanēsis, anticategoria,* and many more are used by Frank with the timing and precision of a master apologist. Against this verbose document, the text positions a "silent," "voiceless" statement of truth (Knightley's proposal), which provides an implicit indictment against rhetoric, a reminder of language's figurality.

Frank has the good sense to begin with *comprobatio,* complimenting his readers: "I know it [the letter] will be read with candour and indulgence.—You are all goodness" (436). Then he asks his readers (the letter is addressed to Mrs. Weston, but Frank knows that she will show it to all affected parties) to consider the entire situation from his subjective viewpoint, disregarding the objective appearances and effects of his actions. In essence, Frank asks his readers to see with his subjective distortions rather than accept what is readily apparent. Believing that all can see the events through his eyes, Frank uses *dicaeologia,* excusing his actions because of necessity: "You must consider me as having a secret which was to be kept at all hazards" (437). Then he resorts to *encomium,* extolling those he has most offended, calling Jane "the most upright female mind in the creation" (437) and praising Emma's "delicacy of . . . mind" (439). In praising Emma for her delicacy, Frank duplicates the unwarranted flattery of his father's conundrum. This alone should alert the reader against falsification. Ever ready to assure his reader of his sincerity, Frank relies upon *donysis,* a dramatic reenactment of an emotion: when he begins to write of Mrs. Elton's manipulation of Jane, he inserts a direct address—"Here, my dear madam, I was obliged to leave off abruptly, to recollect and compose myself" (440). *Dicaeologia* is used tediously, sometimes stretching credulity to its limit—he blames the grief and business obligations from his unloved aunt's death for his mindlessly locking in his desk a letter that, if mailed, would reconcile him with Jane. Typically, the letter ends with an impassioned *eucharistia,* not one but "a thousand and a thousand thanks" (443).

Ignorant of what apparently is its reliance upon conventions instead of sincerity and truth, Emma brings the letter to Knightley and expects him finally to approve of Frank in light of this most worthy epistle. Indeed, he does exclaim, "What a letter the man writes!" (447). But he is quick to see through Frank's reliance on epistolary conventions: "Humph!—a fine complimentary opening" (445). When Knightley charges that Frank in his letter "trifles here . . . as to the temptation" (445), he refers to the young man's stated temptation to view the concealment of the engagement a virtue. Frank refuses to announce the reason for the temptation, and Knightley calls attention to this lapse, this *apoplanēsis* (evading the issue by digressing) or *aposiōpēsis* (leaving a statement unfinished). Knightley brushes aside Frank's dicaeologic excuses for his behavior toward Emma. When he reads that Frank falsely carried on the flirtation with Emma in order to disguise further his engagement with Jane, Knightley declares that he is "too much indebted to the event for his acquittal" (445). And he cannot truly believe Frank when he writes that he believed Emma knew of the secret all along. Knightley refuses to do what Frank has asked his readers—to accept his subjective view of the world as their own. Seen thus "objectively," Frank's letter is a string of rather empty conventions. Acknowledging the grief caused by Frank, Knightley conveys the moral lesson of the novel: "My Emma, does not every thing serve to prove more and more the beauty of truth and sincerity in all our dealings with each other?" (446).

Knightley softens his criticism of Frank, though, when Emma says, "I wish you would read it [his letter] with a kinder spirit towards him" (447). To this he replies, "Well, there *is* feeling here" (447). This statement is one of several instances in which the text implicitly questions the true-false opposition as represented by Knightley and Emma. For one, the latter part of the text subtly indicates that Emma's and Knightley's union is not completely a matter of his raising her to his own superior level. This ekphrasis hints that as Emma acquires keener disjycrimination through reason, Knightley's sternness is softened. Indeed, aside from purely dramatic considerations of humanizing Knightley to make him a credible lover for Emma, the text toward the end blurs the sharp distinction it has made between the two characters. As Ryle notes, this unifying of polarities is a common Austenian technique, for she states, "Must Head and Heart be antagonists? . . . 'No, the best Heart and the best Head are combined in the best person'" (169). Also reminding of the text's movement toward synthesis, Litvak calls special attention to a late speech of Knightley's, in which he pardons himself for the numerous times he has corrected Emma: "My interference was quite as likely to do harm as good . . . I do not believe I did you any good. The good was all to myself, by making you an object of the tenderest affection to me. I could not think about you so much without doating on you, faults and all; and by dint of fancying so many errors, have been in love with you ever since you were thirteen at least" (462). As Litvak indicates, what surprises is that Knightley admits the partial correctness of Emma's behavior, which he and the text had earlier condemned

Also, as he "fancies" Emma's errors, he admits to engaging in the same fictionalizing activity that has supposedly been corrected.

The Democratization of Discourse

Along with other problematic passages, Knightley's tribute to fancy and emotion near the end of the text problematizes conventional interpretations, which see the narrative as a gradual, linear correction of Emma's subjective views. The novel is conventionally interpreted as the rejection of Emma's subjective truth for the objective truth codified by society. But in problematizing this educative process, the text reveals a limitation of the empiricist episteme identified with Locke. Locke's attack upon rationalism was manifest in his theory of knowledge, which denied the existence of a priori truth and essentialist theories of language. In defining the sources of knowledge in the sense experience and reflection of individuals, he denied the possibility of a transcendent reason that could be a foundation for knowledge, inquiry, and morality.

The gap in Locke's epistemology is his inability to erect a foundation for ethics within the framework of sense and reflection. Such a foundation would have to both incorporate and transcend the individual in order to be foundational and not relativistic. And in his theory of language, if words corresponded to ideas, not things, and if ideas were private, not the result of innate inscription, then communication would be totally contingent if an absolute foundation could not be found. Locke attempts to provide a foundation for his moral theory of ideas by affixing it to a category of knowledge separate from those of sensation and intuition, that of demonstration, the mind's innate ability to judge the relation of simple ideas to the complex wholes that they may form quite apart from their correspondence to things. The paradigm for such knowledge is mathematics, geometry, and logic, but Locke also included ethics in this category of the relation of ideas because it is "the conformity or disagreement men's voluntary actions have to a rule to which they are referred, and by which they are judged of" (II.28.4). Locke displays remarkable optimism regarding our abilities to arrive at an objective knowledge of ethics through demonstration; he believed that we could discover the "foundations of our duty and rules of action, as might place morality among the sciences capable of demonstration . . . from self-evident propositions . . . as incontestable as those in mathematics" (IV.3.18). It is this hope for mathematical perfection in the artificial medium of language that Foucault finds characteristic of his late Classical

Age: "If the language in question had been 'well made', there would be no difficulty in pronouncing true judgments, and error, should it occur, would be easy to uncover and as evident as in a calculation in algebra" (*Order* 116). The flaw in Locke's formula is his equating such constants as numbers and geometrical figures with moral laws, which are subject to historical and cultural change. By assuming that moral laws are demonstrable and self-evident, Locke does not allow for a self-examination that could critique social norms.

However, *Emma*, a text produced within these epistemic constraints, implicitly provides such a critique. As Knightley, the voice of the social code, fictionalizes Emma's errors, so is the process of objective codification shown to be fictional. In other words, the novel traces not Emma's imaginist views being replaced by those of objective reason, but rather her views being replaced by other fictional ones, which happen to be socially sanctioned. The foundation of social consensus is shown to exist just as much in the realm of the imaginary. The climax of the novel, in which the omniscient voice "truthfully" states the conditions of truth, ultimately denies the possibility of absolute truth—"Seldom . . . does complete truth belong to any disclosure" (431). This statement, we presume, applies to itself. Another possible argument against the truth-claims of the novel's climax is what the text seems to illustrate about Emma's moral education. One might argue that in spite of their conventional status, Knightley's and the omniscient voice's statements concerning morality, because of their effects, relate more clearly to essential moral truth than do Emma's actions and uses of language. In equating Emma's and Knightley's worldviews, are we condoning Emma's abuse of Harriet and thoughtlessness toward Miss Bates? No, we are, instead, condoning "English delicacy," which, as Knightley illustrates, requires that individuals show dignified tolerance toward those in lower social classes while maintaining a respectful silence toward the cultural conditions that create such a caste system.

Faithful to Kuhn's definition of a paradigm, this discursive formation supports its legitimacy by defining what moral and epistemological questions can be asked. Both the Kuhnian paradigm and the Foucaultian episteme maintain their identities and their power by regulating discourse, the legitimating of those speech acts that are considered serious and meaningful. The disruption of these formations occurs whenever questions are asked for which no answers can be provided. If a foundation cannot be found for meaningful questions, or if meaningful questions expose the lack of foundation, then a paradigm or epistemic shift occurs. The Lockean episteme, in spite of its revolutionary character, could not provide a basis for relating inner and outer experience, nor could it provide an empirical basis for ethics.

The text's final undecidability concerning fancy and understanding represents the Lockean episteme's arrival at a boundary representing ethical knowledge. This boundary is reflected in the moral work of Locke's disciple, Lord Shaftesbury, who wavered between seeing morality as a product of reason and seeing it as a product of feeling. Francis Hutcheson, another Lockean, attempted to solve the dilemma by positing a "moral sense," which gives us out of our experiences the ideas for proper ethical choices. While the empiricists provide the basis for a social theory of morality, they cannot entirely abandon the episteme's definitional constraints on moral knowledge as a product of sense or intuition. Without fully acknowledging not just the arbitrariness of signifying practices but also their implication of social power and struggle, empiricist ethics are limited in their ability to provide a cultural critique that should be the basis of ethics. But *Emma*, a literary exemplar of this episteme, implicitly provides this critique and reveals the discourse's limitations.

In many respects *Emma* is a novel primarily concerned with maintaining the rigidity of caste distinctions through the power of discourse. This reflexive rigidifying of social and linguistic norms could be the product of an episteme's final acts of self-preservation. Just as the idealist skepticism of Hume was the logical product of Lockean empiricism, so was the democratization of discourse the logical direction empiricist philosophies of language would take, in spite of Locke's attempts at consensual regulation. Written in the decades after the French Revolution, Austen's novels portray a world in which social distinctions are collapsing. The contradictory impulses of the text of *Emma* are those that dramatize this collapse and yet struggle to repair it. The farmer Robert Martin is shown to be superior to the reverend Mr. Elton; Emma's flaws are exposed by her inferior's (Jane's) virtues and by her equal's (Mrs. Elton's) vices; and the final elevation of the imaginist Emma to the realm of understanding is portrayed as an act of fancy. In portraying the linguistic and social distinctions upon which the episteme is supported, the text of *Emma* carries them to the point of collapse. Although the world evoked in *Emma* seems one in which persons and words find their designated places within a naturalized hierarchy, the representation of this process exposes its artificial basis. Thus exposed, discourse would find difficulty in assuming anything close to a naturalized correspondence to an uncritiqued reality. One reason that Austen's novels engage the reader as much as they do is that they evoke a sense of nostalgia for what seems superficially a securely regulated worldview. In actuality these texts expose the limits of this security and the abyss underlying its foundation.

The narrative movement of the text of *Emma* seems to be toward a conclusion that completes characters by a final act of nominalization. Foucault describes this as the goal of Classical representation: "to make one's way towards the sovereign act of nomination, to move through language, towards the place where things and words are conjoined in their common essence, and which makes it possible to give them a name" (*Order* 117). As the connotative drift of key abstractions are secured to unitary referents, so are characters nominalized by being matched in marriage. This final act of nominalizing ends the play of character relations as proper objects of desire are defined and Jane and Emma are properly renamed in marriage.[18] This naming describes the conclusion of the narrative but also the end of discourse within the text, since what motivates reading and articulation is the delay of nominalization and the catachretic play of what remains unspoken. As Foucault says, "To reach a name . . . exhausts, and thereby kills, the possibility of speech" (118). The text—which begins with the character's name, Emma, and ends with her being renamed by an authoritarian power described as knowledge—moves toward nominalization itself as its primary theme. Thus, like *Don Quixote*'s, the ekphrastic system of *Emma* serves the purpose of discovering "truth" in naming. But by fixing what was free and hidden within the subjectivity of character—desire—to the closed, open, and objective realm of the social word, the text destroys the motivation for speech. As Emma's subjectivity is absorbed into the objectivity of a sanctioned discourse, "a subjection of the fancy to the understanding" (37), her subjectivity is reconstituted as an object for manipulation. It is the motivation for this reconstituting activity that the text raises as a final issue, leaving at the end not a name but an ellipsis.

---

18. In *Narrative and Its Discontents: Problems of Closure in the Traditional Novel*, D. A. Miller argues that narrative closure consists in finding a proper referent for open signifiers. Echoing Foucault, he claims that texts are narratable as long as closure is not reached and that the suspension of naming is a textual necessity. Analyzing the text of *Emma*, he claims that the novel moves toward a disclosing of concealed meanings and a closure of the excessive play of open signifiers.

CHAPTER FOUR

Tolstoy's Supranatural Sensualism

Parergon and the Kantian Paradigm

In classical rhetoric ekphrasis was defined as a descriptive digression allowing rhetoricians to support arguments with a relevant example. The *Progymnasmata*, the primary writing texts in antiquity and the Renaissance, contain exercises in ekphrasis, or what Quintillian calls *enargeia*: "Let us number *enargeia* among the ornaments of style, because distinctness, or, as some call it, representation, is something more than mere perspicuity. . . . It is a great merit to set forth the objects of which we speak in lively colors, so that they may as it were be seen" (Clark 201). In his *Progymnasma* Hermogenes explains, "An ekphrasis is an account in detail visible . . . bringing before one's eyes what is to be shown . . . the style must through hearing operate to bring about seeing" (Clark 202). The *Progymnasmata*, emphasizing the ornamental and auxiliary nature of ekphrasis, define it as serving the ends of rhetorical appeal but not integral to discursive meaning. By contrast, I argue that ekphrasis in literary narrative, often a digressive description of a work of art laying bare the mimetic devices of the text, problematizes the secondary status defined for it in classical rhetoric. In narratological terms ekphrases are satellites, nonsequential scenes or images appended to kernels, scenes or images that connect causally with other kernels to form the main narrative. However, in translating the main narrative into another level of discourse, these satellites often codify the norms of a mimetic paradigm, provide keys to textual interpretation, and thus form metalinguistic relations with the narratives they enframe and define.

As extrinsic ornament not contributing to intrinsic form, ekphrasis occupies a space in poststructuralist theory similar to such Derridean terms as *différance*, supplement, *pharmakon*, and hymen. The digression, appendage, and ornament serve Derrida as tools for deconstructive readings of philosophical and artistic texts that mystify the relations of inner and outer and privilege the essentialist concepts of unity and innateness. One of his critiques of essentialism is of the Kantian aesthetic distinction between the *ergon*, the artifact's innate form, and the *parergon*, an ornamental or framing device that merely supplements the viewer's aesthetic appreciation of an object's intrinsic beauty.[1] It is interesting that one of Derrida's fullest treatments of Kant, whose philosophical system served as paradigm for well over a century, comes through a commentary upon the *Critique of Judgement* and Kant's aesthetic theory rather than the more widely read earlier critiques. Derrida justifies this by illustrating that through aesthetics Kant "was able to identify in art (in general) one of the middle terms (*Mitten*) to resolve (*auflösen*) the 'opposition' between mind and nature, internal and external phenomenon, the inside and the outside, etc." ("Parergon" 3). In other words, aesthetics can be seen as an important element in the Kantian project of connecting mind and matter or concept and experience. And this justifies introducing his paradigm, the ambitious synthesis of rationalism and empiricism, through his aesthetic theory, which is usually relegated to the background of mainstream Kantian studies.

One of Kant's intents in the *Critique of Judgement* was to find a correspondence between the categories of the understanding and the manifold of sense, which separated understanding from the natural

---

1. In *La vérité en peinture* (English translation of part 2: "The Parergon," in *October* 9) and in "Economimesis," Derrida argues that aesthetics is foundational for Kantian epistemology in treating such central concepts as representation, artistic disinterest ("purposiveness without purpose"), and the privileging of aesthetic experience. Derrida argues that each of these central concepts, from which Kant lays a unitary and changeless foundation, is subject to the figural play of signification. For discussions of Derrida on Kant, see Irene Harvey, "Derrida, Kant, and the Performance of Parergonality"; Cynthia Chase, "Paragon, Parergon: Baudelaire Translates Rousseau"; Richard Klein, "Kant's Sunshine"; Stephen Watson, "Regulations: Kant and Derrida at the End of Metaphysics"; and Jonathan Culler, *On Deconstruction*.

world in which we make moral decisions. In the earlier *Critique of Pure Reason* Kant posited that moral judgments could not become entangled with the deterministic world of nature and necessity without losing the freedom of choice that is the necessary underpinning of morality. But in the third *Critique* Kant correlates the aesthetic pleasure derived from the perception of an object's intrinsic form with the intrinsic harmonic accord of the cognitive faculties of the understanding and, beyond that, transcendent reason. He assigns to judgment the regulative role of reconciling theoretical reason with the categories of the understanding, which then can be applied to the sensible world. Aesthetic judgment is the primary mode by which the faculty of judgment can be seen to operate, because it suggests a relational connection between the phenomenal world of representations and the noumenal world of things-in-themselves, inaccessible to the categories of the understanding. Aesthetic judgment, mediating between the objectivity of things-in-themselves and the subjectivity of individual response, transcends the particular and suggests a *sensus communus*. Through the universal *and* individual aesthetic response, "This is beautiful," Kant postulates a faculty that, while tethered to sensory perception, transcends the determinism of mechanical necessity and points to a realm of freedom in which aesthetic as well as moral judgments can be made. Thus, for Kant, "the beautiful is the symbol of the morally good" (*Judgement* 223).[2]

To Derrida it is ironic that Kant uses aesthetic judgment as both detachable copula and essential component of the correspondence and harmonic accord of the faculties. The problematic status of judgment and, indeed, the motivation for the composition of the third *Critique*—as supplement justifying the authority of the preceding texts—allow Derrida to use Kant's *parergon* as focus for a deconstructive reading. Kant's application of the categories to aesthetic judgment depends upon an ability to distinguish inner from outer, intrinsic from extrinsic. Indeed, the entire notion of a priori categories depends on such an ability. Kant's inordinate interest in parergonal details confirms for Derrida that these distinctions are problematized at the level Kant defines as boundary or frame: "Ornamentation (*parerga*), i.e. what is only an adjunct, and not

---

2. In *Kant and the Transcendental Object*, J. N. Findlay echoes Derrida's valorizing aesthetics in Kantian epistemology. He writes, "Kant's transcendental doctrine of the aesthetic judgement or judgement of taste, in which transcendental objectivity plays a fascinatingly obscure but all-important part . . . helps to gather together Kant's whole thought regarding the relation of the phenomenal to the noumenal" (326). Findlay concentrates on those sections in *The Critique of Judgement* that treat taste or judgment as having a harmonizing role parallel to the harmonic accord of our cognitive faculties and therefore laying a universal foundation from which a metaphysic of morals can be built.

an intrinsic constituent in the complete representation of an object, in augmenting the delight of taste, does so solely by means of its form. . . . But if the ornamentation does not itself enter into the composition of a beautiful form—if it is introduced like a gold frame merely to win approval for the picture by means of its charm—it is then called finery and takes away from the genuine beauty" (*Judgement* 68). Against Kant's claims that *parerga* are excludable adjuncts to a work's inherent form, Derrida argues, "A *parergon* is *against,* beside, and above and beyond the *ergon.* . . . But it is not incidental; it is connected to and cooperates in its operation from the outside" ("Parergon" 20). The *parergon* cooperates in the accomplishment of the work through its literal and metaphoric function as a frame enabling one to distinguish what is intrinsic in form from the extrinsic. It is "an outside which is called inside the inside to constitute it as inside" (26). The *parergon* is therefore essential to the unity of the *ergon* because its frame or boundary separates the object from all that is outside. Serving a definitional function, the *parergon* can thus be considered the primary figure to which the *ergon* is adjunct.

I have given lengthy attention to the Kantian *parergon* and Derrida's critique for two reasons. The first is relevant to my use of extrinsic description and the second to my definition of mimetic paradigms and their representation within novels. Literary texts, even more than plastic arts, highlight the problematic status of ekphrasis as ornament or supplement. *Don Quixote* and *Emma* are novels in which ekphrasis is used to reveal the cultural and linguistic subtexts that are underpinnings of a mimetic paradigm. The ekphrases in *Don Quixote* are more than digressive asides—they produce a system of meaning formulating the episteme's discursive definitions of how the text relates to an external reality. Similarly, in *Emma* the case for the primacy of the ekphrastic convention is aided by the fact that the novel's primary theme is the relation of thought, word, and deed to reality. In this novel the ekphrases of language games that must be deciphered and interpreted by characters mirror the reader's interpretive strategies as he or she arbitrates between the conflicting claims of desire and truth.

My third example, *Anna Karenina,* by Leo Tolstoy, like the earlier ones, is a novel in which important ekphrastic scenes define both the conflict over representation within a paradigm and the text's language use. Thus, it, along with the other examples, fits my definition of a realist text—one that thematizes the world-word relation by dramatizing the referential status of signs. Tolstoy's novel gives one of the clearest depictions of a crisis over interpreting truth through the conceptual vocabulary of a mimetic paradigm, a crisis that motivates its own representation within the text. This crisis occurs as a conflict between nineteenth-century interpreters of the Kantian paradigm's theory of knowledge as a synthesis of concept and experience. Minimizing the synthetic nature of the Kantian project, objective interpreters of Kant emphasized his "empirical realism" and the independent existence of the material world, and subjective and idealist interpreters emphasized his "transcendental idealism" and the formative role of the human mind. Tolstoy, in fact, was aware of at least one part of this debate through his readings in Kant, Schelling, Schlegel, Hegel, and Schopenhauer, for his hero, Levin, directly names them as sources for some of his moral ideas, as does Tolstoy himself in his diaries. Therefore, the treatment of this paradigmatic conflict is not as subconscious as in the earlier examples, thus justifying even more the interpretation of *Anna Karenina* and its use of ekphrases through the conceptual vocabulary of its guiding representational paradigm, the Kantian.[3]

Within this conflict in the Kantian paradigm, the correspondence-and-coherence dialectic is formulated as a conflict between reality and appearances. Even though Kant insists that noumena, the things-in-themselves in reality, are unknowable because we recognize only their representations within the mind, phenomena, many of his interpreters within a subjective tradition, especially Hegel, Jacobi, Schelling, and Schopenhauer, strove to amend his representationalism by expanding his theory of the knowability of reality through the knowledge of self as thing-in-itself, or consciousness directed toward itself, which Schopenhauer calls a manifestation of the essential "Will" and Hegel "Being," in opposition to the phenomena, which are representations creating the "veil of Maya." Tolstoy, however, responded to the romantic angst that accompanied a representational theory that alienates humans from nature; therefore, he follows those in the subjective Kantian tradition in stressing the knowability of noumenon, or will, but differs from them in finding it knowable not in an idealist sense but rather in the empirical

3. Tolstoy was an avid reader of philosophy and at the time of composition of *Anna Karenina* was reading and rereading those same philosophers that his character Levin was reading—"Plato, Spinoza, Kant, Schelling, Hegel, and Schopenhauer, the philosophers who gave a nonmaterialistic explanation of life" (822). Although critics differ regarding the dates he became acquainted with the *Critique of Practical Reason*, it is certain that he was enthusiastic about Kant's moral philosophy, which he called "the crown of Kant's deepest spiritual activity" (Hájnády 291). Even if he read the second *Critique* in 1887 (ten years after the completion of *Anna Karenina*) instead of 1869 (Greenwood, "Tolstoy, Wittgenstein, Schopenhauer" 62), he still was aware of Kant's moral philosophy through Schopenhauer, whom he called "the greatest genius among men" (McLaughlin 188). Of Kant's moral philosophy, Schopenhauer writes that Kant "freed ethics from all principles of the world of experience . . . and showed that the kingdom of virtue is not of this world" (Greenwood, "Tolstoy, Wittgenstein, Schopenhauer" 65).

and particular. Tolstoy, like Kant, rejects both "pure reason," an attempt to achieve knowledge of reality by concepts alone, and mechanical causation, knowledge coming only from phenomena, for a "metaphysics of the body," or a "transcendental empiricism." Seeking to bridge the gap between self and other, or nature, he explores the way things-in-themselves can be perceived through intuition, in this case an aesthetics of pure perception. Tolstoy's dramatic use of intuition and pure aesthetic perception are akin to the Kantian "intuitive intellect," which unites the faculties of sensibility and understanding, but closer to Schopenhauer's "intuitive interpretation," Schelling's "conscious-unconscious activity of the artistic genius," and Jacobi's "supranatural sensualism." In stressing the sensuous apprehension of essential being, Tolstoy carries the Kantian implications about our synthetic knowledge of the empirical world to an end emphasizing a way in which the concepts of the mind and the objects of reality can be correspondently joined. Through his fiction, Tolstoy strives to make the antithetically oppositional terms of phenomenon and noumenon meet in a dramatically enacted synthesis.[4]

The metaphysics of the body and the purity of perception are important dramatic and thematic elements in *Anna Karenina*; in fact, I contend that they are the text's *most* important themes. Their centrality, however, is more than thematic; they also guide Tolstoy's language use. Like *Don Quixote* and *Emma*, the text contains an ekphrastic system thematizing the representational norms of a mimetic paradigm in terms of a debate over an object of representation. In *Anna Karenina*, as in the earlier texts, this debate appears as a conflict of mimetic paradigms that question the relation of word–idea–thing. In this case, one paradigm suggests the knowability of the world through representations, phenomena, or intertextual conventions; the other contrastingly shows how the empirical world can be known through things-in-themselves, will, or noumena. This important element of the text is treated in an ekphrastic scene illustrating the rivalry between two paintings of Anna. The first, by her lover Vronsky, is drawn by conventions representing a possible world of adulterous intrigue and gothic romanticizing. These conventions illustrate the representations of Schopenhauer, the "veil of Maya" that disguises the reality of the world, which can be sensually perceived by intuition in a moment of pure aesthetic perception. This purity of perception and representation is dramatized in the contrasting painting of Anna by the professional painter Mihailov, who so accurately depicts the reality of Anna, or herself as noumenon, that it becomes "a living,

4. For a discussion of the Kantian idealist tradition, see Wilhelm Windelbrand's "The Development of Idealism: The Thing-in-itself," in *A History of Philosophy* 2:41.

breathing woman," epitomizing Anna for all who see it. The painting by Mihailov thus models Tolstoy's own portrait of her in that he attempts to use language in a specular and sensory manner. Like the earlier novels discussed, Tolstoy uses ekphrasis to engage in an exacting critique of language, about which the novel also evidences a distrust for its lack of connection to the world, and thus the novel seeks other, more intuitive correspondences. Also important is how the ekphrastic scene depicts Mihailov's compositional method, as a parergonal detail defining the *ergon* of the work, and explains Tolstoy's use of this digressive aside.

The parergonal details of the ekphrastic scenes of painting define the *ergon* of the work by setting forth the philosophical positions motivating the actions of characters. The text thus, though different in many ways from the menippea, also explores the real-life implications of the guiding philosophies and discourses a character adopts. Conventionality in art is identified by Tolstoy as the larger system of conventions—particularly language—that guide social action and disguise the true motives and inner realities of characters, leading them to unhappiness and disaster. On the other hand, intuitive knowledge, identified with Mihailov's aesthetics, leads other characters to more-lasting truths about the nature of reality. This testing of philosophical and discursive premises is manifest on two possible-world levels represented by the narratives of the two main characters, Anna and Levin, as each struggles to define the inner reality of self in opposition to the overdetermining signification of social conventions and language. In the case of both, this philosophical testing is carried out through a parallel theme—the discovery of a meaning in life in the midst of death. And in both cases, Tolstoy uses the aesthetics developed in his ekphrastic scenes as Kant and Schelling also use aesthetics—to define how practical judgment guides moral action. It must be emphasized, however, that as the text dramatically reenacts the philosophic positions within the paradigm, the intricacies of the dramatic action, as well as the problematic role of language within fictional-world construction, complicate a too simple opposition between the correspondent and coherentist terms and even question their supposed synthesis. Tolstoy's later rejection of his own fiction and almost all art can be interpreted as being at least partly motivated by these problematics.

Character and Description in Tolstoy

There is no doubt that of the texts examined so far, none more skeptically examines conventionality and the abuses of language than does

Anna Karenina. Tolstoy's initial means of dramatizing artistic conventionality, false representation, and the consequent illusory world produced
is the extended ekphrastic scene depicting Vronsky's painting. This
ekphrastic scene sets the terms for the novel's dramatic questioning of
social conventionality and false representation through language. During
this scene, Anna and Vronsky, delaying momentarily the deterministic
flow of events in their tragic affair, are here afforded one brief interlude
of relative peace when they run away to Italy after Anna's near death
from childbirth and Vronsky's aborted suicide. Deprived of his military
and government career, Vronsky decides to imitate the life of a quattro-
cento *artiste* by collecting necessary conventional accoutrements. He
rents a decaying *palazzo*, replete with wall frescoes, mosaic floors,
damask hangings, even an original Tintoretto, and wears hat and cloak
flung over his shoulder in medieval fashion. His re-creation of the actual
textual world by adopting the conventional signs of the possible textual
world of romance is treated harshly by Tolstoy, similar to Cervantes'
critiques of Don Quixote's re-creative signifying. Like the Don's, the
possible world projected by Anna and Vronsky is created partly by the
conventions of art, and thus Vronsky turns to art to further concretize
its existence. "In the agreeable illusion that he was . . . a painter" (492),
Vronsky paints a portrait of Anna in medieval Italian costume, fixing in
oil an image of her shaped according to a conventional artistic ideal. The
painting, like *Emma*'s painting of Harriet, is motivated by a subjective
desire for an alternative world. But before finishing his ekphrastic
portrait, Vronsky commissions a professional painter, Mihailov, another
Russian expatriate living in Italy, to paint a second portrait of Anna, an
ekphrasis about which the text comments:

> The portrait impressed everybody, especially Vronsky, not only
> by its likeness but also by its peculiar beauty. It was strange
> how Mihailov had been able to discover that peculiar beauty.
> "One needs to know and love her, as I have loved her, to
> discover the very sweetest expression of her soul," thought
> Vronsky, though it was through this portrait that he himself
> learned this sweetest expression of her soul. But the expression
> was so true that it seemed to him, and to others, too, that they
> had always known it. "I have been struggling on for ages
> without doing anything," he said one day, referring to his own
> portrait of her, "but he just looks at her once and the thing is
> done! That's the advantage of technique." (503)

Lacking sufficient knowledge, Vronsky attributes the superiority of
Mihailov's painting merely to a more clever choice of conventions.

However, what Vronsky calls technique is more than this—it also suggests the conflict between two mimetic paradigms concerning truth in human representation, one a rationalism relying upon concepts and conventions that illustrate Schopenhaurian representations, and the other a transcendental empiricism that directly portrays an inner will. Additionally, however, the entire ekphrastic scene deserves to be examined for the way in which it also illustrates paradigmatic shifts in the uses of convention in the historical treatment of character in narrative, particularly the ekphrastic convention.

Considered in historical succession, the ekphrases of *Don Quixote*, *Emma*, and *Anna Karenina* reveal that though character is a primary element of realism, the paradigms of representation modify what is considered verisimilar representation; and the ekphrases in these novels reflect that change. The puppet characters of Master Peter's marionette show mirror the characterization of Don Quixote in early chapters—as a flat, one-dimensional character whose static, predictable responses to experience reveal him to be, like the ekphrastic objects of the marionette show, a puppet guided by the strings of an obsessive ideal. But this early treatment of the Don is ultimately discontinuous with the text's implicit mimetic norms, for its ekphrastic satire upon stock characters of medieval romance exists less for making stereotypical knights puppets than for serving as contrast to show how the Don's self-chosen, caricatured image finally becomes realistic, conforming with the wider conception of personality that evolved from Renaissance humanism. This ekphrasis shows a change from the caricature and allegory in early texts that view character types based upon essentialist notions of human personality. After Cervantes, caricature yields to more empirically and socially realistic devices of characterization, reflected by different forms of ekphrasis. For example, characterization is central in *Emma*, and Emma's moral growth is measured by her distance from the novel's primary ekphrastic form, Churchill's epistles. Exchanging personal letters was a primary means of moral edification in the eighteenth century, and as shown by Austen, an ill-intended disguise of motives in letter writing threatens the moral code defining personal relationships. Austen defines character in socially moral contexts, and it is appropriate that a common form of social communication, the letter, is the ekphrasis with which she reveals the moral truth of character.[5]

Since *Anna Karenina* is Tolstoy's "portrait of a lady," the painting of Anna's portrait by Mihailov is symbolic of Tolstoy's own creation. And

5. In *Character and the Novel*, W. J. Harvey chronicles the shifts in novelists' treatment of character according to changes in worldview and social context.

as the puppet and letter were appropriate to illustrate the representational paradigms of the earlier texts' treatment of character, so the painting is the proper ekphrastic form to illustrate the conventional norms of nineteenth-century realism. It should be noted, however, that the ekphrastic scene in which Anna's portrait is painted by Mihailov is based upon the painting of two portraits of Tolstoy by Ivan Kramskoye in September 1873, during Tolstoy's composition of *Anna Karenina*. Mihailov is modeled on Kramskoye, and many of the ideas on art expressed in the scene are based on conversations between the artist and Tolstoy.[6] Sensing the author's identification with his artist-character, T.G.S. Cain remarks that Mihailov's aesthetic "is more accurate as a description of the way the writer works than of the way the painter does" (104). By identifying with Mihailov, Tolstoy provides an interior definition of the representational foundation of his text. Also important is the fact that Tolstoy's theory of character is thinly disguised as Mihailov's. Like Mihailov, Tolstoy is a realist who aspires toward a transparency of medium that gives readers or viewers the illusion they are experiencing life itself. And in identifying his aesthetic with that of a pictorial medium, Tolstoy is able to carry out his questioning of language's representational capabilities, a trait I identify as central to the mode of novelistic realism. But in addition to convincingly reproducing surfaces, both the novelist and his created artist yield to romanticist instincts to represent the inner reality of the human form through external details, thus circumventing the representational limitations of all artistic media. In both novelistic character and painted subject, intricately described phenomenal details suggest noumenal ones, a higher reality in which the represented form's harmony of detail show the essence of an individual.

Tolstoy's and Mihailov's descriptive technique, eschewing earlier conventionality, reflects a paradigmatic shift not only in characterization but also in narrative description. The transcendental empiricism used to achieve an illusion of immediate physical presence epitomizes the emphasis upon the conventions of empirical accuracy in nineteenth-century realistic description and explains why the painting was at that time such a common ekphrastic form in novelistic texts. The pictorial impulses in such novelists as Zola, Hardy, Conrad, and Crane culminated a shift in narrative toward the conventionally empirical and away from the conventionally scenic in natural representation. By scenic I mean the use of familiar topoi. For example, in the natural descriptions of *Tom Jones* and *Joseph Andrews*, Fielding represents nature in the conventional terms

---

6. An interesting discussion of the conversations between Tolstoy and Kramskoye is in Victor Shklovsky, *Lev Tolstoy*.

of a Hogarth or Gainsborough portrait—the humanly ordered garden framing man, the anthropocentric subject. Literary realists and naturalists rebelled against such stock scenes of verdant pastures, grazing sheep, decaying castles, quaint cottages, and picturesque elms. The more stark and unadorned paintings of nature by Millet and Courbet reflected the same impulse literary realists obeyed: to present the reality of nature with conventions that allow for a greater transparency of artistic medium. Realist painters perfected the visual element of mimesis, and the significance of their perceptual and representational insights was diminished only when their photographic realism yielded to the technical accuracy of the modern photograph.[7] But as Wallace Martin notes, realist novelists tried to lay claim to greater empirical accuracy by "calling attention to devices used in other narratives and exposing their artificiality, [and thus] the writer clears a space in which departures from convention will be taken as signs of authenticity" (69). The realist novelist's dilemma is epitomized by the irony of validating the truth-claims of conventions by attacking conventionality.

In aspiring toward transparency of medium, Tolstoy is an excellent example of a realist novelist using the medium of language like a realist painter. As viewers of Mihailov's portrait of Anna think they are seeing a real woman, so do readers of Tolstoy sense that his characters physically come to life. Tolstoy culminates the era's struggle to move beyond the conventional view of character that creates caricature. From Cervantes through Austen to Tolstoy, characters move toward what seems to us now as lifelikeness, the adoption of newer conventions that take into account the nineteenth-century's fuller, sociopsychological view of human personality. Anna's portrait encapsulates her complexity as it is progressively revealed in the course of the novel. The relation of Tolstoy's ekphrasis to those of Cervantes and Austen in respect to character is analogous to the relation between the empirical and the scenic mode of portraiture and nature painting. But even though Tolstoy epitomizes the realist attitude toward natural and human description, he differs in one way. Providing perfect physical imitations of characters was not enough for the prophet-artist—he also strove to reveal their essential realities and hence their spirituality. Mihailov paints Anna so accurately that her physical features reveal what one translator renders as "the sweetest expression of her soul" and another "her unique spiritual expression." This technique can also be seen in Mihailov's masterwork,

7. In "Novel and Camera," Leon Edel writes of the descriptive impulse that led novelists to aspire toward photographic realism: "Whenever we turn in the nineteenth-century we can see novelists cultivating the camera-eye and the camera movement" (177).

"Christ before Pilate," in which the Russian artist paints a Christ emphasizing the physically human incarnation of the divine.

Genius, Imitation, and the Essence of Art

Tolstoy's critique of conventionality is translated to an existential level in his depiction of the possible world created by Anna and Vronsky during the ekphrastic scene dramatizing the painting of the portrait. While living in their *palazzo*, Anna and Vronsky are momentarily able to break their emotional and ethical connections to the outer world and thus avoid the consequences of their actions. Tolstoy here emphasizes the discontinuity of the escapist textual world epitomized by the romantic painting and the actual textual world of action and consequences. Anna feels guilt neither for the pain she has caused her husband nor for abandoning her son; she is, while with Vronsky, "unpardonably happy" (490). Vronsky, on the other hand, responds differently to the satisfaction of desire. Able to live completely what Kierkegaard calls the aesthetic life, the fulfillment of sensual pleasure, Vronsky realizes "the eternal error men made in imagining that happiness consists in the realization of their desires" (490–91). The despair Vronsky experiences comes from the inevitable longing for some meaning in life beyond desire-fulfillment. The shallow Vronsky, however, cannot conceive of a life beyond the senses, and while sensually satisfied, feels "desire . . . in his heart for desires—*ennui*" (491). His desire motivates and informs his haphazard intellectual and aesthetic diversions: "As a hungry animal seizes upon everything it can get hold of in the hope that it may be food, so Vronsky quite unconsciously clutched first at politics, then at new books, then pictures" (491). Also important is the fact that it is his desire that motivates the representation of Anna in his portrait.

By showing the inadequacy of the possible world created by Vronsky and Anna, Tolstoy contrasts worlds created by different modes of artistic and linguistic representation. John Bayley writes that at this point of the novel, Anna and Vronsky, insulated from the textual real world, "have, in a sense, stopped living, and so have leisure for art" (234). Tolstoy here also evidences his hatred of an escapist art motivated by desire, created as an anodyne for ennui, and used as mere diversion by the elite classes who have rejected real life. Some of the most caustic sections of his *What Is Art?* concern the art of the upper class, about which he writes, "For people of the wealthy classes, spending their lives in idleness and luxury, desire to be continually diverted by art: and art, even the lowest, cannot be produced at will, but has to generate spontaneously in the artist's inner self" (92). Tolstoy shows that this lack of spontaneity, similar to Schopenhauerian intuition, precludes Vronsky from being a genuine artist. Vronsky is the embodiment of the latter in Kant's distinction between genius and learning.[8] Kant writes in the third *Critique* that "learning is imitation" (169) and that its product is a mechanical art formed by examples but incapable of being exemplary. To Kant, genius is an activity—"the exemplary originality of the natural endowments of one individual in the *free* employment of his cognitive faculties" (181). This activity "cannot be communicated, but requires to be bestowed directly from the hand of nature" (170). Schopenhauer also derides such received learning when he writes, "The inclination of most scholars is a kind of *fuga vacui* [vacuum suction] from the poverty of their own minds, which forcibly draws in the thought of others" (*World* 2:254). Lacking the "innate mental aptitude" (168) given by nature, Vronsky imitates the conventions of recognizable artistic schools: "After hesitating . . . to decide which style of painting to take up—religious, historical, *genre*, or realistic—he set to work. He appreciated all the different styles and could find inspiration in any of them, but he could not conceive that it was possible to be ignorant of the different schools of painting and to be inspired directly by what is within the soul" (491).

Vronsky's reliance upon imitation is similar to Frank Churchill's dependence upon rhetorical devices in *Emma*. Both use conventions ultimately to mask subtextual truth. In his essay on art, Tolstoy, echoing Kant, writes that through imitation "the artist only transmits the feeling received by him from a previous work of art: therefore every borrowing . . . is but a reflection of art . . . not art itself" (96–97). Needing to find a model to imitate, Vronsky decides to paint his portrait of Anna in the "graceful and effective French school" (491), which Tolstoy held in particularly low esteem. For example, Levin, discussing French art with Anna, says that "the French have carried conventionality in art further than anyone else" (491). More important, this conventionality is con-demned by Tolstoy in that he makes it partly responsible for his heroine's tragic fall. Overdetermined by Vronsky's conventionalized image, Anna

8. See David Lloyd, "Kant's Examples," for a discussion of Kant's distinctions between the exemplar and the exemplum, genius and taste, in the *Critique of Judgement*. The concepts are, Lloyd argues, tied to Kant's notions of freedom and constraint. If genius is outside the constraints of imitation and learning, it is therefore innate—genius and "exemplary originality [are] the natural endowments of an individual in the *free* employment of his cognitive faculties" (Kant, *Judgement* 181). Lloyd says, "The judgment of genius produces for humanity at large exemplary products for the judgment of *taste*. Unlike genius, taste is a progressive faculty and intimately associated with pedagogy" (42).

loses sight of her true self, as depicted in Mihailov's painting, and is thus made incapable of living in the real world.

In this ekphrastic scene, Vronsky's friend Golenischev, according to R. F. Christian, "fulfills the role of the critic" (188), and critics were a group Tolstoy rebuked even more than dilettantes like Vronsky. Tolstoy defines critics as "able writers, educated and clever, but with their capacity of being infected by art quite perverted or atrophied" (*Art* 104). Golenischev particularizes this definition. Condemning Mihailov as having "that everlasting Ivanov-Strauss-Renan attitude" (492), and declaring Vronsky the better painter because he paints "more like the Old Masters" (505), Golenischev, classifying artistic creation, reveals that he understands only convention and imitation. Drawn to create himself, he delays proving his abilities by "deceiving himself with the idea that his theories had not yet matured" (505). Golenischev's false artistry can be viewed in light of Kant's and Schopenhauer's insistence that art is derived from intuition and not concepts. Thus, when Vronsky, Golenischev, and Mihailov meet on the common ground of art, three different views collide—those of the dilettante, the critic, and the true creative artist.

Tolstoy depicts first in the narrative Vronsky's conventional aesthetic and its consequent false world to provide a contrast with the truth of Mihailov's realist aesthetic and accurate picture of the world. Mihailov finally appears in a significant section illustrating his method of creation, an important ekphrastic scene describing him laboring for hours on two sketches of a raging man. Frustrated, he tosses the second sketch to his daughter to play with. Then, dissatisfied with the first sketch, he asks his daughter to return the other, now stained with candle grease. But the stain gives an insight: "He suddenly recalled the powerful face of a tobacconist with a prominent jaw . . . and he gave the man he was drawing just such a face and jaw. . . . The lifeless figure of his imagination had come to life and could not be improved upon. . . . He removed the wrappings, as it were, that partially obscured the form, each new stroke bringing out the action and power of the whole figure that had suddenly been revealed to him by the grease spot" (495–96). Several contrasts between the ekphrastic opposition of Vronsky's conventional method and Mihailov's intuitive one deserve consideration. First is the latter's intuitive, as opposed to the former's intellectual, form of understanding. Mihailov is undoubtedly representative of the Kantian genius creating exemplars and not imitations. Kant defines aesthetic judgment as free of rational concepts, and from this freedom comes disinterestedness, "purposiveness without purpose," or what Schopenhauer calls an effacement of individual self to the inner self of the object, to a will-less contemplation of another inner truth or will. Because of the "free play" of Mihailov's disinterested imagination, the figure becomes "alive" in his intuition, and the "wrappings" obscuring the (inner) form are revealed by an incidental realization coming from the grease spot. In opposition to this, Vronsky, relying upon concepts, learning, and imitation, chooses among conventional signs, motivated not by disinterest or will-less contemplation of the essence of Anna's personality but by his overdetermining desire for her and for the false world created by illusory conventions that promises pleasure, escape, and social prestige. The bulk of the novel explores the consequences of this ruthless overdetermination.

This ekphrastic scene is also important because the structural principle guiding Mihailov's creativity is similar to Tolstoy's. In an essay on the irrelevant detail and narrative form, Martin Price, citing this passage, comments, "Once the artist finds, through contingency, a necessary outward form, that form must in turn be protected from, stripped free of, the merely trivial irrelevancy" (76–77). However, this scene problematizes the definition of irrelevance by dramatically shifting inner and outer, intrinsic and extrinsic detail. The grease spot, the most irrelevant of parergonal details, becomes the focus for the painting's inherent form. Price describes the process as "the arbitrary suggestion in the form of the grease spot, the outward drive of an inner content or vision that seizes upon actual details of any sort to find specification" (76). Similarly, Tolstoy seizes upon the parergonal ekphrastic scenes described above to find a specification for the *ergon* of the main narrative in theme, treatment of character, and structure. Thematically, the text defines as "trivial irrelevancy" the conventions, both social and artistic, whose "wrappings" must be "stripped free" from the necessary internal form of personality.

I have considered how these ekphrases inform theme and characterization and will more fully elaborate these features later, but I would like now to consider how Mihailov's method in this particular ekphrasis also informs the novel's structure. Both the striving of inner form toward outer actualization and an extrinsic detail becoming the focus of inherent form describe Tolstoy's structural methodology. Contrary to Percy Lubbock's and Henry James's famous criticisms of his novels' lack of design, Tolstoy prided himself on their form and structure, particularly *Anna Karenina*, whose "architecture" he praised. Recent books on *Anna Karenina* by Sidney Schultze and Elizabeth Stenbock-Fermor focus on the structure of the novel and confirm its formal artistry.[9] The text's

9. Stenbock-Fermor's *Architecture of Anna Karenina: A History of Its Structure, Writing, and Message* and Schulze's *Structure of Anna Karenina* are the most thorough studies of the structure of the novel. See also in William W. Rowe's *Leo Tolstoy* the section "Structure

subsumption of empirical detail into a classic, severe form reflects, among other things, the division in the author's personality at the time of composition. Drawn to both realism and religious romanticism, Tolstoy sought to paint a broad canvas of society and nature while enframing it in an aesthetic form reflecting an atemporal spiritual pattern. Thus, Tolstoy reflects Schiller's reading of Kant—that in art humans seek to reconcile their dual natures, one binding us to the fleeting world of sensations and one organizing sense impressions into the unity of a formal law. Writing to a critic who praised *Anna Karenina* but complained "there is no architecture in it," Tolstoy replied, "I pride myself . . . on the architecture—the arches are so joined that it is impossible even to notice the keystone" (*Letters* 1:311). He also declared that "the structural link" was an "inner" one—"Not the plot or the relationships . . . between the characters." In another letter, Tolstoy again mentioned the hidden link without identifying it; he instead stressed "the endless labyrinth of linkings in which the essence of art resides" (1:296). He warned that it is "impossible to express the basis of this linking in words," for "each idea expressed in words on its own, loses its meaning . . . when it is taken out of the linking in which it is found." The linking, he writes, "can only be expressed indirectly, by words describing images, actions, situations." Tolstoy's essentialist, specular, and extralinguistic aesthetic is apparent in his description of his novel as having an "inner link," a structural law or inherent form that transcends the surface details of story, character, and language. The law, an a priori unity intuitively perceived in an act of Kantian genius, gives form to the labyrinth of external links by choosing randomly an external point of focus—the grease spot on Mihailov's canvas or the ekphrastic scene in Tolstoy's text. I contend it is the elaborate ekphrastic system—a sequence of parergonal details reflecting Vronsky's and Mihailov's paintings and giving Tolstoy's theory of representational truth—that forms this "indirect" link.

The Wrappings of Convention

There are several other parallels between Tolstoy's aesthetic in *Anna Karenina* and Mihailov's method of invention. First, of course, is the autobiographical source of inspiration: giving the jaw of a real-life

---

and Symmetry" within the chapter on *Anna Karenina*. These and other studies highlight the error of seeing Tolstoy's novels as "loose, baggy monsters."

tobacconist to an imaginary subject of a painting. Nadezhda Garodetzky indicates that as a tobacconist's jaw is used by Mihailov for subject matter, so "a wealth of autobiographical detail and features of contemporary Russian life were naturally absorbed by Tolstoy" (125). A second analogy is the integrity granted the subject of representation—once Mihailov finds the inner truth of his figure, he cannot change it significantly. This, too, reflects Tolstoy's view that characters, once realized, achieve an autonomy and are thus immune from authorial tampering. For example, he wrote, "With Vronsky's suicide, I had never clearly felt the necessity of it . . . suddenly, by some means that was totally unexpected but ineluctable, Vronsky determined to put a bullet through his head, and it later became clear that the scene was organically indispensable" (Troyat 389). But the most significant and ambiguous part of this passage is Mihailov's view that creating character is no more than removing wrappings that obscure the essential form of self. According to Shklovsky, Tolstoy and the painter Kramskoye discussed this principle (440–41). Cain interprets it as "allowing the novel to develop as its own internal logic demanded . . . refusing to impose preconceived or simplified solutions" (105). Christian, however, interprets the passage not as structural metaphor but as descriptive of Tolstoy's quest for his characters' inner truth: "Like Tolstoy he [Mihailov] wants to get at the character behind the conventional facade, to strip off the surface layers and reveal the essence of his subject" (188). Christian's interpretation, conforming closely to the conversations between Tolstoy and Kramskoye reported by Shklovsky, seems more accurate.[10] For one, if the ekphrasis of Mihailov's painting is compared to Vronsky's, the meaning of "wrappings" becomes clearly identified as the conventions that obscure the inner reality of Anna. Tolstoy's technique is, like Mihailov's, to seek beyond the veil, representations, and obscuring phenomena, to seek the inner reality of character, the human object as thing-in-itself. However, this noumenon is, for Tolstoy, apprehensible through an aesthetic intuition akin to a physical response.

The parallel between novelist and painter becomes obvious when considering Tolstoy's manner of character description. Perhaps unequaled among novelists, Tolstoy makes his readers apprehend the essence of his fictional characters by closely delineating their physical selves—their muscles, eyes, and nerves. Dimitri Merezhkovsky, in his classic early study, succinctly states, "By the motions of muscles or

10. See Malcolm Jones, "Problems of Communication in *Anna Karenina*," for further discussion of Tolstoy's technique of characterization as outward revelation of intrinsic personality.

nerves we enter shortly and directly into the internal world of his characters, begin to live with them and in them" (178). Tolstoy is a master in knowing what external gestures or features need to be described, as well as what conventional wrappings need to be removed, in order that the noumenal essence of character be represented, that we "live in them." He is, in this way, like Mihailov, who can see through the facade of Golenischev's polished but empty rhetoric to find his essential identity in his sensible features: "A mass of hair and a very open forehead gave a semblance of distinction to the face, which had only one expression—a petty, childish, restless expression concentrated just above the narrow bridge of the nose" (497).

The full significance of Tolstoy's and Mihailov's aesthetic is revealed in the manner by which it informs the dramatic action of characters. To Tolstoy, wrappings are the socially acquired, conventional traits that overdetermine a character to act in a way contradictory to the instinct and intuition of the essential self. These wrappings may also be considered social conventions, or, in terms of novelistic realism, manners. But, as R. P. Blackmur notes in his essay on *Anna Karenina*, manners are treated differently by Tolstoy, whose protagonists seek a Rousseauistic natural existence apart from society, than by Jane Austen, who usually celebrates her protagonists' codification by social conventions. Blackmur writes of Dolly and Oblonsky, "We see in this couple how it is that manners dictate the roles by which we escape acknowledging reality" (6). To Tolstoy, as with Kant, the apperception of self as noumenon makes noumenal reality accessible to consciousness, and characters lose this ability through extrinsic social roles. This point is the most important derived from the ekphrastic scenes of painting, for it is explored dramatically throughout the text. In the course of the narrative, Tolstoy shows that representational conventions concealing the inner self reflect the way social conventions perform the same function. When counterfeit artists learn technique from recognized schools of art, they become incapable of inner revelation; and when characters acquire social manners, they are blinded to the essential reality of themselves as noumena. Tolstoy's phenomenal-noumenal distinction is most clear as the Schopenhauerian one that separates the phenomenal, external world of appearances from the noumenal, inner will of things-in-themselves. In *The World as Will and Idea*, Schopenhauer writes that "only *internal* processes . . . have true reality . . . because the will alone is the thing-in-itself. . . . Manifoldness is only phenomenal, and the external events are only configurations of the phenomenal world" (2:568).[11] In his characteriza-

---

11. Sigrid McLaughlin has written the most detailed analysis of Schopenhauer's influence on Tolstoy, in "Some Aspects of Tolstoy's Intellectual Development: Tolstoy and Schopenhauer." I am indebted to McLaughlin for the parallels she discovers between

tions Tolstoy is careful to distinguish the extrinsic, usually social elements from the intrinsic, internal, and noumenal ones of will. But Tolstoy's realism forces him to concentrate on the physical manifestation of inner self, thus portraying fictionally a synthesis of mind and external reality.

The conflict between intuitive and conventional knowledge is portrayed in the text as a conflict between two systems of semiotic codes—language and physical gestures. Society functions almost entirely through the linguistic code, but in Tolstoy this code is most fallible and hypocritical. Thus, Tolstoy, like Cervantes and Austen, uses ekphrases to question the word-world relation. But unlike his predecessors, who concentrate upon the "proper" references of words and things, Tolstoy's critique of language is even more exacting in seeking a correspondent reference beyond the fallible medium of language. Tolstoy shows that language can be manipulated to disguise motivation, but through a semiotics of the body the internal processes of self as thing-in-itself communicate instinctively, directly, and honestly. Merezhkovsky notes of Tolstoy's characterization, "The language of gesture, if less varied than words, is more direct, expressive, and suggestive. It is easier to lie in words than by gesture or facial expression. One glance, one wrinkle, one quiver of a muscle in the face, may express the unutterable" (178). Revealing characters less by spoken words than by glances, wrinkles, quivers of muscles, the text strives to make readers unaware of reading literary descriptions, as realist paintings allow viewers to forget they are seeing paint on canvas. Malcolm Jones says of Tolstoyan characters, "We respond to their smiles, the pressure of their hands, just as characters in the book do" (89).[12]

The Eyes and Smile of Anna

The responses that readers and other interpreting characters have to the physical traits of characters in Tolstoy are similar to Vronsky's response

---

Tolstoy's thought in *War and Peace* and *Anna Karenina* and Schopenhauer's *World as Will and Idea* and *Two Basic Problems of Ethics*. Unless otherwise noted, I use McLaughlin's translations from Schopenhauer.

12. Since its publication in 1902, no work has surpassed Merezhkovsky's *Tolstoi as Man and Artist* in analyzing Tolstoy's ability to represent personality through physical characteristics. But Malcolm Jones, developing Merezhkovsky's points more fully by analyzing the ways characters communicate through these physical gestures, writes, "Tolstoy was well aware that people often express themselves and their deepest feelings involuntarily" (90).

to Mihailov's portrait of Anna—these traits capture some element of the characters' intrinsic selves. In fact, all the major (and many minor) characters of *Anna Karenina* are distinguished by unique physical details indexical of their intrinsic selves. There is Oblonsky's habitual smile, which, in its ability to infect everyone with its owner's empty and vacuous good-naturedness, is emblematic of his simple, harmless hedonism. Its untimely appearance during his argument with his wife, Dolly, over his innocuous little adultery sets off the crisis opening the novel. There is Dolly's twitching muscle on the right side of her face, which expresses the uneasiness and self-pity she feels for having to raise a large family while her husband, an incorrigible adulterer, gives little solace. There is Karenin's habit, so distasteful to Anna, of cracking his knuckles, which tells, more directly than words, of his sexual tension with his wife, of his unalterable stiffness and formality. There is Nikolai's constant scowl, which expresses the outrage he feels for the life slowly drawing from him. There is Varenka, who, thin and without color, is described by Tolstoy as a flower past its bloom, an admirable but pitiable human being whose opportunities in life (like the proposal she almost receives from Koznyshev) have faded. There is Levin, whose passion and vitality never fail to register upon his face, blushing easily, jaw trembling when aroused. And, of course, there is Anna, described early by Vronsky, who notices "the suppressed animation which played over her face and flitted between her sparkling eyes and the slight smile curving her red lips . . . as though her nature were so brimming over with something that against her will it expressed itself now in a radiant look, now in a smile. She deliberately shrouded the light in her eyes but in spite of herself it gleamed in the faintly perceptible smile" (75). The animation in her eyes and smile, which first attracts Vronsky to Anna, are more than mere details in Tolstoy's description—they reveal to him and others her essential nature.[13] What her features show "brimming over" is an elemental passion for life, a capacity for transcending emotion that is "suppressed" but expresses itself "against her [conscious] will." Most important, Anna's essentializing trait is rather a convergence of traits combining eyes, smile, radiance, and animation. Like the arbitrary focus the grease spot gives Mihailov, these external features of Anna

13. Several critics remark on Anna's eyes and smile. In perhaps the best analysis of these traits, R. F. Christian comments in *Tolstoy: A Critical Introduction*, "In describing Anna's appearance, Tolstoy emphasizes the features which are an outward and inner reflection of an inner state—the expression in her eyes, her smile, the radiance which comes from within and is not a surface adornment" (194). Michael Pursglove, in "The Smiles of *Anna Karenina*," comments on Tolstoy's use of the smile throughout the novel to differentiate between various characters.

harmonize in such a way to reflect the inner unity of her noumenal self, which Cain interprets as "an excess of vitality that should find release in marriage and motherhood" (109), or what Schopenhauer might call the Will to Life. But her marriage to Karenin offers no such outlet. Merezhkovsky finds in Tolstoy's references to Anna's "unruly curls, so easily becoming unkempt, the same tension, 'the excess of something ever ready for passion' " (176). But Tolstoy more constantly locates this animation, this excess of vitality, this inner will, in Anna's eyes and smile. In fact, the smile is the most often described detail in *Anna Karenina*: it is used to describe eighty-five different characters, and the noun for smile, *ulybka*, and the verb for smiling, *alybat'sja*, appear 613 times in the novel (Pursglove 43). Admittedly, both eyes and smiles are used by many novelists to reveal their characters' emotional states, but the degree and particularity of their uses in Tolstoy are unusual. Characters in Tolstoy's novels smile and show emotion in their eyes involuntarily, thus revealing their inner selves undisguised by social conventions. Michael Pursglove notes, "The spontaneous reactions of the flesh are stronger than the rationalizations of the intellect" (43).

It is interesting that although Anna's indexical expression is used by Tolstoy as an essentializing one, it is nonetheless altered by the subjective responses of her various interpreters. This particular expression affects not only Vronsky—it attracts many to Anna, who give it meanings unique to her relationship with them. To Dolly, when Anna comes to comfort her and reconcile her with Stiva, the expression means compassion: "Under their thick lashes her brilliant eyes suddenly filled with tears" (81). To Kitty, at first, the expression captures the older woman's youthful vitality: "Anna was not like . . . the mother of an eight-year-old son. Her lithe movements, her freshness, and the persistent animation of her face, which broke out now in her smile, now in her glance, would have made her look like a girl of twenty" (86). But later, after Anna has won Vronsky from her, Kitty interprets the expression differently: "She saw that Anna was intoxicated with the admiration she had aroused . . . saw the quivering, flashing light in her eyes, the smile of happiness and excitement that involuntarily curved her lips" (95). For Vronsky, the expression confirms her love: "Her face looked tired and had none of that play of animation which peeped out now in her smile and now in her eyes; but for an instant as she glanced at him her eyes lighted up" (121).

Tolstoy concentrates so much on this expression of Anna's to dramatize externally the internal, spiritual changes that occur as her affair with Vronsky begins and progresses. The trait epitomizing Anna in Mihailov's representation thus becomes a focus to describe her tragic decline. Concentrating on changes in this trait, the text details the distorting of her Schopenhauerian Will to Life, becoming at last a Will to Death. Like her marriage to Karenin, her affair with Vronsky cannot provide adequate release for her vitality. Both lives, both possible worlds, are falsely overwritten by conventional images that deny a natural outlet for the Will to Life, which is then diverted into destructive channels—jealousy, insomnia, and drug addiction. In the end she denies life as ardently as she had embraced it earlier. Tolstoy makes her life-denial apparent through the viewpoint of Dolly, who, when visiting Vronsky's country estate, is shocked by Anna's easy talk of contraceptives and her apparent lack of affection or motherly concern for her daughter by Vronsky. But the change is most apparent in her expression. Dolly notices still the faint half-smile, but a new expression has become more dominant. Dolly notices "Anna's strange new habit of half-closing her eyes. And she remembered that it was just when her inner feelings were touched upon that Anna dropped her eyelids. 'As if she half-shut her eyes to her own life, so as not to see everything' " (659). The expression once showing Anna open to life is replaced by one now showing her closed to it.

But Tolstoy allows another character to observe the change in Anna's expression in a late scene involving the ekphrasis of Mihailov's portrait. That character is Levin, who, as the other major character of the novel, along with Anna, is given a story paralleling and converging with hers. However, Levin knows the earlier Anna only through Mihailov's portrait, one capturing the truth of self. Joan Grossman remarks, "It suited Tolstoy's design that the moment recorded in Mihailov's painting should be that of Anna's greatest happiness as a woman and thus of her greatest fascination" (7). And it suited Tolstoy for Levin to observe Anna on the eve of her tragedy through the ekphrastic work of art capturing "the sweetest expression of her soul": "A full-length portrait of a woman . . . arrested Levin's attention. It was the portrait of Anna painted in Italy by Mihailov . . . which in the brilliant illumination seemed to step out of its frame. . . . It was not a picture but a living, lovely woman with black curling hair, bare shoulders and arms, and a dreamy half-smile on her soft, downy lips" (728–29). Anna's eyes and smile entrance Levin, as they had Vronsky earlier, but only because Mihailov had understood the noumenal basis of that expression and represented it in her sensible features. Then Levin turns to see the real Anna, "not in the same attitude, nor with the same expression, but with the same perfection of beauty which the artist had caught in the picture. She was less dazzling in reality, but, on the other hand, there was something fresh and seductive in the living woman which was not in the portrait" (729).

The "something fresh and seductive" is the change most evident to
Levin, who intuitively compares the ekphrastic painting with the real
woman. When the portrait was painted, Anna's inner beauty was natural,
emanating from her free, joyful love for Vronsky. But now that she has
become so completely overdetermined by the conventional image of the
kept lover in Vronsky's romanticized portrait, she augments her beauty
with those conventions: ample cosmetics, perfume, lavish hair styles and
dresses. And most important, she tries to be seductive rather than rely
on her former, natural charm. And she is seductive with Levin, too:
"She had unconsciously been doing her utmost . . . to arouse in Levin a
feeling of love—as she had lately fallen into the habit of doing with all
the young men she met" (736). This ekphrastic scene illustrates through
external details Anna's slow degradation. The earlier, natural Anna, as
captured in Mihailov's portrait, and the later one, debased by the glitter
of conventional charm, represent both the true and false arts Tolstoy
describes in his essay: "Real art, like the wife of an affectionate husband,
needs no ornaments. But counterfeit art, like a prostitute, must always
be decked out" (166).

This ekphrastic scene is also significant, of course, because it is the
first and only meeting of the novel's two main characters. But more
important, their meeting connects the earlier ekphrastic scene of Mihailov's creativity with a later ekphrastic scene of reading or viewing.
Citing the famous statement by Tolstoy on "the keystone" of the novel's
architecture, Grossman claims that this scene may be that keystone.
While it is inviting to see Anna's and Levin's meeting as an important
link or perhaps even the novel's keystone, its significance is more than
its bringing the two major characters on stage at once. If it is the
keystone, or the detail explaining the whole, it can claim that role only
in relation to the earlier ekphrastic scenes that represent both the acts of
artistic production and consumption. Providing this aesthetic model, the
scene "indirectly," through "images, actions, situations," gives the key
to the text's mimetic truth.[14]

The Limits of Reason

The full significance of the ekphrastic scenes and their debates over
intuition and reason, inner truth and convention, is developed more fully

14. In "Tolstoy's Portrait of Anna: Keystone in the Arch," Joan Grossman argues that
the scene portraying the single meeting of the two main characters can lay claim to being
the "keystone of the arch" of the novel's architecture for two reasons. Not only does it
provide the crucial meeting, it also is important for Levin's viewing of Anna's portrait by
Mihailov whose estimate of Anna stands for Tolstoy's own.

as the text explores their real-life existential implications. As in *Don Quixote* and *Emma*, the ekphrases of *Anna Karenina* reveal both the falsity of a given discourse and the truth of a valorized one, which are then more fully dramatized through character action. Tolstoy's text, however, seeks a more keen discursive correspondence to actuality by exposing even more fully the faults of a coherence view emphasizing the linguistic construction of reality. The valorized correspondent discourse is one that, if possible, would dispense with language entirely. Concentrating so much upon gestures, facial expressions, and characterizing physical traits, Tolstoy shows that they are a semiotic system more accurate and trustworthy than language, which creates a false world through socially conventionalized manners. The text dramatizes that removing the socially and linguistically constructed layers concealing essential character or reality is analogous to Mihailov's "removing the wrappings." Speaking of Tolstoy's use of physical traits as a means of characterization, Malcolm Jones writes, "Such gestures may in a commonly understood context speak more eloquently than a thousand words" (91). The commonly understood context Jones most emphasizes is romantic intimacy, which, for example, allows Levin's cough to be for Kitty a sign of his dissatisfaction or which makes Anna's eyes the means by which Vronsky discovers her need for him. And most remarkably, there is Levin's second proposal to Kitty, in which he spells out on a tabletop only the initial letters of the words to his rather long question. His gestures and expressions allow her to understand first and fill in the words afterward. She replies in the same fashion, and Levin too understands before he knows the words. This scene is reminiscent of the "voiceless" proposal to Emma by Knightley. Jones argues that Anna and Vronsky's later failure to communicate as instinctively as at the outset is the source of their increasing alienation from each other. On the other hand, Levin is Tolstoy's most significant vehicle for revealing the proper method of communicating knowledge, one beyond language and conventions. One of his purposes in the text is to represent the actual textual world of inner reality to contrast with the conventionalized possible world in which Anna increasingly lives. This contrast is most apparent in the text's development of the "death theme," which is framed by the same conceptual vocabulary as the ekphrastic debate.

Levin is consistently represented as virtually refusing to live further unless he comes to an understanding of life's basic mystery, the meaning of death. The novel's death theme is presented first as mere background to more significant action. It is announced by the death of the guard at the train station where Anna and Vronsky meet, builds momentum with Levin's realization of Nikolai's terminal illness and with Anna's near death at childbirth, reaches a climax with Nikolai's death and Anna's suicide, and finally is resolved by Levin's rejection of suicide because of a transcendent vision. Levin is the primary figure in the development of this theme, for throughout he actively entertains all received answers to the question of death but reaches a satisfactory conclusion only when these conventional "wrappings" are removed. Levin's obsession with death begins when he realizes the imminence of his brother's death. Nikolai's visit to his estate precipitates this realization and underscores Levin's early incapacity to understand. The brothers' farewell, one of the most moving scenes of the novel, shows how their innate needs to understand what is happening and to communicate sympathy with each other have been muted by the roles each serves in society, by the insufficiency of manners and language:

> Levin . . . felt that if they both stopped keeping up appearances and spoke straight from the heart . . . said just what they were thinking and feeling—they would simply have looked into each other's eyes, and Constantine could only have said, "You're dying, you're dying!" and Nikolai could only have answered, "I know I am, but I'm afraid, afraid, afraid!". . . But that would make life impossible, and so Constantine tried to do what he had been trying to do all his life, and never could learn to do, though . . . many people knew so well how to do it, and without it life was impossible: he tried to say something different from what he was thinking. (375)

In this scene, Levin struggles to confess an emotion from the most inward part of self but is constrained by the limited modes of communication available to him through overdetermining social linguistic codes. Peter Jones interestingly defines Levin's struggle: "Since any man is to be defined in terms of his internal essence, roles, regarded as existing only in external social contexts, inhibit the realization of that essence" (81). The codes overdetermining the actions and discourse of his social roles as male, estate owner, brother, and human being governed by reason—wrappings, as it were—provide Levin with no means to comfort Nikolai or seek understanding himself.

Already Levin has attempted to find the solution to his problem through reason, a mode of knowing analogous to Kantian theoretical reason in that both Kant and Tolstoy treat it as detached from the sensible world motivating moral action. Reason is embodied by Koznyshev, Levin's eldest brother, whose role in the death theme parallels that of the critic Golenischev in the ekphrastic scene. Koznyshev first appears in the novel when Levin interrupts his discussion with a famous professor of philosophy over psychological and physiological phenomena. Listening, Levin reflects, "He had never connected these scientific deductions . . . with questions of life and death" (37). The conversation frustrates, for "they linked these scientific questions with the spiritual . . . but promptly beat a hasty retreat and plunged back into the sea of subtle distinctions, reservations, quotations, allusions and references" (37). When Levin asks about the existence of the soul after death, they, dumbfounded, reply that insufficient "data" exist to answer. According to Isaiah Berlin, Tolstoy's view of reality makes "logical and scientific constructions—the well defined, symmetrical patterns of human reason—seem smooth, thin, empty, 'abstract' and totally ineffective as a means either of description or of analysis of anything that lives" (63). And Tolstoy shows here that the discourses of science and theoretical reason are totally ineffective in understanding death and the hereafter.

Other characters are used by Tolstoy to compare their conventionalized reactions to death with Levin's evolving intuitive understanding. For example, Vronsky and Karenin, at what they think is Anna's deathbed, show how social manners govern men during such crises. Karenin is a purely social being, a bureaucrat whose actions are overdetermined entirely by social codes. Thus, when Anna reveals her liaison with Vronsky, Karenin orders her to maintain the conventional appearance of a devoted wife, even though he knows that her intuitive affections will never be his again. But Karenin's drastic change when Anna is near death shows that even such a regimented and emotionally stifled man possesses an inner self, guided by intuitive Christian sympathy and struggling to break through the social facade. It naturally emerges momentarily here, for he forgives Anna and Vronsky and cares for their illegitimate daughter as would a father. However, very soon his spontaneous intuition is brutally overwritten by more powerful social codes: "He felt that besides the blessed spiritual force that guided his soul, there was another force, brutal and as powerful, or more powerful . . . that . . . would not allow him the humble peace he longed for . . . he knew in advance that everyone was against him and that he would not be allowed to do what seemed to him now so natural and right, but would be compelled to do what was wrong, but seemed the proper thing to them" (445, 451).

In spite of Vronsky's passion for Anna and the sacrifices he makes for her, he is as governed by social convention as is Karenin, and his reactions to Anna's illness are as predicated upon his social role. The social code with which he originally judged his affair with Anna was based upon what he perceived he could gain in status by such an alliance:

"He was very well aware that in their [fashionable people's] eyes the role of the disappointed lover of a young girl or of any single woman might be ridiculous; but the role of a man pursuing a married woman . . . had something fine and grand about it and could never be ridiculous" (144). And his perception is true, for even his mother thinks, "Nothing . . . gave such a finishing touch to a brilliant young man as an affair in the highest society" (191). With Anna dying, Vronsky attempts suicide not from the intuitive despair caused by the impending loss of his lover but rather out of his humiliation at the hands of Karenin, whom he had earlier viewed as "a pitiful object" (441). Facing the once-ludicrous husband's magnanimity, "Vronsky felt Karenin's elevation and his own abasement" (441). Only because of his disgrace in the terms of social conventions does Vronsky attempt suicide.

Both Karenin and Vronsky serve in the text to exemplify those who shop in the marketplace of social codes to find a standard by which to live and to understand death, instead of turning inward to find the truer signs of intuition. Tolstoy treats Karenin's later search for meaning ironically and comically. When he last appears in the novel, Karenin is under the influence of Lydia Ivanovna, who offers simplistic pseudospiritual answers to his problems, including his fear of dying. The countess enlists the aid of a medium and spiritualist, who, she brags, has so comforted a society matron for the death of her only child that "now she thanks God for the death of her child" (769). The scene of Karenin's session with the medium and Countess Ivanovna is made farcical by being recorded through Oblonsky's befuddled mind: "The most incongruous thoughts whirled through his brain. 'Marie Sanin is glad her child's dead. . . . To be saved, one need only have faith, and the monks don't know the way to salvation but the Countess Lydia Ivanovna does. . . . I wonder why my head feels so heavy? Is it the cognac or because this is so very odd?' " (770). This Tolstoyan spoof of conventional pseudospiritualist approaches to life's mysteries is similar to *War and Peace*'s humorous account of masonic ritual. Tolstoy is as critical of empty mystical solutions to the question of death as of the solutions provided by reason. Berlin writes, "He was against unintelligible mysteries, against mists of antiquity, against any kind of recourse to mumbojumbo" (46).

The scene of the death of Nikolai, attended by Kitty and Levin, is presented as the truly intuitive way death should be approached, in contrast with the falsely conventional solutions offered by manners, reason, and spiritualism. Nikolai's death has haunted Levin throughout the novel, but when news comes that he is dying, Levin is unprepared. Out of an intuitive desire to fulfill her marital vows and comfort her

husband, Kitty offers to come along, but Levin, as much governed by
manners at this point as Vronsky and Karenin, is appalled, for to have
his wife in the same room with Nikolai's mistress, the fallen Agatha
Mihalovna, would violate the overdetermining social code. However,
Kitty's sincere tears persuade Levin, and at the deathbed, she and
Agatha, unguided by convention and reason, are the only ones who
know how to comfort and nurse the dying man. Thinking of how they
deal with death, Levin comes to an important conclusion:

> He had more intellect than his wife and Agatha Mihalovna, and
> he could not help knowing that when he thought of death he
> thought with all the force of his intellect. He knew, too, that
> many great and virile minds . . . did not know one hundredth
> part of what his wife and Agatha Mihalovna knew. . . . Both
> knew . . . what sort of a thing life and what death was, and
> though neither of them could have answered, or even have
> comprehended, the questions that presented themselves to
> Levin, they . . . were never under an instant's uncertainty as to
> how to deal with the dying. . . . But Levin and others like him,
> though they might be able to say a good many things about
> death, obviously did not know anything about it. (523)

The actions of those responding to death in accordance with reason and
the conventional manners of social codes are analogous to Vronsky's
painting through the conventions of artistic codes, and Kitty's natural,
instinctive response corresponds to Mihailov's intuitive response allowing him to paint what is innately within the soul. The distinction is
between a self-conscious lack of spontaneity, motivated by selfish and
subjective desire, and an innate sense giving rise to ethical action. In both
cases, a Kantian *sensus communus* guides aesthetic as well as moral action,
proving that "beauty is a symbol of morality" in its transcendent relation
to the sensible world of human practices. To Tolstoy, death is something
impossible to understand purely by means of theoretical reason or
overdetermining social codes: it is, rather, something understood only
in the context of life's natural activities. "What is to be done?" (15)
thinks Oblonsky in the novel's first chapter, and Tolstoy's late work
What Then Must We Do? (1886) proposes the same question. Both
highlight Tolstoy's requirement that intuitive reflection be tied existentially to innate ethical practices and not artificially imposed social codes.

Tolstoy makes another important use of the death theme to dramatize
the debate over language and representation begun in the painting
ekphrasis. It serves to underscore his own language use. The deathbed is

used commonly by Tolstoy to illustrate how characters transcend the evasive patterns of socially codified discourse and speak eternal truths. Bakhtin writes of this: Tolstoy's search for a monologic language expressing a transhistorical and essential truth, not the dialogic language so fully embedded in social practices. Gary Saul Morson notes that Tolstoy sought "speech centers that are traditionally regarded as privileged, as somehow outside of the interests of everyday life and as protected from dialogue" (136). Deathbed scenes provide speech centers where language attains such a purity of expression that it reveals essential truth.[15] These scenes represent another of Tolstoy's attempts to find an absolutely correspondent representation that transcends the problematics of discourse, whose coherentist and socially constructed relation to reality threatens the foundation of an essentialist source of meaning.

The Light of Unreason

In his ekphrastic scenes, Tolstoy clarifies the distinction between those who approach spiritual questions from the position of convention, manners, and theoretical reason and those who approach them from the basis of natural intuition. Viewing Mihailov's masterpiece, "Christ before Pilate," which expresses "the incarnation . . . of the spiritual life" (500), both Golenischev and Vronsky respond to the ekphrasis within the interpretive constraints provided by their conventionalized ideology. Golenischev, anxious to prove his critical intelligence, selects an obvious aspect of the painting upon which to base a cliché-ridden lecture. And Vronsky, viewing a work articulating the schema of the spirit, attributes its success to the methods he has followed—the imitation of conventionalized methods. "There's technique for you" (500), he cries, ignorant of the compliment's inappropriateness. He would not have understood Mihailov's indignation:

> He was always hearing that word technique, and could never make out what people understood by it. He knew it meant a

15. For a full discussion of Bakhtin's treatment of Tolstoy's monologic language and such privileged speech centers as the deathbed, see Gary Saul Morson, "Tolstoy's Absolute Language." Morson argues that Tolstoy's discourse aspires toward the ahistorical, unconditional, and noncontingent ideal for speech of biblical certainty—as in Tolstoy's description in *War and Peace* of the speech of the Deity (1330), which is "absolute and unconditional in the sense that, unlike any utterance of a man, it is not a function of the circumstances that evoked it, and its meaning is not qualified by an audience whose potential reactions have had to be taken into account" (127).

mechanical ability to draw and paint, quite apart from the content of the drawing. He had noticed that even in actual praise technique was opposed to essential quality, as though it were possible to paint a bad picture with talent. He knew that a great deal of attention and care were required in bringing the idea to birth and producing it; but as to the art of painting, the technique, it did not exist. If the things he saw had been revealed to a child, or to his cook, they would have been able to peel off the outer husk of what they saw. (500)

When Golenischev suggests that Mihailov might have altered his technique in painting the figure of Christ, the artist replies, "I cannot paint a Christ that is not within my soul" (501). He stands then in direct contrast to Vronsky, who "could not conceive that it was possible to be ignorant of the different schools of painting and to be inspired directly by what is within the soul" (491). Vronsky and Golenischev, in relying upon learned technique in interpreting and creating spiritual art, suggest those characters who interpret the spiritual question of death from the social conventions of manners, reason, and esoteric spiritualism. Appropriately, Levin gradually accepts Mihailov's view of spirituality as that which, residing within, is accessible even to a child. It is a knowledge of spirit or inner reality that is innate and not acquired, acted upon and not contemplated.

Although Levin is not directly included in the ekphrastic debate that clarifies the text's representational norm in the correspondence-coherence dialectic, he is the primary figure through which Tolstoy dramatically validates the intuitive, essentialist discourse guiding the novel's language use and theme. It is his world, created by his discourse, that proves false the conventionalized world created by Vronsky and Emma. From the beginning, Levin is dispositionally among those characters given the realization that life is to be experienced, reflected upon intuitively, and not intellectualized through intertextual knowledge and theoretical reason. The rationalist Koznyshev's visit to Levin's estate proves this early in the novel. Through this character contrast, Tolstoy advances dramatically the intuition-convention dichotomy introduced in the ekphrastic scene. He also furthers his critique of language as a false representational medium to validate the specular and sensory mode that informs the novel's composition. For example, Levin is frustrated by Koznyshev's circumscribing nature within the confining categories of reason and the semantic traps of words: "Levin did not like talking and hearing about the beauty of nature. Words detracted from the beauty of what he saw" (261). And Koznyshev cannot understand when Levin explains that he mows with his peasants because it is "so hard that there is no time for thinking" (269). Tolstoy's description of Levin's mowing is one of the great paeans in literature to natural labor: "When he forgot what he was doing, he mowed without effort and his line was almost as smooth and good as Titus's. But as soon as he began thinking . . . he was at once conscious how hard the task was, and would mow badly" (271–72). Tolstoy shows that the inner language of conscious thought weakens the intuition, which is most profitably expressed in unreflective, wordless action. Levin again shows he implicitly understands this when he goes snipe shooting with Vasenka Veslovsky. The loquacious Veslovsky makes Levin self-conscious, and he misses everything at which he aims. Yet when he goes alone the next morning, he submits to instincts and wordless actions and shoots nineteen birds.[16]

These scenes introduce Levin's potential to develop this innate sense, and in the course of the novel his fuller awareness grows. Death is the means by which he arrives at his knowledge. From these earlier illustrations the novel moves toward even more intense realizations of death— the actual and contemplated suicides of Anna and Levin. Through this contrast Tolstoy makes a forceful statement about the existential consequences of knowledge gained by intuition as compared to that overdetermined by social codes. Also important is the fact that he describes these different forms of knowledge imagistically, not through abstract language, which the novel has derided. In both cases Tolstoy uses light and dark imagery. Anna, ruthlessly overdetermined by false ideology, has lost sight of her inner, spiritual nature and has a demonic vision of death: "Suddenly the shadow of the screen wavered, pounced on the whole cornice, the whole ceiling. Shadows from the other side darted across to meet it . . . 'Death!' she thought" (784). After losing all the sources of sustenance temporarily given by her alternative world of false conventions—her adulterous intrigue, society friends, and artificial religion—Anna concludes that death is her only recourse. Her lonely death is described by means of the shifting images cast from flickering candlelight: "The candle by which she had been reading the book filled with trouble and deceit, sorrow and evil, flared up with a brighter light, illuminating for her everything that before had been enshrouded in darkness, grew dim and went out forever" (802).

As opposed to the tragedy caused by Anna's false consciousness, Levin's crisis is resolved successfully because of what he learns intuitively, wordlessly, and apart from the overdetermining conventions that

16. For a full discussion of Tolstoy's rejection of reason in the period he composed *Anna Karenina*, see Boris Eikhenbaum, *Tolstoi in the Seventies*.

enslave the spirit. E. B. Greenwood contends that "Tolstoy's treatment of death is very important . . . in connection with the bounds of sense" (100). Cut loose from the security of social convention, Levin explores the bounds of sense in the metaphysical quest of the last chapters. In the deepest period of his despair, as nearly alone as Anna, he thinks, "In infinite time, in infinite matter, in infinite space, an organic cell stands out, will hold together awhile and then burst, and that cell is Me" (823). And he concludes that suicide is the only escape from this intolerable realization. He is saved, however, from Anna's fate because he has developed the sustaining forces she lacks. His sense of intuition is developed fully enough that a simple statement by a peasant triggers a revelation. While Levin is speaking with his tenant Fiodor about Fokanich, a common acquaintance, the *muzhik* says, "One man lives for his own wants and nothing else . . . but Fokanich is an upright old man. He thinks of his soul. He does not forget God" (829). Though not totally wordless, the statement, because of its laconic simplicity, appeals directly to Levin's innate sense of right and wrong and circumvents both the obfuscating channels of theoretical reason and the discourse of false ideology. And even though the truth of Fiodor's remark affects him so profoundly that he thinks he has discovered the meaning of life, Levin cannot express the thought in words: "I was in search of an answer to my question. But reason could not give an answer to my question—reason is incommensurable with the problem. The answer has been given me by life itself, through my knowledge of what is right and what is wrong. And this knowledge I did not acquire in any way: it was given to me as it is to everybody—*given* because I could not have got it from anywhere" (832). Levin realizes that "the only knowledge I and all men possess that is firm, incontestable, and clear . . . cannot be explained by reason . . . [because] it is outside the chain of cause and effect" (830). Levin repeats Kant's rejection of pure reason because it is outside the categories of understanding, which are defined by the a priori concepts of space, time, and causality. But also rejecting mechanical explanations, Levin turns to "Plato, Spinoza, Kant, Schelling, Hegel, and Schopenhauer, who gave a non-materialistic explanation of life" (822). From Schopenhauer, Tolstoy derived the distinction between materialist knowledge that is limited by causality and innate consciousness that "confirms the freedom of action under the premise of willing" (*World* 3:534). In the epilogue of *War and Peace*, Tolstoy echoes Schopenhauer's concept of freedom but is not optimistic about man's ability to be entirely independent of causes: "To imagine a man perfectly free and not subject to the law of inevitability, we must imagine him all along *beyond space, beyond time,* and *free from dependence upon causes*" (1346). Elsewhere in the essayistic epilogue and more dramatically in *Anna Karenina* Tolstoy suggests, like Schopenhauer, that whatever partial freedom humans experience comes in moments when it is possible to turn away from the phenomenal world of causes and toward the noumenal one wherein lies the freedom of moral choice. As Schopenhauer teaches, that turn is inward, for "only *internal* processes . . . are real . . . external events are only configurations of the phenomenal world" (*World* 2:568).[17] Even though apparently contradictory, Tolstoy is consistent in denying the absolute claims of pure reason and materialism, extremes that he avoids through his own transcendental empirical methodology.

Levin realizes that the internal process defining goodness is available to everyone, just as Mihailov knows that his artistic insight can be achieved by a child. Both characters realize a priori truths that transcend reason. The truth that Levin receives from Fiodor has the tone and the effect of a Kantian categorical imperative. Morson notes that Tolstoy, in searching for a language to express eternal, transhistorical truths, uses a discourse that is "timeless, anonymous, and above all categorical," one that exhibits "characteristics of both biblical commands and proverbs" (128). It is a discourse purified of contaminating socially contingent meanings. However, for Tolstoy the purest communication of truth is one that does not rely on language at all, for language, creating socially constructed realities, fails as intuitive expression of true reality. As Tolstoyan characters do not reveal their real selves by means of spoken words, the medium of reason, so even Levin's final revelation is presented indirectly. It, like Anna's death, is suggested by light and dark imagery. But while her imagery, cast by the shrinking light of the candle, is narrow and claustrophobic, his is expansive—the sudden light and dark of an electrical storm.

The experience of the storm is Levin's encounter with the sublime in nature. Although the ekphrastic scene of the paintings focuses the reader's attention upon beauty, a comforting accord between our theoretical and moral selves, this experience of the sublime destroys all comfortable notions with its terrifying reminder of the complete otherness of nature, its wild and untamed aspect. Kant views the sublime as a reminder of a noumenal world beyond the capacity of our senses and understanding to categorize. This is Levin's experience when "there was a glare of light, the whole earth seemed on fire, and the vault of heaven cracked overhead" (847). Later, Levin is reminded of this world beyond sense and understanding when he again sees lightning, and with "each

---

17. See McLaughlin, 190–93, for a discussion of the similarities between Tolstoy's and Schopenhauer's conceptions of freedom and necessity.

flash not only the Milky Way but even the brightest of stars vanished, but . . . would reappear in their places as if thrown there by some unerring hand" (851). Unable fully to comprehend this experience of the sublime, Levin nonetheless sees in it evidence of a world beyond self—either self-interest or self-knowledge—and thus turns away from those egocentric concerns that have plagued him. Most important, the storm threatens Kitty and their infant son, and the flash of lightning, which he thinks may have harmed them, also shocks him into recognizing what they mean to him. As the sky illuminates Levin's way back to the world and responsibility from his despair, so it lights Kitty's way to Levin: "She would not have been able to make out his expression had not a flash of lightning that blotted out the stars illuminated it for her . . . seeing that he was calm and happy she smiled at him" (852). This experience turns Levin away from self and toward others and moral action, for in Kant's terms, when we encounter the sublime in nature we are forced to defend our insignificance by asserting our moral nature.[18] And according to Zoltan Hájnády, Tolstoy's definition of morality is transindividual: "The reason for individual life cannot be found in itself, but in community life" (289).[19] What is important, the visual imagery associated with Levin's revelation convinces more fully than his exhaustive verbal descriptions elsewhere in the text.

The story of Levin thus completes Tolstoy's dramatizing the ekphrastic contrast between naturally intuitive and correspondent modes of knowing against those derived from the coherent systems of intertextual and social conventions. Intuition as a mode of understanding is valorized because its physical, sensory response reveals the internal essences of reality and thus achieves a synthesis of mind and matter divided by the rival theories of rationalism and empiricism as well as by subjective and objective interpreters within the Kantian paradigm. The fictional means by which the text achieves this synthesis is by positing an absolute correspondence through a perception purified of socially constructed codes, an intuitive perception raised to the status of an a priori category by post-Kantians such as Friedrich Heinrich Jacobi, who called it a supranatural sensualism. However, Tolstoy also reveals that the Kantian

18. For a discussion of Kant's theory of the sublime as it relates to fiction, see Richard Kuhn's "The Beautiful and the Sublime."

19. In "The Starry Heavens Above and the Moral Law Within," Zoltan Hájnády discusses the way in which Tolstoy's novels offer two choices for human action—" 'a life for others' or 'a life for ourselves.' " Tolstoy recognizes that what is needed is a synthesis of the two: "the ideal happiness wherein the individual and the community find each other and universal human fate is reflected in individual life" (286). Levin is Tolstoy's vehicle for discovering this synthesis.

and post-Kantian project of positing a priori categories is problematized by the fictional conventions used to represent them.

Perception as Pure

Rousseau, an early influence on Tolstoy, wrote in *Emile* that he wanted his protagonist to learn to paint not from other men's works but directly from nature. Tolstoy's anti-intellectualism is similar to this concept of Rousseau's.[20] It is made manifest by his avowed suspicions of the linguistic conventions of his medium and his yearning to describe exactly what is in nature. In *What Is Art?* Tolstoy condemns abstract conceptions of beauty and notes that in Russian, "by the word *krasota* [beauty] we mean that which pleases the sight" (13). Tolstoy tries to make language become, instead of symbolic signification, a medium of pictorial representation, "that which pleases the sight." Ultimately, he desires that his readers visualize so distinctly that they see the text not as verbal artifact but rather as life itself. His model for an ideal reader's response is Levin, who, when viewing the portrait of Anna, judges, "It was not a picture but a living, lovely woman" (728). Stylistically, Tolstoy sought to make the medium of language disappear to allow readers the illusion of direct sensory access to the innate realities of his characters. In composing *Anna Karenina* Tolstoy consciously simplified his style as compared to that of *War and Peace.* By using repetitive cadences, deliberately repetitious word choices, and a uniformity of tone, Tolstoy achieves a style in which language is more nearly self-effacing. Boris Eikhenbaum writes that "the entire novel . . . is written in the tone of intent but cold . . . observation from a detached point of view" (134). This transparency of style supports Tolstoy's valorizing intuitive, nonrational modes of communication.

In using a portrait as the ekphrastic simulacrum of representation, Tolstoy invests his model with a truth-value transcending the problematic motivations of social discourse. And in illustrating representation through a specular poetics, he defines a space in the imagination for pure, intuitive perception, in which the harmony of phenomenal detail can correspond to the noumenal harmony of the inner self as both will and thing-in-itself. The parergonal frame of the portrait encloses a space

20. See E. B. Greenwood's "Tolstoy and Religion" for a discussion of Rousseau's influence upon Tolstoy's religious and moral thought. According to Greenwood, Tolstoy felt, like Rousseau, that morality and religion "must be 'natural,' in the peculiar sense that it must be apprehensible without the need for specialist intellectual knowledge" (151).

wherein the extrinsic wrappings of conventionality fall away from an essentializing trait to reveal the intrinsic nature of self. Through a transcending intuitive comprehension, the artist-as-genius renders physical details so concretely that spiritual actualities can be perceived by appealing to the genius of taste in the intuitive viewer. Intuition is the model of knowing the novel promotes, and the romantic literary use of intuitive knowledge has its basis in the Kantian and post-Kantian project of using aesthetic pleasure and practical reason as a bridge between the sensible world of things and the supersensible world of reason and spirit. The etymology of "intuition" (Lat. *intueri*, "to look at") reveals its sensible basis. This is also true for "aesthetic" (Gr. *aisthēsis*, "sensation," including inner sense or feeling). In the first *Critique*, Kant identifies the *transcendental schema* as mediary between the two realms, the thought of a sensible image that can be subsumed by the rational categories of the understanding. The basic categories for Kant, "time and space, taken together, are the pure forms of all sensible intuition, and so are what make *a priori* synthetic propositions possible" (*Reason* 80).

Kant's schematic explanation of how sense impressions are spatio-temporally reproduced in an inner sense through the imagination lays the groundwork for the later philosophies of pure perception in both Husserl and Heidegger—the former emphasizing the priority of consciousness, or inner sense, through intentional acts, and the latter the truth of the being of objects through *alētheia*, unconcealedness. And Tolstoy's work represents the most ambitious fictional attempt at a similar reconciliation of sense and spirit, or mind, in a purified perception evading social contingency. The power and beauty of Tolstoy's work reside partly in his successful stylistic and thematic use of a correspondent epistemology relying upon an inner, intuitive understanding and not strictly an empirical one. However, another significance of this particular text, *Anna Karenina*, is that it implicitly dramatizes the boundaries of this paradigm's attempt ultimately to resolve the oppositional conflict through synthesis. Tolstoy carried the implications of Kantian representation to its logical extreme, tested it, saw its limitations, and ultimately rejected it, as he later did all his early works, including *Anna Karenina*. In these texts, particularly *Anna Karenina*, the appearance of the social, intertextual, and coherentist discourse as false ideology problematizes the textual valorization of an ideal correspondence.

Whether called bracketing, unconcealing, or removing the wrappings, this erasure of medium, a striving for an ultimate correspondence with object or spirit is problematized by the emphasis upon discourse and motivation. For example, Tolstoy also shows that if one converts the frame of the ekphrastic portrait into the frames of the individual perceptions and motivations characterized in the text, the space or frame is not pure—it is easily translated into the subjective modes of ideology and desire, as can be seen by the various ways characters transform Anna's supposedly essentializing expression according to their relation to her. Alexander Gelley, writing on perception in fiction, makes this clear: "The visual faculty can never be presumed to operate as a pure percept in fiction but only in relation to certain modalities of consciousness" (421). Each perspectival mode or frame constitutes a different Anna, even though the novel explicitly attempts to make tangible a unitary presence independent of individual interpretation.

Even more than the problematics of motivation, the necessary appearance of discourse troubles the aesthetics of absolute and pure denotation. Immediacy in representation is, in fact, a classical rhetorical figure, *hypotypōsis*, which can be simply defined as using lively and vivid expressions so that the mind seems to see as though through the senses. John Carlos Rowe's insightful essay situating literary impressionism in Kant's use of *hypotypōsis* and rhetoric in general is relevant to Tolstoy's specular aesthetic in questioning the representational terms of the paradigm from which it emerges.[21] Kant uses the figure in section 59 of the *Critique of Judgement* ("Beauty as the Symbol of Morality") to explain the verifying of concepts by means of intuition. The bulk of this section is devoted to distinguishing between schematic *hypotypōsis*, "where the intuition comprehended by the understanding is given *a priori*," and the symbolic, "where the concept is one which only reason can think, and to which no sensible intuition can be adequate" (221). Symbolic *hypotypōses*, accessible only to reason, give, as opposed to the direct presentation of the schematic, indirect presentation of concepts by means of analogy—"transferring the reflection upon an object of intuition to quite a new concept, and one to which perhaps no intuition can directly correspond" (223). Kant's next strategy is to invest the symbolic mode with the capability of representing ideals. Imagining a postulate of knowledge as representation, Kant concludes "that all knowledge of

---

21. Rowe's essay "James's Rhetoric of the Eye: Re-marking the Impression" (developed more fully in *The Theoretical Dimensions of Henry James*) has influenced my views regarding Derrida's reading of Kant in "The Parergon." Rowe comments on how the figurality and metaphoricity of representation subverts whatever ideal of pure perception or impression can be posited. Commenting on a passage from *The American Scene*, Rowe notes how for James "the illusion of pure perception—its sheer surface—is indeed a kind of 'poison,' which denies the human and living activity of interpretation that always already governs every 'vision' of the world and makes for 'the latent vividness of things' " (247). I am indebted to Rowe's demonstration of the continuum in the arguments of Derrida, de Man, and Gelley on the topics of representation and perception.

God is merely symbolic" and later adds that "the beautiful is the symbol of the morally good" (223). This spiritual and ethical turn is clearly descriptive of Tolstoy's motivation in using the *hypotypōsis* of the portrait as well as the scene of the sublime of the storm. Paul de Man, however, suggests that Kant, by giving metaphorical definitions of representation, introduces an element of indeterminacy because the symbolic *analogon* is metaphor lacking the necessary representational support, or ground, that is definitive of *hypotypōsis* (262B). This perceived insufficiency of ground forces Kant to linger upon examples of metaphor that call attention to the lack—figures such as "ground," "depend," and "substance." By using the rhetorical figure of metaphor and analogy to ground his concept of universals, Kant, according to de Man, threatens the basis of his own system by having to rely upon the indeterminacy of discourse. Possibly anticipating this criticism, Kant attempts to restrain the figural play of metaphor by applying it to the realm of reason. Derrida also calls attention to Kant's use of "analogy" in *The Critique of Judgement* as it "operates everywhere in the book . . . assembles the conceptless and the concept . . . legitimizes the occupation of a nonconceptual field by a conceptual force" ("Parergon" 35). Rowe summarizes the implications of de Man and Derrida on the contamination of reason and understanding by discourse within Kant's system: "The symbolic or metaphoric representation of a 'concept' is always transforming the purity (a priori) nature of the concept, thus threatening the very idea of 'a priori' ideas or faculties" ("Rhetoric" 256).

The lifelike portrait of Anna and the indexical sign of her smile and eyes, signifying the spiritual dimension of character, are novelistic explorations of the human ability to escape the indeterminacy of linguistic discourse and discover a realm of pure perception and representation. But as Tolstoy tests dramatically this Kantian premise, he shows that the *hypotypōsis* of this pictured scene can evade the indeterminacy of discourse only through the rhetorical dimensions of analogy and metaphor that threaten the purity of the represented perception. The text shows that the foundation for the analogy, or the metaphorical vehicle of the representation of spirit, is the very ground of discourse, which is nothing more than the differential play of signifying elements. Thus, the transhistorical and essentializing representations of *Anna Karenina* attain their privileged status only through the differential relations of the ekphrastic and linguistic representational systems of the historical and existential text. The conventional representation of a pure perception establishes its truth-claims only through the necessary representation of false conventions. Tolstoy's later remarks on *Anna Karenina* and this attempt artistically to represent inner, preverbal realities show him aware of how problematic is an attack upon language through language, or upon a conventional, coherentist epistemology through literary conventions. They also emphasize his realization of the novelist's allegiance to both word and world.

Beyond the Picture

Tolstoy's choice of a portrait as the basis of an ekphrasis is significant for two reasons, both of which highlight his position as consummate master of nineteenth-century realism. As a portrait, the ekphrastic form represents realism's movement toward character as primary—unique, individual character as opposed to stereotyped caricature. Marvin Mudrick notes, "In nineteenth-century fiction, the image of the individual personality emerges for the first time as an identifying feature of a literary genre" (213). In Tolstoy, individual, rounded characterization reaches an apotheosis. And as painting, the ekphrastic form represents the impulse of nineteenth-century realism toward empirical accuracy in description. The result of these two impulses is the novel as a truly representational art form, one that attempts to create the illusion for readers that they are not reading words describing a character but are instead actually "seeing" a "living, lovely woman."

But as E. H. Gombrich notes of the painter's art, "The artist cannot transcribe what he sees: he can only translate it into the terms of his medium" (36). Tolstoy, like Austen, presents an argument against the conventional uses of his medium, language. But in retreating from conventional uses of language to what he considers more faithful representations of nature, correspondences to essences, Tolstoy must rely upon the creation of newer conventions that present a more convincing illusion of being. Like Cervantes' poets and historians, both Vronsky and Mihailov, through their respective paintings, create no more than illusory pictures of reality. Mihailov's is more "real," more "true to nature," because, in more clearly reflecting the moral, epistemological, and aesthetic values of the Kantian paradigm, it confirms the guiding historical definition of discourse. It is interesting, however, the way in which the text both confirms and tests the limits of this paradigm.

Anna Karenina stands at a crossroads in Tolstoy's career, for it represents the point at which he began to strive beyond the boundaries of art in the apprehension of spirituality. The novel's curious blend of high emotional drama and didacticism is the result of the converging of Tolstoy's artistic and prophetic impulses, which soon thereafter moved toward irreconcilability.[22] And the ekphrastic scene of Anna's portrait is significant not only in respect to Tolstoy's attitude toward character and description but also because it illustrates how necessary it was for him to confirm a correspondent representational paradigm when he began to doubt that art, because of its conventional knowledge, could bring him closer to an actual truth. These doubts, however, later overwhelmed him and culminated eventually in the sometimes bitter *What Is Art?* (1880), in which he summarily dismisses *Anna Karenina* and all his other works (except "God Sees the Truth and Waits," which he calls his best work), as well as the creations of Sophocles, Aeschylus, Dante, Milton, Shakespeare, Raphael, Michelangelo, Bach, Beethoven, Liszt, Brahms, and Wagner (148–49).[23] When Tolstoy completed *Anna Karenina* in 1877, he gave this answer to those who praised the novel: "What's so difficult about describing how an officer gets entangled with a woman? There's nothing difficult in that, and above all nothing worthwhile. It's bad, and it serves no purpose" (Troyat 375). This statement represents more than the moralist's victory over the artist; it shows the frustration of an artist who would attempt directly to transcribe nature. The painter Lucien Freud writes, "A moment of complete happiness never occurs in the creation of a work of art. The promise of it is felt in the act of creation, but disappears towards the completion of the work. For it is then that the painter realizes that it is only a picture he is painting. Until then he had almost dared to hope that the picture might spring to life" (Gombrich 94). Like Freud, who is disappointed at the end because his work is "only a picture," the later Tolstoy rejected *Anna Karenina*. That he would later reject his artistic creations is implicit in the text of *Anna Karenina* itself. For one, he confirms the validity of a foundational, correspondent representation of the actual world by showing the tragic consequences of the possible-world constructions of art, yet he achieves this victory by constructing one of the most magnificent edifices of fictional possible worlds. But more important, the perceptual correspondence beyond language implied by the paradigm he tests dramatically

22. *Anna Karenina* is Tolstoy's most autobiographical novel. The most significant autobiographical element in the novel is, as I argue, the representation and reconciliation of the dualities in Tolstoy's life. In "The Autobiographical Heroine in *Anna Karenina*," Doris V. Johnson comments on this aspect of Tolstoy: "a conflict between Tolstoy the artist and Tolstoy the moralist, between the simultaneous influence of the Iliad and the Gospel, between the antagonistic demands of his teaching and those of his family life, between thinking and being, or as an impersonal result of the general breakdown in art and culture during this period of Russian history" (111).

23. In my discussions of the relation of *Anna Karenina* to *What Is Art?* I am indebted to John Bayley, *Tolstoy and the Novel*, especially the chapter "*Anna Karenina* and *What Is Art?*"

must lead to a rejection of the everyday language creating the coherent structures of fictional reality.

Tolstoy's rejection of his literary endeavors represents more than the conventional view that the artist in him died as he became consumed by his prophetic self. In attempting to reveal his characters' noumenal essences through their phenomenal selves, and in giving an open-ended, partial solution to Levin's spiritual crisis, Tolstoy tries to get beyond the boundaries of the conventions of representation that he had perfected. After perfecting the novel as a picture of life, he indicated the need for something more: out of his prediction would come the modern novel's questioning of the "ineluctable modality of the visible."

CHAPTER FIVE

Ulysses and the Journey from the Tonic of Discourse

From Correspondence to Coherence

Realism is more than just a mode by which novels claim fidelity to actuality. It is a tradition in which novelists examine dramatically and narratively the central focus of philosophic realism, the relation of word and world. Moreover, the structure of this examination is often the same, as can be seen in each of my previous examples. Ekphrastic scenes portray the conflict between and within mimetic paradigms and suggest how the conflict originates from a continuing linguistic debate over the truth-claims of correspondence and coherence theories of representation. Regardless of whether the different historical paradigms assume different vocabularies and horizons of expectations, the dialectical struggle remains the same as the focus shifts between word and world. However, with few exceptions, most philosophical paradigms espouse a metaphysical realism, emphasizing a correspondence theory of reference. But the twentieth century has witnessed perhaps the most dramatic shift in this dialectic, as recent forms of a coherence theory of truth and linguistic meaning have emerged. Their relation to other forms of coherence and their contrast with correspondent theories are worth elaborating.

The tradition of language as correspondence, in placing an object of knowledge outside the realms of human discourse, interprets our various languages—such as the philosophic, scientific, or literary—as adequate approximations of this object, whether we define it as God, transcendental spirit, or matter. From this perspective, science is an effort to translate into human terms the otherwise invisible operations of the universe and to refine by evolutionary knowledge a more perfect mirror upon nature. Ethics is an endeavor to discover a model of human behavior approximating a transcendental norm for morality. And philosophy is an attempt to perfect a set of normative sentences exhibiting a logical, a priori match with the objects and facts of reality. In summary, this view posits that meaning is based on truth and correspondent reference, reason is transcendental, and, most important, there is a single, God's-eye view of reality that can be discovered. By contrast, the other tradition defines the history of science as the succession of conceptual schemes that create more-workable concepts of nature through which practical scientific and epistemological advances may be achieved—the success of a conceptual scheme is measured not by the adequacy of its approximations of nature but by the theoretical and technological answers that can be formulated by the kind and quality of questions it allows. From this viewpoint, ethics is a description of modes of behavior that do not approximate absolute morality but refine moral practices proven by cultural experience most capable of allowing people to live happily and in harmony. And philosophy is a cultural tradition in which practitioners attempt to develop a consensus on concepts whose common goal is not to reflect nature but, in Wilfrid Sellar's words, "to see how things, in the broadest possible sense of the term, hang together, in the broadest possible sense of the term" (Rorty, *Consequences* xiv).[1]

How the latter tradition became dominant in the twentieth century is an interesting story revealing the way in which different cognitive and epistemological models joined to question the possibility of objective knowledge. The phenomenological and existentialist tradition of Husserl, Heidegger, Merleau-Ponty, and Sartre posits a basis for human

1. Throughout his writings, Richard Rorty discusses the correspondence-and-coherence dualism in neopragmatist terms. Beginning with *Philosophy and the Mirror of Nature*, in which he chronicles philosophy's search for foundations or privileged representations, he aligns empirical and transcendental thought as but different manifestations of the same definition of knowledge—as a "Mirror of Nature . . . an assemblage of accurate representations." He writes further, "Then comes the idea that the way to have accurate representations is to find . . . a privileged class of representations . . . [to be] the foundations of knowledge" (163). Against such unitary views of knowledge, Rorty posits a pragmatist theory of knowledge dependent upon social practices, which he variously defines as a conceptual framework, intersubjective solidarity, or communal consensus.

knowledge in inner consciousness and intersubjectivity. The pragmatists Dewey and James, and more recently the self-styled neopragmatists—Sellars, Quine, and Rorty—see truth as a matter of social practice and discourse. Allied to both the phenomenological and pragmatist groups is the hermeneutical school of Dilthey, Gadamer, and Habermas, who constantly stress the role of subjective interpretation, a hermeneutic activity for natural sciences (*Naturwissenschaften*) as well as human sciences (*Geisteswissenschaften*). And philosophers of language as diverse as Wittgenstein, Peirce, and Derrida remind that there is no way to talk about the world outside of our talk about the world, no way to separate our linguistic knowledge of reality from whatever reality may be. And, last, the questioning of objective knowledge in science by the philosophers of science Feyerabend, Popper, and Kuhn is an effect of the same questioning that has emerged in the work of such theoretical scientists as Einstein, Bohr, and Heisenberg.[2] Heisenberg, for example, speaks of the implications of quantum mechanics' theoretical inability to distinguish natural "objects" from scientific instrumentality:

> When we speak of a picture of nature provided by contemporary science, we do not actually mean any longer a picture of nature, but rather a picture of our relation to nature. The old compartmentalization of the world into an objective process in space and time, on the one hand, and the soul in which this process is mirrored, on the other—that is, the Cartesian differentiation of *res cogitans* and *res extensa*—is no longer suitable as the starting point for the understanding of modern science. In the field of view of this science there appears above all the network of relations between man and nature, of the connections through which we as physical beings are dependent parts of nature and at the same time, as human beings, make them the object of our thought and action. (134)

Perhaps the most relevant to fiction of recent coherence models is the constructivism of anthropologists, social psychologists, and cyberneticists, such as Clifford Geertz, Jean Piaget, Ernst von Glaserfeld, Rupert

---

2. For an interesting discussion of "postmodern science," see Stephen Toulmin, "The Construal of Reality: Criticism in Modern and Postmodern Science." Toulmin argues that contemporary science is no longer a value-neutral enterprise theoretically allied with logical positivism but rather is more aligned with the hermeneutic tradition. The postmodern view of scientists does not interpret their role as that of objective spectators but rather subjective human beings intimately bound to and limited by perceptual and technological instrumentality.

Reidel, Michael Gazzaniga, and Marvin Minsky. These theorists emphasize the process by which individuals construct realities out of experiences, cultural myths, beliefs, and expectations. Rather than claim the validity of a single, foundational reality that can be discovered, constructivists argue that individuals compose multiple realities according to different social situations and individual desires. The proper object of study, then, is not the world "out there" but rather the process and products of world construction. It should be obvious by now why the coherence-constructivist theory of knowledge has troubled the texts governed by a correspondence paradigm. Novelists themselves are in the business of world construction, and when alternative worlds are constructed *to valorize* one as correspondent, the process of fictional-world construction, particularly of multiple possible worlds, makes problematic the claim of its being single or foundational. And since language is the primary means by which individuals construct reality, language itself has recently become the dominant model for all of human knowledge.[3] With language as primary cognitive model, foundationalist claims for truth outside discursive contexts give way to views of truth and reality as verbal constructs. Reflecting this coherentist paradigm for world construction, many modernist and postmodernist realist novels place in the foreground linguistic conceptual schemes that are implicitly vital to a reader's understanding of textual verisimilitude and, indeed, external reality itself. The way in which they often foreground the formation of conceptual schemes and their consequent possible worlds is to make the theme of possible-world construction a much more central element of dramatic action and style.

However, the novels from the twentieth century that I have chosen to examine hardly celebrate the liberation from correspondent relations. Like their counterparts written from correspondence paradigms, they are also troubled by the opposing term of the referential dialectic. For one, the fear of relativism haunts the epistemology of multiple worlds and realities. This fear, or rather troubling uncertainty, leads inevitably to the desire for a return to an originary reference by which language can be reconnected to a primal reality, untainted by motivated signifying relations. Also, most novelists would agree that a primary motivation behind fictional-world construction is to make claims about the nonfic-

---

3. In his preface to *The Prisonhouse of Language*, Fredric Jameson discusses the history of ideas as various shifts in conceptual models: "The history of thought is the history of its models." Reviewing the various "objects or systems . . . called upon to illuminate reality . . . [c]lassical mechanics, the organism, natural selection, the atomic nucleus or electronic field, the computer" (v), Jameson argues that the most recent model for knowledge, language, is an extreme reaction to the substantialist models of the past.

tional world consensually agreed to be the actual one. Although corre-spondent reference is unprovable, perhaps even an illusion, it is nonethe-less a socially imposed presupposition that talk is talk about something, not just its own processes. What I call the modernist paradigm is that which makes language the central tool for world construction, as can be seen in the works of Wittgenstein, Heidegger, and Saussure. But it is also one troubled by the fear of solipsism and alienation from a nostalgi-cally evoked picture of the world of actuality.

The Worlds of Language in *Ulysses*

The modernist novel treating most fully the relation between language, conceptual schemes, and reality is James Joyce's *Ulysses.* By foreground-ing numerous linguistic conceptual schemes in adopting multiple narra-tive styles, Joyce questions the possibility of objective knowledge sepa-rate from our modes of discourse. These multiple narrative styles set *Ulysses* apart from the texts of preceding centuries that I have examined thus far. The earlier texts attempt to valorize a mimetic norm by illustrating the conflict by means of ekphrases that represent competing versions of correspondence and coherence theories of reference. The ekphrastic system of signs generates artistic models of some form of correspondence that are continuous with the novel's linguistic norm. In each case, however, the paradigm of correspondence is implicitly problematized by coherence models of discourse that are also represented within the ekphrastic system of the text. This relatively simple dualism between continuous and discontinuous ekphrases is made more complex, however, when a text explicitly refuses to privilege a unitary view of language. For example, *Don Quixote* thematizes the plurality of language by creating various poets and historians who portray the limitations of both correspondent and coherentist language. However, *Ulysses* does more than merely thematize language's plurality. The text, an encyclo-pedia of literary styles, reveals the polysemous nature of signs by giving numerous examples of correspondent and coherentist expressions. Not explicitly prioritizing these discrete modes of representation but rather exploring their potentials and limitations, *Ulysses* approximates and problematizes the expressive values of *Don Quixote.* Whereas Cervantes merely questions the mimetic accuracy of his internal narrators, Joyce actually adopts different rhetorical modes for different chapters, each creating different realities and worlds. The point Marilyn French makes of "Cyclops" and "Oxen of the Sun" is true of the entire work: the novel "demonstrates the dependence of what we take as real upon its linguistic rendering" (173). By not privileging a single referential structure or voice, Joyce creates in *Ulysses* an indeterminate reality, or rather shows how the concept of the actual world is contaminated by the numerous possible worlds that can be evoked by language. Hugh Kenner, among many others, finds this linguistic questioning of reality and realism one of the most interesting aspects of the novel: "Deprived of reliable criteria for 'reality,' we have no recourse, save to read the text as though everything in it were equally real: the phantasmagoric street, the crowds, the lists, the processions, the instantaneous costume changes, even Bloom's change of sex" (*Ulysses* 126–27). By questioning the adequacy of all representations, Joyce questions whether any one in itself provides what Kenner describes as "reliable criteria for 'reality.' " Thus, the text problematizes the terms of the menippean satire in not providing an extended foundational discourse compared to which inserted genres and other discourses can easily be called departures.

One way in which *Ulysses*, like *Don Quixote*, questions a correspondence view of language is by revealing the arbitrary nature of the sign in a manner reminiscent of Cervantes, who allows his hero to rename and transform an ordinary article of toiletry from a "barber's basin" to the "helmet of Mambrino." Stephen's ashplant, for example, is transformed symbolically from its empirical form in "Telemachus" to the apocalyptic sword of Siegfried, *Nothung*, when in "Circe" Stephen renames it and uses it in its symbolic function; and as a result, the possible world of Germanic saga replaces or supplements the empirical: "Time's livid flame leaps [with] the ruin of all space" (583; 475). The distance between the possible-world signifiers and the signifieds of the textual actual world is felt most acutely in "Cyclops," "Oxen of the Sun," "Circe," and "Ithaca," where the text renames characters—for example, Boasthard (Stephen), Sir Leopold (Bloom), the cap (Lynch), Bello (Bella)—with a transformative logic echoing Don Quixote's. In "Circe" the symbolic transformations so dominate the empirical level of reality that the objective scene and characters become secondary to the hallucinatory conceptual scheme. The change from the conventional view of the sign, matching signifier and signified by unmotivated, empirical necessity, to a view in which the signifier works intertextually toward another signifier, a signifying mythic frame, describes the formal technique of the novel. In other words, what applies to individual signs applies to the entire sign system of the novel as well. The shift of realistic conventions can be seen in the contrast of early chapters, in which the extralinguistic "signatures of things" communicate empirically to the individual human subject through the "*nacheinander*" (temporal mode) and the "*nebenei-*

nander" (spatial mode), to the later ones, in which the ruins of time and space are given as the multitude of linguistic signatures through which time and space have been created by the discourses of fictional language communities. The styles of all the chapters are not, as popularly interpreted, detached from the dramatic action of event and character. They are intimately related to the narrative action as Joyce, following Cervantes, Austen, and Tolstoy, illustrates dramatically the effects on human life of determining discourses.

From the Certainty of Ithaca

The most significant way in which the latter part of the text questions correspondent signifying relations is by adopting different narrative styles.[4] It thus contrasts with the first part of the novel, the first six chapters, which are governed by a correspondent epistemology and are characterized by their exclusive use of dialogue, narrative description, and stream of consciousness or interior monologue. Objectively reporting inner states and outer reality, these early chapters assume that a relatively stable world of space and time can be humanly interpreted by a stable system of signs.[5] The perceptual focus of the first six chapters, the attempt by the human consciousness to interact with an external reality, culminates the early modernist emphasis on consciousness and the representation of subjective states.[6] Joyce here furthers his experi-

4. One of the most significant shifts in Joyce scholarship in the past twenty years or so has been from a heavy critical emphasis on the text's use of myth, theme, and character to the text's style and narrative voices. Instrumental works using this approach include David Hayman, *Ulysses: The Mechanics of Meaning;* Hugh Kenner, *Joyce's Voices;* Marilyn French, *The Book as World: James Joyce's Ulysses;* Karen Lawrence, *The Odyssey of Style in Ulysses;* John Paul Riquelme, *Teller and Tale in Joyce's Fiction: Oscillating Perspectives;* Weldon Thornton, "Voices and Values in *Ulysses";* Ben D. Kimpel, "The Voices of *Ulysses";* William B. Warner, "The Play of Fictions and Succession of Style in *Ulysses";* and Monika Fludernik, "Narrative and Its Development in *Ulysses."*

5. Several critics comment on the first six chapters as establishing a reliable and changeless relation between language and world. For example, Karen Lawrence writes that this section "provides us with a sense of the real world of the novel . . . it functions for us as a narrative norm" (43). Monika Fludernik agrees: "The initial episodes mostly serve as a point of reference, against which later innovations, characteristic of a 'second half' of the novel, may be measured" (17). And Weldon Thornton emphasizes that the initial style serves to establish a moral foundation, which is the real "rock of Ithaca": "The 'initial style' . . . expresses the stance of Joyce himself and the underlying values of the novel most clearly" (244).

6. Recent perspectives on the movement have revealed the naïveté of seeing modernism as a unitary movement. My emphasis upon the basic split in modernist thought and

ments in subjectivity begun in *A Portrait of the Artist as a Young Man*. Moreover, he heightens the major dramatic conflict of *A Portrait*, the alienation and estrangement of the artistic sensibility from both the sustaining and imprisoning elements of external reality. By focusing on the deliberative mind, Joyce portrays a consciousness cut off from a sustaining foundation in externality.

"Proteus" is the chapter probing most fully an isolated subjectivity's estrangement from the external world. In both theme and narrative, the chapter presents the problem of consciousness attempting to "read" or interpret the inscrutable text of the world. Although each of the first six chapters shows Stephen or Bloom, isolated by heightened self-consciousness, attempting to translate the texts of their lives and of life in general, it is "Proteus" that most vividly renders the world as untranslated text. Reading as understanding is here defined in its most empirical form—Stephen at first views auditory and visual stimuli as stable signs that, in giving access to externality, confirm a basis for existential identity. The first two chapters, tracing the progress of Stephen's disillusionment with self and others, dramatize why he now seeks such a confirmation. Alienated from such foundations as father, country, religion, and a mother's love, his extreme isolation threatens the very basis of his identity. If identity is defined relationally, Stephen's loss of or refusal to accept these external foundations drives him inward to a self-consciousness so painfully isolating that he resorts, in "Proteus," to seeking a foundation for identity in primal perception. Through the intentional acts of the mind that he had defined elsewhere as epiphanies—the radiance surrounding an object that shines forth as object to consciousness—the objective reality of the world might reveal itself, freeing him from the prison of inner language and self-consciousness. Stephen defines empirical perception as reading, for he refers to objects

---

expression, upon its divided interest in subjectivity and consciousness and in aesthetic form, has been suggested by other critics as well. Monroe K. Spears's *Dionysus and the City: Modernism in Twentieth-Century Poetry* posits "two primary impulses in modern literature. . . . The first is the drive toward aestheticism, toward the purification of form. . . . This is countered by the opposing impulse, to break through art . . . to insist that the immediate experience, the heightening of life is the most important thing" (62). Malcolm Bradbury and James McFarlane, in "The Name and Nature of Modernism," citing Stephen Spender's distinction between the "moderns" and the "contemporaries," state that modernism "is not made up of one essential strand, but of two—roughly antithetical" (24)—one a style "in which art turns away from realism and humanistic representation towards style, technique, and spatial form" (25); the other, quoting Alfred North Whitehead, the expression of "the quality of human experience peculiar to their day" (24), which, ironically, is an extreme subjectivity, "when public notions of language have been discredited and when all realities have become subjective fictions" (27).

as "[s]ignatures of all things I am here to read," which he outlines in empirical form: "seaspawn and seawrack, the nearing tide, that rusty boot. Snotgreen, bluesilver, rust: coloured signs" (37; 31). Losing himself in his own subjective discourse, he seeks to refute by means of an experiment the idealist disbelief in the existence of objects separate from consciousness. Closing his eyes a few moments, questioning, "Has all vanished since?" and opening them again, he is convinced of the separate existence of reality: "See now. There all the time without you: and ever shall be, world without end" (37; 31). Stephen tries to solace himself by not having to add solipsistic despair to his list of miseries. In "Proteus" and its companion chapters of the first section, Joyce dramatizes Stephen's desire to believe in a real and not artificial and socially contingent world. Jules David Law notes Stephen's striving in "Ithaca" for a redeeming belief in referential certainty: "Stephen fears . . . the straying of words from their metaphoric home . . . [and] does not want language to be—as it is in Wittgenstein's view—a habit or way of life, in which meaning is established by social context rather than by intrinsic significances" (51). However, it is ironic that this chapter presents the possibility of a verifiable, external world yet is so utterly subjective that the reader loses a sense of a world outside Stephen's consciousness.[7]

In the rest of the text, Joyce destroys the comforting notion of reference sought by Stephen in "Aeolus" and thus dramatizes the crisis within the modernist paradigm as it moves from an empirical scientism to a view of reality as socially contingent. Beginning with the headlines of "Aeolus" and the intercalations of "Wandering Rocks," and culminating with the musical devices of "Sirens," the next few chapters announce their intent to exploit the notion that if the things of the world are what Stephen calls them in "Proteus"—"signatures" and "signs"—they are subject to the differential play of signification. In these later chapters, Joyce self-consciously questions the earlier chapters' belief that discourse corresponds to a stable, empirically verifiable world. He wrote to Harriet Weaver about the later chapters: "I understand that you may begin to regard the various styles of the episodes with dismay and prefer the initial style much as the wanderer did who longed for the rock of Ithaca" (*Letters* 129). "The rock of Ithaca" is the "initial style's" presentation of a stable ego reading or interpreting a world existing apart from the discourse that describes and interacts with it. However, in the later chapters Joyce shows that as signifiers the "signs and signatures" of the

7. In " 'Signs on a White Field': Semiotics and Forgery in the 'Proteus' Chapter of *Ulysses*," Murray McArthur shows that in "Proteus" Stephen reads signs of the empirical world as signifiers occupying the visible and audible realms of writing and speech.

world do not correspond to external objects or referents but to signifieds, mental signs pointing to other signs—in other words, other signifiers. In abandoning correspondence and denotation to present meaning as an endless relay of signs, Joyce anticipates poststructuralist theories of signification. Studying the referential system of Joyce's texts from the perspective of poststructuralism, Steven Heath comments, "Crucial to the action of a *vraisemblable* is . . . a context of reference, producing . . . a fixed meaning. Joyce's texts, by contrast, in their unstabilization . . . refer . . . not to a 'Reality' . . . but to an intertext" (39).[8] As Heath's reference to an intertext indicates, it would be a mistake to consider completely arbitrary Joyce's substitution of signified for referent, signifier for signified. The first series of substitutions for the empirical level of the text is an intertextual network of mythic and literary signs that point primarily to Homer but also to Dante, Shakespeare, Dumas, Mozart, Sacher-Masoch, and others. This mythic frame provides continuity of theme and character development. However, as each chapter after "Hades" gives a different series of substitutions supplementing the mythic, each substitution displaces another semiotic system, and illusions of unitary, univocal signifying are incrementally eroded. Joyce dramatizes Derrida's theory that "there have never been anything but supplements, substitutive significations which could only come forth in a chain of differential references, the 'real' supervening, and being added only while taking on meaning from a trace and from an invocation of the supplement" (*Grammatology* 159).

The text does more than merely supplement one sign with another; it substitutes entire systems of intertextual signs whose internal coherence is achieved by what Wittgenstein refers to as family resemblances. As the discursive practices in each of these chapters do not merely reflect a "real" world but rather constitute different ones, the overall effect is to contrast the realities or possible worlds constituted by language communities or language games. Discourses motivated by the effects of music, hallucination, clichés, hunger, jingoism, sentimentalism, lust, ribaldry, and hatred suggest that the logical atomistic discourse of the first six chapters can be endlessly supplemented, contaminating what is perceived as actuality with the endless chain of possibilities. In the first six chapters language is treated as having a relatively stable and objective

8. The poststructuralist studies of Joyce highlight the claim that we are still learning to be Joyce's contemporaries. Notable is the number of Joycean studies Derrida has written. For introductions to these approaches, I recommend *Post-Structuralist Joyce*, ed. Derek Attbridge and Daniel Ferrer; *International Perspectives on James Joyce*, ed. Gottlieb Gaiser; *James Joyce: The Augmented Ninth*, ed. Bernard Benstock; and *New Alliances in Joyce Studies*, ed. Bonnie Kime Scott.

system of reference, but the later chapters show that since no discourse is unmotivated, no world is objective. This latter language use is defined by biological, environmental, cultural, and traditional motivations. The elaborate schemata Joyce provided for *Ulysses* do more than give structural unity. His headings—such as "Organ," "Art," "Colour," "Symbol," "Technic," and "Correspondences"—classify the extent to which emotions, desires, fears, physiology, and traditions shape language games and constitute different realities. Thus, Joyce shifts his dramatic test of the consequences of a character's discourse. Whereas the first six chapters illustrate both the comfort and constraints of the foundation coming from unitary and univocal signification, latter chapters dramatize the terrifying freedom consequent to losing correspondent relations to the world.

As several commentators have pointed out, the odyssey in *Ulysses* from the "rock of Ithaca" belongs as much to the text and readers as to the correspondent Homeric characters. Karen Lawrence's "odyssey of style" and Daniel Schwarz's "odyssey of reading" can also be interpreted as an odyssey of language, and since language is constitutive of reality, it is also a journey through different worlds.[9] A travel metaphor more compatible with the peregrinations of characters through the asphalt mazes of this very urban novel would be the journey through the suburbs of language. The metaphor is, of course, Wittgenstein's: "Our language can be seen as an ancient city: a maze of streets and squares, of old and new houses, and of houses with additions from various periods; and this surrounded by a multitude of new boroughs with straight regular streets and uniform houses" (*Investigations* no. 18). Joyce and Wittgenstein share the modernist fascination with the city as primary metaphor for modern life. For both, the city, whose identity consists of the relation of part to multitudinous part, best represents the socially contingent construction of reality. More important, Joyce and Wittgenstein share a similar defining relation to the modernist paradigm.

Joyce, Wittgenstein, and Modernism

In their respective discourses, literature and philosophy, Joyce and Wittgenstein are the paradigmatic figures of modernism, for the parallel

9. Several critics have remarked that Joyce's changes in style are not just changes in perspective; they rather construe different realities. I acknowledge Marilyn French's *The Book as World* as a relatively early study that emphasizes the linguistic basis of reality. As her chapter "The World as Book" claims, our sense of what is real is based on its expression: "If what happens is almost totally contingent on how it is described, act and word are equally potent" (11).

turns of their careers can be seen as defining the paradigmatic and epistemic boundaries of the discourse that we call the modern. Although not chronologically parallel, their careers follow a remarkably similar course in the way in which they shaped the discourses of literature and philosophy—from an early confidence in a correspondent theory of language to a later view stressing the motivational determinants that create language communities. Stephen's (and Joyce's) early aesthetic of epiphany and authorial effacement shows the early modernist desire for an objective, scientistic theory of meaning, which, in Pound's words, is the "direct treatment of the thing." Even though he emphasized impressionism over empiricism, Joyce's early writings reflect the objectivist credo of imagism and the aesthetics of Pound, Williams, Stein, and Hemingway. This confidence in a world apart from discourse, which is nonetheless correspondent to it, runs through the *Tractatus*, beginning with the opening aphorism: "The world is all that is the case" (no. 1). Also throughout is the early modernist desire to purify language by finding its logical match with the world. Stein's and Hemingway's sculpted, transparent prose, the perceptual immediacy of imagism's "direct treatment of the thing," Williams's "say it, not in ideas but in things," and *Dubliners'* "style of scrupulous meanness" can be seen in both the style and theme of the *Tractatus*. The *Tractatus* calls for a discourse that, by circumventing the ambiguity inherent in ordinary language, finds a series of empirically truthful expressions that picture reality. These elementary propositions mirror facts, correspondent elements in the external world. One could consider the aphorisms of the *Tractatus* as such elementary propositions whose truth-values are derived from the abstract beauty of mathematics as well as the empirical precision of scientific analysis. The *Tractatus*, in fact, epitomizes the early modernist valorizing of scientific knowledge and opposes the late modernist and postmodernist privileging of social modes of knowledge. As mirrors of facts that compose the world, the *Tractatus* presents the modernist notion of the objectivist book as empirical description of the world.

Wittgenstein's complete reversal of his position, one of the most dramatic and influential in modern thought, suggests the irreconcilable contradiction in the essential dichotomy of literary modernism—the conflicting interests in the world as revealed to consciousness and in aesthetic form. The modernism of James, Proust, and early Joyce, the rendering of the impressions of a consciousness as it engages an outer world, inevitably led to a modernism that became more interested in the shaping of reality by consciousness and in the variety of forms conceived by this shaping activity. In a similar way, Wittgenstein rejected the correspondence theory of the *Tractatus*, emphasizing an essential form for language, to adopt a view emphasizing the forms and varieties of language usages. In the linguistic view of the *Philosophical Investigations* and other later works, language is not unitary or reflective of facts but is a pattern of communicative behaviors and consensual rules shared by different communities. These rules and behaviors, or family resemblances, define the community as well as its world. The community is thus constituted by a language game deriving its meaning from shared communal activities and traditions that Wittgenstein calls "forms of life." Like Wittgenstein, Joyce moved from seeing language as corresponding to the world through an autonomous subjectivity to seeing it as a language game through which a community creates a reality by means of its social discourse. In fact, these shifts, which foreshadow the transition from the modernist to the postmodernist paradigm, make Joyce and Wittgenstein the representative figures that they are.

In each of the later chapters of *Ulysses* a different discursive pattern shows how social, artistic, emotional, and intellectual language games construct different realities. The stories of Stephen and Bloom, which the text defined earlier as actuality, become distorted by each chapter's different language use and the different worlds they constitute. Marilyn French, accurately calling derisive the tone of several discourses, shows how ultimately they deny the characters' humanity.[10] Distorted by sentimentality, hatred, satire, abstraction, and clichés, the alienation caused by the characters' intense subjectivities in early chapters is replaced by alienating social discourses, "prisonhouses of language." Through the different styles the characters lose the autonomy of self. Karen Lawrence indicates how the later chapters reverse the early chapters' "faith of character not as a 'construct' seen from the outside but . . . as a 'self' that is constant" (52). As we read further in *Ulysses*, we realize that the early chapters' representation of the self as an autonomous ego existing in a stable, external world is invalidated by social discourses that construct individual identity by the often circumscribing rules of language games. A good example of this is in "Circe," where Bloom is denied his humanity by policemen who treat him as merely a word— declining him as if he were a Latin noun: "Bloom. Of Bloom. For Bloom. Bloom" (370; 453). Throughout these chapters, Joyce's technique thus becomes one of the most probing dramatic analyses of the consequences of discourse upon human life.

10. The most important contribution made by Marilyn French's work is her positing of a "derisive narrator," building upon the way Hayman describes the "arranger" assaulting the humanity of the characters. These notions allow Thornton to claim that "the voices of the later episodes represent styles that Joyce wishes to expose as somehow incomplete" (244).

In addition to overturning conventional notions of character, the polyphonic discourses of the later chapters also challenge conventional views of a unitary narrative voice. David Hayman suggests that the narrator plays at least two roles, similar to those played by the poet and historian of *Don Quixote*, and calls the roles those of "narrator" and of "arranger" (78). The narrator, using language in a correspondent and referential function, is seen in the first section of the text, chapters that "contain the clearest exposition and correspond to the four most clear-headed hours of the day" (93). Using objective reportage of stream of consciousness, description, and dialogue, this narrator defines the relatively stable world of the first section. With "Aeolus," however, the objective narrator is replaced by a playful, mischievous arranger of the text's multitudinous voices, who problematizes the fictional reality of the text with these rhetorical styles that transform the signs of objects and characters. As the novel progresses, the arranger seems more arbitrary in assigning relations between signifier and signified, implicitly rejecting the first section's claim to correspondent and empirical accuracy. In becoming an arranger of voices, the narrator guides the reader through language games and communities, along with their constituted realities.

A final comparison between Joyce and Wittgenstein is one that perhaps exposes the limits of the late modernist paradigm. Both figures, having so fully explored language's relativist potential, seek what Wittgenstein calls the "original home" of language, which is "to bring words back from their metaphysical to their everyday use" (*Investigations* no. 116). Heidegger's applying of a home metaphor for language use as the pure expression of being contrasts with Wittgenstein's theory of ordinary language but is related in its call for a return to originary usage and is perhaps, in its emphasis upon the revelation of *Dasein*, related as well to Joyce's theory of epiphany.[11] Both Heidegger and Wittgenstein seek a foundation for discourse to secure its relativistic drift. In the "Penelope" chapter, Joyce does, indeed, return to the basis of language in individual consciousness. More significantly, the wandering of language into the relativity of linguistically constituted worlds is anchored in *Ulysses* by the very archetype of journey and return. Joyce's use of the Odyssean journey myth serves two functions. For one, it reflects how modernists treated the contemporary world as discontinuous and fragmented yet

11. See Jules David Law, "The Home of Discourse: Joyce and Modern Language Philosophy," for a discussion of Heidegger's and Wittgenstein's conception of a home for language and its applicability to Stephen's quest for meaning. According to Law, the text proves that "there is no 'home' for language to retreat to that is not already a 'pawnshop,' its words already *invested* with habitual, cultural, and political significances beyond the individual's entire control" (52).

strove to mend these divisions within the anthropologically and formally secure frame of myth. More important, however, by thematizing the archetypal pattern of journey and return, *Ulysses* dramatizes the return home of language and character from the abyss of meaning to what is at least the illusion of a comforting correspondence with the earth.

The Journey from Ithaca and Stratford

Bloom and Stephen, narrator and arranger, initial style and later style, logical atomism and language games, autonomous individual and socially constructed subject—these and other dualisms define the thematic boundaries of *Ulysses*. Moreover, the above polarities signify in different ways the correspondence-and-coherence dualism that has guided mimetic theory throughout novelistic history. *Ulysses*, then, stands along with other revolutionary novels that, in portraying this dualism, problematize the conventions of a prevailing mimetic paradigm. The debate over representation appears self-consciously in *Ulysses*, as it does in *Don Quixote*, *Emma*, and *Anna Karenina*. Joyce's novel is perhaps exceptional in the extent to which it consciously attempts to resolve the conflict inherent in this dialectic. Joyce left many textual clues defining artistic production as a synthesis of correspondent and coherentist theories of representation. The primary clue, as I later show, is the structure of the novel itself, but this clue is most fully revealed when seen through the perspective of ekphrastic scenes. Like other novels representing mimetic paradigms ekphrastically, *Ulysses* presents the conflict as an argument over artistic production. The ekphrastic argument between Stephen, A. E., and John Eglinton over Shakespeare's artistic creation in "Scylla and Charybdis" defines thematic concerns that appear again in the ekphrases of "Sirens," "Circe," and "Ithaca." Moreover, the argument mirrors the ekphrastic arguments between the Canon and the Don in *Don Quixote*, Emma and Knightley in *Emma*, and Vronsky and Mihailov in *Anna Karenina*. And like these earlier novels, *Ulysses* uses an ekphrastic argument to examine a paradigm shift—in this case from a scientistic, empirical early modernism to the later view of reality as socially constructed.

The ekphrastic argument in *Ulysses* uses the journey-and-return-home motif to reveal the theme and structure of the novel as well as the epistemological foundation upon which it is constructed. This ekphrasis dramatizes the implications for character of a relativistic discourse that journeys from the foundational "home for language" in correspondent actuality. This motif is treated ekphrastically in Stephen's debate on Shakespeare's *Hamlet* in "Scylla and Charybdis," where home and journey are treated existentially and artistically, and, with greater complexity, in musical ekphrases developed in "Sirens," "Circe," and "Ithaca," where home and journey are configured as the tonic and dominant tones of a classical sonata. Together these ekphrases form a system of meaning that defines the major theme of the novel, reconciliation, a return of both characters and discourses from a journey revealing the abyss of meaning. This Odyssean journey motif represents the departure of the characters, text, and language from a sustaining origin. Derrida locates this origin in *Ulysses* as the performative "yes," an affirmation that appears in the text only as a reproduction. Using the text's several examples of "yes" communicated by telephone, Derrida indicates how the discourse of *Ulysses* is one "inscribing remoteness, distance, and spacing in sound" ("Ulysses Gramophone" 39). Searching for the "yes" of Molly's initial acceptance of him, Bloom, in exile, is "hooked up to a multiplicity of voice and answering machines. His being-there is a being at the telephone, in the way that Heidegger speaks of being for the death of *Dasein*" (41). Stephen and Bloom's alienation from self is also one from an external or correspondent affirmation, a being-in-the-world signified as intercourse with the other.[12] The various styles, alienating the reader from the characters' humanity, are the discursive embodiment of this estrangement. The return home, or resolution and reconciliation of the characters, is accompanied by a cessation of language-game experiments and what Wittgenstein calls "a return home . . . to bring words back from their metaphysical to their everyday use."

Numerous commentators have argued that the aesthetic theory proposed by Stephen in his ekphrastic *Hamlet* debate in "Scylla and Charybdis" provides an aesthetic foundation for the novel's major thematic concerns as well as explores the relation between biography and art.[13]

12. The analogue for the confrontation with all that is not-self, signified by the other, is sexual intercourse. Bloom's masturbation and celibate wanderings from Molly's bed and Stephen's essential misunderstanding of women show how these characters are exiled from the world within their confining subjectivities. French defines this theme in sexual terms; what each character must do "is to have intercourse with the real" (35). In "Joyce, Derrida, and the Discourse of 'the Other,' " Christine Van Boheemen-Saaf develops the theme as the text's confrontation with the otherness of feminine discourse.

13. Regardless of the irony with which Stephen is treated in the *Portrait* and in several sections of *Ulysses*, Joyce does commit some of his own beliefs to his character. Brook Thomas, in *James Joyce's Ulysses: A Book of Many Happy Returns*, treats the scene as autobiographical in an analogical way—the theory allows Joyce to enter his work narratively and symbolically: "Having given himself theoretical justification for the return of the artist to his handiwork, [Joyce] embarks on his odyssey of return that enfolds in the second half of the book" (67). In addition to those already cited, other studies treating this scene as

And because this ekphrastic debate also foregrounds the representational dialectic that the text seeks to reconcile, it deserves a full examination—both the ekphrastic scene as framing digression and the ekphrasis of *Hamlet.* Brook Thomas's very helpful book interprets the entirety of *Ulysses* within the terms of the *Hamlet* debate; he writes, "Just as Stephen constructs the history of Shakespeare's art as one of escape and return, so we are invited to see Joyce's art conforming to the same pattern" (66). Daniel Schwarz also anchors his book-length study of the text with an analysis of the *Hamlet* debate because "this chapter educates [Joyce's] reader to read his novel in terms of the aesthetic principles with which he interprets Shakespeare" (12). John Hunt, exploring the human and existential elements of the debate, argues that the crucial terms are Stephen's "sundering and reconciliation," which connote the broader textual pattern of "exile and return" (298). He writes that " 'sundering' refers to an alienation of the self from the world in which it lives, from other human beings, and from its own past, while reunion signifies a process of projecting selfhood back into the empirical world and seeing its preoccupations and desires reflected and consummated there" (298). These several studies thus confirm the centrality of the journey-and-home motif in the *Hamlet* ekphrasis to the structure and theme of the entire text.

In his theory, Stephen elaborates several configurations of the journey motif. Initially he alludes to a common belief that Shakespeare played the role of ghost in *Hamlet* and liberally defines ghost as "[o]ne who has faded into impalpability through death, through absence, and through change of manners" (188; 154). According to Stephen, the role is appropriate, for Shakespeare became a ghost by absence when Ann Hathaway's aggressive sexuality and later adultery drove him from the maternal, incestuous hearth into a tortured self-consciousness borne out of his sexual self-doubts. By departing from Stratford to go to London, he faded through absence into impalpability to nurse his sexual wounds. What Stephen calls "banishment from the heart, banishment from the home" (212; 174) is caused by the recognition of sexuality, an "original sin, committed by another in whose sin he too has sinned" (212; 174). Shakespeare's return to home and Stratford through his works proves to Stephen that "[w]here there is a reconciliation . . . there must have been first a sundering" (193; 159). Sexual knowledge is the "sundering" that drove him to London and "into a new passion, a darker shadow of the first, darkening even his own understanding of himself" (196; 161).

---

symbolically significant include Richard Ellmann, *Ulysses on the Liffey,* and S. J. Goldberg, *The Classical Temper.*

While in London, he explored the new, dark passion: "Twenty years he dallied there between conjugal love and its chaste delights and scortatory love and its foul pleasures" (201; 165). The implied homosexuality of the sonnets and the reputed promiscuity with Penelope Rich represent Shakespeare's immersion in the otherness of sexuality. Through this surrender of self, a correspondence of self with other, Shakespeare learned to immerse himself in his art, the lives of his characters. Transforming the real facts of his life throughout the entirety of his creation, he gave birth to and is now one with all of his created characters, so that "[t]he boy of act one is the mature man of act five. All in all. In *Cymbeline*, in *Othello* he is bawd and cuckold. He acts and is acted on. Lover of an ideal or a perversion, like José he kills the real Carmen. His unremitting intellect is the hornmad Iago ceaselessly willing that the moor in him shall suffer" (212; 174). Joyce proves correct Mulligan's description of Stephen's theory of Shakespeare, "that he himself is the ghost of his own father" (18; 15). As creator, Shakespeare shares a common identity with both the ghost father and the son Hamlet, and though "sundered by a bodily shame," they achieve a consubstantial state through art. Creativity is defined as fathering because of the mystery of paternity: "Fatherhood, in the sense of conscious begetting is unknown to man. It is a mystical estate, an apostolic succession from only begetter to only begotten. On that mystery and not on the madonna which the cunning Italian intellect flung to the mob of Europe the church is founded and founded irremovably because founded, like the world, macro and microcosm, upon the void. Upon incertitude, upon unlikelihood" (207; 170).

Stephen compares the uncertainty of paternity with maternal certitude: "*Amor Matris* may be the only true thing in life. Paternity may be a legal fiction" (207; 170). Stephen (and Joyce) choose paternity over maternity as a metaphor of artistic creation because the certainty of the maternal bond between mother and child connotes a necessary, correspondent relation between sign and referent. On the other hand, paternity, a "fiction," connotes the seemingly arbitrary relation between the signifier and signified of the literary sign. This view of signification also illuminates why Joyce used as the sign of the reconciliation of father and son the story of Stephen and Bloom. The fleeting, momentary coming together of these radically different men reflects the mystery of both fatherhood and signification—both are "founded like the world, macro and microcosm, upon the void. Upon incertitude, upon unlikelihood" (207; 170). This view also explains why Stephen refuses to believe in his "mixture of theolologicophilolological" (205; 168). If belief must be based on complete certainty, then the fictions through which we live our lives, though more significant because created, must be sustained in a less absolute way. Finally, this view of fatherhood and signification does not invalidate the possibility of consubstantiality or correspondence; it merely comments upon the abyssal foundation of such a union.

From Dominant to Tonic

The text's primary dramatic theme of reconciliation and consubstantiality, if combined with the subtextual theme of referential relations, can thus be interpreted as the desire for correspondence. However, though few critics deny that the reconciliation of father and son is a primary theme of Joyce's *Ulysses*, many argue against such a reconciliation occurring on a dramatic level between Stephen and Bloom. To adopt this latter view a reader would have to assume that the multiple signs of the father and son reconciliation theme are empty markers, false symbols leading him or her to anticipate a resolution that does not occur dramatically in the text. But it should be obvious that the myriad symbolic variations of the theme at least suggest a pattern of reconciliation. In addition to the Odysseus/Telemachus and Bloom/Stephen variations of the theme, other motifs are formed by "Scylla and Charybdis's" Shakespeare and Hamlet, Hamlet and the ghost, God and Christ, and the artist and his or her creation. Elsewhere other motifs appear as Reuben J. Dodd and son, Siegfried and the parent gods, Bloom and Rudy, Bloom and his father, Rudolph, Daedalus and Icarus, Simon and Stephen, Patrick Dignam and Patrick, Jr., and the false father and the croppy boy.[14]

Also, in "Ithaca" Joyce suggests that Stephen and Bloom attain a consubstantial state when he refers to them as "Blephen" and "Stoom." Transposing the letters of their names suggests a merging of selves, even if the merger seems, in the dramatic context, slight and transitory. I believe, however, that *Ulysses* moves ineluctably toward the union of these characters, and Joyce both foreshadows and describes the nature of this union in the ekphrastic scenes of the text describing the consubstantiality of father and son. The ekphrastic debate on *Hamlet* in "Scylla and Charybdis" presents the way in which Joyce defines consubstantiality through the journey-and-home motif, but the definition is completed only when the theme is represented through musical ekphrases in

14. For the recognition of the multiplicity of the theme of father-son reconciliation, I am indebted to Zack Bowen, *Musical Allusions in the Works of James Joyce.*

"Sirens," "Circe," and "Ithaca" as the musical resolution of a dominant
tone into a tonic one within the diatonic scale, also structured according
to the terms of journey and home. This musical structure is an important
ekphrastic code on several different levels in the text: it dramatizes
Bloom's and Stephen's consubstantiality, describes the formal unity of
the text as resolution, completes Stephen's argument on artistic creativity, and reflects the paradigmatic notion of the sign. The entire musical
ekphrasis, extending and resonating throughout the text, is a semiotic
system that constrains the indeterminacy of textual meaning by making
the multiple intertextual signifiers refer ultimately to a signified representing consubstantiality and thus at least the comforting illusion of
correspondence.

The first chapter in which the sonata theme is ekphrastically rendered
is "Sirens," where Joyce creates an encyclopedia of musical devices. The
most dramatic use of music in the chapter, however, is Simon Dedalus's
sentimentally rendering the aria "M'appari" from Freidrich von Flotow's
opera *Martha*. The ekphrastic scene is more than a digression, for the
musical effects of this ekphrasis upon a melancholy Bloom follow closely
the affective aims of the sonata form, which is structured according to
the journey-and-home pattern so crucial to the meaning of the text. The
aria also thematically mirrors Bloom's own journey from the home of
Molly's love. The song, quoted in fragments by the text, deserves a
full quotation for a better understanding of its dramatic significance
to Bloom:

When first I saw that form endearing;
Sorrow from me seem'd to depart:
Each graceful look, each word so cheering
Charm'd my eye and won my heart.
Full of hope, and all delighted,
None could feel more blest than I;
All on Earth I then could wish for
Was near her to live and die,
But alas! 'twas idle dreaming,
And the dream too soon hath flown;
Not one ray of hope is gleaming;
I am lost, yet I am lost for she is gone.
When first I saw that form endearing
Sorrow from me seem'd to depart!
Each graceful look, each word so cheering
Charm'd my eye and won my heart.

Martha, Martha, I am sighing
I am weeping still; for thee;
Come thou lost one,
Come thou dear one,
Thou alone can'st comfort me:
Ah Martha return! Come to me!

Bloom is struck by the ironic significance of his writing a letter to Martha Clifford while listening to the aria from *Martha*, but his thoughts are with Molly. The opening line appeals to his "remembered lives" (274; 226), and with the repetition of "When first I saw that form endearing," Bloom remembers when he met Molly at Matt Dillon's in Terenure. The line "Each graceful look . . . charmed my eye" makes Bloom think of when he first saw Molly's "Spanishy eyes" (274; 226). The aria is a siren's song for Bloom, for the memories it arouses cause him to despair upon realizing how far he has journeyed from the originary home of requited love. Stanley Sultan interprets the ekphrasis as dramatically rendering what Molly's impending adultery really means to him: "Where Bloom was resigned in the sixth chapter (post office) and troubled in the eighth (Byrne's), he is now fully, consciously aware of his situation and of its significance" (227). Singing silently along with Simon—"Bloom sang dumb" (276)—he identifies with the hero of *Martha*, Lionel, who "cried in grief, in cry of passion" (275; 226). The cry of passion, "Martha! Ah, Martha!" (275; 226), is sung in notes that build to the climax of the song, the moment before "the dominant to love [is] to return" (275; 226). The dominant note is sung with the word "Come" and is described vividly by Joyce: "It soared, a bird, it held its flight, a swift pure cry, soar silver orb it leaped serene, speeding, sustained, to come, don't spin it out too long long breath he breath long life, soaring high, high resplendent, aflame, crowned, high in the effulgence symbolistic, high, of the ethereal bosom, high, of the high vast irradiation everywhere all soaring all around about the all, the endlessnessnessness" (275–76; 227). Because it is the note most anticipatory of the return to the home key, the dominant note expresses longing, a desire for rest or merger with the home or tonic note. This dominant note, a prolonged dominant seventh, is a high B-flat that is resolved in F major, the key of the song and the tonic note of rest sung in the last word (Fig. 1). When this last word is sung, the dominant resolved in the tonic, then a merger of identities takes place: Simon, the singer, Lionel, the operatic character, and Leopold, the listener who is dumb singing, become "Siopold!" (276; 227). On a dramatic level, the aria presents the way art can bridge otherness, both in production and reception, repeat-

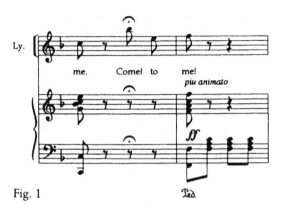

Fig. 1

ing the way the *Hamlet* ekphrasis defines Shakespeare's creativity as immersion with the world through knowledge of sexuality. More important, the ekphrasis uses the return-to-home structure in musical form to underscore and complete the text's major theme.

The first line of the song, sung in the home key of F major, presents an idyllic picture of a past love when Lionel/Leopold believed "[n]one could feel more blest than I." But when the song describes the present plights of both the operatic character and Bloom—"yet I am lost for she is gone"—it modulates or journeys from the home (tonic) key to the active (dominant) one. In the logic of tonal music, the melody of the song cannot be resolved until it returns to the home/tonic tone. And dramatically, the situations of Lionel and Leopold cannot be resolved until they return to the lost bliss of love that was established by the home key. Thus, as the song expresses a desire for "dominant to love to return," it combines the dominant note's longing for the home key with Lionel's and Leopold's longing for the home of lost love. When the melody is resolved with the tonic note, Lionel and Bloom merge in mutual longing with Simon, whose place Leopold will take as the father figure of Stephen.

The importance of this ekphrasis becomes clear when the musical process describing the consubstantiality of Simon, Lionel, and Leopold as "Siopold" is used later to show dramatically the consubstantiality of Stephen and Bloom as "Blephen" and "Stoom" in "Ithaca." The more symbolic fusion of characters in the "Sirens" ekphrasis foreshadows the later dramatic fusion. The "M'appari" ekphrasis, however, is but one of several within the ekphrastic system of the text in which Joyce uses tonal logic to prepare the reader for the merging of characters in "Ithaca."

For example, there are many dramatic and ekphrastic references in

"Circe" to the resolution of dominant and tonic notes. A comic example is when Stephen's hallucinatory projection Philip Drunk (Siamese twin of Philip Sober), cries, "If only I could find out about octaves. Reduplication of personality" (518; 423). Although comic, Philip Drunk's question concerning the octave refers to an important pronouncement that Stephen has made concerning the return of the dominant to the tonic within the boundaries of the octave. Earlier in "Circe" is a brief ekphrasis in which Stephen plays on the piano in Bella Cohen's brothel the series of "empty fifths" (505; 410). In playing empty fifths, Stephen would be striking "with two fingers" a chord consisting only of the tonic and the dominant key notes, which would establish no home key, since a third note is needed to form a triad, the principal chord material of any scale. Thus, Stephen would traverse all keys (by means of the circle of perfect fifths, twelve in all) without establishing a home key, and therefore create a series of chords that have neither departure nor return—creating an apt metaphor to describe his dramatic state at this point in the text.

As he discusses musical theory, he is mocked by Lynch's cap (a symbol of his skeptical companion): "Bah! It is because it is. Woman's reason. Jewgreek is greekjew. Extremes meet. Death is the highest form of life. Bah!" (504; 411). This charge is a defiant attack upon the theories of consubstantiality, which Stephen elaborated in "Scylla and Charybdis." "The cap" denies that "jewgreek" and "greekjew" (Stephen and Bloom) can become consubstantial. Stephen attempts to answer the charge with the analogy of the octave: "The reason is because the fundamental [tonic] and the dominant are separated by the greatest possible interval which. . . . Interval which. Is the greatest possible ellipse. Consistent with. The ultimate return. The octave. Which" (504; 411). When the cap interrupts with further taunting, Stephen pauses. Then a gramophone begins to play "The Holy City," implicitly referring to Bloom as the Messiah, the builder of the "new Bloomusalem" (484; 395). This annunciation triggers in Stephen a sudden realization about his *Hamlet* debate, connecting the earlier ekphrasis with this later musical one: "What went forth to the ends of the world to traverse not itself, God, the sun, Shakespeare, a commercial traveler, having itself traversed in reality itself becomes that self. Wait a moment. Wait a second. Damn that fellow's noise in the street. Self which it was ineluctably preconditioned to become. *Ecco!*" (505; 412).

Stephen's revelation answers the crucial questions he proposed in the "Scylla and Charybdis" ekphrasis concerning Shakespeare and his works, an artist and his or her creation, God and the world. In this later ekphrasis Stephen advances his theory of *Hamlet* from an aesthetic to personal, religious, and epistemological levels:

He found in the world without as actual what was in his world within as possible. Maeterlinck says: "If Socrates leave his house today he will find the sage seated on his doorstep. If Judas go forth tonight it is to Judas his steps will tend." Every life is many days, day after day. We walk through ourselves, meeting robbers, ghosts, giants, old men, young men, wives, widows, brothers-in-love. But always meeting ourselves. The playwright who wrote the folio of this world and wrote it badly (He gave us light first and the sun two days later), the lord of things as they are whom the most Roman of catholics call *dio boia*, hangman god, is doubtless all in all in all of us, ostler and butcher, and would be bawd and cuckold too but that in the economy of heaven, foretold by Hamlet, there are no more marriages, glorified man, an androgynous angel, being a wife unto himself. (213; 175)

Before Shakespeare, as artist, can become "all in all," he must encounter all that is nonself, making the "world within as possible," "the world without as actual." This actualizing of possible worlds, symbolized by the journey to London, is motivated by a sexual knowledge threatening the boundaries of self. Driven by feminine sexuality and "a new passion, a darker shadow of the first," he leaves the incestuous, maternal home to experience the world, the not-self, and this experience is both literally and figuratively sexual. Literal sexuality allows him figuratively to "traverse not [it]self," and the result is his ability to transform the personal details of his life into a universe of created characters, so that he becomes "all in all." The only way he can return to the feminine home from which he was cast is to cure his sexual insufficiency by rivaling maternal creativity. As artist he becomes "the creator of his race," the "father of his own son." God's creation of a mortal son suggests the same immersion in the physical world that is required of the imaginative artist.

Stephen's insight into and resolution of his ekphrastic theory is gained only when the later ekphrasis allows him to consider the logical necessity of a tonic note within the octave. The octave represents the greatest interval between one tone and its duplicate in the scale; thus, there is one octave separating C–C, D–D, E–E, and so on. It is the extreme limit that a tone can travel before returning to the home of self-identity. Thus, it represents the extreme limit of Socrates' travels before he returns to himself, of Shakespeare's journey to London and his works before returning to Stratford, of Joyce to Trieste-Paris-Zurich before returning (in his fiction) to Dublin, and of Bloom to the Hibernian metropolis before he returns to Molly. Harry Blamires describes the interval succinctly:

> Thus it reflects the journey of God in making and entering a world intended to return to him, the daily journeying of the sun around the earth, the journeying of a Shakespeare from Stratford to London and back (with all that is produced), the journeying of a commercial traveler (a Bloom presumably) from home and Molly and back to them . . . the earth is the dominant to God's tonic; noon the dominant to midnight's tonic; London the dominant to Stratford's tonic; and the plays he wrote the dominant to Shakespeare's tonic; Bloom's wandering around Dublin the dominant to Molly's tonic. (185)

Frederick Sternfeld notes that Joyce's Jesuitical training in music undoubtedly included instruction in the Christian symbolical significance of musical intervals, as interpreted by Pythagoras, the scholiasts, and Renaissance church scholars. In light of this symbology, Sternfeld offers this theory: "The ultimate return of the octave symbolizes the ultimate return of God in Everyman, the commercial traveler in Dublin, the 'usylessly' Ulysses." (47). The religious, aesthetic, and epistemological interpretations of consubstantiality in these musical ekphrases point therefore to the uniting of Stephen and Bloom.[15]

The Sonata as Structural Device

The theme of consubstantiality, introduced in the *Hamlet* ekphrasis of "Scylla and Charybdis," thus reappears as the reconciliation of the dominant into the tonic in the musical ekphrases of "Sirens" and "Circe," and consequently these ekphrases point toward the dramatic fusion of "Blephen" and "Stoom" in "Ithaca." Joyce prepares the reader for the reconciliation of his two characters by treating them as a musician would two opposing themes in a composition—two themes whose conflict and eventual merger shape the structure of the work.

The musical context most often used to describe the resolution of Stephen and Bloom as the tonic and dominant keys of *Ulysses* is the sonata form. The sonata is a specific structural use of the contrast

---

15. Surprisingly, Bowen does not analyze this scene in his study, which annotates and interprets over seven hundred allusions.

between tonic and dominant keys. The tonic key is the scale of notes or progressions that cluster in an ascending or descending order around the note of rest from which a scale takes its name. The dominant is the next related key whose note of rest is five notes, a fifth above or a fourth below the tonic. The chordal relations of one key are often not compatible with those of the other, and so a contrast between these two keys will cause tension, each striving for its own note of rest. The contrast between tonic and dominant keys is put to use in the classical sonata in a ternary form. In an exposition, a theme is introduced in the tonic key, which is then contrasted with another theme in the dominant. In a developmental section, these themes (called principal and subordinate) are elaborated, and the resulting tension gives the music its dramatic quality. In this middle section, both themes are examined from different perspectives, according to a wide range of relations, and both strive for dominance. In the last section, the recapitulation, the principal theme appears again in its original key and original context, and it is again contrasted with the subordinate theme, which now, however, has modulated from the dominant to the tonic key, and the two themes are united. The three sections (to which a coda may be included) have been metaphorically described in several different ways, such as statement/departure/return and introduction/conflict/resolution, but the closest analogy they bear to *Ulysses* is their cyclic pattern of home/adventure/return.

The internal evidence that *Ulysses* has a musical—especially sonata—structure has attracted critical attention for many years. As early as 1922, Ezra Pound suggested that the novel definitely was a sonata (89).[16] Initially, however, his theory prompted few critics to attempt a detailed musical analysis. Many years later, Anthony Burgess, in *ReJoyce*, applied a sonata metaphor to the novel for the purpose of explaining the relation of "Circe" to the entire book:

> The exposition will not make sense until it has been followed by a development section in which the subjects combine, lend each other their subsidiary motifs, swirl about each other in an area of dream-like fantasy, bump into each other drunkenly, melt into each other in the discovery of previously unguessed affinities. After that—in the recapitulation section—they can appear soberly and singly, properly dressed and tidied up, but they

16. Ezra Pound made this remark in his essay "James Joyce and Pécuchet": "Ce roman appartient à la grande classe de romans en forme de sonata, c'est-à-dire, dans la forme: theme, contre-thème, recontre, développment, finale."

cannot be as they were before, in the exposition. They have learned strange things about each other and about themselves. (158)

Although undeveloped, Burgess's interpretation identifies Stephen and Bloom as themes of a sonata movement; however, by not treating Stephen's "What went forth" monologue, Burgess does not explore the full significance of his revelation. Robert Boyle's "*Ulysses* as Frustrated Sonata Form" is a more sustained and helpful effort to apply a sonata metaphor to the novel. Boyle contributes to a theory of sonata form by describing the tonic and dominant keys of *Ulysses* in terms of the moods created by the contrasting personalities of Stephen and Bloom. Boyle also charts the stages of the text according to sonata form, noting whether the key for each chapter is tonic/Stephen or dominant/Bloom. In the end, however, Boyle rejects the sonata as the basic structural pattern because he denies that the two men become consubstantial. In order to perceive a sonata structure in *Ulysses* one has to assume that the themes represented by Stephen and Bloom are somehow united. Boyle finds this theory inconsistent with textual evidence and dismisses it by fervently denying that the book can be interpreted optimistically:

> The extremes, the Jew Bloom and the Greek Dedalus, meet in the "Oxen of the Sun" chapter, and the results of that meeting, worked out in the Recapitulation, constitute the climax and the catharsis of Joyce's vision of the unsaved. If Bloom could enter Stephen's octave, as he desires to and pitifully strives to, the novel would indeed have something of the "happy ending" tonality which some readers claim to find there. But as above all else the style indicates, passing from the death of nauseating cliché in "Eumaeus" to the rigor mortis of "Ithaca," the paralysis of *Dubliners* operates fully here too. (254)

Before he abandons his thesis, however, Boyle makes several interesting observations about structure. The temporal simultaneity of the first three chapters (treating Stephen) and the second three (treating Bloom) constitutes a structural whole, even though they are separated in the narrative. These simultaneous introductions correspond to an expositional section of a sonata—the classical double exposition of a pair of themes.[17]

---

17. Even though Boyle abandons his analysis of *Ulysses* as sonata, his study is thorough and well informed of both musical structure and its applicability to *Ulysses*. I have been influenced by Boyle's reading.

The opening section of a sonata, the exposition, sets forth both themes in their respective keys. I think that it is more than merely convenient to consider the first six chapters of *Ulysses* an expositional section. The simultaneity of the times of chapters one and four, two and five, and three and six represents the simultaneous introduction of the opposing themes—Stephen and Bloom. And there is more than just the matter of time to suggest that the first six chapters are opposing pairs and not just a triad for Stephen followed by a triad for Bloom. Richard Ellmann gives a most helpful explanation of the structure of the first six chapters:

> Each of the first three chapters is half a circle, to be completed by its parallel chapter in the second triad. Mulligan's transubstantiation of God into flesh in "Telemachus" is completed by Bloom's transubstantiation of flesh into faeces ("Calypso"). The sadism of Christians and Romans persecuting Jews ("Nestor") is completed by the masochism of Christians and Buddhists in their devotions ("Lotus-Eaters"). In the "Proteus" episode Stephen follows the arc of generation through corruption to death, while in "Hades" Bloom begins with death and follows it back to birth. (*Ulysses on the Liffey* 55)

Although I differ with Ellmann in seeing the geometrical shape of the exposition not as a circle but rather as two parallel lines, I agree fully with his matching of themes. As Joyce introduces Bloom and Stephen in the context of matching themes, he is able to establish consistent oppositions. In "Telemachus," Joyce introduces Stephen with a symbolic eating of flesh, the communion bread representing Christ's body; but in "Calypso," he tells that Bloom "ate with relish the inner organs of beasts and fowls" (55; 45). In "Nestor," Stephen rejects secular and sacred history with acts of symbolic rebellion; but in "Lotus Eaters" Bloom submits in manifest acts of compromise to those very same historical forces. In "Proteus," Stephen contemplates the limits of sense and has a vision of the ultimate boundary, death; but in "Hades," Bloom is presented with an actual death and visits Death's own chamber, Glasnevin Cemetery. The contrast of personalities is similar to the contrast that Cervantes found so profitable in the figures of Don Quixote and Sancho, that between the mind and the body, the imagination and experience. Perhaps a more fitting contrast for the characters is between one who has rejected all forms of correspondence with the actual world and another who, although having journeyed from a redeeming correspondence, still is confident it exists and can be found again.

In the developmental section of a sonata, the theme or themes modulate from the home key to a series of foreign keys, and this sequence of shifts from the tonic key increases the tension resisting the theme's inevitable return home. Significantly, both Stephen and Bloom, in leaving home, lose their latchkeys and are keyless. "Aeolus," the chapter beginning the developmental section of *Ulysses,* is obsessively concerned with keys, and the advertisement that Bloom sells for Alexander Keyes— the two crossed latchkeys—suggests that both in theme and musical metaphor the keys of Stephen and Bloom must come together. The sonata's development examines the themes in the widest possible angles, and in *Ulysses'* development, from "Aeolus" to "Ithaca," Joyce shifts his narrative modally by drastically changing language use from chapter to chapter. The alienating discourses of each of the later chapters thus perform the same function as the journey section of a sonata—to suggest the longing for an inevitable return to an originary home.

One device musicians use to increase the drama of the theme's eventual return to the home key is to present hints, in the form of fragmentary phrases, of what the resolution will sound like when the theme is subsumed in the tonic tone. A good example of this is the first movement of Beethoven's *Eroica* symphony when the main theme, a horn call, is attempted by a solo horn in the tonic key of E-flat major but is cut off by the entire orchestra. Similarly, Joyce presages Stephen's and Bloom's consubstantiality in their similar dreams—Stephen's dream of Haroun al Raschid and the Arabic man who in friendship pressed the melon to his face, and Bloom's dream about the exotic east.[18] Joyce provides significant evidence of their coming together in their mutual thoughts concerning Shakespeare. In "Scylla and Charybdis," Stephen thinks of the bard as "greyedauburn" (202; 166); and in "Sirens," Joyce transposes into an interior monologue of Bloom a reference to Shakespeare as "greyedauburn" (280; 230). The same phrase repeated in each section suggests the consubstantiality of these characters in the archetypal pattern of journey and return: "One life is all. One body" (202, 280; 166, 230). Shakespeare is the focus of their merging together also in "Circe," where Stephen and Bloom gaze into the mirror and see the bard's reflection. The characters are referents of the sign representing Shakespeare, because of the way in which they fulfill the terms of Stephen's and Joyce's theory of Shakespeare's, the artist's, and God's authorship. In giving birth to Bloom, Joyce/Stephen fulfills the early description of

18. In his always entertaining and informative *Lectures on Literature*, Vladimir Nabokov treats this common dream as crucial to the text. Connecting the melon of Stephen's dream and Bloom's kissing "the melons of her [Molly's] rump" (734), Nabokov calls the dreams prophetic of Bloom's "wishing to bring Stephen and Marion . . . together as a means of displacing Bloom" (330).

his ekphrastic theory that "he himself is the ghost of his own father" (18; 15).

It must be admitted, however, that at this point the text presents few explicit clues indicating that the characters come together either dramatically or emotionally. Bloom's concerted efforts to achieve a quasi-paternal relationship with Stephen in "Eumaeus" end in failure, since Stephen refuses to agree with Bloom's business schemes, theories on art, history, and religion; nor does he agree to partake in the communal confectionery and coffee. However, these abortive but nearly consummated efforts toward merger can be seen to foreshadow an eventual resolution. Also, a dramatic reconciliation can be seen within the sonata structural metaphor composed within the text's ekphrastic system.

In the recapitulation, the original (principal) theme appears again in its home (tonic) key, and the subordinate theme, too, modulates to the tonic, so there is a merging of themes within a common key. "Ithaca" is *Ulysses'* recapitulation. When they share a cup of "Epps massproduct, the creature cocoa" (677; 553), Joyce suggests a communion, a consubstantial merging, when he refers to them as "Blephen" and "Stoom" (682; 558). And the moment the cocoa is consumed, Stephen sings the ballad "Little Harry Hughes," an ekphrasis that, in contributing to the journey motif, relates to the other ekphrases within the system:

> Little Harry Hughes and his schoolfellows all
> Went out for to play ball.
> And the very first ball little Harry Hughes played
> He drove it o'er the jew's garden wall.
> And the very second ball little Harry Hughes played
> He broke the jew's windows all.
>
> (690–91; 565)

The undercurrent of anti-Semitism becomes more apparent in the subsequent verse of the song with the introduction of a "jew's daughter" who murders the gentile boy after luring him into her father's house:

> She took a penknife out of her pocket
> And cut off his little head,
> And now he'll play his ball no more
> for he lies among the dead.
>
> (691–92; 567)

Bloom has already experienced a merging of identities with the resolution of "M'appari." Then he was called "Siopold" by Joyce; now a merger is suggested when the characters are referred to as "Blephen" and "Stoom." Stephen's interpretation of the song connects it with the themes of the earlier ekphrases: "One of all, the least of all, is the victim predestined. Once by inadvertence, twice by design he challenges his destiny. It comes when he is abandoned and challenges him reluctant and, as an apparition of hope and youth, holds him unresisting. It leads him to a strange habitation, to a secret infidel apartment, and there, implacable, immolates him, consenting" (692; 567). Stephen (like the gentile Harry Hughes in the song) is the victim who consents to immolation (ritual sacrifice) in a secret infidel's (Bloom's) apartment. This proposition can be read through one version of Stephen's theory. It was destined that God (tonic) enter the earth to be there transformed into his own Son (dominant) and then immolated in order to return, as Holy Ghost, to his true state as the Trinitarian God, "all in all"; so, too, was it destined that the god/author of *Ulysses*, Joyce, as his son, Stephen (tonic), enter "the strange habitation" of the father's/Bloom's (dominant) life, and be sacrificed in order to return, as ghost, to the world in his fiction. What Stephen sacrifices (and Joyce exorcises) is the adolescent inward pull of self-consciousness, which threatens both solipsism and the relativism of a foundationless discourse. Joyce implies through Stephen that to mature as an artist, he has to learn to embody some of the traits of the more worldly Bloom, and in doing so return to the home of connnectedness with actuality.

Stephen's interpretation of the song also provides a way of reading his ekphrastic theory of consubstantiality through the ekphrasis of sonata resolution. In the exposition of a sonata, the theme travels from the home (tonic) key to the limit of that scale, the dominant key, which nonetheless strives toward and eventually returns to the tonic. It goes forth to the ends of the scale/world "to traverse not itself" (it modulates to another key). But having traversed that reality/scale, it seeks the inevitable return to itself. Stephen, having rejected tradition, church, state, and paternity, has plunged himself into an isolating self-consciousness, which has made a mockery of his pledge in *A Portrait* "to encounter for the millionth time the reality of experience" (252–53). Such an encounter requires a journey to the extreme limit of his scale of possibilities, where he modulates to Bloom's (dominant) key. This identification with a figure so very different from himself is a crucial step in Stephen's artistic life. Transcending the narrow confines of the isolated self is prerequisite to creating a world outside of self, and such a transcendence implies Stephen's inevitable return to the self as artist where, in conceivably writing *Ulysses*, Stephen/Joyce, as father to the father figure Bloom, becomes "his own grandfather" and "the father of his race."

A strong argument could also be made that the tonic key should apply to Bloom—the correspondent figure to Odysseus, the wanderer who must return. The applicability of Stephen and Bloom to the principal theme analogy suggests that both are tonic to each other's dominant. Joyce offers this as a possibility in the interpretation of "Little Harry Hughes" when he refers to the host (Bloom) as both the "victim predestined" and "secret infidel" (692; 567). In other words, *Ulysses* contains the story of more than one odyssey, and in their own scales, Stephen and Bloom must each identify with the other (if but for a moment) in order to return to a whole self. And it is in "Ithaca" that they literally become "Blephen and Stoom." Boyle's application of the sonata form fails because he identifies the principal and subordinate themes too narrowly with the specific characters of Stephen and Bloom. They are both tonic keys in their own worlds, and they modulate to the other's key at the same moment in "Ithaca." Appropriate for the musical metaphor, their union is preceded by ekphrases, songs they sing and chant to each other "with modulations of voice" (688; 563). Stephen, in Gaelic, sings "walk, walk, walk your way, walk in safety, walk with care" (688; 563). The message could be T. S. Eliot's advice in *Four Quartets*—"Old men should be explorers"—a call for change or progress. Bloom chants a verse from the *Song of Solomon*—"thy temple amid thy hair is as a slice of pomegranate" (688; 563). And after writing phrases to compare Hebrew and Gaelic script, Bloom is inspired to chant the first two lines of a Hebrew song, the "Hatikvah." Both acts represent the necessity of accepting the past and a heritage. The cocoa communion was just a symbol of their union, but the moment each of them recognizes what the other offers and admits it to himself, their fortunes merge:

> What was Stephen's auditory sensation?
> He heard in a profound ancient male unfamiliar melody the accumulation of the past.
> What was Bloom's visual sensation?
> He saw in a quick young male familiar form the predestination of a future. (689; 565)

In this climactic moment, keys change, modulate—consubstantiality is complete. Stephen's recognition of the "accumulation of the past," a paternal obligation, is countered by Bloom's recognition that Stephen represents "the predestination of a future," whereby a father might have his youth restored through his son. They each begin a return—Stephen to a creative future by recognizing the past and history as something more than the "nightmare from which I am trying to awake" (34; 28), and Bloom to a chance of retrieving his happier past with Molly through the prospect of future change. In the Linati schema, Joyce describes the technique of "Ithaca" as "fusion." Each of the two characters gets from the other what he lacks in himself. Stephen senses in the older man's behavior the equanimity and self-assurance that comes from experience, what Bloom likes to call the university of life. And Bloom sees in Stephen the creative energy that is "the eternal affirmation of the spirit of man" (666; 544). Their "fusion" represents Joyce's belief in the necessity of an artistic awareness of body and soul, real and ideal. An artist must have a vision that he implicitly identifies in "Cyclops" as "twoeyed"—a realization of both the actual and possible. F. C. McGrath writes that "the symbolic fusion of Stephen and Bloom at the end of *Ulysses* represents, among many other things, the merging of the artistic with the scientific temperament" (164).[19] It is, rather, that the merging of Stephen's inward imagination and creativity with Bloom's curiosity about the world and experience produces the artistic temperament. It is also symbolic of the novelist's twin indebtedness to actuality and possibility. This artistic temperament, as "all in all," subsumes the actual world in which it lives, and recasts it in the possibilities offered by the imagination and language. The spiritual father and son, Bloom and Stephen, are subsumed in this creative image when they look into the mirror in "Circe" and both see Shakespeare's reflection. A symbol of the artist, Shakespeare represents Joyce's return, as ghost, to Dublin by writing a text he claimed could be used as a guide to rebuild the city were it destroyed, a claim indicative of his tie to actuality. And as the Holy Ghost makes consubstantial the separate entities of God the Father and God the Son, so does Joyce, as ghost returned to his world, make consubstantial Stephen and Bloom.

Joyce does not imply that through some miracle they will remain united. Stephen's unconditional refusal of Bloom's offer of room, board, and wife/daughter should settle any doubt. However, they are united for a few significant moments, and they return to their own worlds changed by the possibilities offered by the other. What is miraculous is that even such a brief union can take place at all. Set against "Ithaca's" background

19. McGrath's study of *Ulysses* ("*Ulysses* and the Pragmatic Semiotics of Modernism") concentrates on synthesis as the dominant element of the text. He argues that of all works of modern literature, Joyce's displays the equivalence of scientific and literary interpretations of reality. Citing Ernst Cassirer, Suzanne Langer, and Nelson Goodman, McGrath argues that Joyce's primary theme is worldmaking through symbolic language.

of the frightening infinitude of the humanless universe, the union reveals the essential character of paternity, which Stephen had defined in the *Hamlet* ekphrasis as founded "upon the void. Upon incertitude. Upon unlikelihood" (207; 170). The absence of human emotion in the narrative voice of "Ithaca" ironically gives the chapter its emotional power for the reader. Within the complexity of coldly analytical relations, the characters of Stephen and Bloom are elevated, not diminished, and the objective, scientific mode in which they are examined draws the reader closer to them and their need for communion, the frail human shelter against the frightening void, enacted against incertitude and unlikelihood. Left alone after Stephen's departure, Bloom is symbolic of individual man naked before the universe:

> Alone, what did Bloom feel?
> The cold of interstellar space, thousands of degrees below freezing point or the absolute zero of Fahrenheit, Centigrade or Réaumur. (704; 578)

Joyce described his technique for this chapter to Frank Budgen: "All events are resolved into their cosmic, physical, psychical, etc., equivalents. . . . Bloom and Stephen thereby become heavenly bodies, wanderers like the stars at which they gaze."[20] Within the play of relations that is signification, the signs "Stephen" and "Bloom" cross momentarily under the signs "son" and "father" and depart across the void of differences. Because of the unlikelihood and incertitude of their convergence, the event is given a prominence in the text reserved for the miraculous. The miraculous relation of Stephen and Bloom as son and father is metaphoric of the mystery of corresponding relations of the sign within the infinite web of signifying elements that is language.

Even though Joyce said jokingly that "Ithaca" was the true ending of the novel, it is, of course, not; nor is it, as the recapitulation, the end of the sonata form of *Ulysses*. "Penelope" is a coda, which, in strict musical terms, is a vigorous restatement of the major themes in the home key—it often celebrates the return to the tonic by restating the themes in new, daring contexts that, according to Joseph Machlis, proclaim "the victory of unity over diversity, of continuity over change" (198). Bloom and Stephen continue their consubstantiality as coreferents of "he" in Molly's sexual musings. But Molly's thoughts revolve around Bloom as surely as his revolved about her during the course of the day. Her return to the Edenesque moment for both of them—the day he proposed to her on

---

20. Letter to Frank Budgen, February 1921; quoted in Richard Ellmann, *James Joyce*, 501.

the Hill of Howth—is a celebration of his return too. And her "yes" is the tonic tone, for which Stephen's *"non serviam"* serves as dominant, and its climactic repetition is the triumph of "dominant to love to return" (275; 226).

Joyce's view of Stephen and Bloom's coming together is not as simple as a merging of identities. In the same way, themes of a sonata do not simply merge—they come together in a common key. And Stephen and Bloom's merger is given its fullest treatment in a key that is common to both of them yet separate from each—Molly, whose sensuality is symbolic of their need for earthly correspondence. During the course of the day, both have yielded to the allure of an ideal of love, independent of the flesh. Bello-Bella's spell over Bloom is broken when he can deny the temptations of the ideal in the form of his dream nymph, who brags of her lack of a physical impurity, the human anus: "We immortals, as you saw today, have not such a place and no hair there either" (551; 449). Bloom realizes, "If there were only ethereal where would you all be . . . ?" (553; 451). Bloom's return to tonic, his "dominant to love to return," is away from the "stonecold and pure" (551; 449) sculpted flanks of ethereal goddesses to Molly's warm, earthly crevices: "He kissed the plump mellow yellow smellow melons of her rump, on each plump melonous hemisphere, in their mellow yellow furrow, with obscure prolonged provocative melonsmellonous osculation" (734-35; 604). Bloom presses his face to Molly's "mellow yellow smellow melons" and fulfills Stephen's dream of the man of the street of harlots—"The melon he pressed against my face" (47; 39)—a dream also suggestive of his need for earthly correspondence. The question Stephen asks throughout the novel, "What is the word known to all men?" (49; 41), is the question of a young man with still adolescent views of mature love. Women are either the ideal, universal, untouchable "She, she, she" (48; 40) or the whores of nighttown. The answer to Stephen's question would come from Bloom and his knowledge of women through Molly, implicitly communicated to Stephen. Stephen's naïveté concerning women blemishes him in the eyes of his creator, who rejected Christ as the complete hero because "he was a bachelor, and never lived with a woman, surely living with a woman is one of the most difficult things a man can do, and he never did it" (Budgen 15).

One could argue that the word for which Stephen searches is Molly's "yes." Stephen hints of this when he speaks of "the eternal affirmation of the spirit of man in literature" (666; 544). But his idealistic, intellectual phrasing pales next to the gregarious sensuality of Molly's expression. As symbol of the Earth, Molly does provide an implicit answer: the word is love—not the ideal of love, but one planted in the "full amoral fertilisable" human body (*Letters* 1:164).

From a Galaxy of Signs to a Signifying Ground

The merging of Stephen and Bloom is still one of the most controversial questions concerning *Ulysses*. Because Joyce provides at best only hidden clues concerning his characters' coming together and because their meeting seems to have little immediate effect on each other, readers appear to be free to arrive at their own conclusions. Richard M. Kain, in "The Significance of Stephen's Meeting Bloom: A Survey of Interpretations," shows how Joyce's interpreters divide evenly on this issue. Two commentators, Frank Budgen and Edmund Wilson, gave early expressions to the opposing positions, which are still hotly debated. Budgen writes, "They are like two ships bound for different ports that come within hail and disappear into the night" (259). Wilson counters with the belief that their coming together will alter the life of each: "It is possible that Molly and Bloom, as a result of Bloom's meeting with Stephen, will resume normal marital relations; but it is certain that Stephen, as a result of the meeting, will go away and write *Ulysses*" (202). Kain attempts to reconcile these positions by positing an ambiguity theory based on Joyce's reticence on the subject both in the text and in comments and notes given to interpreters such as Linati and Gilbert. Kain writes, "The ambiguity of *Ulysses*, and Joyce's own ambivalence, render neither the negative nor the affirmative conclusions completely satisfactory. . . . Joyce, like the author of *Hamlet*, achieved an artistically viable ambiguity" (151). This notion of ambiguity fits well with one of Joyce's most famous statements on the novel: "I've put in so many enigmas and puzzles that it will keep the professors busy for centuries arguing over what I meant, and that's the only way of insuring one's immortality" (Ellmann, *Joyce* 535).

However, while the story (Gennette's *histoire*) of the characters' actions may give an ambiguous picture of reconciliation, the text (or *récit*) constrains interpretation in such a way that one sees a reconciliation at another level of textual meaning. The reader is guided by mythic signs and an elaborate ekphrastic system to read Bloom and Stephen as spiritual father and son in the same way that he or she is guided to read Bloom as Odysseus. Aligning the sequence of events of Bloom's day with that of the travels of Odysseus, Joyce shows how this unlikely hero is conduit for an archetypal pattern. Hugh Kenner defines Joyce's practice in terms of the Pound vortex: "In Zurich James Joyce was drawing the 18 hours of Leopold Bloom through a patterned integrity defined by Homer: a tough self-interfering pattern through which, he discerned, Shakespeare had already drawn the skein called Hamlet (Telemachus, Stephen) and Mozart his Don Giovanni (Antinuous, Boylan) and even the elder Dumas his Monte Cristo, returned avenger (Odysseus at Ithaca, the stone guest at the banquet, the ghost at Elsinore). Time, place and personnel alter; the pattern remains" (*Pound* 147). Just as the text imposes a system of signs constraining our reading of Bloom so that we see him as a simulacrum of Odysseus, it also imposes an ekphrastic system that guides our reading of Stephen and Bloom as reconciled father and son. Joyce supports the archetypal and ekphrastic systems with a sequence of tropes that symbolize Stephen and Bloom's consubstantiality, including their mutually engaging in micturition, their communal cocoa, their common vision of Shakespeare, and their simultaneous sighting of "a star precipitated with great apparent velocity . . . towards the zodiacal sign of Leo" (703; 577). However, of all the tropes of consubstantiality, the use of music, completing the ekphrastic system begun in the *Hamlet* debate, is primary to the structure of the text. The primacy of music is reinforced by Joyce's earlier use of song as a medium of consubstantiality. Through Bartell D'Arcy's singing of "The Lass of Aughrim," Gabriel Conroy in "The Dead" merges momentarily with the deceased Michael Furey and, with "his own identity fading out" (*Dubliners* 223), has an epiphanic vision uniting him with all the living and the dead.

The musical sonata form as an extended ekphrasis metaphorizes the structure of the novel to explain both character development and Joyce's use of different language games in the various chapters. The sonata's form of simultaneous opening of opposing themes, their development, and their resolution through consubstantiality describes Stephen and Bloom's odyssey. It also describes the journey of language. The introduction, the first six chapters, establishes a home for discourse in the conventional presentation of inner and outer speech. The subjective thoughts of the characters and the objective reportage of the narrator characterize the opening section, what Monika Fludernik calls "a point of reference, against which later innovations, characteristic of a 'second half' of the book, may be measured" (15). Although the interior monologue and narrative voice often blend in indirect discourse, these poles represent a correspondent ground, a form of life manifest in language. The developmental section—the next ten chapters, "Aeolus" through "Circe"—illustrates how loosely anchored language is to this ground. Each chapter of this section shows how language use can be distorted by social, physical, and psychological determinants, and its referential relations redefined by these pressures. In these chapters Joyce unleashes the sign's potential for disseminating a galaxy of meaning within various coherentist structures.

"Ithaca" and "Penelope" illustrate a return to the initial frame of objectivity and subjectivity, purified of contamination by alienating social discourses. They represent what a purely objective or purely subjective discourse might be like. "Ithaca" and "Penelope," the return home of the hero in the Homeric correspondence, represent language's return to its home, an originary ground of meaning that assumes a correspondent relation between sign and world. That this assumption is merely an assumption, that and no more, has been proved by the motivated substitutions of signs in the middle section. But Joyce ceased the relay of substitutions to return to a ground erected upon the void and show how precarious and valuable this ground is as presupposition for linguistic meaning, communication, and bridging otherness. In this sense, Joyce compares with the late Wittgenstein, who, after illustrating the conventional basis for language, rejected linguistic relativism. According to Wittgenstein, a language game, or form of life, "is not based on grounds"; it is, rather, as the basis of our knowledge, the very ground itself: "It is there—like our life" (*Certainty* 559).

Language's connection to the world, as conventional and unprovable as it might be, is an assumption that a community of speakers must share, and the text's return to this originary assumption is signified by the mysterious consubstantiality of the sign. The tenuous relations of sign and referent, signifier and signified, can be seen in the tenuous human relations in the text. Stephen's and Bloom's seemingly casual alignment under the signs "son" and "father" is accomplished by means of a third term—"Molly," the unfaithful wife and mother who nonetheless provides the fleshly substance of consubstantiality. Molly's "full amoral fertilisable" flesh provides a worldly home for wandering father and son. And meaning is brought home from the rhetorical dissemination of the middle section to a certain, if illusory, connection to the world.

CHAPTER SIX

The Postmodern Subject in the Paracinematic Reality of *Gravity's Rainbow*

The Postmodern Motivated Sign

From a coherentist perspective, a correspondence theory of linguistic meaning merely privileges one of the several systems of signifying relations to make it appear naturally determinative, originating not from cultural discourses but from nature itself. The structuralist challenge to this theory of normative signification originated with Ferdinand de Saussure's positing of an unmotivated, arbitrary relation between the signifier and the signified of a linguistic sign. Saussure argued that the two components of the sign, the "sound image" and the "mental concept," are but arbitrarily connected and that meaning is derived solely within the linguistic system, not from correspondent, extralinguistic relations. Although appearing to provide an ideal critique of correspondent theories of language, Saussure's theory does not detail how such theories are actualized as normative. By neglecting the role of motivation, Saussurean linguistics fails to define the process by which certain signifying relations are privileged. However, many theorists since have provided such accounts by ascribing motivation to such various factors as cultural myth, ideology, and phallocentrism.[1]

Roland Barthes, in *Mythologies*, details how ideology (or, using his term, mythology) can be seen as a second-order signifying system underlying and motivating that of the first order. His famous example from this text—a photograph of a black soldier saluting the French flag—shows a denotative signified in the first-order relation embodying the concept "a black soldier is saluting the French flag" (116), but in the second order, the order of connotation, the sign is a connotative signifier pointing toward such connotative ideological signifieds as militarism, patriotism, the racial equality of colonial France, and so forth. Barthes argues that because ideology works through connotation, a more unconscious source of association, it can appear to consciousness as inherently natural, instead of culturally motivated; however, in reality it is the primary source of motivation. In *S/Z*, Barthes, revising his earlier theory, argues that denotation, the apparently more natural correspondent relation, is the primary field of ideological signifying. He defines denotation as "the superior myth by which the text pretends to return to the nature of language, to language as nature" (9). By analyzing connotation, the cultural intertext, a reader frees the sign from the illusion of normative denotation to reveal the fictionality and ideological motivation of signs purportedly denoting "the real."[2]

Other theoreticians have extended Barthes's theories by illustrating how the human subject is also determined by cultural semiotic systems

1. C. S. Peirce's semiotics places greater emphasis on a motivated signified than is posited by the Saussurean sign's arbitrary relation. Barthes, influenced by Peirce and Hjemslev, develops perhaps more than any other semiotician the idea that signifiers are used to determine the dominant values of a culture. In his analysis of the black soldier saluting the French flag as signifier, Barthes says, "Let us look at the signified . . . it is determined, it is at once historical and intentional; it is the motivation which causes the myth to be uttered" (*Mythologies* 118). The myth expressed is that which denotes and determines a whole series of signifieds that glorify French imperialism. Michael Riffaterre calls the workings of motivation an overdetermination in which "each word appears to be necessary many times over, and its relations with other words appear to be multiply imperative" (*Text* 44). The cultural myth denoted by such motivated relations Riffaterre calls the hypogram.

2. Barthes has enlarged upon his idea of connotation from such early works as *Elements of Semiology* and *Mythologies*. In the latter, he explores more fully the relation between what he calls a connotative signifier and the connotative signified. The cultural codes that support ideology work through this second-order signifying system. What the dominant mythology desires to do is make this second-order system seem primary, the connotative signified a denotative one. Denotation, closing off the play of signification that connotative systems offer, therefore limits the literary and cultural text's plurality of meaning to give politically motivated meanings the appearance of natural reality.

that attempt to elide the formal boundaries of artificiality and reality for ideological purposes. In *The Order of Things*, Foucault remarks that the illusion of a natural signifying relation is attained by the inscription of ideology upon the human unconscious. He writes that "the double articulation of the history of individuals upon the unconscious of culture, and the historicity of those cultures upon the unconscious of individuals," is such that "the signifying chain by which the unique experience of the individual is constituted is perpendicular to the formal system on the basis of which the significations of a culture are constituted" (*Order* 379–80). Foucault argues a psychological position that Jacques Lacan, Gilles Deleuze, and Felix Guattari extend: the human psyche is structured according to systemic social discursive practices. Guattari is especially forceful in arguing that culturally motivated signifying practices implant dominant values through the acquisition of language: "Languages are not mere supports to communication among individuals; they are inseparable from the social and political context in which they are used. What could be called arbitrary in the relationship of signification (the relationship between signifier and the thing signified) is only a particular manifestation of the arbitrariness of power" (103–4). The ramifications of this conclusion are central to separating modernist from postmodernist thought, and they extend into every human arena—science, philosophy, literature, and ethics. To my mind, this is the central theme of the postmodernist paradigm—the artificial construction of human reality through language, which is motivated by ideological ends. For this reason, many texts of the postmodern era provide some of the most exacting critiques of the effect of discourse upon human lives. Paramount among these critiques is the conclusion that a motivated discourse deprives the individual human subject of a perspective extrinsic to social discourses from which a culture can be critically evaluated.[3]

The valorizing of myth, art, and the unconscious within the early modernist paradigm stemmed from a confidence in a privileged perceptual locus in subjectivity, from which the real could be distinguished from narrower social artificialities. However, in much postmodernist theory, all discourse, including the artistic, is a cultural appropriation of both reality and the possible relations of the self to that reality. These are the terms by which Louis Althusser defines ideology: "not the system of

---

3. Peirce posited the notion that "the word or sign which man uses is the man himself" (5.189). Emile Benveniste, in *Problems in General Linguistics*, draws an even more radical formulation, that the human subject is inseparable from the discourse he or she uses: "*I*" is "the individual who utters the present instance of discourse containing the linguistic instance *I*" (218). Louis Althusser and Jean Baudrillard argue that the subject is identical with the cultural discourse, positing no way to step outside ideology.

real relations which govern the existence of individuals, but the imaginary relations of those individuals to the real relations in which they
live" (164–65). Defining the real as the actual conditions of production
and class relations and the imaginary as the means of inscribing these
conditions upon the subjectivities of individuals, Althusser illustrates
how the appeal to reality and nature is a cultural stratagem for disguising
the exploitative use of artificially conceived definitions of what is real. In
"White Mythology," Jacques Derrida quotes Nietzsche—"truths are
illusions of which one has forgotten that they *are* illusions" (217)—and
illustrates, following Althusser, that the forgetting is a motivated forgetting, that a privileged signifier denoting reality is an illusion inscribed
by ideology.

Althusser's separation of the real from the imaginary, however, repeats
what many postmodernist theoreticians thought as modernist error—the
assumption of a perceptual objectivity anterior to social discourse. It also
reveals to them the inadequacy of classical Marxism fully to explain
postmodernist phenomena and theories of discourse. Marxism's utopian
yearning to move out of history by effecting a change in economic
relations is tied to the ability of the proletariat to separate the ideological
from the real, the cultural codes from the actual conditions of production. The tendency in postmodernist thought, by contrast, is to reduce
everything that signifies to the level of the ideological. As Jean Baudrillard states, "All the repressive and reductive strategies of power systems
are already present in the internal logic of the sign, as well as those of
exchange value and political economy" (163). Baudrillard effectively
destroys any notion of ideological signs as mystifications of the materi-
ally real by pointing out the politically encoded and motivated nature of
every sign.

According to Baudrillard, "ideology is actually *that very form* that
traverses both the production of signs and material production" (144).
The signifying practices of postmodern, postindustrial capitalist societies
commodify the sign to such an extent that the relation of signifier to
signified reflects the commodity's relation of exchange value to use
value. Furthermore, if signs and commodities share a common structure,
they are put to the same ideological use, and as a result economic
and discursive practices essentially converge in the postmodern, which
Baudrillard defines as "the stage where the commodity is immediately
produced as a sign, as sign value, and where signs (culture) are produced
as commodities" (147). In a postmodern society so weighted toward
conspicuous consumption, the exchange value determines a commodity's use value, and not, in classical economic terms, the other way
around. As Baudrillard describes it, the fundamental principle "is *not* use

value, the relation to needs, but *symbolic exchange* value, the value of social prestation, of rivalry and, at the limit, of class discriminants" (31). Value is not inherent to any commodified object; it is, instead, something added by the system of exchange, which is a semiotic code of value. By the same token, an individual sign has no inherent meaning; meaning is, instead, derived from the differential relations within the coherentist structure of a broader semiotic network. What results economically and linguistically is a privileging of coherent system over correspondent object, form over sign. Consequently, as exchange value overdetermines use value in the commodity, so the signifier overdetermines the signified. The signified, apparently connected correspondently by the referent to the world, is, in actuality, only "the moving shadow of the Sr. [signified]," and meaning is only "the reality effect in which the play of signifiers comes to fruition and deludes the world" (152). By making the signified (or referent) virtually an interchangeable appendage of the signifier, the relation of the two parts cannot be determined by empirical necessity—"the only relation thinkable, the only concept under which the articulation of the phenomenal (psychological) and the sign can be thought is that of motivation" (153). Baudrillard defines motivation in both political and psychological terms. He isolates "the drive for appropriation and satisfaction, performance and supremacy, which is supposed to be the deepest of human motivations" (204) and "has all of psychology behind it" (154), and positions it centrally within all ideological production, both material and semiotic.[4]

With the political encoding of every sign within a system of power and domination, users of signs cannot free themselves through the agency of linguistic concepts. If, as Baudrillard argues, the entire concept of the individual is based upon signifying systems that are economically and politically motivated, then the individual has no recourse but to be entrapped by those systems with every utterance. The plight of the postmodern novelist is that to provide a critique of culture, he or she must enter the politically encoded system of signs that is language and have that critique appropriated, transformed, and silenced. Fredric Jameson provides an essentializing definition of the postmodernist novelist when he describes E. L. Doctorow's attempt to convey the truth of the American radical tradition: "He has had to convey this great theme

4. Jean Baudrillard's early embrace and later rejection of Marxist thought is perhaps emblematic of postmodernism's uneasy alliance with Marxism generally. In *For a Critique of the Political Economy of the Sign*, Baudrillard rejects the Marxist claim of a naturalized use value that relates to essential human needs and exists prior to commodity production and exchange. This naturalism positions Marxism with other essentialist theories that posit a realm of human freedom outside of sign and commodity production.

formally . . . and more than that has had to elaborate his work by way of that very cultural logic of the postmodern which is itself the mark and symptom of his dilemma" ("Postmodernism" 70–71). The practice of many postmodern novelists has indicated that the only viable escape from entrapment within the system of signs is by thematizing what Jameson elsewhere calls "the prisonhouse of language." The self-conscious narrative techniques of much postmodern writing are an attempt to display the repressive features of linguistic worldmaking. Through self-consciousness, a writer is no longer blindly entrapped by a system that creates a reality to perpetuate itself; the writer can instead show the relation between system building and worldmaking by positing alternative systems and worlds.[5] And like the other texts that I define within a realist tradition, the postmodern realist novel is one that displays centrally the discursive relation of word and world within the terms of its guiding linguistic paradigm.

Cross and Circle: Sign and Thing

Because of its comprehensive depiction and critique of the role of language in the postmodern paradigm, Thomas Pynchon's *Gravity's Rainbow* is probably the period's essential text. It is also, like the earlier realist novels examined, centrally concerned with the theme of referentiality and with discourse's effect upon human lives. As in *V, The Crying of Lot 49,* and *Vineland,* one of Pynchon's major concerns in *Gravity's Rainbow* is motivated discourse's power to entrap lives by actualizing artificial and created possible worlds. And like his earlier novels, his masterwork is structured like a detective novel in which the mission of both readers and central characters is to interpret a mysterious and fetishized text, symbol, or object. Moreover, the interpretive task in *Gravity's Rainbow* is similar to the interpretations of ekphrastic objects examined in earlier texts in that the object is paired against another one, each representing some element of correspondence or coherence. In *Gravity's Rainbow,* the Rocket is the primary phallocentric text/symbol/

---

5. Several studies of postmodernist fiction declare that the motive of self-consciousness is to expose system building and the artificial nature of reality. In *Metafiction: The Theory and Practice of Self-Conscious Fiction,* Patricia Waugh argues that "composing a novel is basically no different from composing one's 'reality'" (24). Linda Hutcheon, in *A Poetics of Postmodernism,* makes similar claims of the postmodern self-reflexive novel: "Its theoretical awareness of history and fiction as human constructs . . . is made the grounds for its rethinking and reworking of the forms and contents of the past" (5).

object of Western civilization because it literally embodies the culture's essentializing meaning, death and transcendence, for, as Pynchon reminds, there are two rockets—one for the earth's salvation, the other for the earth's suicide. As the privileged cultural signifier, it is both "the one Word that rips apart the day" (25) and a "holy Text" (520) with "a promise, a prophecy, of Escape" (758). Through its frequent associations with the image of the cross, the Rocket assumes the hierarchical symbolic status of the crucifix, and with it the sanctioning authority of Christianity, for the text makes clear that nuclear holocaust and planetary escape are but modern technological fulfillments of biblical apocalypse and resurrection. And through even more frequent associations with the phallus, the Rocket also signifies the material source and method of Western civilization's bent toward destruction. Its shape suggests the phallocentric culture whose mode of production culminated in "the Rocket [. . .] an entire system *won*, away from the feminine darkness, held against the entropies of lovable but scatterbrained Mother Nature" (324). The rape and pillage of the earth by human technology is suggested by Enzian's realization about the Rocket's mission: "Do you think we'd've had the rocket if someone, some specific somebody with a name and a penis hadn't *wanted* to chuck a ton of Amatol 300 miles and blow up a block full of civilians? Go ahead, capitalize the T on technology, deify it if it'll make you feel less responsible—but it puts you in with the neutered, brother, in with the eunuchs keeping the harem of our stolen Earth for the numb and joyless hardons of human sultans, human elite" (521). The mysterious relation between Slothrop's erections, which prefigure V–2 blasts in London, and the erections of the 00000 and the 00001 rockets further establishes the sexual basis of the cultural drive for power and domination that culminates in death and destruction. And as the Rocket represents the tragic victory of Western civilization over the Earth, so does it suggest the postmodern valorizing of artificial coherence over natural correspondence, form over content, signifier over signified—or over that shadow of the world, the reality effect, the referent.[6]

One of the most important features of *Gravity's Rainbow*'s thematizing of discourse and reference is its postmodern theory of signs in which the relation of signifier and signified, or sign and referent, is not a utopian one of equivalence but rather one marked by the powerful domination

6. For a discussion of the Rocket as canonical text, see Khachig Tölölyan, "War as Background in *Gravity's Rainbow*." See also Alec McHoul and David Wills, *Writing Pynchon: Strategies in Fictional Analysis*, particularly the chapter "*Gravity's Rainbow* and the Post-Rhetorical."

of one term, the signifier, over the other. Pynchon shares with Foucault, Deleuze, Guattari, Barthes, and Baudrillard the belief that all social relations are characterized by power, especially the coherentist relations of signs from which ideology fashions the world. *Gravity's Rainbow's* view of language is a critique of the excesses of postmodern coherentism, for it dramatizes how systems of signs are equated with systems of control that eventually destroy all correspondences with life and, indeed, destroy life itself.[7] Pynchon views postmodern language as an imprisoning system of internal coherence that has replaced an idealized correspondence with reality and the earth. Throughout the text, there is a nostalgic longing for this correspondent relation, a connection to the world, in which, as Blicero describes, "words are only an eye-twitch from the things they stand for" (100). The form in which language exists now is instead a motivated, coherent system of differential relations between signifiers that, in Baudrillard's terms, "delude the world."

If the Rocket is the text's privileged signifier, its subordinate, oppositional pair in the economy of the sign, the signified, is represented by the Earth in its symbolic form of the circle. The conjoining of the two into the form of the sign is realized by Slothrop when, "with a piece of rock, he scratches this sign:

Slothrop besieged. Only after he'd left it half a dozen more places did it dawn on him that *what he was really drawing was the A4 rocket, seen from below*" (624). After he contemplates the numerous spiritual and political manifestations of this sign, he comes across its most essential form in the sandstone of a cathedral, "the mark of consecration, a cross in a circle" (625). Representing a potential for earthly correspondence, all of the values associated with the various manifestations of the circle in *Gravity's Rainbow* oppose those associated with the Rocket. Like Earth, cosmic egg, womb, mandala, Kazakh and Herero communal and tribal circles, and the Herero *Erdschweinhöle*, the circle signifies the natural designs of fertility, life, and unity. The dominance of the system signified by the Rocket suggests the victory of death over life, singularity over unity, and abstract form over material content. This domination is

7. In my discussion of language as system of control, I am influenced by Charles Russell, "Pynchon's Language: Signs, Systems, and Subversion." Russell's essay is the best short introduction to language as theme in *Gravity's Rainbow*.

dramatized by the numerous possible worlds that are created and artificially actualized for the purpose of exploitation—the elite over the preterite, men over women, western Europeans and Americans over their colonies, industrialists/capitalists over the masses, death merchants over their victims—but the text's thematic of discourse makes clear that this actualization occurs because of the tyranny of the signifier shaping the world in artificial forms motivated by power and greed.

One of the most significant meanings associated with the circle is the concept of "Holy-Center-Approaching" (508). The concept actualizes the circle's inherent meaning as mandala or maze whose center contains a correspondent and unitary meaning. Noting the derivation of this concept in quest romance, Molly Hite describes the Holy Center as "the terminus of the quest, the epiphanic point in both time and space where the questing hero realizes the full meaning of his search and his world" (121).[8] All the major characters—Slothrop, Tchitcherine, and Enzian—are quest heroes searching for that interpretive center where the mystery of their existences will be revealed. But as Hite points out, "The pattern of the quest is an infinite approach, which brings the seeker closer to a terminal revelation without allowing him to reach it" (121). In searching for unitary and correspondent meaning, an absolute denotative, signified, referent, or world, the seekers are lost in a maze of signifiers, a motivated, coherent system of meaning that reveals nothing more than itself. All the quests for the "Holy Center" of denotative meaning result in discoveries of labyrinths of systemization, self-referentiality, and stagnation, for in *Gravity's Rainbow*, meaning is relational only within a coherentist system. Tragic for all the quest characters, however, this maze, or labyrinthine system, manifest in all grammar and socially imposed structures, is motivated by the selfish desire of the chosen elite to transcend death through the sacrificial deaths of the preterite seekers. The monster in the labyrinth is the labyrinth itself.[9]

8. Molly Hite, in "Holy-Center-Approaching in the Novels of Thomas Pynchon," considers the imagery of the circle in terms of the possibility of closure that a center might give. However, according to Hite, this closure or origin exists in Pynchon's texts only as a myth: "He constructs his decentralized texts around the idea that the Center is unaccountably missing" (122). What results is a lack of closure or terminus for both character and reader. Thomas Schaub, in *Pynchon: The Voice of Ambiguity*, interprets the symbol similarly; to him, the circle represents the mandala, which is "meant to invoke an integrating force which spars with the disintegrating forces of analysis" (52). Schaub echoes Hite in claiming that the unity the mandala represents is lost: "The mandala is a visionary image of reality in which its parts are united, though this same reality is experienced as multiplicity, and unity remains a doubtful and ominous possibility" (54).

9. The labyrinth imagery pervading *Gravity's Rainbow* undoubtedly reflects the ways Jorge Luis Borges uses the labyrinth theme to suggest the endless systems of self-

Illumination as Transcendence from Signs

Like the other novels I have examined whose realism is characterized by a central concern with the representational potential of language, *Gravity's Rainbow* portrays the representational conflict between correspondence and coherence theories of language in ekphrastic scenes. The most direct ekphrastic expressions of language as ideally correspondent are the songs of the Aqyns, whose power comes from their immediacy and their theme of an ideal communication unmediated by words. Because of these mystical elements, the Russian Tchitcherine, when hearing the songs for the first time, realizes that "soon someone will come out and write these down in the new Turkic alphabet he helped frame . . . and this is how they will be lost" (357). The replacement of oral signs with written ones represents a loss of correspondent presence and further entanglement within rigidifying coherentist structures. And the oral signs themselves are but empty replacements for direct revelation and apprehension, a substitution of secular sign for divine thing.[10] One song Tchitcherine hears, part of a singing contest between tribal members sitting in a circle, tells of a superior communication that is diminished even by the oral expression of their song, which must rely on words:

> In a place where words are unknown,
> And eyes shine like candles at night,
> And the face of God is a presence
> Behind the mask of the sky—
> . . . .
> If the place were not so distant,
> If words were known, and spoken,
> Then the God might be a gold ikon,
> Or a page in a paper book.

referentiality that make up what is known as reality. Although he does not fully develop the implication of his title, David Seed, in *The Fictional Labyrinths of Thomas Pynchon*, argues that the novel "is constructed on the basis of a worldview that even the most diverse cultural and natural phenomena are interconnected. The repeated metaphors of its own assembly are the lattice and the mosaic" (158).

10. In *The Gnostic Pynchon*, Dwight Eddins interprets this scene as epitomizing a central conflict in *Gravity's Rainbow*—that between "Word and Earth." Eddins describes the conflict as between "language as a compartmentalized shadow world of Apollonian representations, as a system of insubstantial units that depend upon their individual autonomy and upon their dissimilarity to each other for the power of signification . . . in a conflict . . . with the Dionysian unity of life itself, the primordial and preverbal oneness that Pynchon valorizes" (133).

But It comes as the Kirghiz Light—
There is no other way to know it
. . . .
And my words are reaching your ears
As the meaningless sounds of a baby.
(358)

Another ekphrasis, an African Herero myth, represents the pattern Pynchon believes all essential meaning follows after it has been tainted with the rigidifying coherence of grammar, structure, and death. A leader of the nearly exterminated tribe, Enzian recalls the ancient Herero belief that each brilliant sunset is a battle between the sun-god and monstrous warriors who spear it to death "until its blood runs out over the horizon and sky. But under the earth, in the night, the sun is born again, to come back each dawn, new and the same" (322). However, with near extermination and the loss of a tribally sanctioning context, this resurrection myth, as detached words merely representing belief, becomes just an approximation, a compromise, since the signs are once-removed from real divinity—"There may be no gods, but there is a pattern: names by themselves have no magic, but the *act* of naming, the physical utterance, obeys the pattern" (322). As replacement for the gods, the pattern, the system of signs, offers a hope of meaning. Yet the pattern proves imprisoning, and words quite often bring, instead of true experience, its falsification, as in the Herero myth: "The history of the old Hereros is one of lost messages. It began in mythical times, when the sly hare who nests in the Moon brought death among men instead of the Moon's true message. The true message has never come. Perhaps the rocket is meant to take us there someday, and then Moon will tell us its truth at last" (322).

As artifact, the Rocket becomes an artificial substitute for a truer, mystical experience of essential meaning associated with light and illumination for each of the three quest characters seeking the Rocket's mysterious signified: for Slothrop, it is his experience when, as a child, he sees the Northern Lights; for Tchitcherine, it is the Kirghiz Light song; and for Enzian, it is the lost Herero myth of the Sun and Moon. As signifier, or substitute for true experience or "real" thing, the Rocket becomes the "Kabbalist Tree of Life" (747) and the "Word" (25). Finally, Enzian comes to the conclusion that the Hereros "are supposed to be the Kabbalists out here [. . .] to be the scholar-magicians of the Zone, with somewhere in it a Text, to be picked to pieces, annotated, explicated, and masturbated [. . .] that this holy Text had to be the Rocket" (520). But he also realizes the paradox inherent in substituting secular sign for sacred thing: "Its [the Rocket's] symmetries, its latencies, the *cuteness* of it enchanted and seduced us while the real Text persisted, somewhere else, in its darkness, our darkness" (520). Speaking from beyond the grave, "the other side," through medium Peter Sascha, the economist Walter Rathenau indicates that this darkness is in the Earth, the primal circle that has "hugged to its holy center the wastes of dead species, gathered, packed, transmuted, realigned and rewoven molecules to be taken up again by the coal-tar Kabbalists of the other side" (590). For the preterite, like the Hereros, what truly signifies the transcendence of death is the Earth and its capacity to bring further life out of apparent death, a circularity of eternal life that is epitomized by its physical shape. Contrastingly, the Rocket's physical shape, as a line with a beginning and end, signifies life's temporal move toward terminus. But to the unenlightened, the Rocket's threat is ambiguous. Like the hare in the Herero myth, it can bring the truth of the Moon or the complete dominion of death, for there are "two Rockets, good and evil [. . .] a good Rocket to take us to the stars, an evil Rocket for the World's suicide, the two perpetually in struggle" (727). The parabola of the Rocket's flight, the rainbow of the title, connotes another religious symbol—God's covenant signaled by a rainbow in Genesis 9:8–17— which also promises destruction and/or redemption.[11]

Causal Tyranny

The means by which modern culture appropriates essential meaning is by naturalizing it through a form of linearity that is symbolized by the Rocket's shape—through appeals to analysis and cause and effect as ultimate determinations, what Charles Russell defines as "the belief in . . . the continuity of identifiable and controllable forces" (271). As the ghostly voice of Rathenau reminds, the two essential questions for

11. The parabola of the Rocket's flight has several interpretations within the text. Other than the hopeful one signaling God's covenant, it also represents the inevitability of gravity, a predetermined fall that ties together behaviorism, analysis, and Puritanism. As Joseph Slade, in *Thomas Pynchon*, indicates, the fall can be broken down into units of time represented spatially, as the Germans used the trajectories of cannonball flights for rocket ballistic diagrams. In a letter, Pynchon associated these cannonball diagrams with the invention of calculus and with "German Christianity [and] . . . the whole Western/analytic/ 'linear'/alienated shtick" (quoted in Seed, 242). Pynchon here contrasts the Hereros' "unified theory of creation," the cyclic forms explored in *Gravity's Rainbow*, with the linear and determined forms of the West. See also John R. Holmes, " 'A Hand to Turn the Time': History as Film in *Gravity's Rainbow*."

meaning within these determinations are the following: "First, what is the real nature of synthesis. And then, what is the real nature of control?" (167). Analyzing, synthesizing, and perceiving causes to control natural randomness, require objectifying and killing lived experience and are, therefore, "structures favoring death" (167), according to Rathenau. From the other side he can see that "all talk of cause and effect is secular history, and secular history is a diversionary tactic" (167). Acknowledging the motivated manufacture of reality and history, Pynchon writes later, "History is not woven by innocent hands" (277). Causality is parodied by an ekphrastic object, *The Book*, a single copy, shared and exchanged by an esoteric group of readers of (although never explicitly identified in *Gravity's Rainbow*) Pavlov's second series of "Lectures on Conditioned Reflexes," *Conditioned Reflexes and Psychiatry*. The mission of the behaviorist Edward Pointsman, a disciple of Pavlov, is to confirm another death-oriented linearity, his master's assumptions of "a pure physiological basis for the life of the psyche. No effect without a cause, and a clear train of linkages" (89). The desire to prove causality gives significance to Pointsman's continuation of Jamf's experiment with Slothrop. Conditioned to erect in the presence of Imipolex G, Slothrop's penis also erects on future sites of rocket bomb detonations in London. Unless one reads Slothrop's erections as *causing* the rockets to fall on a particular site, this clearly reverses and challenges causality. If Pointsman can find a causal reason for this most aberrant example, then, he says, "we'll have shown again the stone determinacy of everything, of every soul. There will be precious little room for any hope at all. You can see how important a discovery like that would be" (86).[12]

In a debate over the truth-values of an ekphrastic artifact reminiscent of those between the Canon and the barber, Emma and Knightley, Vronsky and Mihailov, and Stephen and A. E., Roger Mexico argues with Pointsman over the validity of *The Book*'s premises and advises that "the next great breakthrough may come when we have the courage to abandon cause-and-effect entirely, and strike off at some other angle" (89). The "other angle" is most explicitly stated in an important film ekphrasis, which is a part of the most important ekphrastic system within the text. While watching Fritz Lang's *Die Niebelungen*, Leni Pökler corrects Franz for watching films by nodding in and out of sleep and piecing together the fragments of plot. "You're the cause-and-effect man" (159), she says. Using the analogy of astrology to explain narrative interpretation, she describes the structure of *Gravity's Rainbow*—"Parallel, not series. Metaphor. Signs and symptoms. Mapping on to

12. For a discussion of Pointsman and behaviorism, see Schaub, 90–94.

different coordinate systems, I don't know" (159). Pynchon parodies his abandonment of causality when he writes late in the novel, "You will want cause and effect. All right" (663). After a few causally connected paragraphs, however, he consciously digresses from causal narration. Another important way in which Pynchon challenges causality within his narrative is by not allowing the stories of his major characters to reach final closure. However, the significance of these ekphrastic scenes becomes clearer when interpreted as part of the extensive ekphrastic system informing the structure, theme, and style of the entire text.

These ekphrases show that, as opposed to causal narration, *Gravity's Rainbow* presents "parallel" but "different coordinate systems," operating under roughly the same patterns of domination and submission. These parallel systems of coherence are arranged analogically.[13] The intricate complexity with which Pynchon describes these systems can be seen in Kathryn Hume's and Stephen Weisenburger's comprehensive works on *Gravity's Rainbow*.[14] Russell writes about this systemization thematized in the text: "All behavior, all knowledge, all *reality* seem to exhibit the same structure and logic" (255). Indeed, the text is designed to lead the reader to "the discovery that *everything is connected*, everything in the Creation, a secondary illumination—not yet blindingly One, but at least connected" (703). The connected systems extend from the human in two directions—transcendentally to the realm of spirit and physically to the level of molecule and atom. The hierarchical structures of the Calvinistic God as well as the bureaucratic other side provide parallels for human action from the spiritual level, as molecular and atomic structures provide material parallels. That these systems correspond to one another and that language itself is structured along similar lines prove the possibility of a redeeming correspondence theory of truth and meaning. But the redeeming myth of such a correspondent order of signifying is lost in the human past. As Pynchon writes:

13. Possibly the best discussion of the parallel systems of control in *Gravity's Rainbow* is Molly Hite's section "Structures Favoring Death" from her book *Ideas of Order in the Novels of Thomas Pynchon*, 100–31. See also Russell, "Pynchon's Language."

14. Hume's and Weisenberger's work represent what Bernard Duyfhuizen calls "the third phase" of Pynchon criticism in a review-essay ("Pynchon Criticism: Third Phase") of several works on Pynchon, written roughly twenty-five years after the publication of *V.* The first phase he defined as "narrow readings of 'paranoia' and 'entropy' as distinct themes rather than integrated features in a full textual matrix" (75–76). The second phase he calls a "deconstructive" one tracing the indeterminate nature of Pynchon's text. The third phase is characterized by "not just a recognition of Pynchon's use of details drawn from the 'real' world, but also a thematics of the mythic and religious patterns in *Gravity's Rainbow*" (77). Hume's work particularly indicates the intricacy of the shaping structures of the novel and reclaims not only its thematic structure but also its worldview from the readings that find it undecidable and indeterminate.

> The rest of us, not chosen for enlightenment, [. . .] must go on
> blundering inside our front-brain faith in Kute Korresponden-
> ces, hoping that for each psi-synthetic taken from Earth's soul
> there is a molecule, secular, more or less ordinary and named,
> over here—kicking endlessly among the plastic trivia, finding in
> each Deeper Significance and trying to string them all together
> like terms of a power series hoping to zero in on the tremendous
> and secret Function whose name, like the permuted names of
> God, cannot be spoken. (590)

Although the secular words and molecules over here correspond to the
"transmuted, realigned, and rewoven molecules" (590) over there on the
other side, this correspondence provides no escape from the imprisoning
structures of coherent secular systems. In fact, the same imprisoning
structures exist in all systems, as the voices from the other side prophesy.
The secular versions of these coherent structures are perhaps best observ-
able through their manifestations in multinational cartels and monopolies, such as IG Farben and GE, which have altered natural processes
for the self-perpetuating design of exploitation and victimization. But
Rathenau also tells of members of "an astral IG" (590), who have
discovered and communicated to their secular counterparts the means by
which their system can be preserved.

Immortality in Molecule and Word

One of the most profoundly significant revelations communicated from
the spiritual monopolies to the secular ones is the dream "sent" to
August Kekulé leading to his discovery of the aromatic ring that became
"a blueprint, a basis for new compounds [. . .] so that there would be a
field of aromatic chemistry to ally itself with secular power, and find
new methods of synthesis that would become the IG" (412). Pynchon
speculates about the transmission of this dream of the "Great Serpent
with his head in his mouth" (412), signifying to Kekulé the circular
structure of benzene as well as the circularity of all existence: "Doesn't
that imply a switching path of some kind? a bureaucracy? Why shouldn't
the IG go to seances? They ought to be quite at home with the
bureaucracies of the other side" (410–11). What is important, the dream
gives the secular and spiritual elite the basis by which capitalist exploitation can reconfigure natural processes:

> The Serpent that announces, "the World is a closed thing, cyclical, resonant, eternally-returning," is to be delivered into a system whose only aim is to *violate* the Cycle. Taking and not giving back, demanding that "productivity" and "earnings" keep on increasing with time, the System removing from the rest of the World these vast quantities of energy to keep its own tiny desperate fraction showing a profit: and not only most of humanity—most of the World, animal, vegetable and mineral, is laid waste in the process. (412)

The capitalist extraction of surplus value is one of numerous examples of the violation of circular, cyclical natural patterns. The example of the benzene ring shows that natural forms can be manipulated to serve the ends of profit. This is the lesson Jamf gives to his then student Pökler. Instead of telling us that "we had been given certain molecules, certain combinations and not others [. . .] the Serpent whispered, *They can be changed*, and new molecules assembled from the debris of the given" (413). The reassembling of molecules allows for the invention of synthetic materials that are more stable and hence more controllable than natural ones. However, their stability depends upon their artificiality, upon their existing as compounds of inorganic forms. These synthetic and inorganic compounds, "structures favoring death," give the elite power through a multinational, monopolized economic structure called "the Firm." This synthetic process has configured all semiotic and language systems, which also have replaced a natural correspondence.

The products from synthetics, including the Rocket, extend the elite's and the Firm's dominion over nature. After revealing specifically the elite and more broadly the human role as "God's spoilers [. . .] holding down that green uprising" (720), Blicero realizes, "*It is our mission to promote death*" (720). The Firm "promotes death" by extending the "structures favoring death" from the linguistic and industrial to the molecular level. Jamf taught that from synthetics one learns to move beyond the covalent bond, common to animate forms, to the ionic bond, common to inanimate ones. The covalent bond is formed by a sharing of electrons between atoms, and the ionic by the complete transfer of one or more electrons from one atom to another. Jamf is appalled that "something so mutable, so *soft*, as a sharing of electrons by atoms of carbon should lie at the core of life. [. . .] How much stronger, how everlasting was the *ionic* bond—where electrons are not shared, but *captured, Seized!*" (577). The transfer of power by the greater force of the stronger underlies the secular, sacred, linguistic, and molecular economies. And the victory of these structures represents a furthering of the dominion of death over life, as Jamf lectures that the future of synthetics is to abandon animate structures in favor of the inanimate: "You have two choices [. . .] stay behind with carbon and hydrogen" or "move beyond life, toward the inorganic. Here is no frailty, no mortality—here is Strength, and the Timeless" (580).[15]

Jamf's experiment with Slothrop is a primary example in the text of the bonding of organic forms with inorganic ones. Jamf's invention, Imipolex G, the synthetic plastic that has the organic feature of sensuously erecting, was the conditioning element causing Infant Tyrone's penis to erect. And Slothrop's later, mature erections in London establish his bond with another inorganic erection—the launching of the V–2 rockets, whose falls he predicts. Because Imipolex G was used as the conditioning agent, one might read this relation of Slothrop's erections and the V–2 as being caused by it. But paradoxically Imipolex G was used in only one rocket—the 00000 carrying Gottfried, cradled in an Imipolex shroud, to his death. Both Slothrop and Gottfried are conditioned by Imipolex G to accept a parodic sexual union with the inorganic Rocket, another violation of living forms by the synthetic and manufactured. In fact, Gottfried's launch in the 00000 is described as a wedding ritual. And, significantly, both Slothrop and Gottfried react the same way to the smell of gaseous Imipolex G, the form in which the causal agent was administered to Baby Tyrone. For Slothrop, childhood memories mean that "something was done to him, in a room, while he lay helpless" (285); and Imipolex G is "a smell before his conscious memory begins, a soft and chemical smell, threatening, haunting, not a smell to be found out in the world [. . .] essence of all the still figures waiting for him inside, daring him to enter and find a secret he cannot survive" (285). And for Gottfried, Imipolex "is a smell he knows. It doesn't frighten him. It was in the room when he fell asleep so long ago, so deep in sweet paralyzed childhood . . . it was there as he began to dream" (754). For both Gottfried and Slothrop, the rooms represent the imprisoning structures of social conditioning that supplant unconscious dream and shape conscious memory. The giving up of Slothrop and Gottfried to these enclosures are betrayals by cultural fathers, as both are actualized in the texts as topoi of the figure of the sacrifice of Isaac by Abraham. As Abraham was willing to sacrifice his son for the promise of his own eternal life, so Broderick Slothrop and Blicero sacrifice Slothrop and

---

15. In analyzing the Pynchon cosmos (*Pynchon's Mythography*), Kathryn Hume invests the mineral world with much of what the novel treats negatively—death and sterility. Hume notes that "also belonging to the negative side in the realm of the inanimate and the mineral are the artifacts that we build from such inert matter" (72).

Gottfried for their own selfish ends. Throughout the text sons are sacrificed for the furtherance of the patriarchal system.

As creator of Imipolex G, Jamf is the text's archetypal "Pernicious Pop." The plastic represents all inherited synthetic structures by which humanity attempts to transcend its own life by promoting the death of others. This transcendence is portrayed as various manifestations of the human desire for personal immortality, eternality of the individual self. Jamf's name is a variation of "I am," and Imipolex is a "-polex," synthetic structure, that signifies "imi-", or "I'm I," a play on God's description of himself in the voice from the burning bush. One could read "Imipolex" as meaning "I am I" through the agency of "polex," or synthetic form. "I" signifies the human ego and phallus, as well as the linear designs fashioned egocentrically for immortality, such as the Rocket, the transcendental signifier, and causality. The human (and primarily male) desire for deification of self through immortality, power, and control is such that living sons are surrendered to death and living forms translated into synthetic, dead systems. When he is carried in the 00000 rocket toward the astral universe and to his sacrificial death, Gottfried, through "a tiny speaker [that] has been surgically implanted," carries with him "the words of Weissmann" (751). In the same way, the "word" of Jamf, "I," is carried into the molecular universe through the invention of his synthetic material, Imipolex G. Imipolex G alludes both to the "IG" in IG Farben, the industrial cartel, and to the acronym "IG" formed by conjoining "I" and "God." The manipulations of molecular structure are the most insidious ways in which humanity, through technology and economic power, has attempted to play God in creating and destroying nature. Imipolex G is one of two inventions by Jamf that attempt to subject the human "I," as "God," upon the molecular universe. A variation of Jamf's hallucinatory drug Oneirine (about which I say more later) is Oneirine theophosphate. Before he injects it, Tchitcherine questions Wimpe: " 'You mean *thio*phosphate, don't you?' Thinks *indicating the presence of sulphur.* . . . Wimpe: 'I mean *theo*phosphate, Vaslav,' *indicating the Presence of God*" (702). The synthetic drug, whose name is derived from the Greek for dream, symbolizes all synthetic systems of meaning that replace reality with analgesic, deadening dream. As what Tchitcherine earlier calls them—"political narcotics . . . [o]piates of the people" (701)—these systems secularize the Marxist view of religion as an opiate and indicate a new shift of power from divinity to the human ego.

Pynchon implies that monopolized capitalism pursuing the selfish ends of the elite is the most recent and destructive version of the human desire to transcend nature and destroy it in the process. However, the text shows that this desire is inherent in humanly created signs. If the Rocket is the "Word," the signifier is "I," whose root is the vertical sign that opposes the circle. The vertical cipher signifies all human efforts to transcend the circular cycles of life and death. But in the text, the conjoining of line and circle is the parabola, the arc of the rocket's flight, gravity's rainbow. The rocket's parabolic flight shows that this desire, rather than lead to transcendence, will lead instead to human extinction.

Pynchon makes clear that the reconfiguring of natural systems at the molecular level, leading ultimately to "the Rocket [. . .] an entire system *won* from [. . .] Mother Nature" (324), was made possible because of the extension of the tyranny of the ultimately privileged signifier, "I," as well as the semiotic system of exchange that supports it. Thus Pynchon's thematizing of representation is not merely an exercise in self-referentiality; it is an exploration of the linguistic basis of power. The human elite first learned how to manipulate signs to create a synthetic reality and then applied their semiotic successes to a molecular level. This is Blobadjian's realization when comparing his work on linguistic and molecular structures: "How alphabetic is the nature of molecules [. . .] 'See: how they are taken out from the coarse flow—shaped, cleaned, rectified, just as you once redeemed your letters from the lawless, the mortal streaming of human speech. . . . These are our letters, our words: they too can be modulated, broken, recoupled, redefined, co-polymerized one to the other in worldwide chains that will surface now and then over long molecular silences, like the seen parts of a tapestry' " (355). Pynchon indicates that underlying all human analysis and synthesis is the extraction of form from essentializing content and then the manipulation of that form to serve selfish human ends. The separation of signifier from signified and of sign from referent allows for the creation of artificially coherent systems of meaning that operate under their own internal logic and not those dictated by a correspondence with nature. So too does the separation of molecules from natural forms to be "modulated, broken, recoupled, redefined" allow for these human systems of meaning to replace natural ones.[16]

The Spliced Frames of Reality

As I have indicated, Pynchon portrays the political manipulations of signs in numerous ways, but the most interesting and important one is

16. See Russell, "Pynchon's Language," and Hite's *Ideas of Order* for further discussion of the relation between the linguistic and molecular manipulations by Jamf and the formulators of the new Turkish alphabet. See also Eddins's *Gnostic Pynchon* and "Paradigms Reclaimed: The Language of Science in *Gravity's Rainbow*."

the extensive system of filmic ekphrases and devices that lead one to assume that the text of *Gravity's Rainbow* is a film. Film serves the ekphrastic function of mirroring the major themes and techniques of the novelistic text, as well as the assumptions of the postmodernist representational paradigm, because it embodies many of the features of *Gravity's Rainbow*'s critique of the politically encoded sign. For one, its physical form of linear frames represents the linear structure of causal logic as well as that of the Rocket. Moreover, the technique of splicing frames to create an illusory reality illustrates the synthetic rearrangement of natural forms, such as practiced by the Firm. More important, however, film's emulatory effect upon the audience represents the imposition of artificial, coherent structures upon a naturalized reality. To prove that all representations have been "mediated" by film, Pynchon makes the actual-world reality of *Gravity's Rainbow* that of a film.

Many critics have noted that film is probably the most commonly mentioned art form in *Gravity's Rainbow*.[17] Pynchon uses film in two basic ways, thematically and formally. In his thematic use, Pynchon creates an elaborate system of filmic ekphrases, and by also creating textual situations to parallel their plots, he shows how their synthetic, fictional realities have become the empirically real. Pynchon ties his formal use of film with his thematic use and illustrates the synthetic nature of reality by making *Gravity's Rainbow* an imitation of a film. The scenes in which the novel seems a film culminate in the closing one, in which the novel is the film its readers, "old fans who've always been at the movies," view at the Orpheus Theatre, what Tony Tanner calls "the old theatre of our civilization" (55), before the fall of the apocalyptic rocket.

Pynchon has several reasons for choosing filmic ekphrases to illustrate bhow ultimately determining are artificial systems of signs. First and most obvious is the pervasive influence of film upon culture. Our culture has learned to kiss by the example of Clark Gable and Elizabeth Taylor, to walk like Gary Cooper, to talk with the affected coolness and nonchalance of Marlon Brando, and finally to accept Hollywood premises about reality. Film, Pynchon illustrates, has had an enormous emulatory effect upon our culture. Second, the photographic realism of filmic signs gives them the greatest illusion of unmediated vision and communication and hence makes them easier to manipulate to create

17. I have written elsewhere on Pynchon's use of film. Other works on this widely written-about topic include Cowart, "Cinematic Auguries"; Clerc, "Film in *Gravity's Rainbow*"; Simmon, "Beyond the Theater of War"; Lippman, "The Reader of Movies"; Sherill E. Grace, "Fritz Lang and the 'Paracinematic Lives' of *Gravity's Rainbow*"; and McHoul and Wills, *Writing Pynchon*.

false belief. But more important, Pynchon adopts filmic conventions, formulas, perspectives, and even narration to show that no perception is unmediated by shaping structures. In fact, Pynchon makes clear that every aspect of human life is mediated by media; as he writes in *Vineland* about the pervasive effect of the mass media: "If mediated lives . . . why not mediated deaths" (218). By foregrounding these fictional signs, Pynchon makes the reader aware of how much his or her responses are conventionally governed. The primary narrative voice, in fact, is "an old movie fan" speaking to other "old fans who've always been at the movies." By analyzing tone and temporal distance, one can identify the implied narrator of *Gravity's Rainbow* as a knowledgeable, hip, moviegoing late-sixties dropout viewing World War II through cultural framing systems. In *Gravity's Rainbow*, Pynchon illustrates with more amplitude what Fredric Jameson says of E. L. Doctorow's *Ragtime*: "This historical novel can no longer set out to represent the historical past; it can only 'represent' our ideas and stereotypes about the past" (71). For this reason Pynchon rejects an objective narrative voice that would imply the lack of mediation. By using free indirect discourse, the narrative voice changes styles often when describing different characters, thus extending *Ulysses'* experiment with menippean inserted discourses. These changes are shifts from one mediating frame—the filmic—to those that may govern other characters. For example, the Rilkean prose used in many of the Blicero passages indicates how the spiritual yearning of romantic poetry and prose have shaped Germanic sensibilities. In this way, Pynchon adopts *Ulysses'* menippean technique of changing narrative styles to illustrate the effect of discourses upon human life and perceptual reality.

As pervasive is Pynchon's "art of allusions," the frames of film connote better than any other form the "framing" of reality, and in *Gravity's Rainbow* both formal and colloquial definitions of the term are actualized—framing as both the placement within a defining grid and the false implication of the innocent. To Thomas Moore, the concept is central to the text:

> Framing in *Gravity's Rainbow*, then, generally connotes the imaginative or cognitive energy, analysis, the will to order and systematize, which both divides and unites, separates and links subject to object, inside and outside. Self conceives and projects a patterned reality (in Pynchon, grids, labyrinths, systems, structures, assemblies), such that the pattern is imagined to have preexisted and can be introjected, coming back to the self as observation, intuition, revelation, in a reflex arc. (33)

Moore insightfully argues that the filmic frame connotes all human framing—artistic, mathematical, historical, religious, and linguistic. Another important element of the film frame is that it can be spliced together and rearranged, similar to the way Pynchon describes a Jamf-like chemist working with molecular structure. The synthetic structures that result in both cases are a manufacturing of the real. Film represents a wedding of art and technology in the same way that the Rocket is the culmination of the union of technology and political power. It is not insignificant that the text's archetypal scientist, Jamf, invents a film stock—Emulsion J—which director Gerhardt von Göll believes can reveal an underlying reality. And Jamf's supreme invention, Imipolex G, perhaps derives its erectibility from "the projection, *onto* the Surface, of an electronic 'image,' analogous to a motion picture" (700). The linear structure of film thus illustrates the pervasive power of all linear forms that are emblematic of phallocentrism—causal reasoning, molecular structure, the phallus itself, and the Rocket.

The artificial arrangement of the frames of motion pictures are, like the synthetic arrangement of molecules, betrayals of natural sequence and succession. Felipe of the Argentine anarchists suggests the possibility of perceiving this succession when he argues for a greater human sensitivity to rocks and minerals. This is also the implicit argument of this apocalyptic novel, whose only redemption is the penultimate line's hope for "a soul in ev'ry stone" (760). Felipe

> believes [. . .] in a form of mineral consciousness not too much different from that of plants and animals, except for the time scale. Rock's time scale is a lot more stretched out. "We're talking frames per century," Felipe like everybody else here lately has been using a bit of movie language, "per millenium!" Colossal. But Felipe has come to see, as those who are not Sentient Rocksters seldom do, that history as it's been laid on the world is only a fraction, an outward-and-visible fraction. That we must also look to the untold, to the silence around us, to the passage of the next rock we notice—to its aeons of history under the long and female persistence of water and air (who'll be there, once or twice per century, to trip the shutter?) [. . .] (612–13)

Opposed to the slow progress of natural time, lasting "frames per century," humans have succeeded through "the rapid flashing of stills to counterfeit movement" (407). Through the technology of the Firm, the human elite have succeeded in accelerating the natural cycles of birth and death through overpopulation and planned extinction. Global extinction is but the last result of the genocidal thrust of humanity that has led to the extinction of the various species and races mentioned in *Gravity's Rainbow*, such as the Hereros and the dodoes. Pynchon illustrates that in seeking truth and reality we must look to the "persistence of air and water" through aeons rather than be fooled by "persistence of vision," the phenomenon of image retention in which fabricated frames give the illusion of reality.

Reality as Paracinematic

Pynchon writes that "history is not woven by innocent hands" (277). According to Pynchon, history—or historical reality as a system of consensual "facts"—is a manufactured product. This manufacture as an act of creation is as motivated as the creation of art; in fact, Pynchon demythologizes the romantic view of art as spiritually liberating to show it complicit in the political motivations that fabricate a reality. Consensual reality in *Gravity's Rainbow* is a fabrication by "Them," the elite, who manipulate the preterite masses by producing illusory, imprisoning realities that are naturalized as the empirical, linguistically correspondent "real." Because of its source in and access to the unconscious, art serves the elite in a way that is similar to "Their" use of dream, as in the example of Kekulé, whom Pynchon calls "Their brilliant employee" (413),[18] and his dream of the aromatic ring. The narrative voice wonders about the hidden motivation behind determining dreams in speculating, "How is it that we are visited [in dreams] as individuals, each by exactly and only what he needs? Doesn't that imply a switching path of some kind? a bureaucracy?" (410). Jamf also hints of the existence of the "astral IG" when, in lecturing on Kekulé, he wonders: "Who, sent the *Dream*?" (413).

One of the most significant characters exemplifying "Them" in *Gravi-*

18. See Sanford Ames, "Pynchon and Visible Language: Ecriture," for a brief but interesting discussion of the relation between Pynchon's concerns regarding language and those of Deleuze and Guattari (*not* the writers of the *Italian Wedding Fake Book* in *Vineland*). Like Deleuze and Guattari, Pynchon "dramatizes the idea of systems programming a human reality" (170). In Pynchon, "the whole world becomes the visible language of invisible structures, images projected in a darkened theatre" (170). Evoking both Pynchon's cinematic metaphors and his treatment of Kekulé's dream, Ames continues with this analogy: "This theater of guilt and bad conscience is eloquently evoked by Deleuze and Guattari and parallels Pynchon's demonstration of how men are colonized in their most intimate thoughts" (171).

ty's Rainbow is the film director Gerhardt von Göll, a manufacturer of a
kindred form of dream—the dreamworld of film, the commodified
products of Hollywood and Ufa dream factories—and the creator of
several of *Gravity's Rainbow*'s filmic ekphrases. Through references to
von Göll and an extensive ekphrastic system of filmic allusions and
descriptions, Pynchon defines film as a primary means by which the
elite have made an illusory reality in order more easily to exercise power
and control. Film, in fact, is metaphorical of the entire process by which
"They" have fabricated a reality. Von Göll symbolizes an important
aspect of the elite, its ubiquitousness. In his various roles he can control
several forms of cultural production—political, commercial, artistic, and
technological. Like the Firm, he is multinational, working both for the
Germans and the Allies. In order to harness both technology and trade
for dream manufacture, he has business connections with both the
scientist Jamf and the drug dealer Seaman Bodine. He assumes the name
"Der Springer" to conduct illicit trade but also establishes financial
arrangements with the American tycoon Lyle Bland and IG Farben. As
Der Springer, he is the "white knight of the black market" (492).

As "white knight," he is both to be compared and contrasted with
another white knight, Dominus Blicero, Weissmann (white man).
Through their relationship Pynchon displays the routinization of the
charismatic element of hierarchical, knightly status. Blicero—
forbidding, mystical, Rilkean—parodically represents the romantic motif of the quest for immortality that drives Western society. Springer—
the debased, commercialized version of that same longing—eventually
achieves the timeless in escapist "mindless pleasures," drug-induced
states. Springer's symbol, a white knight chess piece (significantly, it is
plastic), gives him the totemic ability to leap over the squares of the
board, beyond the individual frames that would enclose. He describes
his freedom: "You are no longer an actor, but free now, over on the
other side of the camera [. . .] *'flight has been given only to the Springer!'* "
(494). His belief that as a manipulator of frames he is free from the
external frames that control is but one aspect of his megalomania.
Another is his assumption of privilege as one of the elite, the chosen
ones for whose benefit the preterite must suffer and die. When he meets
Slothrop, he guards with a pistol a turkey stolen from the hungry masses
and gleefully comments that because many of them will starve by
tomorrow, there will be fewer with which to contend. When Slothrop
expresses disgust for this remark, von Göll says, "Despise me, exalt
them, but remember, we define each other. Elite and preterite, we move
through a cosmic design of darkness and light, and in all humility, I am
one of the very few who can comprehend it *in toto.* Consider honestly

therefore, young man, which side you would rather be on. While they suffer in perpetual shadows, it's . . . always . . . [breaking into the song 'bright days for the black mar-ket' (fox trot)]" (495).

Pynchon uses von Göll to symbolize the operations of the elite when von Göll creates filmic ekphrases, whose possible worlds are accepted as actual-world reality. With his filmic creations accepted as empirically real, von Göll accomplishes the elite's God-like mission to control reality through its manufacture. Commissioned by the Allies, he directs actors "in plausible blackface" (113), in a film about Herero rocketeers, "the fictional Schwarzkommando" (113), in whose real existence few Allied intelligence officers then believed. But later, when it is proved that Schwarzkommando indeed exist, von Göll is overcome with the belief that he and his film have created them: "Since discovering that Schwarz-kommando are really in the Zone, leading real, *paracinematic* lives that have nothing to do with him or the phony Schwarzkommando footage he shot last winter in England for Operation Black Wing, Springer has been zooming around in a controlled ecstasy of megalomania. He is convinced that his film has somehow brought them into being" (388) (my emphasis). Von Göll believes that the real Schwarzkommandos are "paracinematic" versions of the fictional, cinematic ones filmed by him. Through another filmic ekphrasis created by von Göll, Pynchon illustrates how fictional designs have engendered realities on personal as well as cultural levels. Von Göll is unaware of his greatest paracinematic success—Pökler's daughter, Ilse. In conceiving a child after being stimulated by the torture-rape scene in von Göll's masochistic and porno-graphic *Alpdrücken*, in which a child is also conceived by the actress Greta Erdmann, Pökler makes his daughter, Ilse, a paracinematic version of Greta's Bianca. "How could they not be the same child?" (577), Pökler asks Slothrop. Through this particular ekphrasis, Pynchon indi-cates through film how discourse shapes human identity.

To von Göll, the creations of his imagination, once existing only cinematically, have become tangible, physical, real—or in his terms, paracinematic. Using the prefix "para-" in the sense of beyond, he believes that his possible-world creations have moved beyond a merely imaginative realm and have begun to populate the actual world thought to be objectively real. Pynchon's source for the concept of the paracine-matic, the fictional object become real, is probably the Borgesian "hrönir," the objects from the fictional world of Tlön that begin to intrude upon reality in "Tlön, Uqbar, Orbis Tertius." When von Göll discovers that his cinematic Schwarzkommandos have given birth to real, paracinematic ones, he is overcome with a megalomaniac urge to make all of life paracinematic by encompassing it entirely within a film. For example, Francisco Squalidozzi, the leader of the Argentine anarchists, expresses to von Göll his desire to re-create the myth of Martin Fierro, the gaucho of the once-open pampas. Von Göll assures Squalidozzi that by making a film, *Martin Fierro*, he can make the mythical gaucho and his free plains real by creating paracinematic versions of them, just as with the Schwarzkommando: " 'It is my mission,' he announces to Squalidozzi, with the profound humility that only a German movie director can summon, 'to sow in the Zone seeds of reality. The historical moment demands this, and I can only be its servant. My images, somehow, have been chosen for incarnation. What I can do for the Schwarzkommando I can do for your dream of pampas and sky' " (388).

From the Schwarzkommando to Martin Fierro, von Göll enlarges his ambition of making a world. His godlike omnipotence becomes clear when Slothrop complains to von Göll that life is not a film. Von Göll replies, "Not yet. Maybe not quite yet. You'd better enjoy it while you can. Someday, when the film is fast enough, the equipment pocket-size and selling at people's prices, the lights and booms no longer necessary, *then* . . . then . . ." (527). The seemingly mad director envisions a time when technology will allow the filming of every detail in life, so that the actual world will become his paracinematic version. The irrepressible Springer is not one to wait for technology to catch up with his ambitions, however, and by the end of the novel, Pynchon introduces an ekphrasis to show that von Göll has started his project of making reality paracinematic: "There is a movie going on, under the rug. On the floor, 24 hours a day, pull back the rug sure enough there's that damn movie! A really offensive and tasteless film by Gerhardt von Göll, daily rushes in fact from a project which will never be completed" (745).

The ekphrasis of von Göll's endless film of reality is similar to another encyclopedic ekphrastic narrative described in *Gravity's Rainbow*: Brigadier Pudding's history, "a mammoth work entitled *Things That Can Happen in European Politics*. Begin, of course, with England. 'First,' he wrote, 'Bereshith, as it were: Ramsay MacDonald can die.' By the time he went through resulting party alignments and possible permutations of cabinet posts, Ramsay MacDonald had died. 'Never make it,' he found himself muttering [. . .] it's changing out from under me. Oh dodgy—very dodgy' " (77). Pudding's project fails because he misuses causality. By trying to anticipate and chronicle the mercurial sequence of unforeseen events, Pudding is at the mercy of random causality and always lags one step behind. On the other hand, von Göll, believing himself to be the causal agent of the reality he creates, manufactures the sequential arrangement of images in his films. When they become paracinematic, or "real," he has imposed his chosen patterns upon life.

In making a film about life, he makes life conform to the artificial, synthetic patterns of film. Thus, his perceptual rearrangement of images can be equated with the synthetic rearrangement of molecules in chemistry or the motivated alignment of words with chosen meanings. All three are artificial structures that impose rationalized and manipulable patterns upon reality. One can see von Göll's cinematic pattern emerge in an ekphrasis near the text's conclusion; the set and design—the frame—of his film *Martin Fierro* are as much an empirical as a cinematic reality: "The sets for the movie-to-be help some. The buildings are real, not a false front in sight. The boliche is stocked with real liquor, the pulpería with real food. The sheep, cattle, horses, and corrals are real. The huts are weatherproof and are being slept in. When von Göll leaves—if he ever comes—nothing will be struck. Any of the extras who want to stay are welcome" (613). Von Göll has realized the anarchist dream of the open Argentinean pampas by positioning it paracinematically in the open Zone. By presenting the world as paracinematic, *Gravity's Rainbow* echoes the conclusion of Borges's "Tlön Uqbar," in which all the world has become Tlön, all the world's objects hrönir. Discussing the theme of the artificial becoming real, William Plater writes that in Pynchon, film illustrates that "life and illusion are both a matter of form" (124). Through film one can see the process by which illusory and artificial forms have been naturalized, how the synthetic perceptual frames imposed upon reality actually have replaced it.

Filmic Suppression and Repression

Edward Mendelson writes of Pynchon's use of popular art in general and film specifically, "The popular modes that Pynchon assimilates into his encyclopedia of styles are never modes of liberation from the systems of oppression, but instead are a *means* of oppression and extinguishing" (184). Plater, agreeing with Mendelson on Pynchon's portrayal of film as a system of oppression, says, "Films, drugs, and sadomasochism are typical systems . . . used to create illusions that victimize their adherents" (209). A primary way that films oppress and victimize is the way in which their plots—synthetic, artificial systems—have come to shape reality and affect or create the lives of characters. Literally dozens of films are mentioned in *Gravity's Rainbow*: *Going My Way, White Zombie, The Bride of Frankenstein, Dumbo, The Return of Jack Slade, A Day at the Races, The Cabinet of Dr. Caligari, Freaks, Flying Down to Rio, The Mask of Fu Manchu*, and many more. However, the films given greatest prominence by being ekphrastically described are those whose narratives shape reality into forms of victimization and oppression.

A director/creator with whom von Göll must share the creation of the Schwarzkommando is Merian Cooper, director of *King Kong*.[19] The classic 1932 movie of a giant ape brought by civilized man from the heart of primitive darkness to New York, the white metropolis he nearly destroys, is one of *Gravity's Rainbow*'s key ekphrases illustrating the appropriation of the actual world by the fictional. For example, Cooper's words to Fay Wray, his leading actress, are the epigraph of part 2 of the novel: "You will have the tallest, darkest leading man in Hollywood" (179). Thereafter, Fay Wray's relation to the darkness of her leading man models the psychology of several characters. Jessica Swanlake has a "Fay Wray number" (275), which Pynchon describes as "a kind of protective paralysis [. . .] for the Fist of the Ape, for the lights of electric New York white-waying into the room you thought was safe, could never be penetrated . . . for the coarse black hair, the tendons of need, of tragic love" (275). But later in the novel, Slothrop assumes the role when wearing "a blonde wig and the same long flowing white cross-banded number Fay Wray wears in the screen test with Robert Armstrong on the boat" (688). Among other reasons, Slothrop's sadomasochistic fantasies of being sodomized by blacks qualifies him for this role.

Immediately after Slothrop is transformed into Fay Wray, Pynchon modulates the prose of his novel into verse—a poem that, while never expressly stating it, is to be interpreted as Fay Wray's soliloquy at the time she was tied to the sacrificial altar, waiting to be taken by the fist of the ape, King Kong:

> At that first moment, long before our flight:
> Ravine, tyrannosaurus (flying-mares
> And jaws cracked out of joint), the buzzing serpent
> That jumped you in your own stone living space,
> The pterodactyl or the Fall, no—just . . .
> While I first hung there, forest and night at one,
> Hung waiting with the torches on the wall.
> And waiting for the night's one Shape to come,
> I prayed then, not for Jack, still mooning sappy
> Along the weather-decks—no. I was thinking
> Of Denham—only him, with gun and camera

19. See Charles Clerc, "Film in *Gravity's Rainbow*," for a lengthy analysis of *King Kong* as intertext for several themes within the novel.

Wisecracking in his best bum actor's way
Through Darkest Earth, making the *unreal reel*
(689) (my emphasis)

In this section, Pynchon makes one further reference to Fay Wray, implicitly alluding to other characters who model her archetype: "We've seen them under a thousand names . . . 'Greta Erdmann' is only one, these dames whose job it is to cringe from the Terror" (689). The significance of the *King Kong* ekphrasis as topos is thus revealed. In their own contexts, Fay Wray, Slothrop, Jessica Swanlake, and Margherita Erdmann are blonde, white symbols of civilization's fear of and fascination for darkness, alternately described as "the Fist of the Ape," "the night's one shape," and "the Terror." As a sign of this darkness, the ape also represents "the tendons of need, of tragic love," instinctual, natural urges that are suppressed by the modes of escape from this fear of the dark and unknown. Through analysis and technology, humans seek to escape death, the darkness of biological destiny, in the immachinated, artificial forms they assume in the "white Metropolis" and the "Raketen-Stadt." In culturally psychic terms, the ekphrasis of the ape killed in New York is a fable of the victory of repression.

Cowart remarks that the Fay Wray soliloquy alludes to "the magical ability of directors to make the unreal *real*" (*Pynchon* 36). The pun, "making the unreal reel" (689), suggests that throughout *Gravity's Rainbow* motivated possible worlds of the unreal, or fictional, hover in the individual filmic imagination, ready to be made culturally real. In culturally political terms, the *King Kong* ekphrasis is the prophetic text of psychic repression becoming suppression—the white/European imprisoning and manipulation of primitive darkness through colonialism. The prophecy of *King Kong* is fulfilled when the film generates an empirical event in the text's actual-world reality: "The legend of the black scapeape we cast down like Lucifer from the tallest erection in the world has come, in the fullness of time, to generate its own children, running around inside Germany even now—the Schwarzkommando" (275). The biblical analogy satirizes the role humans play as God lording over primitive nature, and privileges the role of "the black scapeape" as sacrificial victim. As the "unreal" King Kong, abducted from his primitive lair, mounts civilization's highest tower, the Empire State Building, and threatens the white metropolis, so the "real" Schwarzkommandos, abducted from Südwest Afrika, are brought to Germany, where they mount civilization's most powerful tower, the 00001 Rocket, actualizing a threat of cultural destruction. Ironically imitating the 00000 launch, the Schwarzkommando mission engenders great fear in the bureaucratic powers because it results from the deadly combination of repression and technology. The psychic repression of instinctual urges, the colonial suppression of primitive cultures, and marketable technology combine to threaten apocalypse.

According to Charles Clerc, Pynchon is ambivalent "in imparting terror of the monster [King Kong] within society while at the same time conveying sympathy for it as pariah" (144). Pynchon's natural sympathies are for the repressed in nature, but he acknowledges that this repression stems from the deepest of instinctual fears—the death of the self. White, Western culture turns instinctively from the darkness and blackness of nature, which, to its egocentric systems, means oblivion. Edwin Treacle tries to convince his colleagues in the Allied psychological warfare section that their repressed fear of darkness, so aptly manifest in *King Kong*, had created the Schwarzkommando: "Why wouldn't they admit that their repressions *had* . . . incarnated real and living men, likely (according to the best intelligence) in possession of real and living weapons [. . .] they are real, they are living, as you pretend to scream inside the Fist of the Ape" (276–77). The archetypal fear derived from subconscious dreams creates a Hollywood dream that, in turn, becomes real. As one of the researchers in "The White Visitation," Treacle is probably more aware than most of the relation between cinematic reality and subconscious desires and fears. Treacle works with the behaviorists, who use a related, film-based form of conditioning on Grigori, the octopus that is trained to attack "The White Visitation's" agent, Katje Borgesius: "The reel is threaded, the lights are switched off, Grigori's attention is directed to the screen, where an image already walks" (113). Treacle correctly suspects that the film of Katje walking worked on Grigori's primitive consciousness as *King Kong* worked on the dreams of viewers—they are both forms of conditioning: one specifically neurological, the other broadly cultural.

Expressionist Nightmare

Pynchon uses filmic ekphrases to show their culturally specific effects upon individual lives. Although Allied scenes are dominated by the escapist dreams manufactured by Hollywood, German scenes have the nightmarish feel of German cinematic expressionism. For example, several episodes involving Franz and Leni Pökler are colored by the somber, distorted landscapes of the German expressionists' obsession with the danger and mystery of streets, which characterize such silent films as *Die Strasse* (The street), *Die Freudlose Gasse* (The joyless street), *Dirnentragödie* (Tragedy of a street walker), and *Asphalt*. Lotte Eisner, writing on expressionist cinema, discusses the sense of the evocative, treacherous street as part of the German character: "The metaphysical vision of German-speaking artists, whether they be Ludwig Tieck, Kubin, or Meyrink creates streets crammed with snares and pitfalls, which appear to have no relation to reality" (251). In German expressionist films, the street is animated maliciously, as it is in the Germany of *Gravity's Rainbow*: "The street reaches in, makes itself felt everywhere. Leni knows it, hates it" (158). Leni's husband, Franz, is even more terrified of the street: "He thought about its texture, the network of grooves between the paving stones. The only safety there was ant-scaled, down and running the streets of Ant City, bootsoles crashing overhead like black thunder" (399). Another way in which the Germany of *Gravity's Rainbow* is an effect of expressionist reality is in the abundance of shadows and their ancillaries—doubles and mirrors. For example, Margherita Erdmann describes Gerhardt von Göll's lighting technique for *Alpdrücken* (Nightmare): "The lights came from above and below at the same time, so that everyone had two shadows: Cain's and Abel's" (394). This filmic play between illusion and reality, which found metaphorical expression in such films as *Schatten* (Warning shadows), contributes to Pynchon's creation of Enzian, the black shadow of his white half-brother Tchitcherine, and of Ilse, Pökler's "shadow child." In fact, the several doubling of characters in *Gravity's Rainbow* may stem from Pynchon's desire to represent the expressionist influence over German perceptual reality.

As he must share creative honors with Merian Cooper for the Schwarzkommando, von Göll must also share with fellow expressionist Fritz Lang the paracinematic successes with Franz Pökler.[20] A Lang film that is treated ekphrastically to show its strong imprint on Pökler and the Germany of *Gravity's Rainbow* is his 1929 *Die Frau im Mond* (The woman in the moon). Produced in the gestation period of Germany's rocket program, the film, telling the story of a rocket trip to the moon, was supervised by many scientists who later worked on the V-2 project; indeed, Pökler "knew some of the people who'd worked on the special effects" (159). *Gravity's Rainbow* presents two rockets, "a good rocket to take us to the stars [and] an evil rocket for the World's suicide" (727). The ekphrastic *Die Frau im Mond* is *Gravity's Rainbow*'s hopeful fantasy

20. See Sherill E. Grace, "Fritz Lang and the 'Paracinematic Lives' of *Gravity's Rainbow*," for a complete discussion of the numerous allusions within the text to the films of Fritz Lang.

of the good rocket and, like *King Kong*, is another example of film myth becoming reality—the first V–2 launched on October 3, 1942, bore the emblem "Die Frau im Mond." Pynchon, when he describes the takeoff of the 00000, credits Lang for contributing to the reality of the V–2: "The countdown as we know it, 10–9–8-u.s.w. was invented by Fritz Lang in 1929 for the Ufa film *Die Frau im Mond*" (753).

The Lang films most significantly shaping reality in *Gravity's Rainbow* are those Siegfried Kracauer calls, in *From Caligari to Hitler*, the tyrant films that depict "the unavoidable alternative of tyranny or chaos" (77), or, in Pynchon's terms, paranoia or antiparanoia. They are, therefore, described extensively as ekphrases to illustrate their effects upon reality. Kracauer argues that Weimar Germans, buffeted by economic and political chaos, yearned for an omnipotently controlling power, like the "supermen-tyrants" depicted in films, and were conditioned by these cinematic figures to accept the real figure that came in Adolf Hitler. Lang's favorite actor for the criminal supermen roles was Rudolf Klein-Rogge, "whom Pökler idolized and wanted to be like" (578). Klein-Rogge is most famous for his role as Dr. Mabuse, a hypnotist like Dr. Caligari who commits crimes by mind control. This and other such films thus thematize the cybernetic control of the masses by film and discourse in general. Of Klein-Rogge's roles, the one that most impresses Pökler is that of Rotwang, the mad scientist-inventor in *Metropolis*, Lang's 1929 masterpiece and one of the text's key ekphrases.

Set in the twenty-first century, *Metropolis* depicts a society fractured by an insuperable division between capitalists and laborers. John Fredersen, the master of Metropolis, controls the masses laboring underground to support the elite few living in sumptuous skyscrapers. His rebellious son, Freder, joins the saintlike Maria, who has secretly led workers to pray for a savior. Afraid of Maria's influence, Fredersen enlists scientist Rotwang (Klein-Rogge) to create a robot that "never tires and never makes a mistake" and that is physically identical to Maria. Inciting the workers to revolt and destroy their machines, the robot causes the underground to be flooded. A complete holocaust is avoided only when the real Maria, saved from the clutches of Rotwang, restores order. Of *Metropolis*'s effect on Pökler, Pynchon writes:

> Klein-Rogge was carrying nubile actresses off to rooftops when King Kong was still on the tit with no motor skills to speak of. Well, one nubile actress anyway, Brigitte Helm in *Metropolis*. Great movie. Exactly the world Pökler and evidently quite a few others were dreaming about those days, a Corporate City-state where technology was the source of power, the engineer worked

closely with the administrator, the masses labored unseen far underground, and ultimate power lay with a single leader at the top, fatherly and benevolent [. . .] whose name Pökler couldn't remember, being too taken with Klein-Rogge playing the mad inventor that Pökler and his codisciples under Jamf longed to be—indispensable to those who ran the Metropolis, yet, at the end, the untamable lion who could let it all crash, girl, State, masses, himself, asserting his reality against them all in one roaring plunge from rooftop to street. . . . (578)

In Nazi Germany, Pökler wins a role in the cinematic world he had dreamed of, but the dream turns to nightmare. The "single leader at the top," Adolf Hitler, is hardly "fatherly and benevolent." However far it may be from Pökler's dreams, the textual reality of *Gravity's Rainbow* has nevertheless evolved from the ekphrastic reality of *Metropolis*. According to Pynchon, the film's utopian social ideal, conditioning a generation to seek rational control in the form of an authoritarian ruler, betrayed it first in Nazism and later in bureaucratized corporations. Charismatic power, such as that exercised by Fredersen and Hitler, has been routinized into the multinational, hierarchical corporate state, governed not by a single leader but by anonymous administrators of cartels, like IG Farben, GE, and Shell. Scientists and engineers work with administrators—Jamf's relationship with Lyle Bland duplicates Rotwang's with Fredersen—but the bureaucratization of technology transforms lion-scientists like Rotwang into state-controlled technicians like Pökler. Far from an "untamable lion," Pökler has a paracinematic part little better than those of anonymous workers. In addition to showing how modern social relations are effects of *Metropolis*, Pynchon also illustrates how there will be a further expansion of its paracinematic reality in the urban landscape of the future: "It's a giant factory-state here, a City of the Future full of extrapolated 1930s swoop-facaded and balconied skyscrapers, lean chrome caryatids with bobbed hairdos, classy airships of all descriptions drifting in the boom and hush of the city abysses, golden lovelies sunning in roof-gardens and turning to wave as you pass. It is the Raketen-Stadt" (674). Raketen-Stadt, or "Rocket City," is established under "the Articles of Immachination" (279). "Immachination is . . . a crucial concept in *Gravity's Rainbow*," writes Kathryn Hume, for in the text, "humanity wedded or welded to the machine is what threatens us" (44). Maria turned into a robot in *Metropolis* is the cinematic equivalent of the paracinematic Gottfried wedded to the 00000 Rocket in *Gravity's Rainbow*. Both represent the elite's extension of nonliving patterns over all natural forms, particularly that most manipulable of forms, the human.

The Hereros therefore exist in the intersection of two semiotic codes created by ekphrases. As the Schwarzkommandos are "real" analogues for the "fictional" King Kong, they are also the workers in *Metropolis*. From Africa, they are brought "to the Metropolis, that great dull zoo, as specimens of a possibly doomed race," and after the war live "down in abandoned mine shafts" (315). In these "underground communities" (315), they use the technology of the elite, the V–2 rocket, against their masters, just as the underground workers in *Metropolis* turn their machines against their rulers and themselves.

Reality Manufacture

Pynchon models the various plots of *Gravity's Rainbow* on the plots of ekphrastic films to illustrate the processes of reality manufacture and the shaping of human lives. The process by which the film myth of King Kong generates the Schwarzkommando can be seen in *Die Frau im Mond*'s stimulating the V–2 program, *Caligari*'s and *Mabuse*'s conditioning a generation of German moviegoers for Nazism, and *Metropolis*'s creating the image of Raketen-Stadt. An explicit example of this process is Horst Achtfaden's description of the secret 00000 project: "We were given code-names. Characters from a movie, somebody said. The other aerodynamics people were 'Spörri' and 'Hawasch.' I was called 'Wenk' " (455). The characters are from Lang's *Dr. Mabuse der Spieler*. Though unstated, the reader can assume that the project supervisor Weissmann/ Blicero gave himself the name Mabuse to impose this story of a superman-tyrant upon the reality of the project and cast himself in the authoritarian role.

Aboard the *Anubis* with Margherita Erdmann, who was conditioned sexually by her role in von Göll's sadomasochistic *Alpdrücken*, Slothrop says of Ensign Morituri's falsified newsreels: "Looks like German movies have warped other outlooks around here too" (474). The outlook most warped by German movies is Franz Pökler's. Pökler is one of Pynchon's most significant moviegoers, for in him the cultural, neurological, and psychic effects of film are brought together. In an ekphrastic scene involving Pökler, Pynchon suggests how art and discourse work on the subconscious to affect the perceptual reality of individuals. When he and Leni go one night to see Lang's 1924 epic *Die Niebelungen*, Pökler cannot stay awake, for he spends his days and nights in inflation-ridden Weimar Germany scavenging for coal:

> He kept falling asleep, waking to images, that for a half a minute he could make no sense of at all—a close up of a face? a forest, the scales of a Dragon? a battle scene? Often enough it would resolve into Rudolf Klein-Rogge, ancient Oriental thanatomaniac Atilla, head shaved except for a topknot, bead-strung, raving with grandiloquent gestures and those enormous bleak eyes. . . . Pökler would nod back into sleep with bursts of destroying beauty there for his dreams to work on, speaking barbaric gutturals for the silent mouths. [. . .] His wife bitched at Pökler for dozing off, ridiculed his engineer's devotion to cause-and-effect. How could he tell her that the dramatic connections were really all there, in his dreams? (578–79)

Film works on Pökler's dreams as it does on the primitive consciousness of Grigori. The "dream work" of film is to reconfigure the subconscious patterns of individuals and then work collectively to create new archetypes.[21] Pökler's acute sensitivity to these subliminal effects of film makes him a likely choice for von Göll's greatest paracinematic success.

Pökler is deeply implicated in the process by which film makes reality, for his personal reality is repeatedly appropriated and made the locus for the transactions of film and reality. During a gang-rape scene in the sadomasochistically pornographic *Alpdrücken*, Margherita Erdmann conceives a child, Bianca, with (possibly) her costar Max Schlepzig. After seeing the film at Berlin's Ufa theatre, Pökler goes home sexually obsessed with the scene: "God, Erdmann was beautiful. How many other men [. . .] carried the same image from *Alpdrücken* to some drab fat excuse for a bride? How many shadow children would be fathered on Erdmann that night?" (397). Ilse, the shadow child Pökler fathers on Leni that night, eventually becomes a film vision to him, as the Nazis allow him to see her for only short intervals, spaced over long periods of time, so that he is not even sure she is the same child as before: "The only continuity has been her name, and Zwölfkinder, and Pökler's love—love something like the persistence of vision, for They

21. In a scene from *Vineland* Pynchon parodies the process by which mediated images work on the subconscious of individuals to create subjectivity; here he describes Prairie's first conscious contact with the outside world as a four-month-old infant: the viewing of the television show "Gilligan's Island" (368). As in *Gravity's Rainbow*, Pynchon shows how the human subject enters a realm of public discourse anterior to the formation of individual identity.

have used it to create for him the moving image of a daughter, flashing him only these summertime frames of her, leaving it to him to build the illusion of a single child. . . . What would the time scale matter, a 24th of a second or a year?" (422).

"Persistence of vision" is the psychological phenomenon that makes motion pictures possible. Still photographs, when exhibited in rapid sequence, counterfeit movement because the separate images persist long enough in the mind to give the illusion of continuity. The Nazis use the same phenomenon to make the different images of Ilse persist long enough in Pökler's mind to give the illusion of a single child. In this case, the phenomenon is used insidiously for control and manipulation. Pökler's terrifying realization—"Isn't that what they made of my child, a film?" (398)—represents how "They" have pressed art into service to fabricate a life. Most insidiously, the pattern of images arranged in Pökler's subconsciousness to represent Ilse are structured in such a way to touch subconscious incestuous desires. The "Ilse" who finally actualizes his desire by seducing Pökler also wins his soul by serving as instrument for Weissman to blackmail him into working on the rocket project. As Richard Poirier writes, "The loved child was . . . begotten of a film and has since become as if 'framed' by film, just as Gottfried is at last 'framed' by the Rocket that Pökler helped develop" (175). Poirier uses "framed" in two senses: "framed" by the movie still and "framed" in a contrived plot. Both senses of the word apply to Pökler's relationship with his daughter and involvement with the rocket project. Pynchon makes this connection clear in describing the photographing of rocket descents: "There has been this strange connection between the German mind and the rapid flashing of successive stills to counterfeit movement, for at least two centuries—since Leibniz, in the process of inventing calculus, used the same approach to break up the trajectories of cannon-balls through the air. And now Pökler was about to be given proof that these techniques had been extended past images on film, to human lives" (407). The flashing of stills that counterfeits movement in a film also counterfeits a life. Ilse (or the several Ilses), conceived through Pökler's sexual dreams inspired by the "frames" of a sadomasochistic film, is herself placed in a "frame" of sexual experience created to "frame" her father with those sexual dreams, now come full circle in the form of his daughter/lover.

Gravity's Rainbow as Film

To forcefully illustrate that reality is a paracinematic object, a manufactured product, Pynchon blurs the distinctions between the novelistic actual-world reality and the filmic realities that have been ekphrastically represented. George Levine, Scott Simmon, David Cowart, Bertram Lippman, and Thomas Moore all conclude that the imitation of film devices in *Gravity's Rainbow* serves to position the implied reader in the center aisle, up close. The major controversy is what kind of film the reader is seeing when watching *Gravity's Rainbow*. Scott Simmon says that "basically *Gravity's Rainbow* is a musical" (352). Charles Clerc calls the text "a big picture, an epic picture" that "reminds one of Jean Luc-Godard" (150). Pointedly disagreeing with Clerc, Sherill E. Grace argues that Pynchon's text, in theme and overall style, more closely resembles a German expressionist film, particularly one of Lang's. Alec McHoul and David Wills call *Gravity's Rainbow* a "war film" (41) in which "most of all the war is played as a movie containing . . . action, scenarios, bombing, shooting and theatres" (39). While these pointed comparisons are useful, it is ultimately futile to seek a single film or cinematic style as model. Presenting a virtual encyclopedia of filmic codes, the text shows the extent to which individual perceptions are culturally conditioned by the subliminal messages within the cinematic lens. In imitating so many cinematic codes, in essence making *Gravity's Rainbow* an imitation of the determining ekphrases it dramatizes, Pynchon imitates their effects by denying the possibility of his own or *any* privileged aesthetic discourse escaping ideological encoding. The only artistic privilege allowed is self-consciousness—the nodding wink of the moviegoing narrator to his readers, "old fans who've always been at the movies" (760).

The narratological implications of writing a novelistic text as film are important for the genre. McHoul and Wills are so convinced of the potential influence of Pynchon's practice that they write, "Some sort of cinema underwrites much of what happens in *Gravity's Rainbow*, so much that one could well ask whether narrative prose is still possible without such reference" (42). Charles Clerc's "Film in *Gravity's Rainbow*" gives a fairly comprehensive listing of Pynchon's cinematic effects. They include the imitation of film-script form for certain scenes, instructions for editing methods and visual effects, directions for camera angles and lighting (141–42). Many other examples can be found. For instance, in his jarring shifts from scene to scene and character to character, Pynchon achieves the montage effect that Sergei Eisenstein defines as "the conflict of two pieces in opposition to each other" (12). Pynchon is one of the few novelists to have orchestrated a musical score for their novels, in the manner of background music for a film. Scenes are accompanied by "mellow close-harmony reeds humming a movement in the air" (196), or "bridge music here, bright with xylophones" (222), or "conga drums and a peppy tropical orchestra" (229). When Slothrop, in the guise of Ian Scuffling, is chased through Zurich, Pynchon makes sure that we know what the music is: "Zunngg, diddilung, diddila-ta-ta-ta, ya-ta-ta-ta William Tell Overture here" (262). The most common form of music in *Gravity's Rainbow* is song. Characters will, if the occasion arises, croon a ballad, as in a romantic musical. Slothrop woos Katje Borgesius with "It's still too soon / It's not as if we'd kissed and kindled" (195), and Roger Mexico laments his loss of Jessica Swanlake with "I dream that I have found us both again / With spring so many strangers' lives away" (627). Many of the songs in *Gravity's Rainbow*, however, fit Pynchon's own description: "tune(s) of astounding tasteless-ness" (619). The abundance of song gives credence to Simmon's conten-tion that *Gravity's Rainbow* is a musical.

Pynchon's use of cinematic descriptions, forcing the reader to view the novelistic actual world through a film frame, shows how all responses are mediated by sign systems and discourses. This is how he describes the former actress Margherita Erdmann approaching Slothrop, who waits for her at the spa in Bad Karma: "When she materializes it is a shy fade-in, as Gerhardt von Göll [her director] must have brought her on a time or two, not moving so much as Slothrop's own vantage swooping to her silent closeup stabilized presently across from him, finishing his beer, bumming a cigarette" (459). A scene is described "from a German camera-angle" (229). Pirate Prentice's daydreams of his former lover, Scorpia Mossmoon, are triggered by a drawing that is "a De Mille set really, slender and oiled girls in attendance, a suggestion of midday light coming through from overhead" (71). The rocket firing range is camouflaged by "German Expressionist ripples streaming gray and black all over it" (513).

More important, character description in *Gravity's Rainbow* illustrates the way in which film has cast roles in human dramas, thus denying the individual subject the freedom of individuation separate from framing discourses. Writing on Pynchon, David Seed acknowledges film's emula-tory effect on personality: "Characters repeatedly act out cinematic roles so that their behaviour ceases to be individually expressive and resembles a set of routines, of culturally determined patterns" (178). For example, Roger and Jessica's affair is "a typical WWII romantic intrigue" (247), "what Hollywood likes to call a cute meet" (38). Jessica has "a Fay Wray look" (57). They speak to each other in a "flip film-dialogue" (121). Pirate Prentice's favorite expression was "learned [. . .] at the films [. . .] the exact mischievous Irish grin your Dennis Morgan chap goes about cocking down" (32). Seaman Bodine assumes the roles of supporting characters like William Bendix, Arthur Kennedy, and Sam Jaffe. Slothrop's identity is also defined by numerous film codes. In fact,

Clerc, saying that because Slothrop "has been brainwashed by all of the movies he has ever seen," is "the perfect instrument by which Pynchon . . . can convey the enormous influence of cinema upon the human psyche" (130). Slothrop calls himself "some kind of a Van Johnson" (182), but later he is "Errol Flynn frisk[ing] his mustache" (248). He speaks in a "Groucho Marx voice" (246), but later "his voice [is] exactly like Shirley Temple's" (493). The text offers one explanation of what happens when the filmic codes that make up Slothrop are "broken down and scattered" (738)—he has been edited out of the film: "They've stopped the inflow/outflow and here you are trapped inside Their frame with your wastes piling up, ass hanging out all over Their Movieola viewer, waiting for Their editorial blade" (694). After being edited from the film, Slothrop's existence is denied. His name is "apocryphal" (696). Even his archenemy's reality is doubted: "Jamf was only a fiction" (738). At the end, "few [. . .] can see Slothrop as any sort of integral creature anymore" (740). Slothrop's disappearance represents the complete dispersal of those cultural codes that compose his fragmented being. By exhibiting the filmic codes underlying human personality, Pynchon defines the postmodernist fictional character as solely the product of cultural codes. The manufacture of human roles in industrial dream factories has produced the ultimate commodity—the human personality.[22]

George Levine writes that *Gravity's Rainbow* is virtually an encyclopedia of the myths of popular and nonliterary culture and that "these myths appear in the frames of motion pictures so that we are at once entertained, engaged, and conscious of the potential artificiality" (188). Pynchon includes an episode that might suggest the reader's response to *Gravity's Rainbow*'s blurring the distinction between a textual actual-world reality and an ekphrastically rendered fictional world—the story of Takeshi and Ichizo. When the two Komical Kamikazes improvise a haiku to describe the epileptic thrashings of Old Kenosho, the loony radarman, the narrative voice addresses the reader: "You didn't like the haiku. It wasn't *ethereal* enough? Not Japanese at all? In fact it sounded like something *right outa Hollywood*? Well, Captain—yes you Captain Esberg from Pasadena—*you*, have just had, the Mystery Insight! [. . .] Yes it *is* a movie!" (691). Captain Esberg's Mystery Insight is a possible

---

22. As *Gravity's Rainbow* is an encyclopedia of the filmic codes that have pervaded our culture, *Vineland* encyclopedically details the way our lives have been "mediated" by television. For a discussion of this topic, see Joseph Slade, "Communication, Group Theory, and Perception in *Vineland*," and Elaine B. Safer, "Pynchon's World and Its Legendary Past: Humor and the Absurd in a Twentieth-Century *Vineland*."

model for reader response—that the reality of *Gravity's Rainbow* is, like the extratextual world, that of a movie.

In fact, the ultimate use Pynchon makes of filmic ekphrases is to blur the distinction between the textual actual world, the textual fictional world of films, and the extratextual world, in which the reader exists. Pynchon presents reality as a series of fictional Chinese boxes that readers open one by one before reaching the last one, in which they are contained. In the course of reading, the reader is conventionally outside the novel in the "actual" world, observing, from his or her own moment, a fictional theatre of war. However, the word "theatre," in relation to the war, has two distinct textual meanings—specifically it denotes the locus of battle, but it also connotes the sense of the war as something staged, directed, a conspiracy about which ordinary partici- pants or actors are ignorant. On the first page the narrator hints, "The Evacuation still proceeds, but it's all theatre." And later Slothrop concludes, "None of it was real before this moment: only elaborate theatre to fool you" (267). Enzian suspects that "perhaps it's all theater but they *seem* no longer Allies" (326), and later realizes that "the war was never political at all, the politics was all theater, all to keep the people distracted . . . secretly it was being dictated by the needs of technology . . . Plastics, Electronics, Aircraft, and their needs which are understood only by the ruling elite" (521). As theatrical event, the war serves the same function as film in casting roles that serve the profit motive. Films also assure compliance to existing roles by disguising their true design.

On the last page of the novel, the narrative voice destroys the bound- aries of actual- and fictional-world realities and addresses readers directly to imply that they have been cast as characters in another "Theatre of War"—a movie theatre in contemporary Los Angeles, over which a nuclear missile is poised for the final apocalyptic fall. The movie we "old fans" have been seeing might be entitled *Gravity's Rainbow*, for the "screen is a dim page spread before us." When the "film has broken, or a projector bulb has burned out," we learn that "in the darkening and awful expanse of screen something has kept on, a film we have not learned to see . . . it is now a closeup of the face, a face we all know—." The face could be the divine signaling of biblical Revelation. It could be Gottfried's, whose 00000, launched in the preceding section, is analogi- cally related to the nuclear missile. Or it could be Slothrop's, whose scattered personalities readers have to reassemble like the daughters that compose Ilse. But if we accept Pynchon's belief in the movie screen as the repository of contemporary archetypes, the face we see upon it is our own—our collective paracinematic self. For in *Gravity's Rainbow*, the self is not a coherent and unitary individual but a collection of social codes that is the postmodern subject. A generation whose collective dream unfolds upon the movie screen can no longer be considered individuals and spoken of in the singular; we are "old fans."

The Analgesic Dream Factory

The ancestry of Pynchon's theatre metaphors is very old, and his text shares some of the earlier usages. In Calderón's Eucharist play *El gran teatro del mundo*, Mankind is the leading actor of the play of life directed by God. Alonso di Orozco, Gracián, and Jaime Falcó all elaborate this convention, which is probably best expressed in Spanish classical literature by de Quevedo's interpretation of Epictetus: "Life is a comedy; the world, a theatre, and all men players; God, the author. It is He who distributes the roles; it is mankind's duty to play them well" (732b). A subsidiary theme of this convention is that popularized by Calderón's *La vida es sueño*—life is a dream from which we awaken only when entering divine reality.[23]

To Pynchon, life is both a play (or film) and a dream. What passes for reality is not the creation of God but the paracinematic artifices of the Firm, routinized ultimately in the figure of Richard M. Zhlubb, the Nixon caricature who manages the Orpheus, "the old theatre of our civilization" (Tanner 55). The example of Pökler shows how the elite restructure and reconstitute dreams as manufactured products in film dream factories. These commodified dreams are sold to the public, "pushed" like drugs, for films and drugs play similar roles in *Gravity's Rainbow* as creators of illusions that pacify, sedate, and destroy. It is no accident that von Göll is both a creator of films and pusher of drugs, nor is it an accident that Jamf invents both film stock and a hallucinatory drug—Oneirine. Wimpe, the omnipresent agent for IG Farben, explains to Tchitcherine, "There is nearly complete parallelism between analgesia and addiction. The more pain it takes away, the more we desire it" (348). Drugs and films are analgesic and hence addictive because their illusions divert users from the pain of life and the acknowledgment of death. The addictive and sedating power of media images is treated similarly in *Vineland*, where characters are committed to "tubaldetox hospitals" to

---

23. A helpful synopsis of the Spanish classical convention of the world as a stage can be found in Otis H. Green, *Spain and the Western Tradition: The Castilian Mind in Literature from El Cid to Calderón*.

overcome television dependence. *Gravity's Rainbow* shows how films can ease the pain of death in the example of John Dillinger, who, killed after seeing Clark Gable's *Manhattan Melodrama,*

> found a few seconds' strange mercy in the movie images that hadn't quite yet faded from his eyeballs—Clark Gable going off unregenerate to fry in the chair [. . .] just wanting to get it over with, "Die like ya live—all of a sudden, don't drag it out—" even as bitchy little Melvin Purvis, stalked outside the Biograph Theatre [. . .] there was still for the doomed man some shift in personality in effect—the way you've felt for a little while afterward in the real muscles of your face and voice, that you *were* Gable, the ironic eyebrows, the proud, shining, snakelike head—to help Dillinger through the bushwhacking, and a little easier into death. (516)

Dillinger's fate is made easier because, as a paracinematic Clark Gable, he is able to accept death arrogantly and nonchalantly, like Gable's cinematic character. Pynchon compares Dillinger with Närrisch, who also suspects that he might be the victim of a bushwhacking, his arranged by the self-serving Springer. But unlike Dillinger, whose fate was made easier by a movie, "Närrisch hasn't been to a movie since *Der Müde Tod.* That's so long ago he's forgotten its ending, the last Rilke-elegiac shot of weary Death leading the two lovers away hand in hand through the forget-me-nots" (516). Närrisch's inability to remember the end of Lang's 1921 film is unfortunate, for in it the actor Bernard Goetzke, according to Kracauer, "brings the humane character of Death to the fore," a character showing "tenderness" and "an inner opposition to the duty enjoined on him" (91). If Närrisch could remember these characteristics of Death, he might be able to accept his fate more easily. But . . .

Films and drugs are shown to be analgesic because of their ability to transform real and historical patterns into artificial ones "not woven by innocent hands" (277). The official versions of history, which Pynchon shows as paracinematic versions of ekphrastic films, subvert individual freedom. For example, Slothrop, like other characters given illusory views of reality, believes "every wretched Hollywood lie down to and including this year's big hit, *A Tree Grows in Brooklyn*" (641). Because of his impressionability, "They" are able to "put him on the Dream" (697), ba Hollywood Dream of "Happyville instead of [. . .] Pain City" (644–45). Pynchon reveals how both film and drugs work similarly to mask a brutal reality, when one of Slothrop's drug-induced visions of the war takes on a Disney-like innocence. Drugged with sodium amytal given by the behaviorists of "The White Visitation," Slothrop has this hallucination: "For a moment, ten thousand stiffs humped under the snow in the Ardennes take on the sunny Disneyfied look of numbered babies under white wool blankets, waiting to be sent to blessed parents in places like Newton Upper Falls" (70). During the Advent Mass, Roger Mexico has a similar vision: "the lads in Hollywood telling us how grand it is over here, how much fun, Walt Disney causing Dumbo the elephant to clutch to that feather like how many carcasses under the snow tonight among the white-painted tanks" (135). War, too painful to accept in reality, must be paracinematically reconstituted and implanted in the dreams of the preterite masses to serve the motives of the elite.

According to Pynchon, films are the "political narcotics" and "opiates of the people" described by Tchitcherine (701). This explains why the ekphrasis of von Göll's endless film, which will make reality paracine-matic, is entitled *New Dope* (745). Hollywood (and Ufa) dream factories contrive perceptual reality to blind the preterite masses from the self-destructive direction in which they are being led. And toward the conclusion of the novel, Pynchon correlates the Hollywood Dream with the American Dream when he makes a caricature of Nixon the manager of a movie theatre, and this manager takes "you" on a fatal ride on the Hollywood Freeway. Before "you" are taken to your predestined encounter with the Rocket at the Orpheus Theatre, Richard M. Zhlubb points to a group of social outcasts and says: "Relax. [. . .] There'll be a nice secure home for them all, down in Orange County. Right next to Disneyland" (756). Like Slothrop and Mexico, other outcasts, we are offered Disneyfied dreams to mask the brutality of death.

With the dream images of Disney, Gable, Cooper, Lang, Klein-Rogge, Bengt Ekerot, and Maria Casares, the reality of the Western world has been manufactured, made paracinematic. Lured into the Orpheus, "the old theatre of our civilization," "we" readers see, through ekphrases, a pantheon of filmic actors and codes upon the screen of the page before finally seeing only ourselves awaiting destruction. But in the end we resign the paracinematic role the text has defined for us, for our roles are finally those of readers who are directed, by the final line of punctuation, a dash, to circle back to the first page of this prophetic text where a "screaming comes across the sky." Is our circling back only a turn in the maze of "Holy-Center-Approaching," or is it a clue to the circular nature of existence, in which "a Soul in evr'y stone" offers redemption?

The preceding analyses indicate that representation in the realist novel is a divided and relational and not a unitary concept, for realism results not from authorial choices to use consistent, unitary representational norms but instead from representational strategies that are rhetorical in nature. As I have shown, this choice is self-conscious, and the rhetorical strategies used are rather consistent, even if conventional norms change from one historical period to the next. By examining these rhetorical strategies, one can easily see how divided and relational is the conceptual status of realism.

For one, the thematizing of representation and the word-world relation through ekphrases and ekphrastic debates posits relational truth-claims. These relations are intertextual and not extratextual, for the signifying system of a representational paradigm can be present in a text only by the repression of the opposing paradigm. Ironically, the repression, suppression, or absence of a representational scheme through the hegemonic strategies of another is accomplished often by an ekphrastic thematization of that opposition, which makes the opposing paradigm present in the text that would attempt to erase it. What this literary phenomenon indicates is that what is true for the smallest signifying unit, a single sign, is also true for the much larger semiotic system of the novel—meaning or representation occurs through the process described by Derrida: "It is because of *différance* that the movement of signification is possible only if each so-called 'present' element, each element appearing on the scene of presence, is related to something other than itself, thereby keeping within itself the mark of the past element, and already letting itself be vitiated by the mark of its relation to the future element" (*Margins* 13). For my purposes, I would define "past elements" as those previous forms of mimetic representation that appear in a revolutionary realistic text by necessity, for realism establishes its truth-conditions through falsifiability, by contrasting its truth-claims with those of an opposing model, a process grounded in a conflictive definition of realism, what André Gide calls "a rivalry between the real world and a [false] representation of it" (Levin 53). But, as I have suggested, the real world can appear in a text only as a representation, so Gide's formula is better stated as a rivalry between representations.

Another, more important reason for the divided nature of fictional realism is the inherent contradiction in the conjunction of the oppositional terms "fiction" and "real." Realist novelists feel the twin pressures of possible-world construction and actual-world representation, which is itself a result of fictional constructions. This pull in opposing directions causes the realist novelist to moderate the more extreme implications of coherence and correspondence paradigms, and is hence one reason the preceding novelistic examples show that while a text may explicitly support the truth-claims of a traditional or revolutionary paradigm, it often contradicts these surface claims subtextually through its ekphrastic system. Another important result of this conflicting loyalty to word and world is that although the validation of truth-claims through ekphrases and debates over representations make realist meaning intertextual, realist novelists attempt to interject this meaning back into actual-world reality by thematizing this debate through the dramatic action of characters. The sufferings, enlightenments, joys, and tragedies of characters are neither adjunct to nor symbolic of self-reflexive debates on aesthetics. The novels indicate that there are dramatic real-life consequences for the choice of discourses that shape our lives. Don Quixote's madness, Emma's delusions, Anna's tragedy of unrestrained will, Stephen's solipsistic despair, and Slothrop's behavioral conditioning all reflect the consequence of living according to the percepts that define and limit a definition of what is real. However strong is the tie to the linguistic basis of world construction, the realist novel is concerned with actuality, the things of the world, and as such is faithful to its etymological foundation in *res*. Hence, the signs of the things existing in the real world are profuse in realistic texts. Although Barthes, in "The Reality Effect," questions a text's signifying seemingly insignificant details that hide their ideological motivation with the claim "We are the real" (148), these details create the fabric of reality upon which realism is woven. Paradigms of representation attempt to provide a model of realist discourse that, by consensus, has a verisimilar relation to human and material actuality.

The choices an author makes, then, when realism is his or her motive are not just those concerning subject matter, theme, or structure—the choices are embodied in representational schemes that are, or aspire to be, paradigms. Why the concept of paradigm is so crucial to the realist novel is that it implies a consensus, a social agreement on the truth of a model, for a model cannot exist in a social vacuum. Realism is a mode in the genre of the novel that can be defined as a collection of rhetorical strategies that appeals to what Douglas Hewitt calls "the shared world" of human experience and by such an appeal aspires to a kind of objectivity—that which is derived from social agreement. Whether a realist text makes use of traditional modes of rendering to arrive at a picture of this world or implicitly argues that those traditional modes are no longer adequate to represent what is common to shared human experience, it still has as its goal an interpretation of the shared world in which we live. Thus, the antithesis of realism is the expression of a subjectivity for which no consensus can be established to validate its truth-claims.

Because of the necessity of social validation, the realist novel makes the adequacy of representations its essential constitutive element. And the analyses of the preceding novelistic examples show that this concern with representation extends beyond the use of mimetic strategies. Each novel thematizes its own language use and the signs that create or reflect an "actual" world. The weight of these examples indicates that no discussion of realism is adequate without considering what a text says about language and its relation to the world. In fact, the search for a normative measurement of a representation's accuracy motivates the realist novel's self-conscious debate over models.

This redefining of realism according to modal processes rather than intrinsic features is an implicit argument against those definitions that attempt to historicize the mode by identifying it with texts of a single period of literary history. In this sense, realism is a dynamic mode, constantly shaping and creating our construal of reality. Of all literary forms, the realist novel has perhaps the greatest potential for fully exploring the imagining self's relation to reality, and thus it has accrued the responsibility of faithfully rendering this relation, forgetting neither the constitutive mind nor the created and interpreted world in which it exists. As an epistemological tool, the realist novel parallels as well as enacts changes in our perception of our relation to the world, and those texts that relate and constitute the change by an adjustment of formal technique have had a rhetorical tendency to examine self-reflexively the truthful signification of the "real" world that is their subject. These novels have as valid a claim to realism as those whose mimetic conventions have been naturalized by tradition. They provide the most explicit ekphrastic self-definitions, for they must renew the dialectic concerning art and representation, justifying themselves and disclaiming the prevailing tradition. Harry Levin writes that "yesterday's realism is today's convention" (57), for realism is not a static form: it is a mode of literary change.

Appendix I: Painting and the Nineteenth-Century Novel

Tolstoy's choice of a portrait as reflexive ekphrastic artifact is consistent with a contemporary interest in comparing novels with paintings. Because of the growing use of descriptive detail in the nineteenth-century novel, novelists began to speak analogically of their art and painting and of perceiving their fictional worlds in visual terms. The effects of this analogy are still felt in the language of novel criticism, developed largely by Henry James, in whose *Prefaces* analogical comparisons of novels and spatial art abound. Hugh Kenner, writing of the "instinct that as the nineteenth century progressed drew writing and painting closer and closer together" (*Pound* 25), lists several Jamesian critical terms derived from spatial art—such as point of view, foreground and background, perspective, outlook, insight, surfaces, depths, and structure.

The impulse toward visualization is expressed in Ruskin's general comments on art: "The greatest thing a human soul ever does in this world is to see something, and tell what it saw in a plain way. . . . To see clearly is poetry, prophecy and religion all in one" (Kenner, *Homemade* 96). It is from nineteenth-century realist novelists and critics, however, that this impulse becomes prescriptive. One of the earliest of many treatises on realism, N. G. Chernishevsky's *Life and Aesthetics* (1853), defines mimesis in the strictest sense of imitation, reproduction: "The reproduction must convey as nearly as possible the essence of the thing reproduced . . . [and] should be least abstract and be expressed concretely in live pictures and individual images" (Becker 70). Zola, later echoing many of Chernishevsky's remarks, gives, in "Naturalism in the Theatre" (1880), prerequisites for novelists that sound like those for a painter: "The novelist . . . must confine himself to observed data and to the scrupulous study of nature" (Becker 208).

The language of the realist movement has such a strong bias for visual metaphors because the movement itself is grounded in painting. Courbet

placed the words "Du Realisme" over the doorway of the room containing his paintings that had been rejected by the Academy of Fine Arts. A
few years later Jules Claretie attempted to synthesize the aesthetic of
Courbet's paintings with the views novelist M. Champfleury espoused
in his volume of essays *Le realisme*. This theoretical synthesis of the two
arts can be considered the basis for a tradition of French novelists,
broadly realists, who use painters as characters in their novels in order to
define their aesthetic. The tradition includes works by Balzac, Stendahl,
the Goncourt brothers, Burty, Rod, Zola, Huysmans, and Duranty and
extends into postrealism in the later work of Huysmans and Proust.

The most exemplary work in this tradition is Zola's *L'oeuvre*. Zola's
novel, more than any other, defines a paradigmatic form for the nineteenth-century novel using painting as reflexive tool. Zola declared that
the novel was a self-conscious attempt to define himself as a novelist:
through the novel, "I shall recount my own intimate life as a creative
artist" (*L'oeuvre* 8). *L'oeuvre*'s main character, Claude Lantier, begins his
painterly career with a declaration much like Zola's—to reflect life
literally: "Life as it's lived in the streets, the life of rich and poor, in
market-places, on racecourses, along the boulevards and down the back
streets . . . the peasants, the farmyards and the countryside. . . . Modern
life in all its aspects . . ." (48). This impulse, reflecting the panoramic
sweep of social detail characterizing Zola's *Rougon-Macquart* saga, leads
Lantier to attempt a single work that could render the actuality of
modern Parisian life, a vast realistic canvas entitled "Apotheosis of
Paris." Originally, Lantier has this view of the work: ". . . the crane and
the barges with all the porters busy unloading them. . . . That's Paris at
work, understand: hefty labourers, with bare arms and chests and plenty
of muscle! . . . Now on the other side, there's the swimming bath, Paris
at play this time" (218). But the execution of the painting does not match
its original conception. Mysteriously, Lantier paints a nude on a barge in
the midst of photographically rendered detail: driven by unknown urges,
he ignores the rest of the painting to devote himself to the nude, which
grows to colossal proportions, overwhelming other figures. Unlike the
nude in his realistic "Plein-Air," who "was smiling into space as she
basked in the golden sunlight" (35), this *symboliste* nude usurps life and
becomes a sun herself, "her body a blaze of red and yellow, a star,
magnificent, unearthly" (347). Lantier's pursuit of the real leads him into
the unreal, an ideal vision so unattainable that, crushed, he hangs himself
in front of his nude, "gazing upon her with his fixed and lifeless eyes"
(356). Many interpret *L'oeuvre* as Zola's critique of the impressionists,
particularly Cezanne and Manet, for forgetting their movement's realist
backgrounds and venturing into nonrepresentational art. Others see it as

a rejoinder to Zola's former disciple Huysmans, whose *A rebours* espoused the later Lantier's "art for art's sake" philosophy. It should be remembered, though, that Zola described *L'oeuvre* as "my own intimate life as an artist." Lantier represents for Zola the danger of losing scientific objectivity in pursuing reality. Lantier's idealism and subjectivism are paired against the views of fictional novelist Pierre Sandoz, who, for all practical purposes, is Zola's persona. Zola uses Sandoz as Tolstoy uses Mihailov—to portray a true artist as opposed to a false one. Like Zola, Sandoz writes with a scientific-like objectivity: "This is the idea, to study man as he really is . . . the physiological human being, determined by his surroundings, motivated by the functioning of his organs" (162).

The continuous-discontinuous conflict over a painting, used by both Tolstoy and Zola, can be observed in numerous nineteenth-century novels. One is Dickens's *Little Dorrit*; although not explicitly a novel about art like *L'oeuvre*, it contains numerous references to the subject. The false artist is the dilettante Henry Gowan, who describes his portrait of the arch-villain Blandois in such a way: "A bravo waiting for his prey, a distinguished noble waiting to save his country, the common enemy waiting to do someone a bad turn, an angelic messenger waiting to do somebody a good turn—whatever you think he most looks like!" (545). Giving numerous alternatives to his subject's identity, among which the truth, "the common enemy," is hidden, Gowan, as artist, evades responsibility for describing things as they are, and his neglect allows Blandois to maintain his disguise in order to achieve his insidious intent. Like so many authors who criticize a work in another medium, Dickens carries his argument against the painting that can be interpreted as anything over into his own medium, language, in subtly criticizing the polymorphous word used by Blandois's acquaintance Cavalleto—"Altro," a "word being, according to its Genoese emphasis, a confirmation, a contradiction, an assertion, a denial, a taunt, a compliment, a joke, and fifty other things" (47). Against such vagueness Dickens pairs the precision of the scientist William Doyce, who as inventor follows a doctrine much like a realist novelist's: "He had the power . . . of explaining what he himself perceived, and meant, with the direct force and distinctness with which it struck his own mind. He never said, I discovered this adaptation or invented that combination; but showed the whole thing as if the Divine artificer had made it" (570). Unlike Austen, Dickens, Zola, and Tolstoy, many novelists match a portrait or painting not against another interpolated art form but implicitly against the norms of the novel itself. The social and moral realism that George Eliot develops in *Middlemarch*, for example, is shown to be a true representation of life, in contrast with the effete aesthetic of her fictional Nazarene painter Adolf Naumann, who so misrepresents character that he paints the deluded, selfish Casaubon as Saint Thomas Aquinas. Often a novelist uses a painting to explore the relation between art and reality, as Oscar Wilde, in *The Picture of Dorian Gray*, shows the two so closely intertwined that the artifact changes in a self-conscious attempt not to mask the true reality of its subject. Poe uses a painting in his short story "The Oval Portrait" to show the parasitic quality of this relation. In his story a painter literally kills his wife by forcing her to sit long hours in a damp, ill-lit tower to pose for a portrait that becomes more beautiful and lifelike as she dies. The most conventional use of painting in the novel is to delineate character. Charlotte Brontë makes Jane Eyre a painter because her paintings reflect her view of herself and the world. James's Milly Theale in *The Wings of the Dove* sees Bronzino's *Lucrezia Panciatichi* as a harbinger of her death.

These various uses of painters and paintings in the novel have in common the novelists' desires to adapt their works to the visual medium. In "The Lesson of Balzac," James writes, "It is the art of the brush, I know, as opposed to the art of the slate-pencil; but to the art of the brush the novel must return, I hold, to recover whatever may still be recoverable of its sacrificed honor" (*Future* 121). Many nineteenth-century novels attempt to give such detailed and rich descriptions as to make the inner eye equal to the outer. Tolstoy, in *Anna Karenina*, achieves this. According to Dimitri Merezhkovsky, "in Tolstoy we hear because we see" (244). And more interestingly, Tolstoy tells his reader how he makes them see by portraying a painting that reflects his creative vision.

Appendix II: Symbolism and Music

The fin de siècle conflict between the realist and symbolist movements in literature can be observed in the contrasting fine arts each uses as analogues of its works. Tolstoy and Zola implicitly compare their techniques to those of realist painters whose representations are so clear they seem real. As painters create forms that correspond to easily recognized details, so realist novelists use a language that clearly refers to everyday details. The major tenet of realism, objectivity, implies an external approach to character, a view of human personality that is roughly analogous to a lifelike portrait that accurately renders the external details of the human form.

The symbolists, on the other hand, in eschewing realist externality, strove to portray internal states that concrete detail and referential language are ineffective in describing. The language of the symbolists is evocatively ambiguous so as to suggest almost ineffable internal states. Music is the closest parallel to the symbolists' aims, so music became the emblem of their aspirations. Charles Chadwick writes that "music possesses just that quality of suggestiveness that the symbolists were looking for, and lacks just that element of precision which words possess and which the symbolists wished to suppress" (5). The symbolist desire to achieve the effects of music fulfills Richard Wagner's prophecy: "In the course of the poet . . . we see him finally come to the limits of his branch of art, where it already seems to touch music: and thus the most successful work of the poet must be . . . entirely musical" (Ellmann and Feidelson, *Modern* 106). Arguing that the ideal art combines music, poetry, and drama, Wagner leaves no doubt that music is supreme. Walter Pater's famous dictum, "All art aspires to the condition of music" (111), does much to enhance this view.

Wagner addressed his ideas on the musicalization of literature to poetry in particular, and poets, both in theory and practice, responded first to his ideas. Mallarmé's "Crisis in Poetry" is partly rebuttal and partly favorable response to Wagner. While agreeing that ordinary language has been debased and that music is more appropriate to suggest spiritual states, Mallarmé argues for a poetic musicalization of language as the basis of a supreme art. Language is musicalized when freed from reference and syntax and developed as a musical theme—along rhythmic rather than referential or syntactic necessity. When divorced from ordinary uses, words no longer refer to external details but suggest internal states that are truer realities. "When I say, 'a flower,' " Mallarmé writes, "then from that forgetfulness to which my voice consigns all floral form, something different from the usual calyces arises, something all music, essence, and softness: the flower which is absent from all bouquets" (Ellmann and Feidelson, *Modern* 112). The poetic use of the word "flower" does not refer to tangible flowers of the outer world; it rather links the imperfect, debased flower in external reality with the ideal flower in the imagination of the poet. The symbolist desire is to search for such linkages, or, as Baudelaire calls them, "correspondences." And it is through a sensitivity to music and rhythm that these correspondences are found. Paul Verlaine writes in "The Art of Poetry," "Music must be paramount . . . and everything else is mere literature" (99).

The symbolist musicalization of literature, so prevalent in the poetry of the period, affected prose fiction much later, but its effects, when fully realized, were significant. The two greatest prose epics of the era, Joyce's *Ulysses* and Proust's *A la recherche du temps perdu*, were profoundly influenced by music, both in structure and theme. Proust's use of music is similar to Joyce's in several ways. Proust, in *Recherche*, describes a search for linkages, Baudelairean correspondences, between real and ideal, present and past, the most famous example of which is the episode in *Du côté de chez Swann* of the madeleine cake and tea. The taste of madeleine soaked in tea evokes for Marcel the distant past when his now dead Aunt Leonie used to give him a piece of the cake dipped in tea, and miraculously "the whole of Combray, and of its surroundings, taking their proper shapes and growing solid, sprang into being, town and gardens alike, from my cup of tea" (36). The madeleine cake, more than mere symbol of the past, is the physical means by which the past, now lost and destroyed in the external world, is resurrected in its more perfect essence in the internal consciousness of Marcel. And the novel Proust writes is the artistic means by which this essence is preserved further from the devastating effects of time.

Proust describes his search for the physical correspondences of eternal essences in terms of music. As did Joyce, Proust used music as a structural model. Like a Wagnerian opera, the major themes and the strategies of *Recherche* are introduced in the "Overture," and henceforth each theme is reintroduced in the form of a leitmotif, surfacing and resurfacing as the symphonic structure of the novel develops. More important, the paradigm for the present object that corresponds to the essence of past life is an ekphrastic piece of music, a little phrase in the composer Vinteuil's sonata for violin and piano that becomes the focal point of the emotional life of first Swann and then Marcel. The story of Swann's love for Odette de Crecy, a break in the autobiographical narrative of *Du côté de chez Swann*, represents the young Marcel's first awareness of romantic love, which, along with art, leads him out of adolescence into maturity. Swann, meeting Odette at the opera, is taken by her into the salon of Mme. Verdurin, where he first hears the little phrase. As their love progresses, the phrase becomes "the national anthem of their love" (167). Time passes, and after thinking he has lost Odette, Swann unexpectedly hears the sonata and phrase again and "now recovered everything that had fixed unalterably the peculiar, volatile essence of that lost happiness" (265). The ekphrastic musical phrase allows Swann to return to a lost happiness as the ekphrastic song "M'appari" suggests to Bloom the "dominant to love to return." Wallace Fowlie writes that "Vinteuil's music evokes in Swann memories of an entire part of the past . . . as drinking a cup of tea in tante Leonie's room had for Marcel" (71). The phrase and the madeleine are among that group of things, writes Proust, that "bear unfaltering, in the tiny and almost impalpable drop of their essence, the vast structure of recollection" (36). Also, the phrase so distills a past moment that Swann feels what Vinteuil must have felt when he composed it. Through the phrase, Vinteuil and Swann symbiotically share the essence of an emotion, merging together for a time, as Bloom, Simon Dedalus, and Lionel merge in "Sirens" as "Siopold" when "M'appari" is sung.

After he grows older, Marcel hears the phrase played by Odette in the Swann household. Years later, after the sonata passes into oblivion, an older Marcel (in *La prisonnière*, the fifth novel of the series) sits at a piano and, playing the music before him, is surprised that it is Vinteuil's sonata; and he hears again the little phrase, which stirs memories of Combray and his desire to be an artist. Later, Marcel, like Swann, is brought to the salon of Mme. Verdurin to hear a posthumous septet by Vinteuil, in which there is a transcription of the little phrase. His artistic urgings become stronger when, like Swann, he feels a communion with Vinteuil, a sharing of the emotion, the essence of which has been preserved in the phrase and in the composer's work as a whole. George Painter writes that the theme "revealed the existence, somewhere deep within him, of a region in which beauty was real and eternal, uncontaminated by disappointment, sin and death" (48). This realization is a harbinger of Marcel's greater revelation in the closing pages of *Le temps retrouvé*, when he comes to understand his own artistic mission—to write the book the reader is now reading. Marcel vows to "extract the real essence of life in a book" (1112).

When he hears the septet, Marcel realizes that Vinteuil had extracted "the real essence of life" in a piece of music. Vinteuil is the text's ideal artist (as opposed to the derivative, stylized writer Legrandin), whose career has culminated in the composition of a work that incorporates all his previous works and preserves in an ideal state the entirety of his life. After listening to the septet, Marcel thinks, "Vinteuil's sonata, and . . . his other works as well had been no more than timid essays . . . towards the triumphant and complete masterpiece which was revealed to me at the moment" (555). Of this quote Fowlie comments, "In the same way, the early writings of Marcel Proust all flow into the final work where they are deepened and transformed" (253). Vinteuil's work is an ekphrastic form continuous with the work in which it is contained.

Proust's use of music, then, is extensive and pervasive; it serves as a structural model for his work. The musician Vinteuil is the ideal artist upon whom Proust models himself. And an ekphrastic musical theme is an analogue of the central experience of the novel—the preservation of the past through first recollection and then transformation into art. Proust's use of music, however, is not as extensive as that of Joyce in *Ulysses*, who carries Proust's strategies even further. Nevertheless, both *Ulysses* and *A la recherche du temps perdu* are novels that aspire to conditions of music.

WORKS CITED

Aarsleff, Hans. *From Locke to Saussure.* Minneapolis: University of Minnesota Press, 1982.
———. *The Study of Language in England, 1780–1860.* Princeton: Princeton University Press, 1967.
Abrams, M. H. *The Mirror and the Lamp.* New York: Norton, 1958.
Aers, David. "Community and Morality: Towards Reading Jane Austen." In *Romanticism and Ideology: Studies in English Writing, 1765–1830.* London: Routledge & Kegan Paul, 1981. 118–36.
Alpers, Svetlana Leontieff. "*Ekphrasis* and Aesthetic Attitudes in Vasari's *Lives.*" *Journal of the Warburg and Courtauld Institutes* 23 (1960): 190–215.
Alter, Robert. *Partial Magic.* Berkeley and Los Angeles: University of California Press, 1975.
Althusser, Louis. *Lenin and Philosophy.* Trans. Ben Brewster. London: Monthly Review Press, 1972.
Ames, Stanford S. "Pynchon and Visible Language: Ecriture." *International Fiction Review* 4 (1977): 170–73.
Armstrong, Robert L. "John Locke's 'Doctrine of Signs': A New Metaphysics." *Journal of the History of Ideas* 26 (1965): 369–82.
Attbridge, Derek, and Daniel Ferrer, eds. *Post-Structuralist Joyce: Essays from the French.* Cambridge: Cambridge University Press, 1984.
Auerbach, Erich. *Mimesis.* Trans. Willard R. Trask. Princeton: Princeton University Press, 1968.
Austen, Jane. *Emma.* Ed. R. W. Chapman. 3d ed. London: Oxford University Press, 1933.
———. *Northanger Abbey.* Ed. R. W. Chapman. 3d ed. London: Oxford University Press, 1933.
Bakhtin, Mikhail M. *The Dialogical Imagination.* Trans. Ann Shukman. Minneapolis: University of Minnesota Press, 1981.
———. *Problems of Dostoevsky's Poetics.* Trans. Caryl Emerson. Minneapolis: University of Minnesota Press, 1984.
Baldwin, Charles Sears. *Medieval Rhetoric and Poetic (to 1400).* Gloucester, Mass.: Macmillan, 1928.
Barthes, Roland. *Mythologies.* Trans. Annette Lavers. New York: Hill & Wang, 1972.
———. "The Reality Effect." In *The Rustle of Language,* trans. Richard Howard. New York: Hill & Wang, 1986. 141–48.
———. *S/Z.* Trans. Richard Miller. New York: Hill & Wang, 1974.

Bateson, F. W. *English Poetry and the English Language*. Oxford: Clarendon, 1934.

Baudrillard, Jean. *For a Critique of the Political Economy of the Sign*. Trans. Charles Levin. St. Louis: Telos Press, 1981.

Bayley, John. *Tolstoy and the Novel*. New York: Viking, 1966.

Becker, George, ed. *Documents of Modern Literary Realism*. Princeton: Princeton University Press, 1963.

Belsey, Catherine. *Critical Practice*. London: Methuen, 1980.

Benstock, Bernard, ed. *James Joyce: The Augmented Ninth*. Syracuse, N.Y.: Syracuse University Press, 1988.

Benveniste, Emile. *Problems in General Linguistics*. Trans. Mary Elizabeth Meek. Coral Gables: University of Miami Press, 1971.

Bergmann, Emilie L. *Art Inscribed: Essays on Ekphrasis in Spanish Golden Age Poetry*. Cambridge: Harvard University Press, 1979.

Berlin, Isaiah. *The Hedgehog and the Fox*. New York: Simon & Schuster, 1953.

Blackmur, R. P. *Eleven Essays in the European Novel*. New York: Harcourt, Brace & World, 1964.

Blamires, Harry. *The Bloomsday Book*. London: Methuen, 1966.

Booth, Wayne C. *The Rhetoric of Fiction*. Chicago: University of Chicago Press, 1961.

Borges, Jorge Luis. "Tlön, Uqbar, Orbis Tertius." In *Labyrinths*, trans. James E. Irby. New York: New Directions, 1962.

Bowen, Zack. *Musical Allusions in the Works of James Joyce*. Albany: State University of New York Press, 1964.

Bowie, Theodore. *The Painter in French Fiction*. Chapel Hill: University of North Carolina Press, 1950.

Boyle, Robert. "*Ulysses* as Frustrated Sonata Form." *James Joyce Quarterly* 2 (1977): 247–54.

Bradbrook, Frank. *Jane Austen: Emma*. London: Edward Arnold, 1961.

Bradbury, Malcolm, and James MacFarlane. "The Name and Nature of Modernism." In *Modernism*, ed. Malcolm Bradbury and James MacFarlane. Harmondsworth, Middlesex: Penguin, 1976. 19–55.

Bradley, Raymond, and Norman Swartz. *Possible Worlds: An Introduction to Logic and Its Philosophy*. Oxford: Basil Blackwell, 1979.

Brinker, Menachem. "Verisimilitude, Conventions, and Beliefs." *New Literary History* 14 (1983): 253–72.

Brooks, Cleanth. *The Well-Wrought Urn: Studies in the Structure of Poetry*. New York: Reynal & Hitchcock, 1947.

Brown, Richard Harvey. "Toward a Sociology of Aesthetic Forms: A Commentary." *New Literary History* 17 (1986): 223–28.

Budgen, Frank. *James Joyce and the Making of Ulysses*. London: Grayson & Grayson, 1934.

Burgess, Anthony. *ReJoyce*. New York: Norton, 1965.

Cain, T.G.S. *Tolstoy*. London: Elek Books, 1977.

Carrier, David. "Ekphrasis and Interpretation: Two Modes of Art History Writing." *British Journal of Aesthetics* 27, no. 1 (1987): 20–31.

Cascardi, Anthony J. "Perspectivism and the Conflict of Values in *Don Quijote*." *Kentucky Romance Quarterly* 34 (1987): 165–78.

Castro, Americo. *An Idea of History: Selected Essays of Americo Castro*. Ed. Stephen Gilman and Edmund L. King. Columbus: Ohio State University Press, 1977.

Caudwell, Christopher. *Illusion and Reality*. New York: International Publishers, 1955.

Cervantes Saavedra, Miguel de. *The Adventures of Don Quixote*. Trans. J. M. Cohen. Harmondsworth, Middlesex: Penguin, 1976.

Chadwick, Charles. *Symbolism*. London: Methuen, 1971.

Chaffee, Diane. "Visual Art in Literature: The Role of Time and Space in Ekphrastic Creation." *Revista Canadiense de Estudios Hispanicos* 8 (1984): 311–20.

Chase, Cynthia. "Paragon, Parergon: Baudelaire Translates Rousseau." *Diacritics* 11 (June 1981): 42–51.

Christian, R. F. *Tolstoy: A Critical Introduction*. London: Cambridge University Press, 1969.

Clark, Donald Lemen. *Rhetoric in Greco-Roman Education*. New York: Greenwood, 1957.

Clerc, Charles. "Film in *Gravity's Rainbow*." In *Approaches to Gravity's Rainbow*, ed. Charles Clerc. Columbus: Ohio State University Press, 1983. 103–52.

Clignet, Remi. *The Structure of Artistic Revolutions*. Philadelphia: University of Pennsylvania Press, 1985.

Cohen, Murray. *Sensible Words: Linguistic Practice in England, 1640–1785*. Baltimore: Johns Hopkins University Press, 1977.

Cowart, David. "Attenuated Postmodernism: Pynchon's *Vineland*." *Critique* 32 (1990): 67–76.

———. "Cinematic Auguries of the Third Reich in *Gravity's Rainbow*." *Literature/Film Quarterly* 7 (1978): 364–70.

———. *Thomas Pynchon: The Art of Illusion*. Carbondale: Southern Illinois University Press, 1980.

Culler, Jonathan. *On Deconstruction*. Ithaca, N.Y.: Cornell University Press, 1982.

———. *Structuralist Poetics*. Ithaca, N.Y.: Cornell University Press, 1975.

Davidson, Donald. "On the Very Idea of a Conceptual Scheme." In *Post-Analytic Philosophy*. New York: Columbia University Press, 1985. 129–44.

Davidson, Michael. "*Ekphrasis* and the Postmodern Painter Poem." *Journal of Aesthetics and Art Criticism* 42 (1983): 69–79.

Deleuze, G., and F. Guattari. *Anti-Oedipus*. Trans. H. R. Lane, R. Hurley, and M. Seem. Minneapolis: University of Minnesota Press, 1986.

de Man, Paul. "The Epistemology of Metaphor." *Critical Inquiry* 5, no. 1 (1978): 13–30.

de Quevedo, Francisco. *Obras en Verso*. Ed. L. Astrana Marin. Madrid, 1932.

Derrida, Jacques. "Economimesis." Trans. Richard Klein. *Diacritics* 11, no. 2 (1981): 3–25.

———. *Edmund Husserl's "Origin of Geometry": An Introduction*. Trans. John P. Leavey. Pittsburgh: Duquesne University Press, 1978.

———. "Interview." In *Dialogues with Contemporary Continental Thinkers*, ed. Richard Kearny. Manchester: Manchester University Press, 1984. 83–105.

———. *Of Grammatology*. Trans. Gayatri Chakravorty Spivak. Baltimore: Johns Hopkins University Press, 1976.

———. "The Parergon." Trans. Craig Owens. *October* 9 (Summer 1979): 3–41.

———. *Positions*. Trans. Alan Bass. Chicago: University of Chicago Press, 1981.

———. *"Speech and Phenomena" and Other Essays on Husserl's Theory of Signs*. Trans. David B. Allison. Evanston, Ill.: Northwestern University Press, 1973.

———. "Ulysses Gramophone: Hear Say Yes in Joyce." In *James Joyce: The Augmented Ninth*, ed. Bernard Benstock. Syracuse, N.Y.: Syracuse University Press, 1988.

———. *La vérité en peinture*. Paris: Flammarion, 1978.

———. "White Mythology: Metaphor in the Text of Philosophy." In *Margins of Philosophy*, trans. Alan Bass. Chicago: University of Chicago Press, 1982. 207–29.

———. *Writing and Difference*. Chicago: University of Chicago Press, 1978.

de Saussure, Ferdinand. *Course in General Linguistics*. Trans. Wade Baskin. New York: McGraw-Hill, 1966.

Dickens, Charles. *Hard Times*. Ed. George Ford and Sylvere Monod. New York: Norton, 1966.

———. *Little Dorrit*. Harmondsworth, Middlesex: Penguin, 1967.

Doody, Terrence. "*Don Quixote, Ulysses*, and the Idea of Realism." *Novel* 12 (1979): 197–214.

Dreyfus, Hubert, and Paul Rabinow. *Michel Foucault: Beyond Structuralism and Hermeneutics*. 2d ed. Chicago: University of Chicago Press, 1983.

Duyfhuizen, Bernard. "Pynchon Criticism: Third Phase." *Novel* 23, no. 1 (1989): 75–88.

Eddins, Dwight. *The Gnostic Pynchon*. Bloomington: Indiana University Press, 1990.

———. "Paradigms Reclaimed: The Language of Science in *Gravity's Rainbow*." *Markham Review* 12 (1983): 72–80.

Edel, Leon. "Novel and Camera." In *The Theory of the Novel*, ed. John Halperin. New York: Oxford University Press, 1974. 177–88.

Eikhenbaum, Boris. *Tolstoi in the Seventies*. Trans. Albert Kaspin. Ann Arbor, Mich.: Ardis, 1982.

Eisenstein, Sergei. *Film Form*. Ed. and trans. Jay Leyda. New York: Harcourt, Brace & World, 1949.

Eisner, Lotte. *The Haunted Screen*. Berkeley and Los Angeles: University of California Press, 1973.

Eliot, T. S. *The Complete Poems and Plays, 1909–1950*. New York: Harcourt, Brace & World, 1971.

Ellmann, Richard, *James Joyce*. London: Oxford University Press, 1982.

———. *Ulysses on the Liffey*. London: Oxford University Press, 1971.

Ellmann, Richard, and Charles Feidelson, Jr., eds. *The Modern Tradition*. New York: Oxford University Press, 1965.

El Saffar, Ruth. *Distance and Control in Don Quixote: A Study in Narrative Technique*. Chapel Hill: North Carolina Studies in the Romance Languages and Literatures, 1975.

Fielding, Henry. *Shamela*. Ed. Sheridan W. Baker, Jr. Berkeley and Los Angeles: University of California Press, 1953.

Findlay, J. N. *Kant and the Transcendental Object*. Oxford: Clarendon Press, 1981.

Flores, Ralph. "Deconstructing Authors: *Don Quixote*." *New Orleans Review* 10, nos. 2–3 (1983): 100–109.

———. "The Role of Cide Hamete in *Don Quixote*." *BHS* 59, no. 1 (January 1982): 3–14.

Fludernik, Monika. "Narrative and Its Development in *Ulysses*." *Journal of Narrative Technique* 16, no. 1 (1986): 15–40.

Foucault, Michel. *The Archaeology of Knowledge and the Discourse on Language*. Trans. A. M. Sheridan Smith. New York: Harper & Row, 1972.

———. *The Birth of the Clinic: An Archeology of Medical Perception.* Trans. A. M. Sheridan Smith. New York: Vintage, 1975.

———. *The Order of Things.* New York: Vintage, 1970.

Fowlie, Wallace. *A Reading of Proust.* London: Dennis Dobson, 1963.

French, Marilyn. *The Book as World: James Joyce's Ulysses.* London: Abacus, 1982.

Fry, Paul H. "Georgic Comedy: The Fictive Territory of Jane Austen's *Emma.*" *Studies in the Novel* 11 (1979): 129–46.

Gaiser, Gottlieb, ed. *International Perspectives on James Joyce.* Troy, N.Y.: Whitston Publishing Co., 1986.

Galinsky, G. Karl. *Ovid's Metamorphoses.* Berkeley and Los Angeles: University of California Press, 1975.

Garodetzky, Nadezhda. "*Anna Karenina.*" *Slavonic and East European Review* 24 (1946): 121–26.

Gelley, Alexander. "The Represented World: Toward a Phenomenological Theory of Description in the Novel." *Journal of Aesthetics and Art Criticism* 38 (1979): 415–22.

Gide, André. *Pretextes.* Paris: Gallimard, 1913.

Goldberg, S. J. *The Classical Temper.* London: Chatto & Windus, 1961.

Goldknopf, David. *The Life of the Novel.* Chicago: University of Chicago Press, 1972.

Gombrich, E. H. *Art and Illusion.* Princeton: Princeton University Press, 1960.

Goodman, Nelson. *Ways of Worldmaking.* Indianapolis: Hackett, 1978.

Grace, Sherrill E. "Fritz Lang and the 'Paracinematic Lives' of *Gravity's Rainbow.*" *Modern Fiction Studies* 29 (1983): 655–70.

Green, Otis H. *Spain and the Western Tradition: The Castilian Mind in Literature from El Cid to Calderón.* Madison: University of Wisconsin Press, 1966.

Greenwood, E. B. *Tolstoy: The Comprehensive Vision.* New York: St. Martin's Press, 1975.

———. "Tolstoy and Religion." In *New Essays on Tolstoy*, ed. Malcolm Jones. Cambridge: Cambridge University Press, 1978.

———. "Tolstoy, Wittgenstein, Schopenhauer." *Encounter* 36, no. 4 (1971): 60–72.

Grossman, Joan. "Tolstoy's Portrait of Anna: Keystone in the Arch." *Criticism* 18 (1976): 1–14.

Guattari, Felix. *Molecular Revolution.* Harmondsworth, Middlesex: Penguin, 1984.

Gysin, Fritz. "Paintings in the House of Fiction: The Example of Hawthorne." *Word and Image* 5 (1989): 159–72.

Hagstrum, Jean H. *The Sister Arts: The Tradition of Literary Pictorialism and English Poetry from Dryden to Gray.* Chicago: University of Chicago Press, 1958.

Hájnády, Zoltan. "The Starry Heavens Above and the Moral Law Within." *Acta Literaria Academiae Scientarum Hungaricae* 27 (1985): 281–93.

Haley, George. "The Narrator in *Don Quixote*: Maese Pedro's Puppet Show." *Modern Language Notes* 80 (1965): 145–65.

Hardy, Barbara. *The Appropriate Form.* London: Athlone Press, 1964.

Harvey, Irene E. "Derrida, Kant, and the Performance of Parergonality." In *Derrida and Deconstruction*, ed. Hugh J. Silverman. New York: Routledge, 1989. 59–76.

Harvey, W. J. *Character and the Novel.* Ithaca, N.Y.: Cornell University Press, 1965.

Hayles, N. Katherine. " 'Who Was Saved?' Families, Snitches, and Recuperation in Pynchon's *Vineland.*" *Critique* 32, no. 2 (1990): 77–92.

Hayman, David. *Ulysses: The Mechanics of Meaning*. Englewood Cliffs, N.J.: Prentice Hall, 1970.

Heath, Stephen. "Ambiviolences: Notes for Reading Joyce." In *Post-Structuralist Joyce: Essays from the French*, ed. Derek Attridge and Daniel Ferrer. Cambridge: Cambridge University Press, 1984. 31–68.

Heisenberg, Werner. "The Representation of Nature in Contemporary Physics." In *The Discontinuous Universe*, ed. Sallie Sears and Georgiana W. Lord. New York: Basic Books, 1972. 122–35.

Hemingway, Ernest. *A Farewell to Arms*. New York: Scribner's, 1957.

Hewitt, Douglas. "The Conventions of Realism: The Shared World" and "The Conventions of Realism: The Unshared World." In *The Approach to Fiction: Good and Bad Readings of Novels*. Totowa, N.J.: Rowman & Littlefield, 1972. 45–84.

Hite, Molly. "Holy-Center-Approaching in the Novels of Thomas Pynchon." *Journal of Narrative Technique* 12 (1982): 121–29.

———. *Ideas of Order in the Novels of Thomas Pynchon*. Columbus: Ohio State University Press, 1983.

Hjelmslev, Louis. *Prolegomena to a Theory of Language*. Trans. Francis J. Whitfield. Madison: University of Wisconsin Press, 1969.

Hoijer, Harry. *Language in Culture*. Chicago: University of Chicago Press, 1954.

Hollander, John. "The Poetics of *Ekphrasis*." *Word and Image* 4, no. 1 (1988): 209–19.

Holmes, John R. " 'A Hand to Turn the Time': History as Film in *Gravity's Rainbow*." *Cithara* 23, no. 1 (1983): 5–16.

Hough, Graham. "Narrative and Dialogue in Jane Austen." In *Selected Essays*. Cambridge: Cambridge University Press, 1978. 46–82.

Howard, William G. "*Ut Pictura Poesis*." *PMLA* 24 (1909): 44–123.

Hughes, Gethin. "The Cave of Montesinos: Don Quixote's Interpretation and Dulcinea's Disenchantment." *Bulletin of Hispanic Studies* 54 (1977): 107–13.

Hume, Kathryn. *Pynchon's Mythography*. Carbondale: Southern Illinois University Press, 1987.

Hunt, John S. "Sundering and Reconciliation: The Aesthetic Theory of Joyce's 'Scylla and Charybdis.' " *Modern Language Quarterly* 47 (1986): 291–315.

Husserl, Edmund. *Ideas*. Trans. W. R. Boyce Gibson. New York: Collier, 1963.

Hutcheon, Linda. *A Poetics of Postmodernism*. New York: Routledge, 1988.

Jack, Ian. "The Epistolary Element in Jane Austen." In *English Studies Today*, ed. G. A. Bonnard, 2d ed. Berne, 1961.

Jackson, Gabriele Bernhard. "From Essence to Accident: Locke and the Language of Poetry in the Eighteenth Century." *Criticism* 29, no. 1 (1987): 27–66.

Jakobson, Roman. "On Realism in Art." In *Readings in Russian Poetics*, ed. Ladislaw Matejka and Krystyna Pomoroska. Ann Arbor: University of Michigan Press, 1978. 38–46.

James, Henry. *The Future of the Novel*. Ed. Leon Edel. New York: Vintage, 1956.

Jameson, Fredric. "Postmodernism, or the Cultural Logic of Late Capitalism." *New Left Review* 146 (1984): 53–92.

———. *The Prisonhouse of Language*. Princeton: Princeton University Press, 1972.

———. "Realism and Desire: Balzac and the Problem of the Subject." In *The Political Unconscious*. Ithaca, N.Y.: Cornell University Press, 1981. 151–69.

Johnson, Doris V. "The Autobiographical Heroine in *Anna Karenina*." *Studies in Literature* 11 (1979): 111–22.

Jones, Malcolm. "Problems of Communication in *Anna Karenina*." In *New Essays on Tolstoy*. Cambridge: Cambridge University Press, 1978. 85–108.

Jones, Peter. "Action and Passion in *Anna Karenina*." In *Philosophy and the Novel*. London: Oxford University Press, 1975. 70–111.

Joyce, James. *Dubliners*. New York: Viking, 1968.

———. *Letters of James Joyce*. Ed. Richard Ellmann. New York: Viking, 1966.

———. *Ulysses*. New York: Random House, 1961.

———. *Ulysses: The Corrected Text*. New York: Vintage, 1986.

Kain, Richard M. "The Significance of Stephen's Meeting Bloom: A Survey of Interpretations." *James Joyce Quarterly* 10 (1972): 147–60.

Kant, Immanuel. *The Critique of Judgement*. Trans. James C. Meredith. Oxford: Oxford University Press, 1952.

———. *Critique of Pure Reason*. Trans. Norman Kemp Smith. New York: St. Martin's Press, 1965.

Kennedy, George A. *Classical Rhetoric and Its Christian and Secular Tradition from Ancient to Modern Times*. Chapel Hill: University of North Carolina Press, 1980.

Kenner, Hugh. *A Homemade World*. New York: William Morrow, 1975.

———. *Joyce's Voices*. Berkeley and Los Angeles: University of California Press, 1978.

———. *The Pound Era*. Berkeley and Los Angeles: University of California Press, 1971.

———. *Ulysses*. London: Allen & Unwin, 1980.

Kettle, Arnold. "*Emma*." In *Jane Austen: A Collection of Critical Essays*, ed. Ian Watt. Englewood Cliffs, N.J.: Prentice Hall, 1963. 112–23.

Kimpel, Ben D. "The Voices of *Ulysses*." *Style* 9 (1975): 283–319.

Klein, Richard. "Kant's Sunshine." *Diacritics* 11 (1981): 26–41.

Knoepflmacher, U. C. "The Importance of Being Frank: Character and Letter-Writing in *Emma*." *Studies in English Literature* 7 (1967): 639–58.

Kracauer, Siegfried. *From Caligari to Hitler*. Princeton: Princeton University Press, 1947.

Krieger, Murray. *Ekphrasis: The Illusion of the Natural Sign*. Baltimore: Johns Hopkins University Press, 1992.

———. "The Ekphrastic Principle and the Still Movement of Poetry; or *Laokoön* Revisited." In *The Play and Place of Criticism*. Baltimore: Johns Hopkins University Press, 1967. 105–28.

———. *Theory of Criticism: A Tradition and Its System*. Baltimore: Johns Hopkins University Press, 1976.

Kuhn, Thomas. *The Structure of Scientific Revolutions*. Chicago: University of Chicago Press, 1965.

Kuhns, Richard. "The Beautiful and the Sublime." *New Literary History* 13 (1982): 287–307.

Kurman, George. "*Ekphrasis* in Epic Poetry." *Comparative Literature* 26 (1974): 1–14.

Law, Jules David. "The Home of Discourse: Joyce and Modern Language Philosophy." In *New Alliances in Joyce Studies*, ed. Bonnie Kime Scott. Newark: University of Delaware Press, 1988. 48–55.

Lawrence, Karen. *The Odyssey of Style in Ulysses*. Princeton: Princeton University Press, 1981.

Leavis, Q. D. "A Critical Theory of Jane Austen's Writings, II: *Lady Susan* into *Mansfield Park*." *Scrutiny* 10 (1941): 114–42, 272–94.

Lee, Rensselaer W. "*Ut Pictura Poesis*: The Humanistic Theory of Painting." *Art Bulletin* 22 (1940): 197–269.

Lemon, L. T., and M. J. Reiss. *Russian Formalist Criticism: Four Essays*. Lincoln: University of Nebraska Press, 1965.

Lessing, Gotthold E. *Laokoön*. Trans. Robert Phillimore. Wolfeboro, N.H.: Longwood Publishing Group, 1978.

Levin, Harry. "The Example of Cervantes." In *Cervantes*, ed. Lowry Nelson. Englewood Cliffs, N.J.: Prentice-Hall, 1969. 34–48.

———. *The Gates of Horn*. New York: Oxford University Press, 1963.

Levine, George. "V–2." In *Pynchon: A Collection of Critical Essays*, ed. Edward Mendelson. Englewood Cliffs, N.J.: Prentice-Hall, 1978. 178–90.

Lewis, C. S. "A Note on Jane Austen." In *Jane Austen: A Collection of Critical Essays*, ed. Ian Watt. Englewood Cliffs, N.J.: Prentice-Hall, 1963. 225–34.

Lippman, Bertram. "The Reader of Movies: Thomas Pynchon's *Gravity's Rainbow*." *Denver Quarterly* 12, no. 1 (1977): 1–46.

Litvak, Joseph. "Reading Characters: Self, Society, and Text in *Emma*." *PMLA* 100 (1985): 763–73.

Lloyd, David. "Kant's Examples." *Representations* 28 (Fall 1989): 34–54.

Locke, John. *The Philosophical Works*. Ed. J. A. St. John. London: George Bell & Sons, 1894 and 1904.

Lubbock, Percy. *The Craft of Fiction*. New York: Viking Press, 1957.

Machlis, Joseph. *The Enjoyment of Music*. New York: Norton, 1955.

Mancing, Howard. *The Chivalric World of Don Quijote: Style, Structure, and Narrative Technique*. Columbia: University of Missouri Press, 1982.

Mann, Thomas. *Essays*. Trans. H. T. Lowe-Porter. New York: Vintage, 1957.

Margolis, Joseph. "The Logic and Structures of Fictional Narrative." *Philosophy and Literature* 7, no. 2 (1983): 162–81.

Markiewicz, Henryk. "*Ut Pictura Poesis*: A History of the Topos and the Problem." *New Literary History* 18 (1987): 535–58.

Martin, Wallace. *Recent Theories of Narrative*. Ithaca, N.Y.: Cornell University Press, 1986.

McArthur, Murray. " 'Signs on a White Field': Semiotics and Forgery in the 'Proteus' Chapter of *Ulysses*." *ELH* (1986): 633–52.

McGowan, John P. "Knowledge/Power and Jane Austen's Radicalism." *Mosaic* 18, no. 3 (1985): 1–14.

McGrath, F. C. "*Ulysses* and the Pragmatic Semiotics of Modernism." *Comparative Literature Studies* 19 (1982): 164–74.

McHoul, Alec, and David Wills. *Writing Pynchon: Strategies in Fictional Analysis*. Urbana: University of Illinois Press, 1990.

McLaughlin, Sigrid. "Some Aspects of Tolstoy's Intellectual Development: Tolstoy and Schopenhauer." In *California Slavic Studies*, ed. Nicholas V. Riasanovsky and Gleb Struve. Berkeley and Los Angeles: University of California Press, 1970. 5th ser.: 187–245.

Meltzer, Francoise. *Salome and the Dance of Writing: Portraits of Mimesis in Literature*. Chicago: University of Chicago Press, 1987.

Mendelson, Edward. "Gravity's Encyclopedia." In *Mindful Pleasures: Essays on Thomas Pynchon*, eds. George Levine and David Leverenz. Boston: Little, Brown, 1976. 161–95.

Mendilow, A. A. *Time and the Novel*. London: Peter Nevill, 1952.

Merezhkovsky, Dimitri. *Tolstoi as Man and Artist*. Westport, Conn.: Greenwood Press, 1970.

Miller, D. A. *Narrative and Its Discontents: Problems of Closure in the Traditional Novel.* Princeton: Princeton University Press, 1981.

Minter, David. "Aesthetic Vision and the World of *Emma.*" *Nineteenth-Century Fiction* 21 (1966): 49–59.

Moore, Thomas. *The Style of Connectedness: Gravity's Rainbow and Thomas Pynchon.* Columbia: University of Missouri Press, 1987.

Morgan, Susan. *In the Meantime: Character and Perception in Jane Austen's Fiction.* Chicago: University of Chicago Press, 1980.

Morson, Gary Saul. "Tolstoy's Absolute Language." In *Bakhtin: Essays and Dialogues on His Work,* ed. Gary Saul Morson. Chicago: University of Chicago Press, 1986. 123–43.

Mudrick, Marvin. "Character and Event in Fiction." *Yale Review* 50 (1960): 202–18.

Munitz, Milton. *The Question of Reality.* Princeton: Princeton University Press, 1990.

Muste, J. M. "The Mandala in *Gravity's Rainbow.*" *Boundary 2* 9 (1981): 163–79.

Nabokov, Vladimir. *Lectures on Literature.* New York: Harcourt Brace Jovanovich, 1980.

Nadel, Ira. " 'Wonderful Deception': Art and the Artist in *Little Dorrit.*" *Criticism* 19 (1977): 17–33.

Neill, Edward. "Between Deference and Destruction: 'Situations' of Recent Critical Theory and Jane Austen's *Emma.*" *Critical Quarterly* 29, no. 3 (1987): 39–54.

Niess, Robert J. *Zola, Cezanne, and Manet.* Ann Arbor: University of Michigan Press, 1968.

Page, Norman. *The Language of Jane Austen.* New York: Barnes & Noble, 1972.

Painter, George. *Proust: The Early Years.* Boston: Little, Brown, 1955.

Pater, Walter. *The Renaissance.* New York: Random House, 1956.

Pavel, Thomas. *Fictional Worlds.* Cambridge: Harvard University Press, 1986.

Peirce, Charles Sanders. *Collected Papers.* 6 vols. Ed. Charles Hartshorne and Paul Weiss. Cambridge: Harvard University Press, 1931–35.

Plater, William M. *The Grim Phoenix: Reconstructing Thomas Pynchon.* Bloomington: Indiana University Press, 1978.

Poirier, Richard. "Rocket Power." In *Pynchon: A Collection of Critical Essays,* ed. Edward Mendelson. Englewood Cliffs, N.J.: Prentice-Hall, 1978. 167–77.

Pound, Ezra. "James Joyce and Pécuchet." In *Polite Essays.* London: Faber, 1937.

Price, Martin. "The Irrelevant Detail and the Emergence of Form." In *Aspects of Narrative,* ed. J. Hillis Miller. New York: Columbia University Press, 1971. 69–91.

Proust, Marcel. *A la recherche du temps perdu.* Trans. C. K. Scott Moncrieff. New York: Random House, 1934.

Pursglove, Michael. "The Smiles of *Anna Karenina.*" *Slavic and East European Journal* 17, no. 1 (1973): 42–47.

Pynchon, Thomas. *Gravity's Rainbow.* New York: Viking, 1973.

———. *Vineland.* Boston: Little, Brown, 1990.

Raaberg, Gwen. "*Ekphrasis* and the Temporal/Spatial Metaphor in Murray Krieger's Critical Theory." *New Orleans Review* 12, no. 4 (1985): 34–43.

Read, Malcolm. "Language Adrift: A Re-appraisal of the Theme of Linguistic Perspectivism in *Don Quijote.*" *Forum for Modern Language Studies* 17 (1981): 271–87.

Richards, I. A. *Principles of Literary Criticism*. London: Routledge & Kegan Paul, 1926.

Riffaterre, Michael. *Fictional Truth*. Baltimore: Johns Hopkins University Press, 1990.

———. "Intertextual Representation: On Mimesis as Interpretive Discourse." *Critical Inquiry* 11 (1984): 141–62.

———. *Semiotics of Poetry*. Bloomington: Indiana University Press, 1978.

———. "Syllepsis." *Critical Inquiry* 6 (1980): 625–38.

———. *Text Production*. Trans. Terese Lyons. New York: Columbia University Press, 1983.

Riquelme, John Paul. *Teller and Tale in Joyce's Fiction: Oscillating Perspectives*. Baltimore: Johns Hopkins University Press, 1983.

Rivers, Elias L. "Cervantes and the Question of Language." In *Cervantes and the Renaissance*, ed. Michael D. McGaha. Easton, Pa.: Juan de la Cuesta, 1980. 23–33.

Robert, Marthe. *The Old and the New: From Don Quixote to Kafka*. Trans. Carol Cosman. Berkeley and Los Angeles: University of California Press, 1977.

Rorty, Richard. *Consequences of Pragmatism*. Minneapolis: University of Minnesota Press, 1982.

———. *Philosophy and the Mirror of Nature*. Princeton: Princeton University Press, 1979.

———. "Solidarity or Objectivity?" In *Post-Analytic Philosophy*, eds. John Rajchman and Cornell West. New York: Columbia University Press, 1985. 3–19.

Rosmarin, Adena. " 'Misreading' *Emma*: The Powers and Perfidies of Interpretive History." *ELH* 51 (1984): 315–42.

Rowe, John Carlos. "James's Rhetoric of the Eye: Re-marking the Impression." *Criticism* 24 (1982): 233–60.

———. *The Theoretical Dimensions of Henry James*. Madison: University of Wisconsin Press, 1984.

Rowe, William W. *Leo Tolstoy*. Boston: Twayne Publishers, 1986.

Russell, Charles. "Pynchon's Language: Signs, Systems, and Subversion." In *Approaches to Gravity's Rainbow*, ed. Charles Clerc. Columbus: Ohio State University Press, 1983. 251–72.

Ryan, Marie-Laure. *Possible Worlds, Artificial Intelligence, and Narrative Theory*. Bloomington: Indiana University Press, 1991.

Ryle, Gilbert. "Jane Austen and the Moralists." In *English Literature and British Philosophy*, ed. S. P. Rosenbaum. Chicago: University of Chicago Press, 1971. 168–84.

Safer, Elaine B. "Pynchon's World and Its Legendary Past: Humor and the Absurd in a Twentieth-Century *Vineland*." *Critique* 32 (1990): 107–25.

Salvidar, Ramon. "Don Quijote's Metaphors and the Grammar of Proper Language." *MLN* 95 (1980): 252–78.

———. *Figural Language in the Novel: The Flowers of Speech from Cervantes to Joyce*. Princeton: Princeton University Press, 1984.

Schaub, Thomas. *Pynchon: The Voice of Ambiguity*. Urbana: University of Illinois Press, 1980.

Schmidt, S. J. "The Fiction Is That Reality Exists: A Constructivist Model of Reality, Fiction, and Literature." *Poetics Today* 5, no. 2 (1984): 253–74.

Scholes, Robert. *Structuralism in Literature*. New Haven: Yale University Press, 1974.

Scholes, Robert, and Robert Kellogg. *The Nature of Narrative*. New York: Oxford University Press, 1966.

Schopenhauer, Arthur. *Sämtliche Werke*. Vols. 1-5. Insel-Verlag, 1964.

———. *The World as Will and Idea*. 3 vols. Trans. R. B. Haldne and J. Kemp. London: Routledge, 1883.

Schorer, Mark. "The Humiliation of Emma Woodhouse." In *Jane Austen: A Collection of Critical Essays*, ed. Ian Watt. Englewood Cliffs, N.J.: Prentice-Hall, 1963. 98–111.

Schulze, Sydney. *The Structure of Anna Karenina*. Ann Arbor, Mich.: Ardis Press, 1982.

Schwarz, Daniel R. *Reading Joyce's Ulysses*. New York: St. Martin's Press, 1987.

Scott, Bonnie Kime, ed. *New Alliances in Joyce Studies*. Newark: University of Delaware Press, 1988.

Seed, David. *The Fictional Labyrinths of Thomas Pynchon*. Iowa City: University of Iowa Press, 1988.

Shklovsky, Victor. *Lev Tolstoy*. Moscow: Progress Publishers, 1978.

Simmon, Scott. "Beyond the Theater of War: *Gravity's Rainbow* as Film." *Literature/Film Quarterly* 7 (1978): 347–63.

Slade, Joseph W. "Communication, Group Theory, and Perception in *Vineland*." *Critique* 32 (1990): 126–44.

———. *Thomas Pynchon*. New York: Warner Paperback, 1974.

Smith, Mack. "The Document of Falsimilitude: Frank's Epistles and Misinterpretation in *Emma*." *Massachusetts Studies in English* 9, no. 4 (1984): 52–70.

———. "The Paracinematic Reality of *Gravity's Rainbow*." *Pynchon Notes* 9 (1982): 17–37.

———. "The Structural Rhythm in *Ulysses*." *Twentieth Century Literature* 30 (1984): 404–19.

———. "Tolstoy and the Conventions of Representation." *Renascence* 37 (1985): 220–37.

Souriau, Etienne. "Time in the Plastic Arts." *Journal of Aesthetics and Art Criticism* 8 (1949): 294–307.

Southam, B. C. "Jane Austen and *Clarissa*." *Notes and Queries* 208 (1963): 191–92.

———. *Jane Austen's Literary Manuscripts*. London: Oxford University Press, 1964.

Spears, Monroe K. *Dionysus and the City: Modernism in Twentieth-Century Poetry*. New York: Oxford University Press, 1970.

Spitzer, Leo. "The 'Ode on a Grecian Urn' or Content vs. Metagrammar." In *Essays on British and American Literature*, ed. Anna Hatcher. Princeton: Princeton University Press, 1962.

Steiner, Peter. *Russian Formalism: A Metapoetics*. Ithaca, N.Y.: Cornell University Press, 1984.

Steiner, Wendy. *The Colors of Rhetoric: Problems in the Relation Between Modern Literature and Painting*. Chicago: University of Chicago Press, 1982.

Stenbock-Fermor, Elizabeth. *The Architecture of Anna Karenina: A History of Its Structure, Writing, and Message*. Lisse: Peter de Ridder, 1975.

Sternfeld, Frederick W. "Poetry and Music—Joyce's *Ulysses*." In *Sound and Poetry: English Institute Essays—1956*, ed. Northrop Frye. New York: Columbia University Press, 1957.

Streuver, Nancy. *The Language of History in the Renaissance*. Princeton: Princeton University Press, 1970.

Sultan, Stanley. *The Argument of Ulysses*. Columbus: Ohio State University Press, 1964.

Tanner, Tony. "V. and V–2." In *Pynchon: A Collection of Critical Essays*, ed. Edward Mendelson. Englewood Cliffs, N.J.: Prentice-Hall, 1978. 16–55.

Tave, Stuart. *Some Words of Jane Austen*. Chicago: University of Chicago Press, 1973.

Thomas, Brook. *James Joyce's Ulysses: A Book of Many Happy Returns*. Baton Rouge: Louisiana State University Press, 1982.

Thorburn, David. "Fiction and Imagination in *Don Quixote*." *Partisan Review* 42 (1975): 431–43.

Thornton, Weldon. "Voices and Values in *Ulysses*." In *Joyce's Ulysses: The Larger Perspective*, ed. Robert D. Newman and Weldon Thornton. Newark: University of Delaware Press, 1987. 244–70.

Todorov, Tzvetan. *Mikhail Bakhtin: The Dialogical Principle*. Trans. Wlad Godzich. Minneapolis: University of Minnesota Press, 1984.

Tölölyan, Khachig. "War as Background in *Gravity's Rainbow*." In *Approaches to Gravity's Rainbow*, ed. Charles Clerc. Columbus: Ohio State University Press, 1983. 31–68.

Tolstoy, Leo. *Anna Karenina*. Trans. Rosemary Edmonds. Harmondsworth, Middlesex: Penguin, 1978.

———. *Letters*. Ed. and trans. R. F. Christian. New York: Scribner's, 1978.

———. *War and Peace*. Trans. Aylmer Maude. Ed. George Gibian. New York: Norton, 1966.

———. *What Is Art?* Trans. Aylmer Maude. New York: Scribner's, 1917.

Toulmin, Stephen. "The Construal of Reality: Criticism in Modern and Postmodern Science." *Critical Inquiry* 9, no. 1 (1982): 93–111.

———. "Ludwig Wittgenstein." *Encounter*, January 1969, 58–71.

Trilling, Lionel. Introduction to *Emma*. Boston: Houghton Mifflin, 1957.

Troyat, Henri. *Tolstoy*. New York: Doubleday, 1967.

Tsomondo, Thorell. "*Emma*: A Study in Textual Strategies." *English Studies in Africa* 30, no. 2 (1987): 69–82.

Valdés, Mario. *World-Making: The Literary Truth-Claim and the Interpretation of Texts*. Toronto: University of Toronto Press, 1992.

Van Boheeman-Saaf, Christine. "Joyce, Derrida, and the Discourse of 'the Other.' " In *James Joyce: The Augmented Ninth*, ed. Bernard Benstock. Syracuse, N.Y.: Syracuse University Press, 1988. 88–102.

Van Ghent, Dorothy. *The English Novel: Form and Function*. New York: Harper & Row, 1953.

Verlaine, Paul. "The Art of Poetry." In *An Anthology of French Poetry from Nerval to Valery in English Translation*, ed. Angel Flores. New York: Doubleday, 1958.

von Glaserfeld, Ernst. *The Construction of Knowledge*. Salinas, Calif.: Intersystems Publications, 1988.

Wardropper, Bruce W. "*Don Quixote*: Story or History?" In *Critical Essays on Cervantes*, ed. Ruth El Saffar. Boston: G. K. Hall, 1986. 80–94.

Warner, William B. "The Play of Fictions and Succession of Styles in *Ulysses*." *James Joyce Quarterly* 15 (Fall 1977): 18–35.

Watson, Stephen. "Regulations: Kant and Derrida at the End of Metaphysics." In *Deconstruction and Philosophy*, ed. John Sallis. Chicago: University of Chicago Press, 1987. 71–86.

Watt, Ian. *The Rise of the Novel.* Berkeley and Los Angeles: University of California Press, 1957.

Waugh, Patricia. *Metafiction: The Theory and Practice of Self-Conscious Fiction.* New York: Methuen, 1984.

Weber, Eugen, ed. *Paths to the Present: Aspects of European Thought from Romanticism to Existentialism.* New York, 1962.

Weiger, John G. *In the Margins of Cervantes.* Hanover, N.H.: University Press of New England, 1988.

————. "The Prologuist: The Extratextual Authorial Voice in *Don Quixote.*" *Bulletin of Hispanic Studies* 65 (1988): 129–39.

Weisenburger, Steven. *A Gravity's Rainbow Companion.* Athens: University of Georgia Press, 1988.

Wellek, Rene, and Austin Warren. *Theory of Literature.* New York: Harcourt, Brace & Co., 1942.

Whorf, Benjamin Lee. *Language, Thought, Reality.* Ed. John B. Carroll. Cambridge: MIT Press, 1956.

Wiesenfarth, Joseph. "*Emma*: Point Counter Point." In *Jane Austen: Bicentenary Essays,* ed. John Halperin. Cambridge: Cambridge University Press, 1975. 207–20.

Williams, Raymond. *Keywords.* London: Fontana, 1983.

Williams, William Carlos. *Paterson.* New York: New Directions, 1951.

Wilson, Edmund. *Axel's Castle: A Study in the Imaginative Literature of 1870–1930.* New York: Scribner's, 1939.

Windelbrand, Wilhelm. *A History of Philosophy.* 2 vols. New York: Harper & Row, 1958.

Wittgenstein, Ludwig. *On Certainty.* Ed. G.E.M. Anscombe and G. H. von Wright. New York: Harper Editions, 1969.

————. *Philosophical Investigations.* Trans. G.E.M. Anscombe. 3d ed. New York: Macmillan, 1958.

————. *Tractatus Logico-Philosophicus.* Ed. D. F. Pears and B. F. McGuinness. New York: Humanities Press, 1972.

Woolf, Virginia. *To the Lighthouse.* New York: Harcourt Brace & World, 1927.

Worringer, Wilhelm. *Abstraction and Empathy.* New York: International University Press, 1953.

Young, James O. "Coherence, Anti-Realism, and the Vienna Circle." *Synthese* 86 (1991): 467–82.

Zola, Émile. *L'oeuvre.* Trans. Thomas Walton. Ann Arbor: University of Michigan Press, 1978.

————. *Thérèse Raquin.* Trans. L. W. Tancock. Harmondsworth, Middlesex: Penguin, 1962.

Hume, David, 82 n. 5
Husserl, Edmund, 150, 158
Hutcheson, Francis, 82, 112

Jacobi, Friedrich Heinrich, 119–20
    supernatural sensualism, 148
Jakobson, Roman, 1, 6
James, Henry, 168
    Prefaces, 243
    The Wings of the Dove, 246
James, William, 159
Jameson, Fredric, 2
Joyce, James
    "The Dead," 193
    Dubliners, 168
    A Portrait of the Artist as a Young Man,
        164, 187
    Ulysses, 15–16, 17, 36, 39–40, 108,
        158–98, 215
        compared to novels of Proust,
            247–49
        consubstantiality as theme in,
            175–76, 185–94
        Hamlet debate in, 14, 171–75, 180
        the journey motif of, 173–74
        linguistic conceptual schemes in,
            161–63
        narrative styles of, 183–87
        and poststructuralism, 166
        and the problem of consciousness,
            164–65
        on reference, 165–67
        sonata as structural device in,
            181–92
        styles of, as possible worlds,
            166–67, 169–72
        tonic and dominant themes of, 15,
            32, 172, 175–81

Kant, Immanuel, 119 n. 3, 146
    on beauty and morality, 142
    categorical imperative, theory of (in
        Anna Karenina), 147
    Critique of Judgement, 116–18, 152
    Critique of Pure Reason, 117
    epistemological theory of, 119–21
    on genius and learning, 127–28
    on *hypotypōsis*, 151–52
    intuitive intellect, theory of, 120, 150
    noumena, theory of, 119–20
    the sublime, theory of, 148 n. 18

Kekulé, August (in *Gravity's Rainbow*),
    209–10, 217 n. 18
Kramskoye, Ivan (painter of Tolstoy),
    124
Krieger, Murray, 27–28
Kuhn, Thomas, 2, 159
    paradigm theory of, 5–7, 6 n. 3, 111

Lacan, Jacques, 197
Lang, Fritz, 225–29, 231, 237
    Die Frau im Mond, 225
    Die Niebelungen, 228–29
    Dr. Mabuse der Spieler, 228
    Metropolis, 226–28
Leibniz, G. W. P., 20, 87
Locke, John
    correspondence theory of, 83 n. 6
    *An Essay Concerning Human
        Understanding*, 78–81
    on ethics, 110–13
    on fancy and understanding, 85–87,
        104
    language theory of, 78–83, 79 n. 1, 79
        n. 2
Longus, 11

Mallarmé, Stephane, "Crisis in Poetry,"
    247
Marxism, 198, 199 n. 4
menippean satire (Bakhtin), 21, 49
    Gravity's Rainbow as, 215
Merleau-Ponty, Maurice, 158
Millet, Jean François, 125
mimetic discontinuity, 16–22
Minsky, Marvin, 160
modernism
    emphasis on consciousness of (in
        Ulysses), 163–65
    Joyce, Wittgenstein paradigmatic
        figures of, 167–71
    as unitary movement, 164 n. 6

nominalism, 43

Orozco, Alonso di, 235
Ovid, *Metamorphoses*, 10–11

paradigm shift
    in Russian formalism, 7
    from tradition to innovation, 7–8

Printed in the United States
204408BV00001B/354/P

27506534R00177

Made in the USA
Middletown, DE
19 December 2015